Feminist Auteurs
Reading Women's Films

Feminist Auteurs
Reading Women's Films

GEETHA RAMANATHAN

WALLFLOWER
LONDON & NEW YORK

First published in Great Britain in 2006 by
Wallflower Press
6a Middleton Place, Langham Street, London W1W 7TE
www.wallflowerpress.co.uk

A catalogue for this book is available from the British Library.

ISBN 1-904764-69-X (pbk)
ISBN 1-904764-70-3 (hbk)

Printed by Replika Press Pvt. Ltd. (India)

Contents

In memory of
Janaki and Lakshmi
and for
Kehan and Dhario

Acknowledgements

This book has been many years in the making, and was first conceived during a conversation at the 'Feminism and Representation' conference in Rhode Island College in 1989. Dazzled as I was by the insights of feminist film theory, I was disheartened by what I perceived to be the relative lack of attention to women's own creative production despite, of course, the work of many pioneering scholars in the field such as B. Ruby Rich. I chose films whose politics of enunciation seemed feminist for the time of its production, and equally importantly, films that I have been able to access. If feminist film culture is to remain vital, we should be able to screen these films in women's film festivals, and in our classrooms.

I am deeply grateful for the enthusiasm, commitment and commentary of the students of my course on 'Women and Film'. The responses of the students from 1988–95 helped to shape the book. In more ways than one, this book is for those students.

Very early versions of slivers of the manuscript have been read at various conferences. A small section of Chapter 2 at the National Women's Studies Association's conference in Baltimore in 1989, of Chapter 6 at the Semiotics Project at the University of Oklahoma in 1990, of Chapter 3 at the American Comparative Literature Association's conference in Columbia in 1992, another segment of Chapter 3 at the Comparative Literature Circle's Race and Film conference at the University of Florida in 1997, and at the Northeastern Modern Languages Association's conference in 1998, sections of Chapter 4 at the African Literature Association's conferences in Guadeloupe and Egypt in 1994 and 2003, and a portion of Chapter 2 at the American Comparative Literature Association's conference at the University of Michigan in Ann Arbor in 2004. An earlier version of a section of Chapter 2 was published by *Quarterly Review of Film and Video* as 'Aesthetics as Woman' in April 2000, and a section of Chapter 6, 'Reading Women's Films: Feminist Aesthetics', by *Deep Focus: A Film Quarterly* in January 1999.

I am deeply grateful to the following organisations and people for use of stills in the book: Women Make Movies for *Illusions* and *La nouba des femmes du Mont-Chenoua*, Kino International for *Daughters of the Dust* and *Hour of the Star*, Zimmedia for *Flame* and Mr Prettymana at Kathleen Collins' estate for *Losing Ground*.

Special thanks to Andi Hubbard of College Literature and Meera Vaidyanathan of Princeton University Press for last minute saves. And many thanks also to the editorial staff at Wallflower Press for their assistance.

Many people made this book possible. I am not able to thank all of them by name, but I offer my warmest thanks to the following parties.

The Feminist Research Group at West Chester University: Madelyn Gutwirth, Anne Dzamba, Stacey Schlau, Deborah Mahlstedt, Elizabeth Larsen and Ruth Porritt read earlier versions of sections of Chapter 4. Helen Berger was part of the group that read the first draft of Chapter 1. Lynette McGrath read and commented on the entire manuscript.

The College of Arts and Sciences made it possible for me to do archival research in India, and a sabbatical in 2002 made it possible for me to undertake valuable work on the book.

I am indebted to Charles Silver of the Museum of Modern Art's Film Library and Archive, New York for making the material accessible to me, the Curator of the National Film Archive in Pune, India for the great assistance the institute gave me, the film librarian of the Library of Congress Washington DC for making prints available, the Fine Arts curator at Chitra Kala Parishad, Bangalore and Kamakshi, librarian at Max Mueller Bhavan, Bangalore for giving me access to printed material. Thanks also to Mr Nair of the Chennai National Film Development Corporation, and Ms Usha of the Mumbai NFDC for reproducing material for me.

Finally, the library staff at West Chester University have been extraordinarily helpful: Tracie Meloy and Dana McDonnell; special thanks to the Inter-Library loan staff who were impeccable in their ferrying of arcane items, Kimberly Klaus in particular. Thanks to the audio-visual department for procuring audio-visual material, especially Trish Lenkowski and Joe Silvestre. My gratitude too to the university's instructional media centre, particularly Aubrey Hays.

Divya Ramamurthi helped to format the first draft. Profound thanks to George Kutty for his support. And of course mom and pop. Lastly: Vek, thanks.

Introduction

This book looks at how feminist films from diverse cinematic and cultural traditions have exceeded the limits that highly specific culturally-embedded aesthetic and visual practices have placed upon the representation of women. The inscription of feminist authority in film is a consequence of the filmmakers' efforts to overwrite established forms of cinematic power.

The genre of feminist film is rich and while composed of many strands, I have chosen to work with three elements that are crucial to its growth: the effort to enhance feminist authority; visual, aural and narrative restructurings that occur because of the inhibitions placed on the cinematic representation of women; and the aesthetics that emerge as a consequence of a shift in the strategies of representation.

In addressing problematic issues surrounding women's visual representation, the feminist filmmakers studied here use visual, aural and narrative strategies that attempt to bypass extremely restrictive cinematic constructions of women. The films that I have chosen to study are symptomatic of the kinds of responses that have been able to counter features inimical to the representation of women.

My interest lies in understanding how women filmmakers have locked horns with problematic aspects of a history of aesthetics that women confronted and endured much before the first film was ever cut. I take issue from chapters 2 to 6 with the broader legacies of this history: (a) women's 'to be looked at' status; (b) black women's exclusion; (c) women's subject status confined to certain genres; (d) women's lack of voice; (e) the repression of female desire; and (f) the absence of culturally-sanctioned feminist narratives. So much of the work of the last forty years has gone toward documenting the troubled status of women in the aesthetic scene – their exclusion except as models – and of black women – their invisibility – that I do not wish to recapitulate that entire history except what is pertinent to an understanding of women filmmakers' specific response to that negative legacy of aesthetics.

Much feminist criticism of the last forty years has studied classical Hollywood to discuss the representation of women and consequently theorises that the conditions of representability for women are hampered in several different arenas.[1] The visual apparatus, techniques of subject formation and treatment of raced subjects have been identified as deeply flawed. Laura Mulvey's classical formulation of woman's 'to be looked at' status, Mary Ann Doane's study of the woman as 'hystericised subject', Jane Gaines' contribution to our understanding of black women's representation in the context of white privilege, and other studies have emphasised the difficulties of the seventh art in representing both European/American and African American women.

Other developments in film theory and criticism also added to our understanding of the influences subtending the representation of women. Apparatus theory of the 1970s was particularly illuminating on the role of technology in producing culture and positioning subjectivities.[2] Current research on the screen's racial coding is exciting in following up on the earlier research in a more nuanced way. In 1930, in a discussion on screen dimensions, Sergei Eisenstein was already keenly alive to its ideological usage. Eisenstein was all for doing away with the horizontal shape of the frame which he felt excluded '50% of composition possibilities'.[3] The reasons he ascribed for his distaste for the horizontal frame were its passivity which he viewed interestingly enough in gendered terms, as being feminine. While one may quarrel with Eisenstein's general attribution of male and female characteristics, I find the intuition that the screen is gendered particularly powerful because it acknowledges that the ground on which the composition is done is already marked culturally and more specifically with reference to masculinity/femininity. Teresa de Lauretis's observation on the dominant cinema would also confirm the notion that cinematic aesthetics are prefigured on elements that are male: 'The camera (technology), look (voyeurism) and the scopic drive itself partake of the phallic and thus somehow are entities or figures of a masculine nature.'[4]

Challenges to readings of the Hollywood system as monolithic came from two directions: by those who sought female subjectivity in the ruptures of the text, and those who regarded the reactions of the audience as transgressive. The influential work done on Dorothy Arzner helped locate women's discourse even within the classical paradigm.[5] Granted, women's perspectives were not completely obliterated; it still appears that the scene of the visual included women within a male theatre[6] that precluded women's representation outside these fairly well-defined patriarchal perimeters. The woman's film, for instance, is one such example of cinema where female roles are important but the conditions of representability, circumscribed as they are by what is allowable in patriarchal culture, does not permit for any nuanced comment on the roles of women which are presented in extremely commonsensical, if not essentialised, ways.[7]

Moving from the limits of the text to issues of spectatorial subjectivity, feminist critics argued that the 'double consciousness' of oppressed groups,[8] rendered lesbian identification possible in films either because of the community's investment in 'the hypothetical lesbian heroine',[9] or because of other kinds of looking relations in the films that resisted the objectifying male gaze. In a similar vein, Michele Wallace has written of how she and her family identified with 1940s female heroes and regarded them as coloured women because of their (her family's) empathy with them.[10] Given that the discursive boundaries of the authority of the text were questioned in literary studies in general, for women certainly, it was crucial to assert the power of viewers, if we were to have a place at all in the transaction, and in that sense the divestiture of the male auteur's authority was timely. However, if meaning in the text is produced because of the signifying relationships in the text, i.e., the context allows us to 'read' the film, notwithstanding the progressiveness of the intervention on behalf of the viewer, one must concede that ruptures in the text permit such entrances, and allow for the *jouissance* of the reader. Logically then even during the highpoint of the death of the author, the author, albeit without patriarchal authority, enters the scene of writing[11] due to the emphasis on textuality and context. For women, the thematic of textuality and auteurship in film recurred as it did in (male) literary/post-structuralist studies. While including the female viewer in film criticism was most influential in lending direction to feminist film criticism and remains empowering for women critics and viewers alike, the question of auteurship has also received considerable attention, partly because it holds out the promise of a tradition of feminist filmmaking.[12]

Early feminist critics, including Claire Johnston and Pam Cook[13], believed that exploring auteurship of women in film was important and Johnston and Cook in a now classic essay showed how Arzner was able to put her stamp on work that came out of mainstream studios. As Patrice Petro avers, Johnston and Cook changed the meanings of traditional auteur study for feminist film critics by insisting that feminist politics and feminist theory were crucial to situating women's film and the writing of feminist film history.[14] Despite the severe criticisms laid on Johnston and Cook, their key insight that the auteur's imprimatur is a 'function of discourse rather than individual intent', as Petro succinctly and economically describes it,[15] is essential to understanding the specificity of feminist authorship of film, dependent as the meanings are on what the representation of women is in that given context and at that historical moment. Although Johnston and Cook discuss the auteur in relation to Hollywood, the emphasis on the difficulty of articulating a vision freely in a patriarchal cultural context that all women artists face makes their insight relevant to women's film production generally.

Meanings around the site of the 'auteur' are not without ambiguity for a feminist film practice/criticism. Judith Mayne observes that despite the call of feminist critics, including Kaja Silverman, to reconfigure the concept of female authorship to differentiate it from the consolidation of patriarchal authority evident in the deployment of the theory, few such attempts have been made. One approach that Mayne suggests would 'bring authorship into a discussion of lesbian representation'.[16] In her comments on the state of feminist film theory in the millennium, Alison Butler suggests that women perhaps turn to women's films for an understanding of women's subjectivity and history. Implied in this position is a perceived need for the acknowledgement of women's historical auteurship.[17] Catherine Grant, a critic on auteur studies in general, notes that the critic about to embark on any study referencing the auteur, inevitably encounters a 'queasy' moment in a bid to take cover from the charge of essentialism.[18] Consequently feminist critical strategy insists on the historical author but concentrates more on the ideological traces of the auteur in the text.[19] Feminist film critics have been caught in this bind for a number of very excellent reasons that Judith Mayne details, one among them being the inevitable shadowing of male models of auteurship despite our well-meaning disclaimers of the same. Mayne herself develops the discussion in two significant ways: by insisting auteurship be regarded in terms of the relationship between women, rather than that of male subject to female object, and by showing in her analyses that female auteurship may be inscribed without necessarily impressing the auteur's authority on celluloid.[20] She moves away from the patriarchal insistence on personal patrimony and individualistic authorial control of the text. Mayne had noted that part of the reason feminist film critics moved in the direction of analyses and left authorship hanging was because the emphasis on authorship might take away from important claims on the difficulties for women in film, both pre- and post-production.

In bringing female auteurship into play with feminist texts, I bring two terms together that have hitherto seemed divided. Feminist auteurship entails the impression of feminist authority, not necessarily that of the auteur herself, on screen. What is at stake here is the films' larger acknowledgement of an informing discourse that is ideological in both form and content. Whether visual, psychoanalytic, aural or narrative, this address transcends the personal; both the place and terms of address are derived from an understanding of the films' relevance to women. Further, such production of meaning that asserts that the feminist standpoint is constructed against the backdrop of very specific strictures in the aesthetic and visual domains that inhibit the authority of women, both behind and on the screen. Through diverse modalities that confront the history of aesthetics, and visuality in film, women filmmakers have succeeded in impressing feminist authority in film, not necessarily or exclusively their own, or even that of the protagonist of the film, but over the representation of women in film in ways that counter prior cinematic renditions. Thus, through the book, I seek to show how the aesthetics of women's film deals with the important themes of the visuality of the medium, and establishing authority in it.[21]

Feminist critics have looked to the work of women filmmakers to find female subjectivity and the claims they have made about women filmmakers have been substantially larger than those made for Hollywood film. The assumptions of both Gwendolyn Audrey Foster and Ann Kaplan in their work on women directors have been that women filmmakers are able to alter viewing relations. The former argues that the directors she studies from the African and Asian diaspora do not reconfirm the hegemonic gaze, and the latter that they offer a mediating position between the colonial and the post-colonial.[22] In a similar vein, the essays in Diana Robin and Ira Jaffe's collection cohere around the notion of 'redirecting the gaze'.[23]

Despite the tremendous scope of all three endeavours, they are defined broadly in terms of area studies or national cinemas. Since my study does not acknowledge national boundaries, but works with films directed by women under the rubric of studying strategies of feminist representation, it is important to address the issue of essentialism. Not grouping the films according to national film histories seems to conspire with patriarchal modes of representation that were uniform and did not differentiate sufficiently between women at all. The fear of falling into the essentialist 'trap' has made it difficult for feminist analyses to offer governing narratives, thus resulting in studies of women or their representations that do not distinguish between hierarchically-structured social positionalities. In other words, the informing power of feminist discourse is itself diminished by the taboo against so-called 'essentialising' gestures. An example of this reigning doxa is borne out by the fact that even commonplace, routine feminist commentary on the objectification of women in media and film has been critiqued for its essentialism. Elizabeth Cowie's rebuttal to feminist arguments about the exploitativeness of images of women in film and the media is to suggest that the feminist standpoint assumes a female subject in some authentic form who is corrupted by male discourse. Rather, she maintains, the image of 'woman' constructed is a function of the discourse, and the feminist view of 'woman' as the object of enunciation in male representation is no more authentic than those produced by men.

Such extreme 'anti-essentialism' that inadvertently masks the power relations between men and women that produce the context of enunciation does not, I believe, do women a service. Far from historicising women's positionalities, the exclusive emphasis on the discursive actually flattens it. While the feminist view may not be more 'real', it does contest masculinist representations. Further, I do want to hold out for an articulated existence of women outside the discursive frame of representation, and would maintain that unrecorded experience does not necessarily mean absence. In other words, female experiences have only been insufficiently and inadequately recorded, and that much remains to enter the discursive. Given that the representability of women is extremely restricted, governed by their positioning in relation to men, other representations of women, specifically and especially constructions by women, are valid, progressive and vital. Finally, discussing the specificity of representation of women itself assumes a very clear historical framework, of genre and culture, that places my study within the discursive, and outside the transhistorical. A comparative framework, then, can be enriching and when contextualised need not necessarily be prey to an unstrategic, or unstudied essentialism.[24] Each of the films marks a feminist approach to an aspect of culture and gender that differentiates it from the others in the study but also connects it through the larger informing discourse of a heuristic, culturally-specific feminism. Putting women's films into narrow nationalist columns can be equally confining, and can easily result in women being relegated to second-class status.[25]

The question of finding female subjectivity and identifying the authorial voice in the text has also been debated. According to Elizabeth Cowie, because the male desiring subject is himself subject to contradictory desires, the delivery of the female has not necessarily been as the consumable object, and that she may be occupying both subject and object positions in the film. Cowie then modifies notions of the objectification of women in film by suggesting that women's object status is not unchanging. However, she regards finding the female subject as an essentialist project trounced out of the representational terrain by the post-structuralists.[26] In the absence of 'a grammatically marking narrating voice' to establish authorial presence, it may seem utopian to make claims about finding female subjectivity in films auteured by women. While the address of the film may not be as clear as the authorial address in a nineteenth-century novel, Kaja Silverman's early commentary on what she sees as an excessive flight from the figure of the auteur, the paternity of his presence, is important to contextualise this critical standpoint as an ideological investment in textually-sealed systems of address to move away from notions of authorship attached to property rights. With great perspicacity, Silverman shows the masculine nature of the struggle to kill the father through a detailed reading of Roland Barthes' essay on the death of the author, and reveals that in fact he did desire the presence of the author in the text. Silverman concludes her reading by finding traces of female desire and subjectivity in the films of woman director Liliana Cavani.[27] Silverman also suggests some ways in which authorial presence is marked in the text: mirror recognition, secondary identification and mirroring in the body of the text itself. Discussions by film critics typically discuss the film in ways in which 'the text' and the proper name of the director of the film occupy the same place. As Kaja Silverman argues, 'although the authorial citation is in this case a formal or narrative "image", it is not any less complexly imbricated with gender, ideology or history'.[28] The highly mediated presence of the auteur in the text in terms of the text's positioning of women, and its impress of feminist authority, is crucial to my understanding of a group of women's films as foregrounding a specific kind of aesthetics, which while not formally similar, theoretically address issues relevant to the representation of women.

In speaking of texts, rather than authorial presence, I assume that the context of enunciation is more crucial to the production of meaning than the auteur outside the text; in using her proper name to describe the actions of the text, I acknowledge the historical contribution of the woman author.

In this book, I bring together the work of women directors who construct feminist authority in the text by *refusing* certain modes of representation. Although from different time periods and cultural contexts, each filmmaker takes issue with the conditions of representability for women at that cultural moment, and rejects the limits imposed on women.

Hotly contested, the term 'feminist' is here used to refer to the work of women filmmakers that is feminist, excluding thereby the work of both male filmmakers that is feminist, and of female directors that is not. In the individual readings of the films it becomes clear how provisional the term is in that it is bound to a specific moment in the cinematic representation of women in a specific culture. Looking clearly at the conditions of representability and recognising the progressive elements has long been useful as a mode of historicising that identifies different moments in the development of a genre rather than the relationship between text, author and production, or between the social and cinematic construction of women.

'Feminist', I aver, is substantively different from 'female', and hence different in tone and range from a 'feminine language' or even from 'écriture feminine'. Feminist ideologies direct the cinematic practices in the genre of feminist film, and while these may have some cross-over connections with the features associated with l'écriture feminine,[29] for the most part, they are not; operating as these films do within the linguistic discursive terrain, although they may seek to move beyond them. In responding to a set of representation issues, these filmmakers have succeeded in registering feminist authority, here defined as acknowledging, or privileging the perspective in the diegesis of the film that would contextually be recognisably feminist. The complex conversations among feminists of diverse political and cultural persuasions has clearly made a singular definition of feminism untenable; therefore the range of feminist practices impressed on film is great, given that *feminist* is an ideological, culturally-specific feature.

By way of introduction, here we shall consider the efforts of feminist filmmakers to deflect visual excess, suggestively delineated as feminine in the history of art and film, through an array of visual practices. The conflation of the overly visual or spectatorial with the female figure while tacitly acknowledged, is in many ways deconstructed through feminist visual codings.[30]

The book spreads out from Chapter 1 which looks at films that advance themes that would seem to subject them to the scopic regimes discussed in feminist theory. This study of three films, Lizzie Borden's *Working Girls* (1986), Aparna Sen's *Parama* (1987) and Nelly Kaplan's *A Very Curious Girl* (1969), examines how visual structurings evade the voyeurist placement of female subjects. Borden, Sen and Kaplan route authority similarly, and all broker it through a self-conscious consideration of the relationship between aesthetics and women. While Borden and Sen favour a deaesthetic of the film format in the former's case, and the figure of the woman in the latter's, Kaplan puts techniques that are normally used to objectify women to different use through the positioning of the female in society. I bring Agnès Varda's *Vagabond* (1985) in as a counterpoint to Kaplan's method of combating received imagery of the feminine through excessive visualisations of the female as alluring. Varda, on the other hand, places her female hero in a context that strips her of femininity, and thus undoes male visual pleasure. Unlike the other three films, feminist authority is not vested in the female in the diegesis, but the auteur's own interpretation of her dilemma. And as a coda to Sen's film, Varda serves to remind us that even when the same theme is treated in similar ways, one's interpretation can be substantively different. In this chapter, I pay particular attention to how the films counter the specific tropes of woman as commodity, and woman as aesthetics. Looking at aesthetic formats, we see how female subjectivity is constituted in diverse ways. The idea that several types of aesthetics put to feminist use locate women as speaking subjects is developed. Although psychoanalytic feminist theory has come in for a fair amount of critique for valorising a few texts, other strands of feminist criticism have paid attention to diverse formats. While psychoanalytic feminist film critics may not have turned to women's films in any ongoing sustained way, their insights certainly frame a reading of the aesthetics of these texts.

In all three films, feminist authority is established through deploying the mechanisms of looking. While none of the three posit 'a female gaze', all do severely curtail the power of the male gaze in the diegesis through controlling the male's vision in the diegesis. By blocking male authority either through looking or through narrative expedients, the filmmakers create an aesthetic that does not allow males in the diegesis visual control and pleasure. The visual field is owned by the women. Varda's *Vagabond* retains the authority of the filmmaker's understanding of the female subject's experience, a feminist understanding.

As aesthetics is not neutral and has in Western history placed an unbearable burden on minorities, black feminist filmmakers have had to employ diverse stratagems to confront the viewer, to challenge the supremacy of the Cartesian viewer. Emphasising the filmmakers' contributions to wrecking the visual paradigm that subordinated minorities, Chapter 2 travels through the spaces of the African diaspora, colonial Africa and the Asian diaspora. Here we see how 'looking power' has radically altered the female's diegetic placement in the text. Films discussed here are Julie Dash's *Illusions* (1983), Claire Denis' *Chocolat* (1988) and Gurinder Chadha's *Bhaji on the Beach* (1993).

Despite the differences in geographic and cultural contexts – Dash from the US, Denis from France and Cameroon, Chadha from England – all three take issue with black/white looking power. The expansiveness of feminism is emphasised by all three who consider race as overdetermining gender identity. A broad colonial context further links these films that destabilise the white male gaze. Feminist authority is here inscribed through race, through ensuring control of the viewer's look. If seeing grants the power of knowing, the films insist that viewers do not know what they are seeing when race is introduced. Despite a broad shared concern in plotting racial looking power in film, each film reveals a different insight about the subject's relationship to visuality. *Illusions* indicates that for black women being seen is as important as seeing, the assumption being that they do see; *Chocolat* debunks white female looking privilege by granting the black man the power to write history, and *Bhaji on the Beach* refuses to give the viewer a recognisable visual field. A brief discussion of Cheryl Dunye's *The Watermelon Woman* (1996) enriches our understanding of the 'invisibility' of black women on screen in the US, particularly lesbian women. *The Watermelon Woman* reminds us again that black women have always seen, but have not been seen. Dunye shatters the viewer's stereotypes of black women, and by establishing her authority directly through a 'talking heads' approach, shows the blindness of heterosexual/white vision. Like Denis, she too questions the sight of white women. A discussion of Marguerite Duras' *India Song* (1975) enables us to contextualise the post-colonial element in Denis, while allowing us to critique the colonial moment in Duras' text, despite its considerable innovativeness regarding the representations of women, both European and native in her film.

Controlling the white viewer's look, all five films, despite different formats, ask that the subjects of colour in the films be read differently; thus conceiving of progressive feminist aesthetics as challenging the white viewer's interpellating gaze.

Moving towards other issues of representation crucial to the construction of feminist authority I turn to genre, the 'house' of form. A key determinant in the aesthetic of a film, genre is also raced and gendered. Chapter 3 argues that the introduction of specifically raced and gendered material, and the mixing of genres, enable feminist renditions of epic, history and myth on screen. These genres are generally considered male and while feminist literary 'types' have been deciphered, filmic versions have not. I focus on Julie Dash's *Daughters of the Dust* (1991), Assia Djebar's *La nouba des femmes du Mont-Chenoua* (1977) and Ingrid Sinclair's *Flame* (1996). Sarah Maldoror's *Sambizanga* (1972) is introduced to contextualise the issues raised by *Flame*. Implicit is the notion that such newer aesthetic contributions expand the possibilities of roles for women. Transformations in genre create spaces for female heroes: women as epic heroes in *Daughters of the Dust*, as subjects of revolutionary history in *La nouba*, as mythic nationalist heroes in *Flame*, and as the seeker of revolutionary truth in *Sambizanga*. The films claim feminist authority through the aesthetics of mixed genres that allow for the positioning of female heroism. Because epic, history and myth are rewritten, the authority of male heroism is seen as corrupt, and female heroism invested with legitimacy as offering more, not just to women, but also to men.

Chapter 4 follows women's desire for cinematic texts that will accommodate much more than what has been possible in cinema's long masculine history. Looking at how feminist theory has understood sound as nullifying female subjectivity on screen leads us to how feminist filmmakers might make use of sound/silence to structure subjectivity in the diegesis. Reading the relationship of the politics of sound to vision in the films reveals the production of new genres and the interpellation of female aural subjectivities, although not in the expected thematic of woman coming to voice. Feminist authority emerges through control of sound. Films considered here are Maria Novaro's *Danzón* (1992), Moufida Tlatli's *The Silences of the Palace* (1994) and Aparna Sen's *Sati* (1989). *Danzón*'s positioning of the female as quest hero is possible only through giving her authority over the extradiegetic music of the romantic hero, *The Silences of the Palace*'s vindication of the women of the palace is effected through granting the voice-over of the female narrator power over the visual flashback, and finally *Sati*'s critique of the inhumanity of the practise through deconstructing the visual, and the contrapuntal relationship between sound and visual. Dana Rotberg's *Angel of Fire* (1992) contextualises and extends the thematic introduced in *Danzón* and offers us a highly nuanced class-specific view of women in the 'other' Mexico. The young female child hero articulates her experience and speaks throughout but is routinely painfully silenced by all around her. This chapter also begins a continued scrutiny of how women's desires are being pictured in these films.

Introducing women as desiring subjects, we follow the filmmakers' travels into and out of the thicket of male construction of female desire and female sexuality. This plotting of female desire in narrative takes the form of rendering women's desires legible in Chapter 5. Discussions focus around Germaine Dulac's *The Smiling Madame Beudet* (1922), Suzana Amaral's *Hour of the Star* (1985) and Kathleen Collins' *Losing Ground* (1982). Some feminist critics have implied that women's desires have only been very incompletely imprinted in the discursive register, submerged as they are in dominant discourses that contain their social recognition and representation.[31] In the films mentioned above, however, women claim desire both consciously and unconsciously. Interestingly, they seek to realise their desires in the world of the social, not the psychic. The different contexts of the films intimate an understanding of women's desires as both complex and located in historical circumstance. The issues in Dulac revolve around the dependency of marriage, in Amaral around underdevelopment, and in Collins around the subordination of women in art, aesthetics and the intellect. Where earlier, women's desires had been seen as devastating their authority, these films show that female desire, as expressed by the women and played out in the narrative, enables them to have authority, as the self-conscious acknowledgement of desire registers a female subjectivity distinct from the patriarchal construction of the female.

In the final chapter, I pay close attention to the narrative issues and visual structurings that are implicated in the authorising of women's texts exemplified by Jeanine Meerapfel's *Malou* (1980), Marleen Gorris's *Antonia's Line* (1995), Prema Karanth's *Phaniyamma* (1981) and Leontine Sagan's *Mädchen in Uniform* (1931). Here I reflect on the narrative turns of the films and find that they bear no real relationship to established classical male paradigms. *Malou* challenges mother/daughter narrative trajectories, *Antonia's Line* male modernist myth, *Phaniyamma* colonial and post-colonial renditions of the self, *Mädchen in Uniform* the classic male oedipal narrative. The aesthetics of feminist narration here suggests ways of telling women's stories of women to women that promise to remap narration.

The book concludes by foregrounding strategies of representation that contest dominant modes, and that enhance the conditions of representability for women. Key to this project is the registration of feminist authority, and the delineation of diverse modalities of feminist aesthetics that seek both to confront the limits of the visual and to go beyond them.

1
AESTHETICS AND THE FEMALE SUBJECT

The dependence of cinema on the female form for visual pleasure, the excess of the visual[1] involved in the depiction of the female at the very expense of narrative, was famously demonstrated by Laura Mulvey's anecdote on how Josef von Sternberg maintained that the Marlene Dietrich footage projected upside down would rivet audiences regardless of the error in projection.[2] The objectification that Mulvey identifies has a long history in Western aesthetics.

Elisabeth Lenk speaks of women having to 'bear the brunt of the ideal of beauty'.[3] Women were effectively passive participants of aesthetics as audiences and as idealised portraits. In directing us to film's history in the visual arts, Lenk enables us to understand the processes by which mainstream film succeeded in reifying women as 'to be looked at'. Her linkage of the aesthetic to the erotic is also useful in exposing the explicitly sexual content in aesthetic pleasure.

The aestheticisation of women is not the only trope in the history of art to give feminists pause in any deliberation of the history of aesthetics. David Summers' reading of the analytic categories of art criticism reveal the extent to which the property of aesthetics belongs to males while women function as figures 'to be fetishised' rather than as creators. His summary evaluation of the history of art, including a detailed exegesis on the lasting influence of Plato and Aristotle on aesthetics, leads him to use their work as a point of departure. Summers' quotation from Aristotle clarifies my understanding of aesthetics as owned by males: 'The truth is that what desires the form is matter, as the female desires the male and the ugly the beautiful.'[4]

Summers emphasises the essential role of women in art, but outside the domain of art: 'Our understanding of women and our understanding of art are in dialectical relation to one another, that our idea of art positively excludes the idea of women at the same time that it is absolutely dependent upon the idea of women for its own definition.'[5] Summers' own interpretation of the way in which form and matter are deployed in the rhetoric of art criticism indicates the male/female breakdown in the aesthetic terrain as male: creator of aesthetics, creator of forms/female: aesthetic substance, incomplete of form.

Command over the aesthetic scene has seldom been possible for women, the male artist being exemplary of the creative principle. In film this situation has been exacerbated by the pleasure of the visual lying in the female. And while the films studied here do not engage in that 'destruction of pleasure' that Mulvey called for, they grapple with the difficulties of representing women as subjects in the very medium that extracts both its pleasure and its supplement from the female. Indeed, the medium that bases its art on producing the perfect female fetish.[6]

This chapter seeks to reverse that imprint on the cultural imaginary of the female form as productive of pleasure by examining films auteured by women from different cultural contexts. The films examined here – Lizzie Borden's *Working Girls* (1986), Aparna Sen's *Parama* (1987) and Nelly Kaplan's *A Very Curious Girl* (1969) – explore the relationship between the feminine and the pleasurable visual by engaging in what Teresa de Lauretis called a 'deaesthetic'.[7] The representational scene, the process by which the female becomes 'to be looked at', visual, is shifted by the films through a deflection of the significance of the feminine/visual; i.e., their 'aesthetic' substance is held up for scrutiny and their commodity value exposed. The visual strategies used to do this paradoxically clear the way for a consideration of women as visible beings that does not replicate their object status, and reconfirms their visuality, their creativity.

The principles of feminist theory are paradoxically both challenged and borne out by these texts that counter the central premise of women's 'to be looked at' status. Confronting the trope of woman as commodity in different contexts – the commercial, the familial and the informal – the films, despite different assessments and mappings of the issues, have one element in common. They engage in a brazen testing of the visual fetishisation of women as commodities by lingering on the very mechanisms that reify them: the mirror and the camera. In situating the woman as commodity in the aesthetic terrain, the filmmakers expose the myth of the innocence of aesthetics.

Lizzie Borden's film raises the issue of whether women prostitutes can be presented as subjects when their roles represent an extreme case of female commodification in patriarchal culture. Concerned with our perceptions of femininity and masculinity, Borden's film through its aesthetic strategies asks us to consider the construction of the feminine by showing us the process by which femininity is composed. Looking at the question of how aesthetics has figured as woman in Western culture allows us to understand how value is conferred on woman because of aesthetic excess in Aparna Sen's *Parama*. The painful defeminising of the woman in Sen's film reminds us of how Borden too lent women status by her clinical scrutiny. Kaplan's text, like the others, breaks the ubiquitous, tremendously obvious, male gaze, by holding it up for mockery. The flaws of male vision are here apparent, as is the woman's upstaging through excess of the trope of aesthetics as woman. A comparison with Varda's *Vagabond* (1985) functions as a realistic comment on Kaplan's film; Varda forces the eye to look at the unpleasant, at the unaesthetic as a way of impeding access to the pleasurable visual feminine.

Reclaiming Women: Lizzie Borden's *Working Girls*

That the gaze in Hollywood mainstream cinema is male is an axiom from the 1970s when feminist film criticism started to scrutinise studio productions for their structural and psychoanalytic configurations of femininity. Among the problems of the visual for women was their passive positioning in the politics of looking. Since mainstream cultural productions consumed images of femininity, and rendered women as commodities, feminists found it important to deconstruct these representations, mythologies even. At the same time women were also making films in mixed genres or formats that offered feminist perspectives.

Shifting representational modalities to redirect the viewer to patterns in the film that suggest female authority in a narrative that handles prostitute women requires challenging conventional mechanisms of visual travelling that are, not unsurprisingly, voyeuristic. In her discussion of the multiple psychic and visual valences of the female body in mainstream film, Mulvey observes that the attempt to conceal male psychic anxieties regarding the female body are actually revealed in the theme of the female as enigma.[8] The luxurious travelling of the eye seeks to find or reveal the deliberate presentation of women mysterious. The film *Working Girls* accrues a feminist authority by distancing itself from that plot of silence about those male psychic anxieties by detaching the eye from the lingering game of looking, holding, withdrawing and then finding the female. Lizzie Borden, who had already received some outstanding feminist attention for her work on explicitly feminist themes and techniques, including the possibility of a women's revolution in *Born in Flames* (1983), brings her nuanced attention to issues of representability to the topic of prostitution. *Working Girls* shows that introducing aesthetic strategies such as a quasi-documentary mode that jostles mainstream conventions can radically alter our perceptions of femininity and masculinity by rereading social codes.

The film follows one working day in the lives of three women prostitutes in New York City. The women do their work in the relatively comfortable surroundings of a middle-class apartment. In travelling through the day with three women: Molly, a college graduate, Gina, a jeweller, and Dawn, a college student, the audience gets a close and accurate glimpse into what prostitution entails. We are given a comprehensive account of how the prostitutes deal with their employer, their working conditions and their clients. Much less is revealed of their personal lives, and we are presented with only a very short scene from the life of one of the women, Molly, who while not the protagonist, serves as a primary focus of the film's concerns. The film rethinks prostitution, as evidenced by its title, and explodes the more vicious stereotypes of prostitutes.

Working Girls was not expected to 'cross-over', but it did very well in the mainstream market, raising the disturbing question of whether a film that 'may have fully intended to use the insights of feminism to its benefit, to flatten out the fascination with prostitution', could indeed be hijacked to reiterate the trope of women as commodities.[9] While the publicity for the film may have mockingly played with the trope, the film does not get enmeshed in that particular ideology of consumer capitalism; rather, it interrogates it and even, one could say, appropriates it to identify the relegation of all women, not just prostitutes, as commodities in a patriarchal culture. The recognition functions as critique and in the medium interrupts the mechanisms of identification that would provide pleasure for the male viewer by its relentless insistence on the heterosexual exchange being predicated on the buying of women.

The film represents an achievement in the history of Western film for being a reasonable, rational account of women who work in the sex industry. While reviewers may disagree on aspects of the film, most implicitly assume that the 'deromanticised aesthetic'[10] militates against the surplus pleasure exuded by female bodies in Hollywood.[11] Borden's focus in the film is not a function of the point-of-view of the prostitutes – indeed, there are no point-of-view shots. Rather, a day in the life of these prostitutes who work in a middle-class context is told from a seemingly distant, seemingly neutral camera. In the context of the slew of films on prostitutes which sentimentalise, victimise, destroy and display these women, the use of the searching but respectful camera lends the women an agency/subjectivity.[12] Above all, the film starts out with the assumption that these working girls are women. Both the patriarchal and feminist imaginations have tended to see prostitutes as women who by the virtue of their profession cease to be women, because they no longer tie their sexuality to a single male or female.[13]

The aesthetics of the film is instrumental in the conception of the relationship between the textual subject and the female image; in the gap between the two, Borden is able to articulate the relationship between the social and textual subject, thus using aesthetic modes to qualitatively alter the perception of the commodification of women. Indeed, her earlier film *Born in Flames* was held up as an example of a what might be a feminist aesthetic by Teresa de Lauretis. De Lauretis discusses Borden's cinematic techniques as being deconstructive, as being a process of working towards a revolution for women.[14] She talks about terms of address, of the film working through differences among women. She views these elements as mapping a feminist aesthetic, and specifically insists on the 'deaestheticising' aspect of the film.

Working Girls does not appear, at first glance, to be overtly deconstructive. The documentary method, albeit fictionalised by interpretive moves, seems rather to block the visual excess in fairly direct 'realistic' modes: the woman role being presented as that of the protagonist, or the textual subject; the prostitute role being presented as the constructed image. Of course the two are the same, making a nonsense of the division of female roles in patriarchal societies. The prostitutes on screen, although images, are a far cry from received conceptions of images of prostitutes; their painstaking self-packaging reveals the manufacture of the 'commodity'.

Borden establishes 'working girls' as subjects, capable of making choices, without necessarily suggesting that prostitution itself is a viable acceptable profession for women. Borden's position on the topic, as seen in her text, re-echoes the testimony of many prostitutes who have asked that as long as the commodification of women remains the staple basis of the working of the marketplace, as long as women submit, play and work within the heterosexual economy, prostitutes alone should not be denied access to resources. Yet another banner that was flown during the prostitutes' movement to unionise was 'no bad women, only bad laws'. Accounts of prostitution internationally suggest that prostitutes are denied the rights of citizens, are not allowed to live together with female friends, are not allowed to live with a single male. The moral panic and rage against prostitution has fixated itself on the victim – the prostitute herself.

Borden's departure point is that prostitutes do not make love, they work. The film emphasises the fact in a heavy documentary style by the compilation of realia and by the close attention paid to the rituals of hygiene before and after the working girl meets a trick. One commentator notes that the film 'seems almost obsessed with the quotidian details of running a call house'.[15] Borden does not make a facile comparison between the prostitution of all women, implied by the sexual subordination of women in a heterosexual economy, and the specificity of the prostitute's task. The elision between the whore and the non-whore, however, has a long history beginning with Eve, fallen-woman archetype of all women. Borden's film carefully demystifies the religious 'natural whore' belief which would have one believe that biologically some women are more drawn to prostitution than other women.

Each of these women – Molly the lesbian, Gina the jewellry maker – are in that house because as women, in patriarchy, they have been edged into unemployment, which would not result in misery for them so much as a loss of financial mobility. Molly makes this very clear when she tells Mary on her first night on the job that if she cannot take it, she should leave. Molly herself is there servicing a male client who has the same qualifications but has a highly-paid job.

The emphasis on work rather than sex has been commented on by one reviewer who states, 'the job is a job same as any other, one that leads to burn-out, to overtime'. Interestingly, Leslie Fishbein argues that the film does not diverge too sharply from earlier white-slave films in that it confuses work with play. Examples would be Molly biking to work, one of the women smoking reefer, the women bonding and laughing. I see these elements as making the work routine and making the women and their job more accessible by using conventions of realia.[16] While the sex that the women take part in is definitely work, and eroticism is certainly absent (a lack noted by another reviewer), it is certainly not just another job.[17] On the contrary, the illusion of ordinariness, or bourgeois conformity, of the space in which the clients are received is contrasted with the extraordinariness upstairs, in the bedrooms, where the clients' sexual needs are served. The two *mise-en-scènes* are carefully distinguished to expose the brutal routinisation of female commodification.

Borden does not directly probe into the individual reasons for each woman's work choice but her representation of the relationship between the tricks and the working girls is framed by an explicit critique of patriarchy/the sex industry that neither condemns the working girls nor judges their complicity with the sex industry. Like many other feminist projects, *Working Girls* reclaims a ghettoised group of women who experience a 'double jeopardy' – the disapproval of many women *and* men – by retelling their stories in order to contextualise their lives as ordinary women, not too dissimilar in many ways from us. Germane to this is that none of the women are completely broke and all are members of the middle class.

The narrative begins in Molly's apartment. We are given glimpses of the warmth of the relationship between Molly, her female partner and the child. Interestingly, the partner is black, but we see her only briefly. In this, Borden does lay herself open to the charge that the black female is being used as a signifier within exterior frames of reference. Granted, she signifies positively in the film, but more pertinently she seems to mark the distance between Molly's home and her work. In other words, placed on the exterior, she occupies a fairly conventional space. In terms of the structure of the narrative, this positioning is crucial in insisting that Molly has a life other than work. By not focusing too much time on Molly's personal life, Borden emphasises the structural similarity of her life to that of the other working girls.

The critique of patriarchy is realised through a stripping down process which breaks cinematic codes to focus relentlessly on the commodification of sex/women. The sex in this film works to show that male pleasure in sex is a function of how powerful he is and how submissive the female is. While Borden definitely considers working girls professionals, she does not minimise the masks they have to wear to make their daily living.

Fig. 1: *Working Girls* – the *mise-en-scène* cleverly shows that women's bodies are commodities through the faceless nude in the background

Acting is a very large part of the prostitutes' daily routine. As one reviewer has noted, there are many psychological dimensions of the job: Molly plays the role of a blind girl, a sadist, a companion, a student. Luce Irigaray has written on the subversions women effect by their mimes and masquerades – a guerilla politics – whereby the woman gains some power.[18] Certainly the customers seem menacing and petty but they also appear less self-aware and definitely far less self-conscious about their actions than the women, which places Molly textually in a more privileged position. The women wear masks that are calculated to fulfill the very specific fantasies of the male clients. The women's carefully rehearsed enactment of these fantasies, such as the one of the prostitute being blind, reveal the clients' investment in stereotypical projections of femininity.

The style in which the sex scenes are filmed does not imbue the men with any extraordinary power; rather, it portrays them as powerless and to some extent infantile. During these sequences, Borden uses a stationary camera, or occasional slow pans, to concentrate on certain parts of the female body, which in this case become the instruments of Molly's work. Female nudity here is framed by the opening sequence which shows Molly in bed hugging her sleeping lesbian lover. Thus Molly's body is shown in a different context, an explicitly pleasurable one. The camera uses no soft-focus techniques, nor does it edit the actual job the woman does for the male. These sequences are painful to watch but the female spectator's distress is insensibly, or unconsciously, problematised by Borden's camera, which keeps us at a distance from the session. This sense of distance from the scene, or lack of identification with the characters, is enhanced by the complete absence of any sentimentalisation of the work the women do. Indeed, a radical alienation effect in the Brechtian use of the term, the distance enables us to understand the working conditions of the women without wallowing in a sense of helplessness about their condition. Camera techniques ensure that these women are not presented as abject. Here, the distance of spectator from the scene combines to guarantee the women a measure of privacy despite the nature of their work. Key to this strategy of enstranging the audience is the narrative technique of the film.

Borden does not privilege the working women's points of view through shots that would suture the audience's gaze with the women's looks. Rather, she is able quite successfully to use her impartial kino eye, her documentary camera, to credit the prostitutes with authority over their own lives. Through the female gaze, Borden authorises the women to set up the scene, to understand it and interpret it, but she achieves this through the effects of a camera watching Molly regulate the scene. Thus Molly acquires the objective authority of the directoral camera. Further, Molly's interpretation cannot be dismissed because, as mentioned, control of narration ceded through point-of-view shots is not given her. Borden retains narrative control, but gives Molly the authority of the gaze.

The presentation of the prostitutes as self-knowing individuals further lends Molly an oblique control over the interpretation of the narrative, but not control over the narrative itself. Structurally, most of the segments open with the women conversing among themselves which explicitly directs the manner in which we are to read the session itself. Similarly, many of the episodes come to closure in a purely female environment. Certainly, despite the half-illusion of the film being shot in real time, the women spend more time with each other on screen than they do with the men, and they discuss their lives and their work. This singular feature successfully inserts them as the interpreters of the narrative.

The discussions between the women downstairs covers several topics and ranges from work to romance. Borden stresses their self-knowledge in these conversations. April asks Molly what she is doing there if she has so many choices, Dawn brutally mimics the heteros' whore bashing, Gina and Molly talk about how their work affects their personal lives. They comment on the customers and continuously renegotiate their positions on their work. Each of the sessions pauses on Molly's measured assessment of her task. The tricks, on the other hand, are crassly judgemental about the women without questioning their roles in the process. Although they initiate the encounter and pay for the right to dominate the women, they do not emerge as powerful characters. Rather, Borden stresses the puerile, misogynistic nature of their fantasies. The girls mock the men repeatedly. Not only are the men physically dependent on the women, they are also emotionally dependent on them. Yet Borden does not suggest that the men themselves are powerless. The Japanese trick makes himself obnoxious, the musician plays power games with Molly when she is pinned under him, Fantasy Fred degrades Molly mentally. All three episodes are tinged with menace and reveal that although the women may exert power over the men in these enactments of male fantasies, they do not necessarily control all the sessions, nor are they unharmed by them.

The sheer absence of point-of-view shots as a means of expressing Molly's revulsion reverses the traditional positioning of male and female on the screen. Here, the documentary camera shocks us into 'clinical' awareness of prostitution without reducing the individual female character's size. Through the camera's interest in realia, objects and activities used to signify the work of the women, Borden succeeds in highlighting the institutionalisation and commodification of the women without diminishing them. The virtually stationary camera lingers on a woman's hand flicking a rubber, on piles of towels, on the bloody sink, on the hands incessantly washing away, on the little diary that tells its own story about a session. The *mise-en-scène* places the action in its institutional and societal context. Although the living room appears to be the standard middle-class room, one side of a wall is decorated with a so-called artistic, but essentially tawdry, black and white drawing of a woman with her legs apart. Directly above the sitting space, the drawings flaunt the slogan, 'women on sale'. The subtext relentlessly emphasises this motif. When Molly browses through a magazine, she again sees pictures of the naked female body.

Other popular and avant-garde films on this theme focus on the women as unique individuals who have somehow been led astray and whose death is inevitable. Federico Fellini's romanticisation of a prostitute, for example, in *Nights of Cabiria* (1957) almost legitimises it by playing with the motif of the pure-hearted mind vs. the corrupt body. The cinematic convention of editing further conflates the shooting of romance scenes with the scenes of sexual exploitation. Typically, the camera withdraws after the prostitute has met her client. Further, the concentration on a single subject reconstructs the prostitute as the Other or outsider. Borden is careful not to focus on only one subject. She dismisses the whole notion of romance altogether; one reviewer notes that the relationship between men and women leaves the 'romantic view out'.[19] While Fellini's Cabiria yearns for romance, and a man to come and rescue her, Borden's characters do not particularly admire the heterosexual marriage bond, nor do they specifically yearn for it. The structure of Fellini's film follows classic male plots in that the woman waits for a man to love an after-image of her, only to find that he plans to kill her. Fellini's Cabiria is tragic and pathetic, invites our sympathy, but does not make us enraged about the institutionalisation of the sex industry. Not only does Borden demystify romance, she distances sex in the brothel from love-making, pleasure or desire, and consequently associates it with violence, power and misogyny of the male ruling class.

The visual and verbal exchanges between the women form the bulk of the text and have an interrogative function. In the film, it forms a space of female friendship and bonding which sustains them and gives us a respite from the painful scenes upstairs. These scenes also resemble other models of women's conversations in their frankness and their concern. Their non-ritualised behaviour with each other contrasts starkly with the masks they wear upstairs.

Each of the women is riddled with contradictions. Peter Brunette comments accurately that Borden works with 'an expanded notion of what is "legitimate" female behaviour'.[20] Dawn and Molly do not tell their lovers where they work. Gina is honest with her boyfriend and loses him. Commenting plaintively that if her boyfriend loved her, he could not be expected to go along with her line of work, she is caught between her knowledge of men and the illusions of romantic love; that her boyfriend should want to rescue her from an occupation that she, paradoxically, has chosen in order to guarantee her independence. Two identities, divorced from one another, complicate the worker's sense of displeasure at the work and disenfranchisement from the product. When Molly has to do a 'show', a lesbian display, Mary expresses homophobic feelings. Molly breezily reassures her, 'Do I look like a dyke?' The film manages to convey the women's clear-sightedness about their ideological contradictions and their victimisation in the sex industry without softening the attack on patriarchy that their work indexically and referentially symbolises.

Borden explores these contradictions in some depth through Molly's character. Molly situates the mind and her home as sanctuaries that cannot be defiled by the clients, although the clients may invade her mental space. Borden dramatises the split self in Molly in a grotesque scene, where the highly intelligent Molly plays the role of a blind virgin for the doctor/client. Her separateness from the sessions becomes more and more compromised as the evening wears on, and the men appear more violent and aggressive. Borden thereby calls into questions Molly's distinction between renting the mind and body. Molly tells Dawn, for instance, that she will not write her paper for her because she refuses to rent her mind out. Borden shows that the difference between the private/public is complete for the lesbian woman and helps her get through her daily life. The separation between mind and body is problematic and even perhaps quasi-romantic in its connotations. Unlike *Pretty Woman* (1990), which played out the romantic inferences to a hilt,[21] in *Working Girls* the women may be prey to these notions, but the director is not.

The dialectic of agency and helplessness that the film depicts works within these seemingly rigid binary oppositions between the private and the public. Forced to negotiate between these polarities, the prostitute occupies a voyeuristic site that gives her an uncensored view of patriarchy, knowledge of men, and hence some power. Since the camera is aligned with Molly because of her mind's drastic disjuncture from her body, it enables her to watch herself and the clientele. The curious travelling of the eye to locate Molly's body as object is hampered by Molly's own looking at her body. Her own body, then, is screened through her look which functions as a barricade to the trick's look. The trick might have access to the body, but he sees only what Molly herself has screened. Thus the gaze becomes the condition of Molly's and the camera's perception of the males in a reversal that has been uncommon in films throughout history.

The enigmatic presentation of femininity is also disturbed by our knowledge of the set-up, of the act that the women stage. The viewer does not therefore have the pleasure and fulfillment of the concealed enigma revealed, while femininity itself is buried in some safe place far away from male eyes, but is asked to understand the construction of the mask as an instrument of survival in patriarchal culture. Such knowledge of women revealed establishes their authority over their own representations. Their constructions for the male tricks do not function in the same way for male viewers who possibly find it hard to identify with these men who certainly do not play any active role in looking, but are caught looking at the set-up.

Further, the men, who might expect to have power because they are buying the commodity, do not hold it with any great authority. We see male genitalia, and male helplessness or sexual dependence on the female. The context of the situation mocks the scenes which mimic female pleasure; the woman openly fakes and is hence not vulnerable to the probing camera. Thus, the women's business-like manner of concluding the transaction exposes the men's weakness. Borden is not particularly interested in the men, and neither are we. Nevertheless, we do observe that they come from all walks of life and treat the women as 'whores', not working girls. Borden makes it clear that should we also consider them whores, we would be identifying with the hetero-patriarchs, exclusively in terms of their

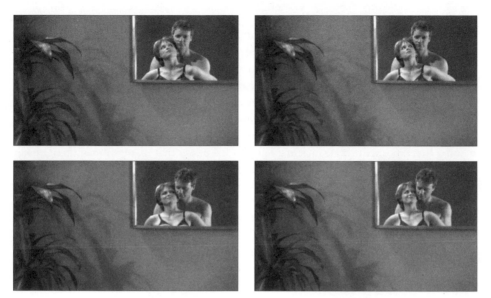

Fig. 2: *Working Girls* – the 'working girl's' gaze controls the session in this stylised mirror sequence

relationship to men rather than looking at them as autonomous individuals or in terms of their relationship to women and children.

Indeed, the power of vision that Molly has is here 'supervision'. Several of the mirror sequences illustrate the camera's oblique sanctioning of the female gaze's narrative and interpretive functions by framing Molly's look as calm, unconcerned – seldom gazing into the man's eyes or looking at his body, but surveying the entire frame to check that her control of the session is not shaken. Further, the shot/reverse-shot trajectory which in Hollywood cinema links the spectator's gaze with male actor's gaze to cut to the next frame, which displays the female as the object of the male gaze, is completely absent in the text. Indeed, the female body is displaced contextually, and the sex so mechanised, that the unequal nature of the sexual exchange is foregrounded without congealing the narrative by focusing on the female body. Brunette, for instance, asks:

> Can naked female bodies be shown performing sexual acts in a way that does not demean them even further, offering them as objects for the prurient male gaze? Somehow Borden manages it. The context of these scenes is so completely economic, and the reminder so insistent that everything we see is cynical performance, that every trace of libido is removed from the sequences, except on the part of the vulnerable, foolish-looking males.[22]

The stress on the commodity value puts the body under erasure in a unique manner that hinders gratuitous excess; in other words, it is not the female body that is the turn-on, it is the fantasy about it that is. But having your fantasy commodified in effect by the women may alter psychic relations of subjectivity, but not market relations.

The prostitutes' mimes are inflected quite differently from the kind of mimicry that heterosexual women practice in the dominant culture. As Marilyn Frye has asserted, we are all in drag.[23] Her statement allows us to understand masquerades in general, but more specially that due to the institutionalised nature of the women's experiences in the film, it is axiomatic that they are playing a role to suit their own ends. In having a facade that is so far removed from themselves, they name patriarchy for what it is – pimpery. Indeed, they can negotiate with patriarchy in a more directly challenging way than most heterosexual women can afford to. The male body is no mystery to them and holds no particular interest. Prostitutes have said, for instance, as Molly does, that when they go home, they do not have sex. It would seem then that prostitutes perhaps negotiate with patriarchy in a manner that exposes the male imaginary and with a power that many women do not have. The prostitutes, whether heterosexual or lesbian, do not have any emotional erotic investment in their clients. This absence of desire for their clients' bodies gives them a different perspective on men.

That prostitutes can scrutinise the underside of patriarchy does not guarantee total control of the agents of patriarchy. While the agent may be reduced to a puny infant, the system still invests him with power. As a non-prostitute feminist, arguably Borden could be charged with presenting prostitution as a viable profession in the name of abstract feminist principles while forgetting the harsh realities of prostitutes' lives: the killing, the exploitation by pimps, police brutality, social disrespect, loss of real citizenship, misogyny, self-hatred. The realist aspects of the film further conspire to accentuate the documentary effect, making the representation more damaging. Yet Borden's film is not a documentary, and the filmic rendition of prostitute women has been so problematic that the survival ethos, the sense of self these women have, cannot but be claimed, despite the difficulties and complexities attached. From *Waterloo Bridge* (1940) to *Mona Lisa* (1986) these films show desperate 'self-hating' women who end up in disastrous circumstances. A film such as Neil Jordan's *Mona Lisa*, ostensibly about the exploitation of a marginal, black, London-based, female lesbian prostitute, succeeds only in exploiting the female body and the image of the prostitute, in satisfying male lust and male narratological cinematic conventions.[24] Bob Hoskins reads the prostitute and we read her; she cannot read. Borden's film choices were no doubt dictated by a commitment to avoid any reproduction of the dominant male gaze.

A feminist ciné artist who wishes to raise popular feminist questions about prostitution need no longer target other feminists as her audience.[25] She can go mainstream, be a director instead of a filmmaker and shape the after-images of hundreds. In so doing she has to follow Hollywood's cinematic codes and avoid documentary and avant-garde. The feminist documentary records women's lives, the avant-garde inserts women's voices, but the mainstream film is the site where meanings of gender are contested within the frame of a recognisable simulacrum. Borden's choice of realism as a mode facilitated her entrance into a cinematic context that lent her the power to construct an image, as opposed to merely reflect it. Constructing the image as excessively feminine in the narrative context, but not visually presenting it as feminine, allows Borden to deflect the surfeit of the feminine visual. The textual subject, then, is not a direct reflection of the social subject but a negotiation achieved in part by a dialogue with the social subject and a quarrel with the object status of the social subject. The textual subject, Molly, and the textual narrative are thus claims that Borden makes to alter and re-conceive the meaning of the lives of working girls. The subjectivity of the working girls is achieved by a troubled negotiation which critiques prostitution without condemning prostitutes. Their ability to understand their commodification, and their investment in using the social object status of women, while valuing themselves and their lives in terms that exceed their commodity fetishisation, is an indication of more than their subjectivity; it suggests a self-conscious resistance to their commodity status, although a haunting sense of an identity outside that of working girl keeps each of them from organising and from claiming that identity in discursive spaces beyond the bordello's confines.

The 'show' aspect of the visual is present even in the familial, as suggested by another film from the 1980s – *Parama* – from the very different cultural context of India. The film itself is in Bengali, not in the dominant mainstream Hindi, and it prompted feminist discussion because of its theme of adultery. Not just exonerating a woman's adultery, but taking pleasure in it, in the 1980s middle-class Bengali or even Indian cultural cinematic context, was definitely unusual. Visual pleasure in the feminine is invoked, predictably, but paradoxically also comes to signify invisibility for the woman in the familial context. Sen too tackles the surfeit of the feminine visual head-on, but in the format of the parallel cinema of India; with no song-and-dance routines, but fairly high production values and the presence of a star, she follows through on the promise of the parallel cinema by engaging seriously in a crucial social issue.

Aesthetics as Woman: Aparna Sen's *Parama*

The deaestheticisation essential to reclaiming women in Borden's *Working Girls* would not at first appear to be important to a discussion on the adultery of a middle-class housewife in Bengal in the 1980s, considering the visible commodification of prostitute women. Yet the deaestheticisation of the woman herself in this case, not the codes of her signification as in Borden's, is crucial to the project of investing the female protagonist with authority.

Cultural context is significant in this instance. Western audiences might find the painstaking record of the woman's relationship outside marriage commonplace and even dull; however, taking the adultery of a respectable middle-class woman to the screen without presenting her as 'other' was quite disturbing for the viewing public of this decade and generated considerable interest.

Within this context, Aparna Sen continues to question the troubled relationship between aesthetics and women in *Parama*. The film's sense of itself as an artefact militates against its aesthetic surplus becoming equated with women and curbs any over-aestheticisation either of the woman or the text.

The notion of over-aestheticisation as problematic would seem to indicate a suspicion of aesthetics. Male traditions of art have been relatively comfortable with aestheticising women and women's bodies. In discussing artistic tropes in the representation of women's bodies, particularly the nude, Lisa Tickner establishes the two modes of articulation between 'Western erotic art and the nude' as fantasist and realist. In sum, decadent or romanticist fantasies set the woman apart quite obviously as sexual repositories while realist work, even in pornography, showed the woman as participating in sex as opposed to being the object of sexual fantasies. However, despite the agency afforded to women in realist work, Tickner's thesis concludes on the note that even realist texts such as porn retained a fantasy element.[26] Fantasy has been a crucial element in both articulations of women as aesthetic. Kobena Mercer emphasises what is at stake in the representation of the female nude:

> The image of the female nude can thus be understood not so much as a representation of (hetero-)sexual desire, but as a form of objectification which articulates masculine hegemony and dominance over the very apparatus of representation itself. Paintings abound with self-serving scenarios of phallocentric fantasy in which male artists paint themselves painting naked women...[27]

Mercer and Tickner draw our attention to the practices of a Western male artistic tradition sealed by heterosexual fantasy.[28] Male cinema, developing on this tradition, albeit in a 'low brow' tenor has also continued to aestheticise women. By aestheticisation of women I mean the artistic appreciation of their beauty, looks, bodies, especially and usually within a cultural sign system that holds such appreciation in high regard as 'artistic' and 'creative'. Mieke Bal's formulation of how '"beauty and truth" are opposed when it comes to women'[29] suggests that for the male artist and critic, a realistic rendition, while truthful, would not be regarded as 'beautiful'.

We feminists might take objection most obviously to an appreciation of the external,[30] but more seriously to the symbolisation and pictorialisation of woman, one that locates her outside history and in the male artistic imaginary. Feminist film, however, has been successful in slipping out of this problematic representational terrain. Borden's realistic presentation of women in *Working Girls* falls outside both traditions of fantasy registered here, high-brow and low-brow, partly because she acknowledges that the male fantasy, and the agency afforded women in the text, is not located in traditions of aesthetics that position women as objects of art, enunciation.

Ostensibly, classical realist aesthetics might invest the woman with a subject position beyond that of carrier of aesthetics that is given her in Western pre-twentieth century schools of art. Outside of Hogarth's gin mills and Defoe's cutpurses, the burden of aesthetic pleasure has been borne by women in art and on-screen. Mukul Kesavan, in a piece that attempts to give women their rightful place in film history, argues that the great stars of the Hindi screen Raj Kapoor, Dev Anand and Dilip Kumar would not be memorable without Nargis, Geeta Bali and Waheeda Rehman, amongst other female stars.[31] Women exude aesthetic pleasure; their presence maps the aesthetic terrain.

Aesthetic pleasure is to be differentiated from Laura Mulvey's visual pleasure not because it is a more innocuous rendition of her reading of male spectator relationships with the female on-screen but because the aesthetic terrain overwrites the narrative and forms the basis from which (male) spectator relationships with the female on-screen can begin.

The truth claims of classical realist aesthetics provided a programmatic way to close off the derivation of the film's aesthetics from the female on-screen. Georg Lukacs, prominent proponent of realism, argues that realism is an adequate mode for the detailing of social phenomena. Defining realism as the artistic dialectic of appearance and essence, Lukacs maintains that 'the richer, the more diverse, complex and "cunning" this dialectic is, the more firmly it grasps hold of the living contradictions of life and society, then the greater and the more profound the realism will be'.[32] For Lukacs, complexity and completeness can be achieved only with realism. Can this be the aim of the feminist filmmaker for whom complete reality may not be aesthetically satisfying? The challenge of feminism, after all, is to imagine what has not happened yet, to articulate unthought-of possibilities.[33] Feminism also quarrels with Lukacs's view that the true aim of art is objective reality. Lukacs appears to have a rejoinder in defence of realism even in this particular instance because he claims that 'it [great realism] captures tendencies of development that only exist incipiently and so have not yet had the opportunity to unfold their entire human and social potential'.[34]

Yet the classical realists have been charged with suppressing the mode of subject production and presenting the subject in a commonsensical way.[35] While this critique of realism was powerful when it first emerged, it is not adequate for an analysis of realist feminist films. Even if the feminist realist film were to present the always already constructed subject, she would still maintain a discursive relationship with a recognisably coherent reality that, because of the subject position of women in patriarchal society, would function as social critique. The possibilities of agency for the female, however, are never guaranteed, and classical psychological realism in film did not live up to the promise for reasons too well known to be documented here. My own sense is that the narrative pressure fractured the possibilities of a female subjectivity that would be unhampered by the aesthetic shackle.

Among the many attempts to release the aesthetic shackle, Aparna Sen's *Parama* stands out as a film that both addresses the problem and steadfastly rejects it, following the female hero's growing awareness of the many shackles that bind her, the aesthetic being the hardest to recognise, to grasp and then to refuse. About a traditional housewife, Parama, in a joint, or extended family, the film traces the changes she undergoes when she is coerced into modelling the 'Indian housewife' for a male photographer with whom she then has an extra-marital love affair. The film follows the relationships in Parama's life that change as a consequence of her sexual liason with the young photographer, Rahul, who has recently returned from the West. The protagonist accrues considerable authority, one that the film testifies to, when she refuses the aesthetic, an action that has to be registered in the film's visual strategies.

In this case, the film's aesthetics is worked out by a process of blockage. Each strand of the film moves according to a nuanced patriarchal teleology, but the film's visual and narrative interventions block the smooth passage of the teleology. Sen does not rewrite, rework or redress any of these movements but begins a new narrative motif that enables the blockage of the patriarchal teleology.

The film begins, very disappointingly, by showing us a woman who is constantly tremulous. Set in a middle-class Bengali household, her tremulousness indicates her relationship to her family. Her obsequious regard for them is irritating and while providing a reason for her tentativeness, it does not engender a sympathetic understanding of her plight. Rather, we become angry with her for the uncertainty she reveals in her interactions with the family. Considering that she is a traditional woman in a traditional household, she should be certain of her role. However, her hesitations imply a perturbation in the traditional as much as the personal. Thus her obsessive tremors show the cracks in the seemingly transparent, seemingly natural way of traditional family life; her personal discomfiture draws attention to the problems of Parama's own participation in that life.

Parama initially presents herself as a woman from a different pre-modern generation. She holds her pallu[36] in a particular way and is a devoted listener to her husband's tales of upward mobility, all with a child-like demeanour. Raakhee's physical gestures capture Parama's somnambulist state quite accurately. She is somatose, not quite comatose, but asleep nevertheless.

The film is both powerful and subtle in showing that domesticity, the joint family, the nuclear family, motherhood, wifehood are conditions that somatise. An early expository sequence in the film grounds the conditions of her waking sleepfulness. Shot in the middle of the frame, she is shown glancing backward to the left as different people assail her with questions. One member wants to know what to wear, one which vehicle to take, one wants her to wait on cousins who are guests. The sequence ends with the family noting that Parama's youngest son, Tutu, has gone to bed without eating.

The story seems to take a decidedly problematic turn when a young male photographer walks into her life. In many obvious ways he would appear to awaken her. Indeed his role as artist implies that the awakening is aesthetic and sexual, complicating and indeed perhaps covering the fact that he is a male who is insidiously connected with the family through Bubu, Parama's husband's nephew. When the New York photographer wants to photograph her because she is a 'traditional Indian woman', Parama's family puts pressure on her to pose for him. His access to her and his power over her are thus through the family network.

Parama's identity is clearly underscored as a traditional one most obviously by the fact that the foreigner, Sarah, does a parody of the unknowing foreigner when she expresses her confusion about the various names, bhabi, kaki, ma, bahu, kakima, and so on, that she (Parama) is called. A circle of male relatives sets the unsuspecting foreigner straight, but we understand that Parama has no individual identity (in the Western sense) as a female.

Three generations of women – Parama, her mother-in-law and her daughter – discuss the issues around female identity at breakfast one morning. The conversation is sparked off by Parama's humble entreaty to be allowed to join an old friends' reunion at her friend Sheela's place. It turns out that Sheela is a divorcee. The mother-in-law thinks that Sheela's divorced status is a shocking waste of her talents. Parama thinks Sheela's lot in life is a hard one, but the daughter remonstrates with the mother in very superior, condescending terms. The daughter stresses Sheela's job as director of the spastic school and also condemns her mother for leading a second-hand life 'through baba (father)'. In this conversation, Parama is clearly linked with the mother-in-law, especially in her insistence that a woman cannot expect what is a man's right to have.

Parama's introduction to an individual identity is through Rahul, the photographer. He refuses to call her kaki or bhabi and joshes her out of the age-bracket that tradition and family have placed her in. He clearly stakes a claim for her as an individual. The glamour around modelling moves her away from the traditional dignity associated with her role as Indian housewife, yet her initiation into an individual identity is through the traditional trope of being the artist's model.

Sen's critique of the photographer challenges his Westernised notions of identity as having to be individualised. Poonam Arora and Katrina Irving also point out that in photographing Parama alone, he isolated her.[37] They mention that Rahul should have done a family portrait, if he wanted to capture the traditional woman. Mercer, in discussing Mapplethorpe's photographs of single male nudes, contends that 'the solo frame is the precondition for a voyeuristic fantasy of unmediated and unilateral control over the other'.[38] Since Parama's life revolves around other people in the home, Rahul's focus on her does tend to have the effect of overpowering her, regardless of his more 'aesthetic' aspirations. Interestingly, Rahul photographs the Durga puja with people all around the frame, with Durga in the backdrop, a fairly fierce and definitely commanding female figure.

Opening shots of Parama are through Rahul's lenses and the middle of the frame is impressed with what looks like the circles of a target range, the circles around professional photographer's lenses. Parama would now appear to be both aesthetically and visually coerced, and as a female, hunted. Sen negotiates these possibilities with extraordinary finesse. The effect of aestheticisation as immobilising and threatening to the woman is shown by the target range occupying centre space right before the advent of Rahul's photographing spree. Yet Parama does not become the object of the male gaze through the relay of looks elaborated in Mulvey's scheme. The very visibility of the camera equipment, the centring of the target range or the exposure of the aesthetic agenda, interrupts the relay of gazes, they do not facilitate it. Visually, the film shows her objectification, it does not objectify her in an unproblematic way.

The dependence of aesthetic pleasure on the female body in both high art and film makes it difficult for the film to cut off the aesthetic pleasure the spectator, male or female, derives from the star Raakhee. De Lauretis, in a discussion on feminist aesthetics in Lizzie Borden's *Born in Flames*, validates one possible approach as the deaestheticisation of women in film. She quotes one commentator's conversation with the auteur: 'The images of women in *Born in Flames* are unaestheticised ... You never fetishise the body through masquerade. In fact the film seems consciously deaestheticised which is what gives it its documentary quality.'[39] Sen takes a more tortuous path in not accepting deaestheticisation as the only way of compensating for the over-aestheticisation of women in film. Instead, with every click she shows the pain of the woman at being caught by the photographer. Typically we see the photographer do his set-up, then we hear the click and see the flash, and then the startled, embarrassed look of the woman as she must appear in the photograph. We never actually see her through his lens or his eye so we are not invited to see her through his eyes. In most of these set-ups Parama is casting a glance at the spectator. Rahul's camera glance is not resealed by her reconfirming look. Parama does not play to the camera in the diegesis.

Parama's appearance on camera foregrounds her invisibility in traditional life. Draped by the pallu, she presents herself as invisible. The visibility she acquires when she becomes Rahul Rai's model has many dimensions. The family seems to notice her attractiveness or her femininity (read: sexuality). Both visually and narratively, Parama tries to elude the camera's searching but her evasiveness becomes increasingly tentative. She is conflicted by her sense that this acknowledgement of her attractiveness may take her out of the traditional milieu. The film situates the dilemma of her awakening in her growing desire to explore herself as aesthetic and sexual.

While the location of her individual growth, placed so overtly around the new-found public acknowledgement of her body colludes with the blatantly patriarchal motif that equates a woman's sexual awareness with her individual awareness, it provides Sen with the opportunity to explore women's own conflicted desires to be visually noticed, to be aestheticised. Parama has never been noticed and she begins to take pleasure in being visible. The film then underlines her aesthetic visibility, her attractiveness as the terms by which her presence will be acknowledged. Sen attempts to work through the dialectic of an invisibility traditionally conferred and a sexualising, aestheticising visibility.[40]

Aestheticisation does not seem dangerous especially because the sexualisation is covert. Indeed, in this context both are liberating for the woman. Yet Sen's exploration of the male camera effect reveals that woman as aesthetics is deadly for the woman's subjectivity. Take the photographic routine of clicking Parama at work in her home. Sen had already established that Parama's life was an endless repetition of domestic, care-giving tasks. When Rahul wants to capture the traditional housewife, he tells her not to bother about him but to go about her work. His claims to *ciné-verité* are immediately counterfoiled by his elaborate light and camera-angle set-ups. Soon, he asks that she wear mehndi, as she had earlier. As a New Yorker with an opportunity to be in a native space and to the work/private routine of an Indian housewife, his photography is also an anthropological invasion. As a photographic subject, Parama is supposed to offer herself in all innocence. In photographing her, Rahul renders her as a curiosity, albeit one that offers aesthetic pleasure.[41] The photography aestheticises her work and in so doing denies her her historical reality. The anthropological eye takes the meaning out of her daily work and smoothes over the film's initial premise that Parama's life is a burdensome round of daily tasks. The male artist's eye negates that truth in aestheticising the woman.

Even as the male artist's eye obliterates the truth, Sen's insistent focus on his constant photography has the effect of exposing or bringing to the fore the fabricated nature of her seemingly natural role as housewife. The photography works to take us out of the seamless classical realism that the film favours. For instance, in one set-up Rahul manages to get a pose of the middle-class memsahib reclining in her chair, with the dhobi (launderer) in the forefront of the frame on his haunches, clothes scattered around him. We do not notice him despite his place in the frame until Parama snaps at him: 'What are you staring at?' While we are forced to pay attention to Parama's tasks and what they imply in terms of her role in the family and in society, we also see her place in the family as a function of her privilege, of her class – a price she pays for class privilege.

Clothed in saris with the pallu over the shoulder, Parama is the invisible traditional wife. Photography brings her out of the traditional world and renders her visible. Both traditionalism and modernity are functions of the 1980s Bengali middle-class family's notions of the role of women. As the film progresses and Parama becomes more separate from her family, her body loses both its traditional aesthetic and its concomitant class significance. Her body and her appearance become declassed. Parama loses class.

If Borden's *Working Girls* highlights the commodification through a stripping-down process that breaks cinematic codes, here, a relentless process of stripping down declasses Parama herself. The aesthetic codes are broken down in the former, the same effect is achieved later in Sen's film by the protagonist's breakdown. She begins to look faded and out of sorts when the photographer leaves for the Aegean. Dark lines under her eyes emphasise her lack of interest in her family and her life. When Rahul publishes a close-up of her more than a trifle *déshabillé* with the inscription, 'Remember? Love, Rahul', her literal objectification at the narrative level is made clear. More importantly, the film concerns itself with her loss of authority and privilege as consequences of her independent actions.

The loss of class privilege, the family's hostility and, interestingly, the children's lack of tenderness drive her to attempt suicide. Divested now of family bonds and societal privileges, Parama looks totally different. Sen uses the glamorous appearance of Raakhee to signify Parama's change. In the hospital, Parama has no colour, either in her face that usually had the big red bindi, or her clothes. She wears a hospital bed-jacket and she is shorn of her hair. Without her long black hair, usually shiny and in a bun, or down in a glossy length to her buttocks, she looks completely unlike the feminine memsahib of the earlier portion of the film. The declassing has stripped her of her aesthetic qualities as the 'traditional housewife' and of erotic attraction. The declassing is crucial because it is also the physical gestures and forms and the costumes of her class that render her aesthetic as the traditional woman. Sen thus shows the tie between tradition, aesthetics and class as bound by the invisible woman.[42]

The relationship between morality, visibility and madness is explored in the film after Parama's husband discovers her photograph in Rahul's rag. The whole motif of hystericisation, or its institutional procedure, is introduced by the neuro-surgeon after Parama's head injuries following her suicide attempt. The attempt to hystericise her further can be seen as another class effort to control the female. In a discussion on Foucault's research on the bases of the bourgeoisie's power/knowledge, Griselda Pollock cites the 'hystericisation of women's bodies' as one of the instruments of such sex-centred knowledge.[43] While Luce Irigaray and others have spoken of how women's hysteria can be seen as a way for women to manoeuvre outside patriarchal control, their very hystericisation can here be seen as a punishment for such efforts.[44]

Pollock also maps out what she calls the 'bourgeois semiotics of class and gender'. Her scheme of the proletarian and bourgeois bodies clarifies our understanding of Parama's status as traditionally aesthetic and.as hysterical after her sexual adventure. Under proletariat she lists, for instance, 'sexual, immoral, bestial, body, diseased, disorderly, unclean, corrupting', and under bourgeois she has 'asexual/sexually controlled, moral, spiritual, soul, healthy, orderly, clean, purifying'.[45] Under 'bourgeois', I would only add 'aesthetic'. Rahul's first photographs of Parama are insets in his series on the Durga puja that he is covering. The credits unfold through the puja sequences. Not only Parama, but the rest of the women on-screen are in white saris with red borders, with the pallus draped over their heads, signifying demureness, modesty, restraint. Rahul later photographs Parama on their visit to the temple when she is a little less restrained, but still very traditional. In fact, she tries to call Rahul to book by asking him to call her boudi if he will not call her kaki. Despite the cultural anthropological tone of Rahul's project, that of featuring the Indian housewife, its sexual overtones became visible in the photographs, when they were screened in the home slide projector. However, the family glosses over it, contenting themselves with a few jokes. Their tune changes when they see Parama, semi-naked in glossy photographs in *Life* magazine. She is obviously regarded as both sexual and immoral. Her presence is shunned by the family, almost as though she has contaminated herself. Her mother-in-law refuses to acknowledge her presence, her children run away and her husband refuses to sleep in the same room with her. He also tells her, 'I don't want a whore teaching my children'.

More cutting because more publicly humiliating is the sequence where Ramesh the servant asks Parama for his salary. Husband Choudhry, on his way out, in the far left of the frame, shouts to the servant that he can collect the money from him in the evening.

Clearly she is considered corrupting and out of control. After her suicide attempt, she is set aside even more profoundly as crazy, diseased and a terrible burden to the family. One sequence reveals their total disengagement from her since she is no longer one of them, one of their class. The doctor comes and tells them that he might have to operate on her. They mistakenly believe that this is emergency surgery and try to talk him out of it. They are disappointed when they find out that the surgery is to forestall cranial damage.

Such a scheme that assigns greater social and moral values (albeit skewed) to the swathed, dependent woman and that even denies full humanity to the sexual woman is startling in a film that is so perceptive about Parama's historically subordinate status. Sen does not, however, endorse this scheme.

It is important to note that Parama does not become hysterical; she is constructed as such by the doctor and family. Their hystericisation allows them to skim over Parama's actions. The implications would be graver if they were to accept that all her actions, both the infidelity and the suicide attempt, were performed through her will or agency.

Sen does not imply that Parama becomes distraught because of her failed love affair. Rather, she shows us an extraordinarily sleepwalking Parama before the hospital and a more stable Parama later. Speech marks the difference between Parama, 'somatose', without agency and Parama, active, with agency.

Parama is luminous in her routine tasks; hysteria cloaks her. She is never animated before she meets Rahul except through the colours of her clothes and face. She always speaks with hesitation, almost like a child. She is speechless when the family cracks jokes in bad taste about her photographs, slow of speech when a visitor questions her, silent when her husband talks of his great plans. She begins to have conversations with Rahul, but her animation still comes from the aesthetic colour scheme, not from her sense of vitality or life. After all, a model follows the master cut. She is speechless and stuttering when Rahul kisses her, breathless, gasping and speechless when they make love, crying and speechless when she asks her husband to come back home. She resembles a startled bird for the major portion of the film; a brilliant portrayal by Raakhee of a woman's disquietude, and her awakenings.

Hysterical women – real and imagined – surround her awakening; yet another way in which Sen contextualises women's hysteria. Parama dreams of a field of marigolds. A woman, in medium close-up, her face absolutely demented, up to her mid-breast in marigolds, with characteristic cracked laughter is running through the fields. Parama wakes up through the slimy mist of the dream. The trope is introduced diegetically when she takes Rahul to her old, dilapidated house. She brings him to an abandoned, desolate, empty space – the room that used to be inhabited by her aunt. A point-of-view flashback then gives us a view of the aunt, behind barred windows, crying to be released. Its inferences for Parama's life need not be laboured, but Parama obsessively speculates on the similarity between their two lives. She asks, 'Perhaps she had a lover?' And she also says that she,

Parama, has started to dream of her often. Hysteria and confinement is very much in the fringe of the lives of these traditional middle-class women.

Parama sees another mad woman strenuously trying to make her escape one day after the photograph debacle. The woman is pulling away at her guards. Three people give chase, four, then a crowd surrounds the woman, and she is taken away forcibly. In all instances we see the hysteria as a function of the confinement. Parama's hystericisation is very much a part of her deaestheticisation. The hysterical women have their hair askew, they are unkempt and are not 'feminine' in the way femininity was provisionally defined by the traditional patriarchal aesthetics of the family and Rahul. Parama's so-called sickness places her outside the pale of aesthetic women.

Parama is confined eventually in hospital. Without colour, without the sitar; without her pallu and its dignity; without her hair and her bindi, Parama confronts herself and her past. She refuses to submit to psychotherapy, refuses to admit to guilt and decides to accept a job. Deaestheticised, declassed and defeminised, Parama finds herself. And she speaks for herself.

Sen makes it a point to tell us that Parama's rejection of her role as aesthetic object has emerged primarily because of her friendships with other women. Early in the film, when Parama meets her cohort, she finds that she is the only one leading a domestic life. Each of her friends is doing something socially useful and personally satisfying. More interestingly, her best friend Sheela is divorced, working class, smokes and is dressed very differently than Parama. She wears glasses, does not have noticeably glamorous hair, and does not have a traditional look about her. Without her accoutrements, Parama, too, does not look so elegantly aesthetic.

Yet Parama's shift to a different lifestyle is not only a matter of divestiture. Through the film she searches for the name of a plant. But the name does not come to her until the end when she interrupts the family confab by saying in sheer wonderment, 'Krishnapallavi, that's the name.' Her daughter moves away from the family circle, comes and stands next to her and in a moment of awakening about her mother, says raptly, 'It is beautiful, isn't it, ma?' Parama now is not herself aesthetic, she has rediscovered aesthetics outside of herself. Although she had earlier played the sitar, Rahul's photography had transformed it into an aestheticised spectacle. That Parama has come to speech as name-giver and has put herself outside the aesthetic frame ensures the explosion of the myth that aesthetics is woman.

Poonam Arora and Katrina Irving – in an article that posits that *Parama*, as indigenous ethnography, cannot be read outside the Indian context, particularly the roles of Indian women, and a knowledge of Indian aesthetics – have a different reading of the conclusion of the film. For one, they find Parama's appearance in the end to resemble a widow's and consequently find the conclusion disempowering. Subtle as the reading is, for it argues that the 'indigenous ethnographer', Rahul, constructs female identity in Western terms that are disastrous for Parama, Sen's film style does not endorse that traditional Indian role at all. While Arora and Irving are correct in pointing to Sen's debunking of the photographer, I would maintain that Sen uses his figure to discuss the difficulties of Western individualised feminism and Western ideas of romance. After all, Sen sets up the romance to expose it. In this context it is important to note that the debate about the relationship between Western and Indian feminisms was current at this time, and further that the trope of the woman's awakening, particularly in the middle-class milieu that Parama and Sen inhabit, was being explored by Westernised, Indian women writers.[46] Arora and Irving note that there are two endings to the film:

> The one [ending] seen in traditional Indian settings shows Parama finally reconciled to her husband and returned to her family after having admitted her guilt in psychoanalysis. The film seen in the West and in Westernised Indian circles shows the woman committed to finding her independence although not knowing exactly how to go about it.[47]

Diegetically, Parama flatly refuses psychoanalysis, read in the film as a gesture of rejection of institutionalised, even Westernised, support. She also flatly denies guilt. Arora and Irving's argument is that she is able to do so because of mythologising her role as Radha to Krishna, played by Rahul.[48] Such a reading also implies that the auteur hystericisises her, abruptly, even brutally, bringing in a mythological code onto a predominantly realistically-coded film without any cinematic signal of the shift in register.

With the difficulties I have with specific portions of Arora and Irving's reading,[49] I find it interesting that they argue that a 'third aspect' is at work in the film.[50] By this, they mean the deconstructive strategies used to debunk the photographer. The anthropological critique is layered by the feminist critique that maps out an aesthetic terrain to be differentiated from the modes of dominant cinema. Wimal Dissanayake suggests that despite the film's effort 'to examine how the subjectivity of women can be rearticulated in terms of the historical experience of gender',[51] it reinscribes patriarchal values in the 'visual codes, narrative strategies and the iconography in general'.[52] Dissanayake maintains that the film's style is neorealist. The film, however, never maintains or establishes any discursive authority for itself as a transparent medium. Rather, the artifice of the male imperial photographer calls such codes into question. The presence of the alien camera through the romance, the use of the alien camera to explode the aestheticisation of Parama indeed suggests the problems with the transparent rendition of reality. Two point-of-view shots in the hospital show us Parama's view of the family. They are seated as in a family portrait and their faces clearly reveal the difference between Parama's notions of a woman's role as opposed to their traditional concerns. It is crucial to note here that a feminist aesthetic cannot be birthed, created, without the social content being engaged. Short of scenarios that have no perceptible relationship to realistic discursive modes, a feminist aesthetic has to emerge from the manoeuvering of the dominant codes if it is to reach a wide target audience, in this case middle-class Indian women. Sen contributes to a feminist aesthetic by revealing how male aesthetics is drawn on specific class and gender imperatives attached to the female.

Dissanayake's more damaging charge is psychological. He contends that female identification with the women characters would inflict pain on women viewers and 'offer male spectators an opportunity to get rid of their feelings of guilt through a process of catharsis'.[53] Narratively, this process seems quite difficult to imagine, granted one's awareness of how different texts are received by audiences. For instance, one sequence where the family expresses hesitation about the brain surgery Parama has to undergo shows without recourse to dialogue that they are hopeful that she will die and not be either a burden or embarrassment to them. Their faces fall when the doctor reassures them that matters are not so dire. Yet their expressions have already let us know that they would prefer to be relieved of Parama's presence. In the context of daily newspaper accounts of how women, especially daughters-in-law are not valued, Sen's observation unveils the middle class's discomfort and cruelty. It is doubtful that female viewers would want to belong to such a family. The film does not stop at that because it shows us a newly empowered Parama, one who has stood the test of family and emerged. Regardless of how female viewers might apply this to their lives, we do not leave feeling weak because Parama has won some independent space, whether in the family or society.[54] Parama has succeeded in establishing an identity for herself that is unconnected to the family, and values herself outside the aesthetic frame, thus proving that she has shaken off the destructive effects of having internalised the dominant culture's values that reify aesthetics as woman.

The feminist strategy of 'deaestheticising' also directs the viewer to the interventions the directors make in the politics of women's sexuality. In both *Parama* and *Working Girls*, the viewer is not only asked to withdraw patriarchal judgement of the character but to approve the feminist qualities of the women's decisions. In their different ways, both films reinscribe the basic feminist notion that what a woman does with her body is her business, which is clearly extremely difficult to maintain and uphold in patriarchal structures. Annette Kuhn, in agonising over the 'feminist' component of a film, its definition clearly changeable, suggests that it is the 'reading' that makes the film feminist, ultimately empowering the viewer, putatively a woman.[55] Teresa de Lauretis emphasises the address to the woman viewer.[56] Aesthetic stratagems that make it possible to deflect the visual surplus clear the representational terrain in ways that make feminist authority visible. Both *Working Girls* and *Parama* are clearly resisting patriarchal understandings of what life for women means. Weaving a critique of patriarchy into the deaesthetics scheme furthers the feminist aesthetics and politics of the texts. We may disagree about what the characters should have done, but the texts' signifying apparatus leaves no doubt as to how the issues of prostitution or adultery should be read: through feminist understandings of the same.

Woman as aesthetic excess, incorporated into the diegesis, seems to fault both aesthetics and woman for this surplus of visual commodification even as the narrative critiques the woman's role in society in Nelly Kaplan's *A Very Curious Girl* or *La fiancée du Pirate* (1969).

The Aesthetics of Eroticism: Nelly Kaplan's *A Very Curious Girl*

While Lizzie Borden's camera attempted to curtail the visual excess of the feminine and Aparna Sen relentlessly stripped the process of female aestheticisation down, the context of family politics in Sen's film suggested that the bigger loss in the deaestheticisation was class. Both, however, ultimately agreed with the intimation that deaestheticisation of the female, whether because of aesthetic format or the result of plot exigencies, was essential to understanding the construction of the female as aesthetic; that is, as valuable, whether as commodity in the market place or in the family. Nelly Kaplan parts company with both directors in her assumption that the erotic uses of visual excess can actually empower women, a point of view closer to third-wave feminists than might be apparent from the date of this film, 1969. Deaestheticisation is not essential to devise a strategy to challenge the surfeit of the visual aesthetic used to represent women; Kaplan's *A Very Curious Girl* promises that feminist authority can be accrued by the use of the erotic without devaluing women or participating in commodity fetishism.

The film is about a young girl in a village in France who is routinely used sexually by various inhabitants of the village. When her mother dies in an accident, she turns to prostitution. The villagers have treated the young girl, Marie, and her mother as outsiders and wastrels. Marie finds that she can have a fair amount of freedom by being a prostitute, given that she had earlier been used routinely by her lesbian farm-owner boss who also expected Marie to be grateful for the servitude she was offered. Marie eventually explodes the hypocrisy of the petit-bourgeoisie who both use her services and mouth their pietistic morality.

Her difficult presentation of women in the film, caught through the heterosexual gaze, does not simply deliver the female to the male voyeur.[57] Were she to do that, the film would be clearly exploitative of women. In seeking, however, to put the male gaze under erasure, or to hold the male gaze hostage, she confronts the male surreal fantasy of the child/woman as passive and innocent. Stella Behar and others claim that in her fiction, under the pseudonym Behlen, Kaplan does not shrink from citing women as erotic, sexually-charged creatures. In making this move, she seems to be shifting towards a discussion of a feminism where sexuality is not just marked as a male domain, but is also viewed as a female impulse. The surrealists, of course, had their well-drawn-out fantasies as did the modernists, and one asks whether in reflecting the gaze back to the male viewer, Kaplan is not after all fulfilling those fantasies for the male viewer rather than introducing female desire or female eroticism. Unafraid of the excesses that emerge from a project so deeply entrenched in a male view of art and women, Kaplan's preferred mode as punishment for viewers is mockery, without altogether shunning the pleasure given to men through the female body. It is all grist to the mill and comes from an acknowledgement shared with the surrealists that eroticism can be liberating, even if it does not completely alter the representational codes by which women are presented, or the images of women. Discussing aesthetics and eroticism, Elisabeth Lenk provides a way of contextualising Kaplan's work: 'Women are experimenting with the erotic. This gives them the temerity to believe that a new aesthetic and even a new human being is in sight.'[58] While the apparatus itself may not be destroyed, or even the codes, a different deployment of the erotic may indeed change the business of aesthetics as usual by, at the very minimum, reminding us as this film does, that aesthetics as usual is predicated on female eroticism as usual. Gertrude Koch makes this point specifically in connection with mainstream film when she states that 'many of Marlene Dietrich's roles are impressive examples of the aesthetic mystification of sexual identity'.[59] The aesthetics and erotics of the female inevitably contribute in large part to the aesthetics of the film, the positioning of subjectivity in general, and female subjectivity in particular. Shifts in rendering aesthetics and erotics, then, do mark differences in perceptions of subjectivity.

The film, however, is quite unlike other prostitution films, whether commercial or art-house, in that the prostitute is not sentimentalised, but neither is the sex regarded primarily as work as in Borden's *Working Girls*. Unlike that film's research impulse, despite some rich cross-overs in thematics, *A Very Curious Girl*'s format works with mainstream techniques to produce a feminist aesthetic. *Parama*, although not documentary, does distance itself from the mainstream Bombay or Hindi film which delights in the spectacle of femininity. Indeed, *Parama* showed that working with women's sexuality in a serious way – that is, concentrating on the woman and her choices, her subject position – was possible only in the 'parallel cinema'.[60] Different from *Parama* because of its overt emphasis on the erotic, *A Very Curious Girl* is also closer to more traditional filmic representations by dealing with women's visual excess, rather than trying to curb it through a deaesthetic.

The opening sequence of the film raises troubling questions regarding Kaplan's visual technique and her approach to the female body. In terms of the economy of the female body in the market place, Kaplan's framing of the narrative clarifies her understanding of it as commodified; however, regarding the economy of desire she asks how the latter can topple the former, and how the economy of desire can be rendered transparent to underscore the commodification.[61] The suffusion of eroticism in the text has reasonably enough been difficult to situate within dichotomous conceptions of visual art products as sexist or feminist, especially in the long history of Western visual art, whether 'high culture' or 'popular culture' as being overwhelmingly sexually absorbing of women. Chris Holmlund attributes this female voyaging through eroticism as the cause of feminist lack of attention to Kaplan's oeuvre.[62] While largely true, the film has not faced feminist neglect. As Holmlund notes, Claire Johnston, Marjorie Rosen and Karyn Kay have written on it. In *The Pirate's Fiancée* (the non-American title of the film), Meaghan Morris's influential book on feminism and post-modernism, her interpretation of the film serves as a matrix for her thinking on women and culture.[63] Morris uses the title itself as a metaphor for the need for narratives that will help women imagine a reality other than one they inhabit. Consequently, she contests the feminist distrust of the lead character's sexual involvement with the men as being steeped in patriarchy. While Morris does pay attention to the young girl's piracy of the story, she is less attentive to the visual structures that represent the girl.

While not overtly surreal, except in a couple of sequences, the film's viewing mechanisms could be said to invite comparison with the surrealist practice set forth by Rosalind Krauss. Negotiating her way through the difficulties surrealism poses for women, Krauss offers an insight that allows us to situate Kaplan's use of various visual structurings, and surreal sequences in the film in the broader context of women's surreal photography as distinct from that of the male masters. Discussing the 'deconstructive logic of surrealism', Krauss accounts for her defence by maintaining that the viewer of surrealist work will 'be stripped of authority and dispossessed of privilege ... trapped in a cat's cradle of representation, caught in a hall of mirrors, lost in a labyrinth' and furthermore that she sees this 'practice [referring to surrealism] as one of feminising the viewing subject in a move that is deeply antipatriarchal'.[64] Kaplan, in this film, does not simply invert the positions, even if that were possible either in the narrative or the culture at large, but she does preempt the male viewer in the diegesis, and consequently perhaps outside also, from retaining the male viewer's privilege of a wholeness of subject positionality.

Ostensibly, the film invites the male viewer's gaze to feast on the girl. Among the obvious suturing devices within the diegesis are the eyes of the old man and the machine eye of the mailman's binoculars. The smooth identification of the male viewer with the two men who have the facilitating apparatus is partly impeded first by the unprepossessing appearance of the two characters, that qualifies the transcendence of perception attributed to the spectator by Christian Metz,[65] second, by the pleasure afforded by the idealised Other in the mirror stage envisioned by Jacques Lacan.[66] Unlike other male voyeurs, here they do not have the power over the woman that renders the viewer's voyeurism pleasurable. The old man is completely helpless; eyes wide open in lechery, but slobbering in an extreme caricature of a lascivious male. His voyeuristic bid is foiled by the girl who stands right in front of him and shows herself, depriving him of the surreptitious pleasure of the power of peeping unseen. When the voyeur is seen by his object, his power is deflated.

The initial shock of the girl performing a show for the old man impedes the match between the spectatorial camera eye and the spectatorial look in several ways. If the fore-grounding of the male eye within the film does not impel the male viewer to question his looks, it does not follow the invisible suturing of the Hollywood tutor code. Extensively theorised, the role of the male subject in attaining mastery over the field of vision because of the effacement of the camera itself is in this context significant.[67] The shot/reverse-shot sequence which empowers the viewer to see both fields of vision through a controlling gaze is also problematised here through a series of simple expedients. The male eye is revealed as un-neutral, and is brought into the field of vision as the 'observing eye',[68] thus challeng-ing the supremacy of the 'Cartesian' viewer and his objective, mastering view of the field of vision. Furthermore, no point-of-view shots impose their vision of the female as the superior, or authoritative view. While the eye is foregrounded to disalign spectator and camera, the camera eye does not serve the male voyeur in the diegesis. The camera retains its authority because it registers that the male in the diegesis is looking, but does not neces-sarily consider his view, and definitely does not impress it on-screen. The camera's retention of authority, a trope in both *Working Girls* and *Parama*, renders it possible for feminist authority, outside the male visual field, to be established in the film.

The sequences with the machine eye, or through the mailman's binoculars, materialise the concept of the camera eye's decoupage from the spectatorial look. The binoculars are detected by the girl, the object of the gaze, and she, by acting, seeks to control both the binocular look and the camera eye. In other words, in these sequences the director puts her own camera under erasure, and shows how her camera is complicit in the visual exploita-tion of the female body, but also in the way in which the camera revels in the surfeit of the feminine through the visual. While potentially damaging to the imaging of women, the context here produces a different meaning. A crucial feature that this strategy engenders is not the self-consciousness of the all-powerful camera, but its relative helplessness when what it seeks to capture as natural has been staged for its benefit. The girl upstages both the binoculars *and* the directoral camera. This double viewing, of the response to the camera, famously discussed in *Dance, Girl, Dance* (1940)[69] continues through the film in various ways. Combined with the directoral camera's confession of helplessness, feminist visuality as a doubled seeing is recognised.

The postman's binocular invasion (four eyes), that would have been threatening if it had been secretive, becomes an open challenge to the specular invasion of female privacy by rendering it transparent. To further limit any of the power that a secret voyeur accrues, Kaplan ensures that we know that the entire village is aware of his voyeurism. The post-man's bid for power through voyeurism is quelled by the girl's awareness of his binocular

Fig. 3: *A Very Curious Girl* – a swish pan foils the voyeur's pleasure

vision. In one sequence, where she makes herself over, the surreptitiousness of the voyeur's gaze is subtly questioned. A swish pan, coming after a shot of Gaston, the postman, glued to binoculars, shows us Marie bathing the goat. Once the goat is taken care of, Marie sheds her clothes. At this point, it is not clear whether she knows the postman is watching her, but it seems fairly certain that she could count on it, since he spent most of his time watching her. Yet her glancing into the mirror, and her conversation with the goat – 'Don't I look nice?' – seems to indicate a degree of privacy that is being threatened, a fact borne out later by the other machine the postman bears, the gun, which he uses to kill the goat. Nevertheless, when she steps out, she is confident that he/someone from the village is going to be outside her door. So even if she does not stage an act for them, she is aware of their intrusiveness. This kind of viewing is rendered as transparent as the old man's ogling, partly because of its ubiquitousness, and acknowledges her representation of her body through her words to the grandfather: 'It's for you, grandfather. You're the only nice one.' The self-valuation of the commodification process brokered through the gaze cuts through the obvious, and the more seemingly sophisticated, considering that almost everyone in the village catches Gaston watching Marie. Many of the other men are also invested in watching her, and the culmination of Marie's 'acting' takes the form of calculated performances that she stages for each of the men, none more calculated than Gaston's. When he proposes marriage, she says he should test the 'goods' first, taking shirt and skirt off, and pressing herself to him, before prodding him out with a rifle butt. Marie's awareness of the male gaze as extending beyond the postman is revealed by her deliberate love-making with the young man in public. In doing this, she is showing that she knows she is watched, that she is commodified, and that a key portion of the male desire she attracts can, through control of the process of watching, be stoked. Certainly, the men had wanted to, and did, have sex with her earlier, but then she had no control. Inflaming their desire by selecting what they see; by staging the appearance of a glamourous woman, she does begin to 'run them'.

Marie's actual control over the 'mad dogs' as she calls them is very restricted, as is evinced by the brutal slaying of the goat, and by their brutality at the end of the film when they try to destroy all the property. Her ultimate control over them hinges around the tape-recorder which tellingly proves more powerful than the binoculars in taping every indiscreet comment made to her in bed by the grocer, the chemist, the priest, the mayor and the postman/warder's son. Their comments are played in church, *ex nihilo*, almost the voice of the supreme authority, here giving the woman the power, albeit through the physical recording of male voices. Kaja Silverman's argument that women are seldom given the authority of the voice-over is relevant here.[70] Marie's voice, which functions in the role of the voice-over, is significant in locating the nexus and context of the speech for the listeners, but the speech of the male voices is crucial to the maintenance of Marie's power. Interestingly, the male voice-over, like the male voyeuristic attempt, usually so invincible narratively, is deflated; here male authority is exposed for being built upon a hypocritical premise. Of course, this does not mean that their authority collapses, as proved by the townspeople's (including the women's) wrath against Marie. Nevertheless, the hearing apparatus apparently triumphs over the seeing apparatuses in this film which is built around the specular, a conclusion quizzically modified by the hero's return to film, to watch as it were, 'The Pirate's fiancée'.

The cruelty of the young woman encouraging these men to talk brutally about their wives is at first disconcerting, in part because of received wisdom that suggests that the woman is held responsible for any kind of disruption. However, since the women do not help her out, and even urge the men on the day Gaston shoots at the hut, Kaplan may well be pointing to the hypocrisy of the village women in condemning the two outsiders. An implied contrast is in their submission to male will as opposed to Marie's manipulation of male desire.

Marie's ultimate escape from the village seems to be unrealistic; fabular, as Meaghan Morris suggests.[71] The majority of the film is shot in a mainstream style, where a certain sort of transparent realism reigns with only a few surreal visual sequences, or fabular narrative turns (such as the conclusion), during which its feminist aesthetic and politics seem to cohere to enable the construction of a sexually-dominant subject.[72] The caveat on whether this construction is progressive insofar as images of women are concerned still holds. Morris is critical of the 'images of women' approach,[73] and understandably so; nevertheless, I do feel that the matter requires attention, but certainly not as the only yardstick, or even the most important yardstick, by which to judge the feminist qualities of a film.

Interestingly, early feminist reviewers of the film did not isolate the images of women in the film, but paid attention instead to its narrative reworking of myths. Linda Greene unapologetically appreciates it as a 'feminist fantasy'[74] and Marjorie Rosen calls Marie a woman in control, a figure she does not see in Hollywood mythologies.[75] The film comes in for high praise from Naomi Gilbert, who, in an essay on women's films such as Leontine Sagan's *Mädchen in Uniform* (1931) and Marta Meszaros's *The Girl* (1969), that posits a dialectic for the cultural female hero, argues for Marie's definition as such, because she overcomes the cultural stereotyping of the sexualised woman, and ceases to function as a conduit between men and their experiences of life. She argues that the film falls into the synthesis stage, where the oppression and the struggle construct a female hero that women viewers can feel socially connected to.[76]

The discursive medium within which the image is presented is clearly of great importance in enabling us to read the image as signifier. Here, Claire Johnston's crucial insight on how myths are demystified by scrutinising their icons is relevant to her assessment of Kaplan as a feminist filmmaker. Covering up the signifiers – the icons and images of femininity – naturalises myths on women, according to Johnston. In a powerful statement that challenges the dominant paradigms of realism, Johnston argues that 'the law of verisimilitude (that which determines the impression of realism) in the cinema is precisely responsible for the repression of the image of woman as woman and the celebration of her non-existence'.[77] Kaplan's discursive modes in this film, including the surreal, serve to draw attention to the construction of images of women, and women's responses to them.

By account, Kaplan sought a rough look for the film, perhaps in a conscious attempt to foreground the signifier, and wanted a rapid, nervous energy in its film style. While the editing seems smooth enough, and certainly not sufficient to disrupt the signifier in any way, other elements do breach the 'transparent realist mode'.[78] Derek Elley has commented that Kaplan does not follow the 'Godard-Expressionist style',[79] observing, for instance, that the *mise-en-scène* of the shack that Marie decorates is brightly and crudely coloured, which serves to undercut the 'transparent realist mode' that is employed.[80] The bright oranges of the shack and the fire, the backdrop of vibrant colour for the men, who are caricatures in many respects, invest many of the sequences with surreal humour, and question the 'naturalness' of what occurs between Marie and her client. Her exaggerated movements, and the afflatus of their sexual response, owe something to the visual art of Germaine Dulac.

A Very Curious Girl is closely connected to its politics.[81] Linda Greene observes that the incredibleness of the narrative and its 'anecdotal quality'[82] lend the film its surreal quality, particularly in the presentation of Marie who is shot in certain sequences with more than a touch of the surreal. The sequences that show Marie's responses, in medium close-ups, to the villagers after her mother's death illustrate well the politics of Kaplan's surrealism.

The bringing home of the dead mother to her humble shack in the woods on the outskirts of town is extraordinary for its feminist resonance. Here, Kaplan makes a double play, showing 'the contradiction of surrealism which glorified women as natural and vital with a total ignorance of their thoughts and desires',[83] and creating a feminist surreal scene. While the village men hardly glorify women, like the surrealist male painters that Kaplan knew, they are indifferent to the living sentient Marie, let alone having an awareness of her thoughts and desires.

The sequence begins with the men bringing the dead body into the shack, a scene that is both grotesque and surreal for the complete lack of attention which is paid to the dead. We do not recognise Marie's mother as a human being, or even as a human corpse. Rather, she is presented as a drawing in the middle of the frame, a drawing of a still female, with hair visible, eyes not visible and completely quiescent. She is scarcely noticeable. Her stillness alone is not remarkable; in conjunction with the tremendous animation of the men attempting to dispose of her remains, it draws attention to her daughter Marie, also depicted as a still life in the right-hand corner of the frame. When the men come in with the body, Marie averts her face and sits down, covering her eyes. The men dominate this composition. Smoke around her, Marie is on the edge of the frame, and looks away from the body, only half of her visible for the scene's duration. There is a congruence between her placement in the frame and her mother's stillness. Almost imperceptibly, she is pushed out of the frame when the priest comes in. The camera cuts to the theft of the underwear, and then without any specific narrative reason, to Marie in the centre of the frame looking out at the audience. She reasserts herself and does not let them invade her space. The shift from the surreal to the transparent mode of realism brings us back to the action of the narrative. The surreal composition has reminded us of the devastating oblivion that women can be subject to, making reference to Kaplan's difficulties with surrealism as indifferent to women's thoughts while glorifying them in artistic terms. Metaphorically, the band of men in the sequence can be viewed as artists arranging their composition, or, à la Kaplan, discussing the disposal of the remains. If the men hold sway over this sequence, in the next sequence of the mother's body, the young Marie is the artist, and she is in control of what happens.

If the men are dominant in a surreal composition, the woman is in an expressionist one.[84] The men jostle amid the dark shadows while Marie directs the burial of her mother. Again, Kaplan moves out of the transparent realist mode to the expressionist to comment on the girl's ability to triumph over the men's obviation of her mother and herself already shown so brilliantly in the surreal sequence.

Three close-ups of Marie draw special attention because of their stylistic difference from the rest of the film. Brenda Roman notes that the last of these – of Marie, looking into the flames instead of the burning house – is problematic, because it 'draws too much attention to the camera viewpoint'.[85] On the whole, however, according to Roman it is the narrative that is important in the film, not the camera work. Kaplan herself regards her cinema as more classical than her fiction, but admits that playing with the code is part of her method,[86] a feature noted here in these shots. This departure in camera technique to differentiate the medium close-ups of Marie from the other shots, registers Marie's will to act, acknowledging her profound understanding of the situation in no uncertain terms. The director's gesture in authorising Marie's visuality establishes both Marie's and the film's feminist strategies.

The shot of the girl looking into the distance while centred in the frame is repeated. Shortly after her mother is buried, Marie gives the men directions, and then looks into the distance. Again, after the men shoot the goat, she lays claim to the centre of the frame and that look into the distance. While this type of shot could be seen to suggest a character looking into the camera and hence, at the audience, Kaplan uses this look to signify Marie's claim to independence, freedom and autonomy. These shots isolate Marie's look, and underline her self-conscious look outside the diegesis, outside the world of the film. The fourth time we see that look is when Marie burns her shack, and looks right into the fire: both are in the same frame, both are centralised. While Marie looks into the fire, she seems to see something other than the burning house which remains out of frame, again to emphasise Marie's vision outside the narrative constructs.

As Marie is able to stage-manage the field of vision, so is she able to understand her opponents, through that observing look which is detached from the relay of looks that privi-

Fig. 4: *A Very Curious Girl* – medium close-up of Marie in an expressionist scene reveals her power over the men

leges the male gaze. Consequently, it is not that she has the power of the look, but that she grasps the reality of the village, a fact suggested by Kaplan not only once, but four times.

Marie's bid for independence is signalled by that look and is borne out partly by the narrative which shows her charging men for sex, a logical enough move since they all 'have their way with her anyway', including Julian and Irene, her employer and her mother's landlord. We do not know why this solution did not occur to Marie earlier; perhaps it is the result of the lechery and cruelty of the postman when her mother is killed, or because she asks the men if they can bury her mother in return for sex. There are other enigmatic moments in the film: why does she not go with the wandering male film projectionist, another male with a machine? Again, Kaplan's investment in Marie's independence provides an answer of sorts for her actions, which have as much to do with the commodity-controlled marketplace as with the market trading the commodity. If, in the economy of desire, the female is the commodity, Marie trades very well with it. She stays one step ahead of the game, always valuing herself higher than the market value that is placed on her. For instance, the underwear representative says that she is charging Paris prices, and she seems to be charging 35 francs more than the going rate. The issue of value is also reassessed in liberating terms: for Marie this monetary value is the price of her power, but not, as it were, freedom. For that, she tosses it all away, but reveals their desire through the tapes that play in the church. That economy is now materialised; hitherto seen as part of her witchery, but now recognised as male expenditure of desire. The scene where the men meet and cut to the chase – 'Well, she's taking our money' – becomes the most important issue for the men. But in raising prices, the commodity, the female, gains value – here, power – while the buyer loses value, because the economy of desire has rendered the transaction both patent and unpredictable in terms of the almost feudal servitude that the two illegal migrant women, Marie and her mother, endured. There is some hint about their Roma status, and their foreignness is brought up time and again, as though the village can use it to justify their scapegoating, which in the case of Marie, is sexual.

The portrayal of Marie's sexual dominance over the men has generated some interest amongst feminist reviewers of the film. Diane Waldman, for instance, sees her as a Circe figure, and sees the film as part of feminist efforts to assign 'positive value to historically maligned female images'.[87] Karyn Kay too has recourse to literature to find a model for Marie, Brecht's Pirate Jenny, who, however, does not really escape but only fantasises about it.[88] Kaplan recounts that Marie was a difficult figure for male viewers who somehow wanted her to die in the end, clearly an appalling comment for Kaplan who analyses the male reaction as their discomfiture with the practice of sex without sin. Kaplan also identifies Marie as a witch who might have been burnt in an earlier time, but who now has the power to do the burning, a comment that adds a layer of meaning to Marie's burning of the house. Kaplan believes that the revenge motif is central to human impulses, and attests that after the revenge is effected, one can go on.[89]

The last shot of the film sequence reverts to the transparent realist mode of the French New Wave but almost with that magical insouciant touch by which Marie seems to escape – into the movies! Certainly, Kaplan meant the conclusion to be tongue-in-cheek; to include both the image of the actor and the female fantasy ego idealised in cinema. In working through the commodification of the female in a transparently realist aesthetic,

Kaplan nevertheless redeploys both looking relations and cinematic mode through holding the male gaze hostage, and through it freeing the narrative. In playing with excess, Kaplan's film shows that it can be manipulated so entirely that the issue of 'to be looked at' can be reformatted to show women's active control of their representational scene. Its authority then lies in an aesthetic that does not depend on subjective points of view, but the doubled seeing of both directoral camera and the eye of the protagonist.

Refusing Femininity: Agnès Varda's *Vagabond*

That magical insouciant moment of stepping onto the road, or into the movies, might very much be a function of 1969, and the possibilities of that moment. What would happen to Marie on that road? Agnes Varda, herself a doyenne of the French New Wave, and maker of several films pertinent to women, would appear to answer the question in her feature *Vagabond*. About a young woman who is on the road and who leads a hand-to-mouth existence, the film flashes back to find out why she died. It touches on all the people Mona, the female hero of the film, met while on the road, and offers partial narratives of each person's encounter with her. Mona takes to the road, and lives outdoors, even in winter.[90] The film begins on an entirely distrait note with the camera drawing closer to a tent in the background, and then the twigs, before it lights on the body of a young woman that is barely discernible as such. The body of the woman, her lack of corporeal beauty, begins the process of curtailing the excess of the visual. As Varda herself comments about the beginning of the film: 'It's clear that she died. Alone in a ditch, frozen, which is an awful death. And the way she looks – she's a mess – she's the colours of the ditch almost, like the colour of a gun.'[91] As one critic points out, the dead female body is the classic patriarchal narrative cue for the male hero to step in and solve the mystery.[92] The opening premise is different here, but the investment of the narrator implicates the *cinema-verité*-style narrative in an unavoidable voyeurism, despite the difference in narrative motivation. Varda then works with a voyeuristic narrative structure, reminiscent of stories that seek to solve the enigma or riddle of femininity.

A quick comparison with Kaplan's film reveals some similarities and differences. While both are aware of visual excess, Varda's training and sensibility direct her to a style that would lend itself to an ideology of deaesthetics, comparable to Borden. Varda's narrative strategies, however, would appear to negate that deaesthetic by its search for an answer to the woman's death and involve her in a politics of looking that would reveal the protagonist's life, allowing the travelling eye to light on its choice object: the female. Impugning all narrative claims could be one way of cheating the curious eye, but destabilising all truth claims would also defeat any feminist perspective on the woman, or the feminist significance of the director's visual design. Subsequently, Varda maintains her curiosity and the viewer's, but complicates both the narrative and the pleasures of the travelling eye by introducing a radical process of deaestheticisation that averts the travelling eye, and substitutes the voyeuristic rendition of the narrative for the feminist.

The female voice-over narrator, Varda herself in a direct auteurial gesture, seeks to find out about her life; her concern is the only indication of any lasting affection for Mona. The corpse of the woman, its refusal to offer any kind of pleasure in the female form, is

Fig. 5: *Vagabond* – although deaestheticised, the dead body of the young woman elicits the viewer's curiosity; here her posture leaves her open to preying eyes

complicated by the auteurial investment, shared by the spectator, in trying to find out how Mona ended up as she did. The narrative answer is chilling: Mona's insistence on freedom from both capitalist and patriarchal structures brings her to this end. The voyeuristic narrative structure that Varda works with is problematic because it shows the process by which Mona becomes deaestheticised. But unlike the stripping down that releases Parama in Sen's film, Mona pays for not retaining the cultural marks of her femininity with her death. Sandy Flitterman-Lewis claims that Varda 'disrupts the patriarchal logic of vision by reconceiving the voyeuristic gaze',[93] but that challenge is posed only towards the end of the film, although Royal S. Brown suggests that Mona's 'body repulses the gaze rather than [attracts] it'.[94] Joanne Klein, too, comments that male spectators had identified Mona as 'scary', and had felt visually distanced.[95] The defeminisation is presented in terms of contrast, which accomplishes the task of repelling the voyeuristic gaze to some extent; the visualising of the feminine becoming increasingly more economic, without succeeding in complete deaestheticisation, except in two instances. While the many narrators of Mona's story are partial and hence cannot claim ownership of it, the systematic deaestheticisation of Mona works as a deliberated destruction of femininity, whose poignance is so great, that the narrative paradoxically acts much in the way that Dorothy Arzner's film *Christopher Strong* (1933) does, suggesting that the social world is not ready for the female hero. The critique of the social world is just not as ruthless as the process of Mona's radical divestiture of beauty, and then most importantly, of life. The voyeuristic gaze persists through much of the film, pleasurably marking the female in the beginning, and although narrative filters mediate the 'story', the look itself is unmediated, partly to accentuate the contrast by which the male gaze is then completely averted because of the horror that would be involved in the looking. While not overly aestheticised, in most of the episodes Mona clearly pulls in the erotic look, but as the film goes on, she becomes more physically straggly; not out of choice, but of necessity. Here, the narrative seems to suggest that she is being ground down because of the free choices she makes, rendering her deaestheticisation troubling. The narrative also implies that her freedom costs. She walks into the woods and is brutally raped. Indeed, the opening flashback by the beach features two young men talking about how they might have had her; her face is in the darkness, suggesting a brief shuttering of access to her. Another sequence close to the end of the film illustrates the extremity of the stripping down; Mona is on the streets when she runs into some carnivalesque merrymakers who terrify her because of their masks, and she too is plastered with the mud. Here, her face defies any prospect of visual excess, and access to her is closed off. However, the body of the corpse is prey to all eyes, and to the curiosity of the narrator/auteur who, although hardly omniscient, seems to have pretty complete access to Mona, allowing her the same privilege as the viewer. Varda maintains that we do not find out much about the girl, leading us perhaps to believe that the inflexion of the narrative is elsewhere, in our access to the voyeurism of the characters that Mona meets. While we do understand the latter, Mona is not as opaque as Varda would have it. Each narrator's tale and view exposes Mona. The difference between partial narrator and auteur, however, lies in the latter's insistence on getting to the bottom of the story, by not stopping at the partial, but forcing her own eye to follow Mona to that last ditch, then to the cut that shows the discovery of her body, oddly aestheticised in the conclusion of the film which returns to the beginning. Auteur and viewer are both privileged, in observing the voyeurism of the partial narrators, and in enjoying it themselves. The rub though is that neither auteur nor viewer like what they are forced to witness: the defeminisation of Mona.

The shocking contrast between the earlier Mona and the later Mona, who is out of control, functions almost as visual punishment. Monstrous when plastered with mud, and paranoid, she clearly represents the harsh difficulties of freedom on the road for females. While the road movie, as presented by Varda, 'explores other cultural and other gendered geographies', in not marginalising women as the road movies of the 1950s and 1960s had done, Mona's relationship with the road is ultimately deathly, thus throwing into question the road as being liberating for women at all.[96] Roger Ebert also believes that the road almost destroys Mona, and that she is represented in extreme terms towards the end, 'animal-like', he suggests, in her desperation.[97]

In a different vein, Flitterman-Lewis maintains that Mona is ultimately feminine,[98] and perhaps its expression outside the familial space that the other women in the film inhabit is threatening for society. Mona, however, puts herself outside female space each time she shakes off a shelter offered to her, or is forbidden to stay because of her refusal to follow the rules. By the end of the narrative, Mona explicitly says she is tired of moving around, an unambiguous expression that leaves no doubt that she is searching for an alternative life, not necessarily a punishing freedom. Visually, she begins to be less conventionally pleasurable to look at as the movie comes to an end, which marks her exit from conventional femininity. Discussing Sandrine Bonnaire's performance in the film, Jill Forbes notes that 'in her physically repulsive appearance [she] is obliged to deny everything that a member of her profession lives by', confirming the fact that Mona cares little even about the rules that the road lays down for women.[99]

The film's conclusion is chilling on two counts. The woman's freedom on the road ends in death, a thematic comment critical of 'society's contradictions'.[100] Further and more

Fig. 6: *Vagabond* – punishment for the viewer; Mona has reached the end of road, and the camera scrutinises her, plastered with mud, and defeminised

profoundly, Varda seems to suggest that her freedom is from packaged 'femininity', a point emphasised by one of the narrators, that inevitably destroys her even as it forces the narrators to acknowledge a quality in the woman over and above her femininity by forcibly removing the signifiers of visual femininity from her depiction. As Amy Taubin puts it, 'although she's young, strong and willing to work, her refusal to accommodate anyone else's standards or desires – she doesn't bathe, she's demanding, she'll fuck for a joint and take off without a thank-you – guarantees that she won't survive'.[101] In other words, it is her refusal of femininity – definitely more of a bind than the resolution suggested by Kaplan – which seems oddly utopian in light of the Varda film. Marie made herself up in Kaplan's film and survived. Perhaps the two conclusions do not contradict each other after all. What happens to Marie on the road? We never find out.

Varda believes that 'even though Mona dies in a ditch, she's a survivor'.[102] In terms of specifying the agency implicated in Mona's choices, Varda is correct. However, the implication that this death specifies the limits of possibility for women at that moment is shocking.

Locating feminist authority in the life of a female who died because of that life is even more disheartening; however, the authority of the film lies in its feminist understanding of why Mona died; not because she was a slut, or a bum, but because she insisted on not following the rules of femininity. That is a powerful insight, and one that reclaims women. Had Mona died beautiful, erotic, holding out the possiblity of sexual/visual pleasure even in death, the voyeuristic narrative would have been upheld. Dying as she does, that narrative falls apart to be replaced by the feminist one that refuses femininity.

The films discussed in this chapter approach the problem of the relationship between aesthetics and the female subject through the limits of the visual for the construction of female subjectivity. They suggest that the visual imperative, however compelling, can be checked by strategies that challenge the visual reification of women, their conflation with aesthetics, and with aesthetics and eroticism. Visuality is held accountable for the woman's 'to be looked at' status.

Working Girls reprises the voyeurism that the working girls experience by the self-consciousness of the female's 'staged show'; *Parama* includes class as a marker of woman's embodiment of aesthetics as a way of demystifying the voyeuristic look; *A Very Curious Girl* succeeds in holding the male gaze hostage by excessively replaying its look as spectacle; *Vagabond* reverses the image of the female fetish by refusing her female character any femininity by the end of the narrative.

All of the films work through complex tropes that merge – the aestheticisation of woman, woman as aesthetics – while working within a visual apparatus calculated to foreground the construction of both. In order to establish feminist authority each uses a different tactic. Borden handles the difficulties of the hostile medium and the history of woman in aesthetics by switching the format; Sen by deconstructing the trope and by compromising the evidence of the visual; Kaplan by exaggerating the visual commodification while stressing woman's role in exploiting it; Varda works with the very image of the female by deaestheticising her while adhering to some fairly conventional features of filmmaking. In hailing the female as subject, all proffer an aesthetic that tampers with the surfeit of the visual to expose its limits.

2

BLACK/WHITE LOOKING POWER

This chapter deconstructs the blindness of aesthetics to race; and the films discussed take issue with the exclusion of black women as aesthetic. The history of the representation of black people in Western aesthetics has been fraught with difficulty, and replete with images of Otherness, often non-humanness. While aesthetics was typically figured as woman in Western culture, black people's entrance into the aesthetic scene was barred. Visual practices were highly racially coded, as in colonial photography that attempted to set up racial visual taxonomies. Early psychoanalytic and Marxist feminist film theory too had its own blind spots, but interventions by other feminist critics indicate the special burden placed on black women in Western representations.

In an early article, Robert Stam and Louise Spence call for a shift away from the 'positive images' approach, and in a very pertinent analogy with the cinematic representation of women maintain that 'the cinematic and televisual apparatuses, taken in their most inclusive sense, might be said to inscribe certain features of European colonialism'.[1] In the study of film, this intransigence of the apparatus regarding race has been seen as axiomatic as Mulvey's formulation on woman's 'to be looked at' status.

The presence of an aesthetic of a different kind in both Third Cinema and feminist cinema has been acknowledged, albeit with the recognition that an aesthetic framework cannot be laid out without foreclosing experimental possibilities. Paul Willemen, for instance, defines the very condition of Third Cinema as a cinema attentive to the 'historic variability of the necessary aesthetic strategies to be adopted'.[2]

As is usual, the challenge to aesthetics comes from several different traditions of film-making – all different from one another but all of which were constrained to find a way of communicating that was unique to their historical positionalities and their national aspirations and\or social\individual subjectivities. Black (African American, Third Cinema in the West), Third Cinema (Latin American, Asian, African) and feminist cinema (in the West and from all of the above mentioned)[3] have all struggled with the desire not to define themselves against the dominant codes. Speaking of feminist cinema at once seems suspect, almost as though one were speaking exclusively of Western women's feminist film and thereby resealing the 'all the women are white' phenomenon.[4] My purpose here is to mark differences among film feminisms even while establishing commonalities.[5]

Even as these departures from normative Western film aesthetics were emerging, definitions, especially of specificity, became extraordinarily uneven in that the minority text begins to bear the burden of specificity. The assumption behind such insistences is the belief that the text is worthy of study because it is representative of third world, black or feminist issues; more commonly one would combine or invoke all three. The dream of specificity, the urgency to claim a speaking space then battles with the impositions of authenticity. In metropolitan centres these texts are commended for their adequacy or inadequacy in fully-fledged representation. Sumita Chakravarty, in her discussion of New Indian film's responses to the dominant aesthetic, finds that 'authenticity', the delivery of the 'real India' to the celluloid screen, is an iterated trope in the debates and manifestos of the 1970s. Chakravarty herself hesitates to endorse such authenticity claims in the context of what, after Homi Bhabha, she terms 'hybridity'. Chakravarty tosses out the idea of an 'authentic aesthetic', as does Kobena Mercer.[6] He rejects 'authentic' aesthetics because of their recourse to 'populist modernism'.[7] I myself am not willing to give up on a 'specific' aesthetic, contingent, arising from historical circumstance but particular, if not exclusive, to that space and that content that emerges from that history.

Of course, authenticity itself becomes tenuous, with the minority community deciding on one set of exposures and the dominant group deciding on another. Of late, dishearteningly, critics from minority communities have on occasion fallen into the trap of judging which third world, black or feminist text is 'more authentic', depending on the social/semiotic code of authenticity that is prevalent. As Mercer asserts: 'When the trope of "authenticity" is used to define the question of aesthetic and political value, it often reduces to an argument about who does, and who does not, "belong" in the black communities.'[8] My point here is not to reassert the problematic of reception and minority representation but to argue that aesthetic criteria are often falsely essentialised when the creative work of minority and women artists are under scrutiny.

Griselda Pollock discusses the manner in which aesthetic criteria get warped when women's art is considered. Different aesthetic criteria may not be problematic if the woman is regarded as a creating subject in a specific culture rather than as a cultural 'object'. She summarises her findings in the history of art criticism as follows: 'All that women have produced is seen to bear witness to a single sex-derived quality – to femininity – and thus to prove women's lesser status as artists. But what is the meaning of the equation of women's art with femininity and femininity with bad art?'[9]

The difficulty of establishing aesthetic criteria is accentuated twofold because minority art is not taken seriously. Mercer touches on an important set of related issues in his discussion of the minority community's tendency to celebrate whatever black films are made by blacks because of their paucity.[10] Neither dismissal nor celebration help to lay out an aesthetic framework. Ultimately the work is not critiqued with the same earnest attention granted to other, more normative texts.

Even more damaging to the process of paying sustained attention to work by minority artists is the institutional bracketing of diversity paradoxically and unintentionally in league with the backlash against diversity. bell hooks critiques the 1993 Whitney Biennial Museum's curating of black art under the rubric of protest. Much of the art in the show did not reference protest in any way, but mainstream culture was central in framing the show in these terms. The backlash, however, is unmistakable in statements that claim that minority art is now at the centre of the art world, and, further, that skill and technique are disregarded in the interests of diversity.[11]

Lacking an acknowledged visual tradition, bombarded by a loathsome visual iconography, a black visual aesthetic nevertheless continues both to combat the old iconography and create a new one.[12] Michele Wallace comments on the effacement of Afro-American visual history by using the case study of European modernist art. The obliteration of a tradition leaves both artists and critics of African American visual art with few relevant documented aesthetic paradigms.[13] Her work indicates that the history of visual arts is particular in the effecting of a rejection of a rich visual tradition that she calls 'the negative scene of instruction' between Africans and Europeans compared to the 'positive scene of instruction' in music and the hailing of a tradition.[14] Hal Foster, in a close reading of the Museum of Modern Art's exhibition-cum-book 'Primitivism in 20th Century Art: Affinity of the Tribal and the Modern', foregrounds the institutional stakes in the West's investment in absorbing primitivism. Foster argues that although the exhibition displayed the affinity between the tribal and the modern, in decontextualising both, it obliterated imperialist history and consequently appropriated primitivism into the Western tradition. Foster contends that the decontextualisation of forms can restore hegemonic relations as in the relationship between empire and colony in the gestalt of the exhibit. More crucial to our own understanding of the significance of aesthetics in the formation of an ideology is his uncovering of the assumptions that informed the show: '...that the final criterion is Form, the only context Art, the primary subject Man.'[15] A visual tradition, and a paradigm for visual aesthetics then, are both withdrawn from the cultural nexus and creators that produced it. In such a context, it would be impossible to emerge with a new aesthetics or a 'specific' one because one such has already been taken over because of imperialist, capitalist history, very broadly speaking. In such instances, the writing of the deletion of the history becomes the writing on the aesthetics.

Clyde Taylor's intervention in the debate on the relationship between marginal subjects and aesthetics is decisive. In his discussion of Marxist theorists on aesthetics, he notes that they 'allow themselves to get stuck to the aesthetic tarbaby, unable to concede that this is one baby that can conscionably be thrown out with the bath water'.[16] He calls for a 'post-aesthetic', one that would be coterminous with the politically-aware liberation movements of the world. His 'zero-aesthetic' is powerful because it acknowledges that aesthetics is class- and race-bound and that those who do not belong to these privileged groups are narrowly categorised, classified using aesthetic criteria.[17] In other words, aesthetic criteria are used to separate human beings hierarchically. Taylor is referring specifically to the ascription of racial differences but the point about how aesthetics is used to justify the subordination of a group has wide relevance. In the case of Western middle-class women, woman was aesthetics, or at the very least, she embodied aesthetics but was otherwise outside the aesthetic scene. Black women were of course 'invisible', unfit to be seen, certainly not aestheticised.[18] All others, except the bourgeois gentlemen, were also outside the aesthetic scene.

Taylor's position is liberating in that one can imagine versions of aesthetics that are not contingent on form for their aesthetic value. The old dichotomy between form and content that has maintained that form bear the burden of aesthetic value is no longer valid as a method of criticism of the creative product. Taylor uses the term 'liberative' strategies in opposition to 'aesthetic' designs.

Whether the films studied in this chapter are instances of authentic black viewing within the diegesis or outside is not of special importance. In shifting the critical burden from the tropes of black viewing to the context of relationships within which power positionalities are marked, the films scrutinise the politics of black/white looking power and its impact on feminist politics. The aesthetics that emerge, in large part, cannot endorse the politics of deaestheticisation, but struggle to establish the authority of black subjects as part and parcel of a larger view on the meaning of feminism.

Julie Dash's *Illusions* (1983), Cheryl Dunye's *The Watermelon Woman* (1996), Marguerite Duras' *India Song* (1975), Clare Denis' *Chocolat* (1988) and Gurinder Chadha's *Bhaji on the Beach* (1993), via very different themes, nevertheless protect the racial subject's in-between status, neither the whole Cartesian subject nor the racially-marked complete non-subject, by strategies that block the Cartesian viewer. The Cartesian viewer, akin to the spectator of classic cinema, can best be defined by Linda Williams' formulation of the relationship among Western philosophy, classical cinema and spectatorship:

> A classical cinema, and a classical cinematic apparatus, seen as the continuous extension of Western idealism, seemed to produce a hegemonic, masculine, Oedipal, bourgeois spectator, who was subject to its vision but who gained an illusory power and coherence in that very subjugation.[19]

The terrain is marked differently by each film. Dash plays with veiling, concealing and revealing, and uses vision itself to withhold knowledge from the viewer. Dunye produces the black lesbian viewer, and constructs both herself and her filmic subject as director and actor respectively. Duras problematises male vision through both sound and image. Denis, while employing vision as a decoy mode, shifts to the haptic. Both vision and tactility as modes of knowledge are set aside by Chadha for a moment, while she presents the viewer with an unknowable visual field. The corporeality of the viewer, both of race and gender, is assumed by the filmmakers. All invite you to mis-see.

The films discussed in this chapter implicitly critique not only practices of representation, but challenge them by confronting the sovereign Cartesian viewer. The sovereign viewer in Western scopic regimes was presumably reaffirmed in 'his' superiority by the subject in the painting; complete mastery of the subject being guaranteed by the clearing of the visual field for him. Lola Young comments: 'Historically, whether under the guise of scientific investigation or the production of visual culture, it is white bourgeois men who have had privileged access to looking rights'.[20] While such generalisations have been challenged by the historicisation of visuality by Jonathan Crary, who argues that vision's attachment to perception resulted in a consequent lack of authority of vision,[21] historically Young's point is borne out by the research on white bourgeoisie looking at black people.[22] Nevertheless, the exclusivity of the apparatus approach – the authority of the look in the diegesis sutured to the look outside – is limiting of course from a feminist perspective that would seek to locate authority in diverse sites; thus Crary's theoretical insights do pave the way for acknowledging a less monolithic viewer, and understanding efforts that reveal that viewer.

The challenge posed by the raced subject opens the way to an understanding of a fractured viewer. The invitation of the gaze, the supremacy of the viewer, the Cartesian regime of referentiality are all deflected by the substitution of the racial subject for the universal subject.

Racial Fractures in Visual Paradigms: Julie Dash's *Illusions*

Inasmuch as women's subjectivities in art forms are intimately connected to discursive modes and genres, their power in the social is even more forcibly entangled with the entitlements attached to certain aesthetic markers. Such female positionalities are further remapped by the warping of aesthetic markers by racial impress. Julie Dash's *Illusions* illustrates what is at stake for black women caught in the mainstream scopic regime.

The passing narrative, with its problematisation of white vision as an absolute guarantor of difference, works with the trope of vision within and outside the diegesis to scrutinise visual interpellations of the black woman's role in the national imaginary and national self-representation. The film, made in 1983, returns to a particular mode and a particular time to discuss issues that are relevant to its own post-civil rights moment. Dash chooses the genre of passing used in African American literature to cross the boundaries between white and black societies during slavery and segregation. The light-skinned African American could 'pass' or enter white society because of his/her light skin.[23] The filmmaker adroitly manipulates the staples of the genre to explore the US's representation of itself and places the relationship between the black woman and her role in the nation-state at the centre of the drama.

Illusions freezes a moment in the long history of the black woman's dilemma in the US. The film is about Mignon Duprée, a black female executive who passes, and Ester Jeeter, a playback singer. Set in Hollywood during World War Two, the film interrogates the imperative of nationality. The framing of one particular sequence guilelessly presents the conventional and compulsory emptying out of the black woman's body into the construction of a national mythology.

The screen in the diegesis cannot image the black singer's body; it must focus on the white body. From the margin of the frame, a black woman belts out a song; the central ground of the frame is taken up by a screen imaging of a white woman in a luxurious, obviously Hollywood *mise-en-scène*; the front ground reveals the control booth. The black singer, Ester Jeeter, has been asked to mimic her sound, her voice to the Hollywood star's lip movements. The lighting is unashamedly Manichean; the black woman is in darkness, the white in light. The screen radiates its light on the white star. White woman sings with black woman's voice. White swallows black. S. V. Hartman and Farah Jasmine Griffin correctly claim that 'Ester's voice is excised from her body so that the black body can be contained and the white body animated'.[24]

Three fields of action in a single frame wrestle with the meaning of nation and its representation for black women. Obvious is the marginal positioning of the singer and the powerful central fascination exerted by the screen, here presented as metaphor of the national will. The screen then highlights the power of whiteness, indeed the equation between whiteness and nation. However, whiteness and the white screen stand in a specific relationship to blackness. Blackness, rendered visible, unwraps the illusion of the white screen. Outside of the illusory white screen the white gaze is challenged by the narrative and visual mechanisms of the film.

Overseeing the production of the national myth on-screen is Mignon Duprée, the executive, who 'passes'. The film uses passing to fracture the white gaze, to suggest that the scopic, essential to Western orderings of knowledge, fails. Through the negotiation between diegetic and extra-diegetic levels, the screen, framed as meta-visual, exposes the flaws in white vision. The fracturing of the white gaze indirectly questions the supremacy of the white screen and its definition of the nation. The rupture of that gaze also marks the decisive break in that scopic ordering of racial hierarchies and their concomitant national hierarchies.

At the narrative level, the film approaches the issue of the black/white gaze through the voice. The collective voice appropriates the marginal one in order to present a unified moving picture of the nation's interests in World War Two. The introduction of the white woman's assumption of the black woman's voice challenges the meta-diegetic film's historiography. History as a national enterprise is short-circuited by the entrance of ethnic histories. In terms of voice, then, the emphasis is only partly on the black woman's loss of voice. The problematic of loss of voice is overdetermined by the manipulation of that voice in the construction of a nation that disallows her visibility and denies her existence. Exit: rhetoric of national investment in democracy; enter: race politics.

Dash's period piece lingers on the massive conscious effort undertaken in Hollywood to construct nation as a fantasy, as a society where good boys went off to slay bogeymen for blonde girls who held down the fort. D. W. Griffith's *The Birth of a Nation* (1915) stakes its worth in white racist hegemony.[25] As though alluding to *The Birth of a Nation*, *Illusions'* Mignon Dupree is sharply aware of Hollywood's ability to fabricate 'the nation'. Indeed, she accounts for her 'passing' by citing the power of the industry to make history. In an utterly utopian fashion, Dupree has hoped to make an impact on the way 'nation' is scripted.

Dupree's role as one of a rare group, a woman executive in Hollywood in the 1940s, makes her passing a necessity. She is neither one of those front-line blacks whom Walter White in the 1920s described as storming into forbidden white enclaves in the name of the 'race', nor is she one of those who passes merely to avail herself of opportunity.[26] As she tells her mother, she aspires to be among the covert architects of the changes that will enable her race in the aftermath of the war. However, Ester Jeeter's entrance solicits Mignon's discontent, for Ester's role paradoxically emblazons both women's invisibility. Ester's obvious effacement in the public sphere (screen) reminds Mignon of her own absence in that space.

The fact that Ester's tones come through the white star leaves Mignon more diminished than it does Ester. Ester is accustomed to being an off-screen voice. Mignon realises that she too is off-screen in a space where the screen holds power over both nation and history. The screen defines what the US stands for and it also determines that it will rewrite history according to its prescription of what US nationalism comprises. The film ends with Mignon's resolution to stay and fight for the power to refashion her own image and consequently the image of 'nation' on-screen. The film unravels the complex relationship between this black woman's actual role in the production of a national image that deletes her body and that image on-screen. The deletion is tantamount to an obliteration of her culture's contribution to the US, specifically the war effort.

If the screen holds power over conceptions of the US, Mignon has to project her cultural self off-screen, change her self-presentation in order to be able to intervene in the screen imaging of the US as a white stronghold, shaped by white vision. The film connects

Fig. 7: *Illusions* – Ester matches her lip movements to the white star's, suggesting the appropriation of the black woman's voice

the self-image of the black female off-screen with her non-participation on-screen. Screen here is metonymical for the national imaginary: a site where ideals of nationhood and subjectivity are drawn.

The frame that articulates the relationship of white power to black labour, in which Ester moulds her words to the white star's lips, even as she sings while Mignon watches, is paradigmatic of the politics of eracinated vision. As Hollywood's history shows, the white gaze forbids screen imaging of the black woman as subject. The screen gulps Ester, it leaves Mignon as unseen as Ester, as much of an illusion as the embellished star.

Yet both women enjoy looking privileges. Mignon plays with the blindness of white vision to secure her position in the Hollywood film industry. Ester knows that Mignon is black: she sees what eludes others in the diegesis. The film emphasises that neither woman is the object of the white or male gaze; it shows us that it is Mignon who surveys the office when she enters. She also looks at the boss, scrutinising. Further, the costuming discourages roving glances. The veil she uses literally prohibits visual knowledge of her and she therefore enjoys a certain amount of power because she is not visually objectified. Ester, of course, is not objectified either, but in her case knowledge of her role in the industry does not empower her. The knowledge of vision here does not guarantee the power of vision.

The black gaze does not grant either Mignon or Ester the privilege of claiming their vision because they cannot be seen; the film does not maintain that these women's precise knowledge of their excision from the national project empowers them. Ester desires to usurp the space of that icon, the white woman. She has the voice and she wants the image.

That Ester's voice is not articulated without her image on the screen, that she does not have the word, is metaphoric of the silencing of her race. Ester herself clearly lipsynchs Ella Fitzgerald's voice. The mechanics of the sound synchronisation suggest that Ester's words cannot harmonise with the image. She is extraneous to the production of a national culture that is racially exclusive. Viewers of the sequence have also suggested that the slight gap between lip movements and diegetic utterances, the 'marbles' in the star's mouth, hints that both the black and white women surrender their voice to the screen. My own sense is that all three readings, in privileging the screen, lead us back to the trope of visual disfigurement, as opposed to oral expression. They refer back to one immutable: the imaging of the white woman in place of the black woman. It is important to remember that the black woman's voice is transmitted, but not heard as black, because of the masking of the image and appropriation of voice.

The framing of this central sequence does not present the silencing of the race as absolute. More importantly, the race is neither silent or voiceless. The silencing itself is subtly placed in the context of the visual image. The black woman's inability to be heard is a given, considering the masking of Mignon. Mignon's self-exploration of her relationship to the film industry and its version of nation is sparked by Ester's place in the shadows. On the other hand, the silencing is literally not a function of the black woman's silence, whether the black woman is Ester or Mignon. Both Ester and Mignon have a voice, one that is taken over by the vision of whiteness on screen, the white singing star who represents what the nation deems worthy of preserving and who embodies the allure and security of the US.

Less obvious and more crucial than the metaphorical vocal silencing is the link between speech and invisibility which renders the speech itself marginal, the diegetic sound extra-diegetic and gives the image the power of speech. Although the song is clearly diegetic, it is understood to be extra-diegetic in and of itself, even without the elaborate framing.

Both Mignon and Ester are shown to have made a decisive contribution to a construction of the US that deliberately fantasises the war situation as distant, the internal lifestyle as coherent but threatened, inevitably saved by the representational value of the white female. While the convention of diegetic music involves a singer or speaker who is not projected on the screen, Ella's voice, Ester's song and Lila's face on screen, with Mignon as producer of the image, tells not the story of simple substitution, but complex super-imposition.

According to Mignon, the dredging of the black voice, its reified appearance in the form of the white woman, eliminates her people's participation in US history. Her invisibility is occasioned by the threat her racial identity would pose to the screen imaging of the country as white. In the case of the black female body, the body has to be (dis)figured to form part of the national family. Merger with the national involves the masquerade and divestiture of the black female body.

There is no space for the black female body in the cinematic version of US history. Stereotypes of black women as mammies pervade the screen.[27] Indeed, Deborah White's comment that black women in historical records are presented as either mammies or jezebels is also verified by their representation in popular cultural texts.[28] Following Jane Gaines' brilliant analysis of *Mahogany* (1975) as a domestication and exoticisation of the black female body, one could argue that Julie Dash extends that thematic by showing that the 'passing' of Mignon and Ester renders both of them acceptable to white society.[29] Dash's

analysis becomes more poignant because she locates this problematic in the image industry and thereby indicates that the disfiguration wrought on black women is no accident
of history. It is a price that they have to pay if they are not to be debarred from earning a
livelihood in the industry and, by extension, white America. Mignon masquerades, Ester
is divested of body.

The trope of passing uncovers what is at stake in Mignon's invisibility: the myth of racial purity and its legitimate offspring, nationality. Seemingly safe in that it plays with the
desire to be white, the trope actually mocks the very construction of race. In so doing, the
film challenges the conflation between US nationals and the races that are white-skinned.
Mignon's attempt to combat this veiling of black folk is further contested by the contradictions inherent in striving for the space of the white female in national representations.
The film then demythifies the role of the white woman in the construction of nation and
through the metaphorics of passing questions that very construction and its pseudo-demo-
cratic rhetoric.

Lila Grant, the dancing star, is the chosen vehicle for conveying the ideology of nation.
The boys fight to stave off the barbarians at her gates. But what of Mignon's husband, who
says that a war will not keep him away from her? Or the Navajo Indians who use their
tongue to foil 'enemy' operations? Mignon tells the Lieutenant towards the end of the film,
'I never once saw a film showing "my boys" fighting for this country, building this country'.[30] What then would it mean if Ester's fantasy were to become reality, and she were to
be on-screen? Lila Grant is presented on-screen for the visual edification of her audience:
very much the object of the white male gaze. To Ester's black looks, she embodies the unat-
tainable: woman as nation.

Curiously, the introduction of a racialised discourse stands feminist film theory on its
head. Lila could justifiably be viewed as sexualised desire, she also functions as icon for
another female. Ester desires the iconicity because of its sacral overtones and because of the
gift of femininity. Mignon sees the same picture iconoclastically. The film suggests that she
knows that the black woman's acceptance of the white woman's image implicates her in the
white supremacist/sexist refigurations of herself as a black woman.

The strength of the film lies in its calm assumption that neither Ester's nor Mignon's
passing ultimately endangers their self-identities as black women. Valerie Smith, in her
overview of narratives of passing, considers that Dash's film belongs to the 'revisionist'
category, unlike earlier narratives which tend to punish the protagonist. What Smith calls
Mignon's 'discontinuous' passing certainly enables the protagonist to tell the difference between masquerade and self; a distinction the film industry she works in has difficulty maintaining.[31] The film claims that Mignon's passing is not a splitting. The overt comparison
between the two women in the industry and their developing relationship bears witness to
their racial affiliation. Then, their racial heritage is brought into the narrative by invoking
the figure of the absent black mother.

When Ester and Mignon first converse after Mignon has worked out an equitable arrangement for her, Ester speaks of her mother. Her mother waits for her outside the studio
after each singing arrangement. Ester confides that she appreciates her mother's waiting
presence. Mignon, aware of feeling isolated from her people, has already called her mother
after the scene has been shot, provoked by Ester's marginalisation in the shooting of the

song. Although we do not hear Mignon's mother, we understand that Mignon confronts herself when she speaks to her mother. She speaks from an assimilationist place when she tries to assure her mother that things are changing for black folk. Even as she reassures her mother, a poster on the booth mocks her. It denies her assertion and boasts of a 'positive message for people of German descent living in America during the war years'. What of the people of African descent? Mignon also reassures herself, 'I'm still me, Mama'.[32] While this little interchange is symptomatic of the difficulties she has with her sense of self, it reveals that she is conscious of her subject position as a black woman fighting for black peoples and values under a white guise.

Ester and Mignon recognise each other. Mignon, because of her consciousness of both race and gender can understand Ester's situation in the industry and society. Ester also recognises Mignon by the way Mignon talks to her. In fact, the white staff members comment on how well Mignon gets along with 'them'. Perhaps Mignon works well with black folk because she does not think of them as different from, but akin to, her. Her displeasure at the manner in which the camera assistant speaks disparagingly of blacks is evidence of her identification as a black.

The bond between the two women, both black, one who passes, while the other does not, both invisible, underscores the distance between them and the star on-screen. The space between both women and the screen is the critical gap between them and the national icon. Lila Grant appears to symbolise more than whiteness or femininity: a deliberately mysterious quality that transcends both entities. The screen has converted her into the repository of national values but has transmuted these so that she simultaneously symbolises a singular formulation of universal decent humanity. History has conspired to make her the singing star. She bears the burden of representation, but she has the privilege of representing. Mignon and Ester, veiled as they are, suffer contradictory impulses in seeking to claim iconicity, because it scarifies, scars them even as it brings them opportunities in the United States.

The historical legacy of African peoples in the US mutilates them and the burden of representation that black women bear seems immutable in the face of Hollwood's role as architect of national ideas and aspirations. Claiming that iconicity, taking the white woman's place, would effectively be yet another mode of 'passing', a deletion of the contributions of black women. It would cover up their roles as actors, deny them their cultural specificity as beings who struggle against what seems to be 'manifest destiny'. Yet the white woman's place is coveted, because she is seen as an integral part of the nation.

The film consequently refuses to pass judgement on Ester for her desire to be on-screen, or on Mignon for passing. Nevertheless, because Dash presents Lila as a stylised screen image, the film moves beyond a simple indictment of the black woman's marginalisation and begins to question what the stakes are for a black woman who seeks to contribute to the nation, represent it or bear some of its symbolic burden.

The disfigurement wrought by participation in the industry is the price these women pay for taking their places as US nationals. The cicatrix that identifies them is the gap between the voice and image: between body and icon; between the self and its disarrayal by white looking power. Ester has the voice but cannot own the image; her voice is transformed into Lila Grant's. Mignon has the task of crafting the image but is loath to subscribe to it. The female black body cannot presume to bear the burden of representation; it certainly cannot embody the values of the US. Both women are self-conscious and have well-thought-out subject positions as black women and yet the flawed white gaze passes over both Ester's and Mignon's blackness. The film does not work only on that level but also explores the inadequacy of white vision in its imprinting of racial identity.

Hartman and Griffin, while acknowledging Dash's subversion of the passing plot, find nevertheless that the film inadvertently reaffirms the power of the racist gaze insofar as the dramatic climax turns on Mignon's 'unveiling'.[33] That unveiling, however, also reveals the infatuated Lieutenant's prejudices about blacks irrevocably smashed by Mignon's identity. If either blackness or whiteness were biological markers of race, surely the Lieutenant should have known that Mignon was black. On the contrary, he stumbles his way onto the truth only after he has snooped and found a photograph of Mignon's husband.

Undoubtedly, the very notion of passing reconfirms the privilege of the white gaze, but in the film itself, that gaze is exploited by the person who passes and who shows America what it wants to see. It is important to notice that Mignon does not veil herself; whiteness curtains her. As Mignon tells her mother, she has not told them who she is, but she has not veiled herself either. She does not disclaim her identity as a black woman, she just cannot afford to claim it. When the Lieutenant confronts her, she says:

> Why didn't I what, Lieutenant? Why didn't I report to you that I wasn't a white woman? Why didn't I warn you not to make such a fool out of yourself ... or why didn't someone stop me before I got so far?[34]

Mignon's appearance, seemingly important, taken to be consonant with her race, becomes insignificant to the Lieutenant when he stumbles upon her heritage. Far from reconstituting the white gaze, the film fractures it by challenging the equation between colour and race. The seemingly differentiating signifier, blackness, is recognised only by the black people themselves. The white gaze cannot hope to see. Seeing is no guarantor of knowledge. Ester tells Mignon that 'they can't tell like we can'.[35]

Dash plays successfully with what Mary Ann Doane has observed is the 'potential confusing of racial categories and the epistemological impotency of vision' implicit in significations of the mulatta narrative.[36] Dash's medium allows her to play sound off on sight in many intricate ways. The use of the screen as metonymical of the national imaginary is instrumental to this project. She finds an entrance into the trope of passing by problematising visual knowledge of the racial and the national. While it may seem paradoxical to suggest that black characters who pass struggle to retain their blackness or are always conscious of it, one could also argue that the very tension and fear involved in passing serves as a constant reminder of differences attributed to black people. If these white constructions of blackness were completely absorbed, the character who passed would be a 'self-hating' black. Mignon does not assimilate these stereotypes of black folk, nor does she hold on to any simple notion of blackness. Interestingly, she hangs on to other women to retain her sense of self. Passing dramatises the difficulties of 'talking back, thinking black'. It also emphasises their emotional distance from whiteness. Passing teases out the knots tying nationality and race.

While the text cannot conclusively stake a claim for an alternative utopian community, it does concretise the delusions of the national imaginary. In so doing, it mocks the racial basis of the construction of this nation.

The film's complex aesthetics revolves around the politics of whether black women can be seen; whether, in fact, the representational terrain allows their visibility. The concluding moments of the film make this powerful gesture of suggesting that black women can ultimately be seen in this terrain through the work of the black feminist director, an auteurial comment on the power of authorship in film.

The invisibility of black women in film[37] is picked up on in Cheryl Dunye in *The Watermelon Woman*, which like *Illusions* invents a tradition of black women in film, this time a black feminist lesbian actor. The film is remarkable for 'bringing out' some of the same themes but in a different vein: the presence/absence of the black female actor. The diegesis of the film suggests the 'disappearance' of the black lesbian actor, while the extra-diegetic sequences portray her in roles that are open to contemporary black feminist criticism. In search of the presence of black lesbians in Hollywood subject,[38] the main character of the film, the would-be black lesbian director, researches the 'Watermelon Woman'. The framing of the film is so artless that many viewers really believe that the invented 'watermelon woman' and her lesbian lover, a white film director, actually existed, and are extremely disappointed with Dunye's pseudo-documentary. Dunye, however, is taking us 'in search of our mother's gardens', the philosophical assumption here being that this tradition of black lesbians in Hollywood needs to be invented in order for contemporary lesbians in film to have that lineage. Alexandra Juhasz describes the process by which Dunye decided to 'document' a tradition that did not have visible evidence, but had a tremendous impact on her identity as a black lesbian filmmaker as 'the relationship between missing precedence and contemporary identity'.[39] In an interview with Juhasz, Dunye is extremely conscious of the connections between her identity, and identity politics in the culture at large:

> Most of us have received some sort of academic training and know what are hot issues in popular culture: identity politics, multiculturalism, issues dealing with race, sex, class. My life story as an individual, I realised at some point along the line, is all about that. I am my own text. So I talk about myself, and that becomes interesting. If I am honest, I'm being theoretical.[40]

In *The Watermelon Woman* Dunye is 'inventing' both the black lesbian actor in Hollywood and her own identity as black lesbian actor and filmmaker; no wonder she calls the genre she invented in this film a 'Dunyementary'.[41] The aesthetics of this film goes towards uncovering the non-visibility of black lesbians in film. At the same time, it establishes the needs and presence of black lesbian spectators by situating the 'Cheryl' character as both director and spectator. This combination works to challenge audiences to accept the validity of 'personal narrative', a theme she had tested earlier, according to David Van Leer.[42]

The Watermelon Woman's contribution is in inventing a different way of looking at the history of exclusion, a direction that Julie Dash had pointed to in her use of a black female executive as protagonist of her film. In that film too, because of its semi-documentary feel, covering as it does Hollywood, many viewers leave thinking it is a 'true' story. Interestingly,

Fig. 8: *The Watermelon Woman* – an invented image of a black female star, supposedly on videotape and played by the documentary filmmaker in her search for a black female tradition in film history

Dunye takes care to draw attention to the fact that she is presenting a pseudo-documentary by covering the contemporary life of the filmmaker in fictionalised terms that seem to follow the biography of 'watermelon woman's' life with her lover. In both scenarios, the white woman seems to wield power. In Dash's film, this power had some hypnotic quality because of screen presence; in Dunye's it is deconstructed as white privilege. For both Dash and Dunye, the power of screening the history of blacks in film lies with the black director.

The self-positioning of both films as serious interpretations, histories and criticisms of Hollywood demands some contextualisation with other studies of blacks in Hollywood. Anna Everett titles her account of black film criticism, culled from black newspapers and articles between 1909 and 1949, 'Returning the Gaze', a metaphor for black responses to white constructions of blackness.[43] This notion of the relationship of blackness to whiteness is replayed in bell hooks' ideas on 'the oppositional gaze' of black film spectators, and also the idea of 'decolonising the gaze' in Gwendolyn Audrey Foster's work. hooks explicitly cites Dash as one of those spectators who spent hours resisting mainstream film, a trope that initiates both Dash and Dunye's film. Certainly, shifting Dash and Dunye's positionalities as auteurs to black female spectators; i.e., locating the identity of the auteur would demand that we see these responses in this light, and the films certainly can fall into that rich context of productions that are offering versions of black subjectivity other than those presented by Hollywood.[44] I would only add that it is equally important to note that efforts such as Dash's do also respond to feminist politics in suggesting that unlike white women who are fighting not to be objectified, black women are struggling to be seen, not objectified. The politics of the aesthetics of the film asks us to acknowledge black women's presence, an authority established by Mignon in *Illusions* seated at the executive table as 'producer', and the title credits of Cheryl's film rolling out in *The Watermelon Woman*.

The Space of the Watched: Claire Denis' *Chocolat*

Given that the politics of racial viewing challenges gender hierarchies depicted in mainstream film, Claire Denis' *Chocolat* offers an instance of a film that is scrupulous about challenging the racial privileges granted the white female subject. Her venture into racial/ gender relations in the colonial arena had been anticipated by Marguerite Duras' radical script for *Hiroshima, mon amour* (1959) and the film that she later directed, *India Song*. The differences in the issues that the two directors tackle, and their understanding of the role of the female in the colonial venture, is instructive for marking the difference between an authorial colonial stance and a post-colonial one.

Duras' *India Song* has received a great deal of press for its aesthetic, particularly *le cinema différent*, which she defines as dealing with the sociological, ideological and political, that uses style to comment on content. From material culled from her novels, particularly, *The Vice-Consul* and *The Ravishing of Lol Stein*, *India Song* opens and closes with the death of Anne-Marie Stretter. The action of the film follows one ball in Calcutta where Anne-Marie dances with Michael Richardson, her lover, and converses with the Vice-Consul who has been 'shamed' for having shot at some lepers in Lahore. Two other events that play into the thematic are the dramatic quality of Richardson's failed love affair with Anne-Marie, and Lol. Stein's investment in seeing them. A key feature of this text which is very unusual in cinema is that none of the characters in the diegesis speak at all. Even when they are supposed to be speaking, the sound comes through voice-over effects, although they lip-synch the words. There is no synchronous sound at all. The voice-overs are dialogues between Voice 1 and 2 who are female, and later in the third movement of the film, two voices: one masculine and one feminine; this time the feminine voice is the auteur's. Duras identifies the latter two as being authorial.

The film itself is exceedingly slow-moving: the deliberately-posed quality of the shots and its double articulation – the voice-overs that discuss the past of Anne-Marie Stretter – render it almost text-bookishly Brechtian. Delphine Seyrig, visually and narratively, is presented as the quintessential object of male desire. Men surround her in several different shots, gazing at her, the arranged nature of the shot calling attention to her femininity rather than to her role as Stretter in the film. Stretter herself signifies desire so the battery of gazes, including the camera's and those of the men in the diegesis, are pointed at Anne-Marie Stretter. W. B. Worthen comments generally about Duras' techniques that she shows that 'the stage necessarily animates desire and makes it visible'.[45] The film, however, forestalls the audience from enjoying the visual depiction of desire because the voice-overs of Voice 1 and 2 sharply cut into the viewing. As the *mise-en-scène* is composed of one room, reflected by a mirror, where you see the action reflected before you see the camera's view, the overall effect is claustrophobic and brings Jean-Paul Sartre's *No Exit* to mind. The dispersion of the male gaze through the authenticity of the narrative voices that are partial and are authorised by the auteur does not, however, deflect the issues surrounding colonial desire and visuality that Duras raises.

The overwhelming impact of the monotony of male colonial desire for the white woman is deconstructed in this film which resists the white gaze through its stylisation of image, mismatched narrative cue, flatness of imagery and thinness of narrative line. Elisabeth Lyon has commented that the psychoanalytic scenarios in the film – such as the elaborate theatricalisation of the 'primal scene' fantasy, here that of Lol watching herself absent in the scene between Anne-Marie Stretter and Richardson – brings up issues crucial both to our understanding of desire and its representation.[46] The techniques of filming showing the fantasy of Lol watching Anne-Marie Stretter and Richardson, being a doubling of the primal scene, searches not for solutions to that fantasy but asks questions about desire, its compulsions and manifestations. While this is largely true, it is also an extravagant universalisation of a specific set of desires arising out of a colonial context. It is important then to add that the film questions colonial male desire, specifically through its rendition of the colonial experience of Indo-China (Vietnam and India). The torpor and lassitude presented in the first part of the film that shows Anne-Marie, Richardson and an unknown friend lying still, almost dead, is linked to the heat and the isolation of India from Europe. The voice-over discusses the plight of the young Anne-Marie, aged 18, married and travelling through various postings in Indo-China. The Europeans wonder what she does with her time. This sense of the place as a non-place, but one that consumes, pervades the visual and the aural. In this context whiteness, especially the whiteness of the women, is stressed several times, including commentary about the white women remaining indoors. Themes of murder, adultery and suicide are woven in, suggesting the classic colonial trope of projecting these 'horrors' on the landscapes and peoples of Indo-China, rendering Indo-China a site of colonial desire gone awry. Disturbingly enough, Duras herself says that Anne-Marie is Calcutta, and that the Vice-Consul is Lahore. She adds that 'we see nothing of Lahore outside of him'.[47] The metaphor of madness that pervades the text holds equally for male desire and India, suggesting that the white female is destroyed by male desire driven mad because of India. Paradoxically, India is both absent and present in this representation; absent because the desires of the colonial masters are significant and the colony irrelevent, present because the colony functions to 'drive' the desires in particularly 'inexplicable' ways such as murder and suicide; all of it edged by intermittent discussions on leprosy.[48]

Martine Loutfi identifies this colonial trope in Duras' film as coming from a general European sensibility extending back to Hegel's idea of India as 'the region of phantasy and sensibility' and therefore 'the perfect metaphor of the unspeakable, the French *indicible*'.[49] She notes that this exoticisation is 'undermined' by the banal talk on famine, poverty, disease, and so on.[50] The exoticisation is not corrected; rather, it is augmented by the talk of leprosy, the fear of infection, of the orient 'catching', like Africa caught Kurtz.

Duras' sophisticated construction through the visual of Anne-Marie Stretter as the object of colonial male desire, and through the aural as a female hero who had to endure the ravages of that desire and the complicity of Voices 1 and 2 with Stretter's subject position, could indicate the deconstruction of colonial male construction of India, as much as the destabilisation of colonial male desire. Moreover, the mechanisms of the presentation could suggest the authenticity of the aural/feminine and the visual/masculine, and could perhaps be supported by the fact that the same soundtrack used for *India Song* was later used for another film, *Son nom de Venise dans Calcutta desert* (1976). While the film does deconstruct colonial male desire, its position regarding the colonial construction of India is ambiguous, problematic and even imperialistic. *India Song* is framed by the song of a Savannakhet beggar woman who has travelled from Burma to Calcutta; the same distance, but by foot, as Anne-Marie has. The woman has lost all her children and comes barren to India's holiest river. Shot one is part of the credits which linger over the setting sun while the beggar woman sings. When Voices 1 and 2 begin, they start the conversation by talking about her and how she was together with Anne-Marie in Calcutta. That linkage between the two women would seem to suggest that both were destroyed by imperialism. It is clear through the text that despite differences, the woman is Anne-Marie's alter-ego, her secret sharer, as many critics have noted.[51] Such a positioning of the subaltern woman seems to pay attention to the West European psyche at the cost of the economic, political and historical, indeed the ontological existence of the subaltern woman. The film then seems to represent a moment in feminist film that challenged and subverted male colonial desire, but is so hampered by its own artillery that what it accomplishes theoretically for European women through the use of sound is not matched by its political progressiveness either for European or subaltern women.[52] While access to taking pleasure in the European woman's image is hindered, her role, as enmeshed in male desire, is not overturned. The white male gaze is questioned when it is on the white woman, but its general sway over the land is unchecked. Clare Denis' work marks a shift from the colonial understanding of race and gender, although she too is not able to lend the subaltern woman any subjective positionality in her film *Chocolat*.

The unsettling of the male colonial gaze is no longer the issue in Denis' work, the politics of post-coloniality being accepted. Denis seeks to map out an aesthetic that would not depend entirely on looking power for specifying its politics. Where Dash introduces the screen and sound in *Illusions* to replot mechanisms of looking, Denis uses looking to reveal its flaws, its fractures – particularly the looking of white colonial women. Authority is removed from looking *per se*, and shifted to another modality; a move corrective of colonial vision, whether wielded by men or women. Profoundly anti-essentialist, feminist authority is problematically located in the space of the black man, excluding the black woman.

The colonial narrative film, with its dramatisation of the unequal contest for power, reveals the supremacy of the white male gaze. Male Western colonial narratives have a history of belittling the black person in terms that are comparable, but not analogous, to the representation of blacks in Hollywood.[53] These epics, whether European or North American, centre the white presence in the colony and present the colonised as masses who are indecipherable.[54] Following Homi Bhabha, Kobena Mercer maintains that 'colonial fantasy attempts to "fix" the position of the black subject into a space that mirrors the object of white desires'.[55]

Given the substantial amount of research on the difficulties of documenting the other without attempting to narrate his/her story, it would seem inevitable that all colonial narratives were doomed to failure in that they could only hope to reenact a variety of colonial fantasies.[56] Naomi Greene charges that one of the difficulties of films such as Pierre Schoendoerffer's *The Drummer Crab* (*Le Crabe-Tambour*, 1977) and Brigitte Rouan's *Outremer* (1991) is that these films blank out history and take recourse to nostalgia: 'Nostalgia impels memory not to "confront" but rather to "reject" history.'[57]

While many films of the colonial genre are exercises in repression and self-mythologisation, of course there are others explicitly anti-colonial. Catherine Portuges maintains that the *'féminin colonial'*,[58] films directed by women that work with the personal and the woman's point of view, can also be seen as texts where 'border crossings translate into a *mise-en-scène* that destabilises hegemonic ideas of nationality, sexuality and the family'.[59] Portuges also credits these filmmakers Claire Denis, Marie Pisier and Brigitte Rouan with handling a subject that France had chosen to forget and with introducing forgotten women into the history of colonialism.[60] E. Ann Kaplan makes a more ambitious claim for Claire Denis and women filmmakers in general and their specific relationship to colonialism when she states that both the 'colonised and the women colonisers become subjectivities in-between'.[61] Denis' film *Chocolat* has more modest aspirations, and achieves something less hybrid in being exacting in its awareness of the demarked spaces of colonialism in which subjectivity is constituted, the very powerful way in which gender relations are disarrayed for the white woman and the black man under colonialism, and finally in its overwriting of cinematic renditions of black maleness and white femaleness without simplistic reversals. Further, the film does not wishfully rewrite history nostalgically, but critiques colonialism through a contemporary post-colonial layer that regards easily-gained hybrid subjectivities with deep suspicion.

Claire Denis, aware of the silence on French colonial history says, 'The French colonial times were never spoken of in France … Maybe it would be interesting to tell a story about it but not a period piece like *Out of Africa* [1985] but something very intimate … that would show the more perverse relations of the colonial regime.'[62] Denis' film explores the relationships of power between subordinated groups in colonial Cameroon. The film, set in Cameroon, is primarily about the relationship between a young French child, France, the houseboy, Protée, and the mistress/mother, Aimée. Denis sees the story of the relationship between coloniser and colonised as being told by the young girl who 'has the advantage of apprehending things in a tactile manner'.[63] Denis provides a framework within which to understand her film when she asserts, 'I tried to be honest in admitting that *Chocolat* is essentially a white view of the "other".'[64]

Unlike the other films of the colonial film genre that efface history, Denis shows her consciousness of that history in her persistent detailing of the articulation between the coloniser and the colonised and in the insistence on the post-colonial. The film's departure point is from the post-colonial moment. France ventures to Cameroon and remembers her childhood there. Both departure and ending points are in the post-colonial timeframe, thus acknowledging that colonial France's presence was temporally, not mythically, marked. We are not set loose in a colonial time period that has neither a beginning nor an end because the whole time span of the film is imaged as memory with edges on either side.

Chocolat's critique of colonialism has been noted by its many admirers who have nevertheless softened the edge of its critique by assuming the attraction between the houseboy and Aimée the colonial Frenchwoman.[65] The critical focus on the love affair that does not happen speaks more to the trope of exoticism current in discourses of the colonial rather than to the film itself.[66] Denis maintained that for her the point of the film was that Pro-tée refused Aimée and that she shot the seduction scene in one take so that the producers would not insist on a steamy love affair.[67] Denis' statement need not necessarily be borne out by the film that to some extent describes an unequal relationship which is only partly overthrown; hence it can easily reinscribe the dominator/dominated fantasy, with a twist, because the dominated here is male. Denis, however, structures black/white looking power in the film in specific ways that resist the fetishisation of blackness and the black body.

The point of view of the narrative of *Chocolat* is that of a young girl.[68] Nikki Stiller observes that 'France becomes the camera, silent observant, remembering'.[69] The power of the look is conferred on a young female child. Denis curtails the power of colonial visual-ity by giving the story and perspective to young France. Visuality becomes insufficient in understanding the complex interaction between the young child and her parents and Protée because of the limitedness of what she sees and understands. The white male eye is here scarcely, if not nowhere, evident. The camera also stays confined to colonial quarters and does not reach the colonised space, thus further confining its supervisory or invasive power.[70]

By virtue of being told by a young girl in the charge of a grown male, *Chocolat* would seem to be reiterative of the normative male gaze trajectory. Protée is, after all, much bigger than France and a normal visual perspective would view him as though through a low-angle shot. Protée, although not framed in low-angle shots, is certainly the most arresting screen presence in the film. Unlike the male gaze trajectory, where we see the male watching the female, here we see Protée without any filtration or relay. Having clipped the power positionality of the watcher, Denis focuses on the watched. Through the spaces inhabited by the two, she makes a clearing ground within which to understand the experiences or life of the watched, but as the watched.

A complex set of relationships determined by the colonial context replaces a contradic-tory and over-determined set of substitutions for the Hollywood relay of looks. The colo-nial white male gaze is replaced by the child's partial perspective, the subordinated female's position is taken by the colonial black male[71] and the returned look is given to Aimée, the mature woman. Each of these positionalities is further negotiated, and the valences carried by the colonial positionings are rendered distraught. The black male lead, Protée, plays a triply subordinated role within the narrative structure of the film. As 'houseboy', his func-tion is domesticated and consequently he is feminised. He also doubles as the young child's 'mammy', a secondary role in the colonial narrative. Finally, as the object of Aimée's desire, he takes the position of one to be found, to be had.

Protée's structural embeddedness in colonial placings is emphasised by the film, which does not romanticise the space the houseboy is caught in by overturning the position-ings easily. Protée's subservient place in the narrative is, however, challenged by his screen presence and the attention Denis draws to the emotions and to the aura of the watched. Two episodes imply the impact of white dominance and give the lie to the harmonious order seemingly produced by colonial hierarchies. In one scene young France is eating at the table, diminutive, while big Protée stands behind her to serve her. The image works doubly. On the one hand, it seems to show that he is waiting on a small child but on the other, the contrast in size lends him a stature that his structural subordination cannot can-

Fig. 9: *Chocolat* – France comes to post-colonial Cameroon

cel. The next shot brings him down to size – literally – as France forces him to kneel and then insists that she feed him. Again, the image works doubly. For one, the child's physical intimacy with him draws him into the circle but his posture belies the possibilities of intimacy. During this section of the film which develops the relationship between Protée and France, another incident reveals his lack of power over her despite his privileged position as her confidante, playmate and caretaker. Protée walks by France who is astride a donkey. Apparently, Protée is sending some money home and availing of the schoolmaster's literacy to write his parents a letter. France is out of the loop both visually and historically. She watches from the far side of the frame, a small figure who cannot understand what is going on. This episode, incidentally, is one of the few where we are privy to what France is not. France calls out to Protée repeatedly, insistently forcing Protée to leave the conversation and to come back and to hold her reins. Protée lies and tells France that he is writing to his fiancée, perhaps to keep something of his life from her, perhaps because she has abused her place as his charge by acting the wilful European employer. A rush of schoolchildren pour into the yard mocking Protée, more particularly making fun of his pliancy as a man to a young girl-child.

While commentators have discussed the so-called taboos involved in the inter-racial 'relationship', the intensity of emotion evoked by the Protée/France relationship has not been registered quite so extensively. E. Ann Kaplan does notice it and asserts that their relationship 'violates colonial mandates and forms'.[72] While the child is set apart from the woman, and not a member of the group of women as Kaplan would have it, their relationship is not extraordinary at all, the colonial mothers' distance from their children reflective of their status. Even so, the development and resolution of their relationship is as indicative of power relations as in the more over-emphasised contact with Aimée.

Protée spends more time with France than with Aimée and has clearly made such a big impact on her that when she returns to Cameroon as an adult, her memories are replete with images of him. He dominates, if he does not overpower, her memories of childhood. Denis lends Protée a certain screen power that commentators have described as majestic, that vitiates his lesser structural position. The power of that screen presence depends on the attention that the narrative pays to his emotions so that a sense of the colonial self is not diminished, but rather created, very partially and through Western eyes, but nevertheless one that lends him some dignity.

The restoration of Protée's 'manhood', knocked down according to Western notions by his domesticated role, is effected through the trope of screen power. As subordinated, and occupying the female position, Protée evades that role by struggling for and wresting some control from woman, girl and less obviously man. That Protée, as male, would control looking relations is fairly obvious for the dominant film; however, as black male he would be plotted lower than the woman.[73] Working through looking relations, Denis shows Protée's structural subordination but does not actually place him as object of the white female gaze in the extra-diegetic narrative of France's childhood. Considering that the opening of the film and its visual perspective is driven by France, all the images of Protée place him as the observed. Nevertheless, Protée evades the positioning decisively. His actions compellingly refute the silence of the observed. For instance, after he has been banished to the garage, France comes to see him. She asks him if the motor is hot. He does not reply but puts his hand on the motor. She does too. Her hand is burnt as is his. While he withdraws his protection of her, he does not necessarily reject her. Indeed, the gesture can be seen as a signature of a new, more equal compact between them. This branding is a continuation of their relationship where France's seeming dominance is belied by Protée's more commanding actions. Protée, for instance, has the power of inscription, of writing.

Denis, in keeping with her notions of tactility as being able to grasp some truths of colonialism not obvious to vision, works extensively with touch in these relationships to create that sense of colonial self; personal, intimate and emotional. The African teaches the Europeans through touch. Among the opening sequences, we see Protée's hand, ants crawling on it. Protée will not let France eat them unless she answers a riddle. His hand is the plate; his palms offer the food. In a more emotionally heightened sequence, following the killing of some wild animals, Protée and France, in one margin of the European scene of hysteria over the killings, look calmly at the dead bloody animals. In one shot they are in the foreground, but on the lower horizontal side of the frame when Protée bends down very gently and dips his finger in the blood and traces it on France's hand, showing Protée's visceral relationship to the natural.

The African, despite the power of inscription, is looked at, but not objectified. Aimée and a European female, atop a hill, look down at Protée and some others. The woman comments on Protée's good looks. While 'women looking sexually at men violates the rules established by men's power base',[74] the colonising woman's look at the colonised male is of course predicated on colonial male authority, a point that Denis emphasises by refusing to invest the white woman with the full authority of the look. The use of the long distance shot forestalls any brutal invasion of his privacy. The European male is explicitly mocked in an exact reversal of the scene, when an African woman checks out Jonathan Boothby.[75]

While Denis uses looking to insinuate Aimée's attraction for Protée and possibly his for her, she uses touch to reveal Protée's engaged act – almost in the Sartrean sense of an existential act that defines the self. On the evening that the woman comments on Protée's looks, Aimée makes a pass at him. She is sitting on the floor with her back to the door and when Protée walks close to her as he draws the blinds, she slides her arm up his leg. He pauses for a moment (almost in arrested motion) and then bends down. She is now passive despite her earlier bold move. In one packed aggressive gesture, he lifts her, stands her up and walks away with firm tread to complete his task.

Protée's definitive rejection of Aimée has resonances through the whole narrative. William A. Vincent's reading of Protée as desiring the Other, and also Aimée, and ultimately as rejecting Aimée because of his 'loyalties to the colonial system'[76] could be maintained only if the film were to be read without reference to the visual – that is, only narratively. Protée's physical cine-presence is extraordinarily commanding, and one could say, checking off the colonial infringement in each of the major encounters, partly by challenging the rules by over-playing his role through impassivity. Keeping boundaries around himself, even if they are based on colonial definitions, ensures his self-respect. Marie Craven supports the idea that Protée's demeanour is 'princely' even if it masks a terribly hurt self. Further, his sense of 'profound alienation' is caused by 'racial domination';[77] not, I would venture to add, because of a desire to merge with the 'Other', as Vincent would have it. Granted, Protée's attraction to Aimée, which Vincent does not doubt, could be due to her whiteness and the desire to own it, a ubiquitous trope in some West African literature, but that would still imply a desire to take the white man's place, not keep it for him. Whether Protée's response is prompted by desire or lack of desire is less important than his refusal of her claiming him as the object of her sexual desire. In refusing her, he reaffirms his masculinity; not a boy, but a man.

That his gesture signifies a reassertion of masculinity is made apparent by the visitor Luc's taunting of Aimée and Protée, and his disparagement of Protée. Luc's goading of Protée as a hapless servant to his masters' and mistress's desires emphasises Protée's will when he, Protée, turns her down.

France also experiences a rejection from the black male, Mungo Park, whom she invites to have a drink with her. At the opening of the film, she watches him bathe in the water barebodied. She travels through her memories as she rides in his car through the African landscape. When Mungo Park drops her off at the bus station, she asks him to join her. His immediate rebuff is a coda to Protée's rejection of her mother. The film defeats the Western stereotypical imagining of the black man as lusting for the white woman.[78]

In this drawn-out rendition of the differences and relationships between white femininity and black masculinity, one may well ask, where the coloured African women are in this space and in the film?[79] Narratively they are invisible, even visually they do not exert any presence at all. None of them have any names, and except for the one woman who gives Boothby the eye, they are not differentiated from one another. One particularly disturbing image is of the coffee planter Delphine's African mistress. Openly condescending to the natives, he characteristically also has a relationship with an African woman. The image of the woman in the enclosed room creates the impression of a caged animal. Delphine does not permit her to mix socially; he comes in and gives her some food, saying 'Here's some seed for my chickadee.' Although a very sliver of a segment, the shot is distressing in its unthinking reification of the image of the black woman. Narratively, the segment could be seen to comment on the difference in power between black men and black women. It also obviously suggests that Protée's acceptance of the 'kept' role would result in such imprisonment.

In insisting on Protée's refusal of a relationship with both Aimée and France, the film reinstates the black male as actor in his own destiny. Protée concludes his protest against colonial domination the night he is in the garage with France when he walks out into the African night, out of Marc's, Aimée's and France's control.

Chocolat lends the black male his authority also through its nuanced, if unspoken sense, of colonial history. Most commentators have noted that Protée is filmed in long shots, framed by the African landscape. When Protée is seen outside the house, his domesticity is obviated by his relationship with the outside space. Several sequences establish his harmony with the landscape including a very powerful sequence when he walks up and down in the night with France on his shoulders as he keeps watch for hyenas on the prowl. He is also shown travelling through the landscape in the back of the truck, his face in the moving countryside. France, whose memories we follow, clearly links Africa with Protée. Her connection is loaded, moreover, because Protée is her guide through Africa, emphasised by Park driving through the land. Through her adult remembrances of childhood, Protée is seen, not just as belonging to the land, but as owning the land.

If the colonial masters hold sway over the interior, Protée commands the outside. France's childish projection of Protée on the landscape resolves into a more adult projection of the landscape on Protée. In other words, she understands that Cameroon belongs to the blacks and that she has no place here. Denis stretches the idea to include Park who, though black, is very much on the borderlands like France, and cannot claim Cameroon as his own. To some extent, Protée's mythical walk into the African night is rendered realistic by the afterword that shows Cameroonians in charge of their own affairs, taking up the space of the screen as they work and play. The singular focus on Protée has been refined to include other Africans, and to reestablish his African identity.

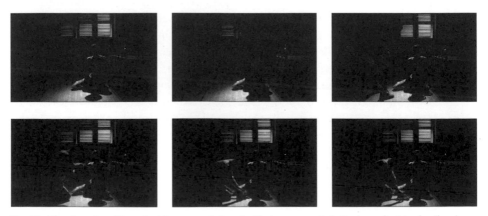

Fig. 10: *Chocolat* – the white colonial comes and gives the black woman a little food, emphasising her 'kept' status, and her total lack of power

Fig. 11: *Chocolat* – Protée's screen presence; in this shot, his relationship to the land lends him a certain power that no European in the diegesis can claim

Protée's physical gestures through the film create a space for him whereby he resists the look. His impassivity and the constant focus on his observation, his looking but not speaking, ultimately gives him power and identity in a colonial context that deny him both. A scrupulous representation of differences in the colonial context, the film does eventually grant the black male subject the authority of inscription on history.

The aesthetic of the film recalls Julia Knight's comment on how feminist aesthetics might devolve into 'a way of looking' and what she considers a 'vertical investigation'. By vertical investigation Knight is referring to a sustained exploration of feeling, of looking at the interiority of experience: 'of what something feels like, of what it means'.[80] Protée's face, the manner in which the narrative's meanings unfold, comes close to bringing the viewer into an understanding of the intimacy of f eeling surrounding everyday colonial relations. In leaving black women in the margins, almost invisible, the film perhaps reveals that its apparatus, its focus on the personal and intimate across cultures, is insufficient in identifying black women as actors in the colonial drama. Nevertheless, in lending the black male authority over the colonial female, Denis does expand the meanings of feminist authority.

Feminist Melodrama: *Bhaji on the Beach*

The politics of looking in the metropolises of the world where the descendents of imperialists and migrants mingle is less rigidly dichotomised than power relations might indicate. Where both Julie Dash and Claire Denis alter traditional viewing relations in the diegesis to create a different aesthetic, Gurinder Chadha presents the viewer with both knowable and unknowable visual fields in confronting the viewer and establishing the presence of

South Asian women in the imperial centre. Feminist authority is cultivated through the narrative, and established very specifically through a politics of subaltern identity.

Taking on the post-colonial woman, passing itself off as a comedy, merging close to the tragic but staying on the register of the melodramatic through the narrative, *Bhaji on the Beach* transforms a woman's weepy into a feminist soap. The film follows one day in the lives of Indian British women of three generations. They take a bus-trip to Blackpool to enjoy a day and bond with the community. Every possible incident that could lead to melo-drama is presented: difficulty in marital relations, mid-life crisis, unexpected pregnancy, inter-racial romance, taboo lesbian relationship. The film is about race matters and the dialogue frames it as such, but race is brokered through women's issues and diminishes in narrative significance. The many women's crises that the text engages pass through the gate-way of cultural difference and complexity presenting an insider's cultural view. The film's intimate view of the Indian community is powerful in that it is not othered but represented as having and struggling to maintain a separate, distinct Indian identity. Very different too from the Merchant-Ivory productions, which though progressive in their foregrounding of the feminine,[81] were redolent of a distant India and a foreign colonised sensibility, not the tough new British-Indian sensibility that was to be displayed in *Bhaji on the Beach*.

The primacy of the women's issues, located in the Indian community and outside it, comes close to obliterating the other England by not imposing it on the main narrative. Setting England apart from the narrative helps Chadha establish the Indian community as centrally English, not peripherally so. She considers that the film constructs Englishness in very specific ways.[82] Routing race, culture and ethnicity through women's issues puts the spotlight on the British Indian community and its positioning of women. The 'black-ening' of the genre, the metamorphosis of the holiday journey motif into a community-type picnic remains important, but when the women's personal lives are unravelled, the journey and the community come apart. The text emerges as a feminist questioning of the community.

The film has come in for some positive feedback for not courting a single conception of India, and for challenging the notion that 'imaginary homelands' are as productive for women in the constitution of their migrant identities as for men in their attempt to retain some sense of home in Britain.[83] Chadha then offers a view of women migrants that shows them as displaced from both the British and the community's concepts of nation that leaves them uniquely positioned to critique the community's reconfiguration of Indian woman-hood.

The challenge to the community is posed in the registers of the melodramatic, comic and satirical. All three registers merge in the extra-diegetic sequences in the Bombay Hindi film industry's style and technique. The flagrant parody of the industry's star-based operas and its transpositioning to the Indian context in Britain makes for the emergence of some startling ideologies on women. Interpolating the Bombay sequences in all their florid in-tensity works as a direct and a cutting comment on the melodramatic incidents that occur during the women's daytrip to Blackpool.

Hyperinflating the emotional from pathos to bathos creates some purely comic mo-ments in the extra-diegetic sequences that punctuate the film. Because of the cruel edge, the filmy sequences transform and constrain the expressive melodrama of the diegesis.

Chadha manipulates these Bombay film sequences by taking an overpowering medium and tinkering with its aesthetics to mock its message on the traditional role of women. In other words, the extra-diegetic in the film shifts the genre of the text from women's tearjerker to a feminist text, and comments on the traditional melodrama's generic exploitation of female emotion.

Traditional melodrama and its solutions for women are flouted by the main narrative line itself that borrows the archetypal quest motif. The epic pressure on the form of the melodrama has created its own difficulties for the readability of the genre for reviewers who find that the 'mixed form' fails. Andrea Stewart[84] and reviewer Farah Anwar,[85] however, point to the mixture of the melodramatic and the political, not the epic movement in the melodramatic form of the film.

Melodrama in the 1940s and 1950s women's film in the US, following the model of late nineteenth-century Victorian melodrama,[86] opted for pathos and the stilling of action, unlike the more artistically valued ones which prized the flow of the narrative action. Thomas Elsaesser's now canonical formulation of the way in which Hollywood family dramas used the melodramatic is well worth remembering:

> Since the American cinema, determined as it is by an ideology of spectacle and the spectacular, is essentially dramatic ... and not conceptual ... the creation or re-enactment of situations that the spectator can identify with and recognise ... depends to a large extent on the aptness of the iconography ... and on the quality of the orchestration ... In other words, this type of cinema depends on the ways 'melos' is given to 'drama' by means of lighting, montage, visual style of acting, music – that is, on the ways the *mise-en-scène* translates character into action ... and action into gesture and dynamic space.[87]

Elsaesser also pointed to what he believed to be the fairly precise relationship of equivalence between the social context and the expressed emotions of the characters.[88] Christine Gledhill, specifically using gender in her analysis, suggests that the Gainsborough melodrama of the 1940s in Britain, because of its emphasis on women's emotion, also became weather vanes of the roles of women.[89] The melodramas measured the extent to which women's roles could be expanded. Given the 'low culture' status of filmic melodrama and its definite generic allowance for the 'women's desire' Chadha's choice in working within this genre as opposed to the more patently 'high culture' form for social protest and expression – realism, particularly documentary realism – seems to be a deliberate attempt to find a genre that would be able to accommodate the emotional overflow and political excess. In the context of discussions on politicising melodrama, Claudia Tate's study of nineteenth-century black women's sentimental narratives is instructive.[90] She comments that because black women did not have varied forums to organise their political platform, the establishment of a certain set of melodramatic incidents around a sentimental hero in a female plot also served to indicate their desires for political change. Black women's insistence on the inhabitation of a certain cultural space was made apparent through the trope of the sentimental female hero. *Bhaji on the Beach* with its uneasy and rapid jostling of race, class and gender issues also speaks for the need for political change in Britain, but unlike 'high culture' forms that do so through experimental, documentary or realist formats, it does so by showing the victimisation of the victim, the psychic tremors caused by the social body. *Bhaji on the Beach* also weighs in so heavily with the 'melos' that it is severely undercut. More profoundly, the victim of melodrama, the passive woman, is here nowhere in evidence, and the last victim is a male whose victim status is qualified by his violence toward his wife.

The film, unlike the Hollywood model, is composed in a double melodramatic mode. Chadha chooses the melodrama genre, in part because of the influence of Bombay Hindi films that are typical melodramas, but dexterously shifts tone so that the Bombay film sequences comment on the female body, 'as the object of fetishised male desire and the inscription of male dominance and power'[91] instead of reifying the female body as in the famed paradigmatic Bombay films *Awara* (1951) and *Sholay* (1975).

In Chadha's film, both the diegesis and the extra-diegetic are melodramatic not just in the touches of melos but in the overpacking of episodes and incidents and in containing explosive elements in each separate incident. The main action of the film covers the lives of Hashida, a young college student involved with a black student who finds out that she is pregnant; Asha, who is going through an identity crisis as a middle-aged woman; Jinder, who gets divorced but is pursued by an unstable and violent husband; Rinku and Tinku, who are out for 'fun' – one of the two of them wants the fun with British boys; and some older women who have to confront a generational onslaught.

Chadha's double dramatic mode, an excess of melodrama, far from typically exploiting female emotion, actually allows women viewers to veer away from it. The extra-diegetic melodramatic sequences in general confer authority and control on the female and para-doxically leave the patriarchal family institutions in the traditional position of being the primary victim of the melodrama.

In a key essay on the shifts in the melodramatic genre in the third world, Dolores Tierney argues that the Mexican melodrama of the 1940s and Maria Novaro's more recent *Danzón* (1991) show that the melodrama was used to compose a nationalist sense and that the entertainment sequences which congeal the narrative and fetishise the female enter-tainer are more than contained by Novaro who actually radicalises these sequences.[92] In *Danzón*, the female protagonist, whose passion is specific to the dance the movie is named for, finds that she can own the dance and express female desire through the dance.

Chadha's women also find that they are able to step out of the formal restrictions of the dance and express their complex desires for both pleasure and political presence. Chadha's film diverges from Tierney's model of the Mexican melodrama primarily through its visual apparatus, or its double melodramatic mode. Without insisting on a neat difference in the visual aesthetic of the diegesis and the extra-diegetic, I want to suggest that the 'melos' in-voked by the extra-diegetic foregrounds a visual aesthetic that confronts the viewer instead of drawing him/her in.

Refusing to use fairly conventional film techniques that reorchestrate reified images of power in the frame that serve to centre the viewer within the disciplinary mechanisms of power, Chadha opts out of that discursive mode, or at least brings with her her own baggage as the migrant does. She draws on Bombay film, and bhangra pop – a Punjabi British musical hybrid – and uses it adroitly to tell her story. The import of the Bombay film is crucial, an important part of the diaspora aesthetic that the film offers. Anne Ciecko worries about whether the film can indeed be considered radical, or 'Third film', film that challenges the dominant aesthetic and offers a radical political ideology.[93] While not exactly following the codes of Third film, arguably the film's aesthetic format is energetic and innovative in terms of interpellating the British viewer. The issue of political radicalness is complex. Compared often with the prolific Hanif Kureishi whose politics are not invested in merely showing the more palatable aspects of the Indian community, Chadha's film retains the same insistence on refusing to give the viewer the 'positive images' sought of the 'progressive filmmaker'. Of course this does not qualify as a radical political ideology, but the aesthetic sensibility, the insistence on another way, style, mode, that prevents making third world women so eminently readable by Westerners, so easy to stereotype, does.

Chadha's film opens with tracking realistic shots of the ubiquitous 'corner shop' in Britain and then sweeps up to a framed photograph of Krishna. Sound effects, or indeed flourishes indexical of the Hindi film's announcement of a dramatic turning point, accompany the flashes of lightning and thunder bolts that prepare us for the deity's pronouncements on duty. The voices are loud and are intended to be a psychic manifestation of Asha's distress, but are presented as 'filmy' in the Bombay sense, as excessive, flashy and self-knowing. The sharp sound of a plate falling – the offering to the gods – brings us to Asha standing there surrounded by her family who are now anxious for breakfast. They circle around her and their questioning seems to diminish the differences between the diegesis and the Bombay sequence. The Bombay sequence brings with it issues of gender that surround that world

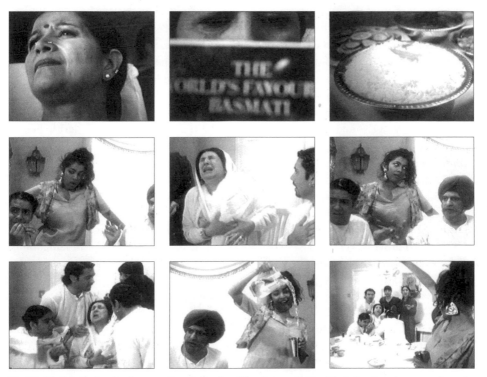

Fig. 12: *Bhaji on the Beach* – the extra-diegetic Bombay 'filmy' sequences that block the viewer's mastery; here, the melodramatic mode gives the woman, Jinder, a power she does not have in the diegesis

into this one. These sequences, of which there are five, are marked very obviously from the diegesis but are germane to it as expressions of a consciousness in a cultural register significantly different from the discursive world of the diegesis.

In using the Hindi film as a lexicon from which to draw the energy of the diegesis, Chadha attempts to move away from the Cartesian regime of referentiality. Borrowing from the Marathi drama and the pre-modern traditions in Indian painting that are foreign to Western notions of depth of perspective and frames of reference, the extra-diegetic sequences picture scenes where the centre dissolves and the image retains the quality of static paintings as distinct from the images that became standardised by the classic Hollywood system and its obsessive gestures to narrativity and seamless suture, not to exclude the endless, seemingly natural flow of action in an illusionistic and enclosed world. Here, the viewer is confronted with images that do not have planes to regularise the eye and is presented with what might in the Western lexicon be called *tableaux vivants* without the ordering that the latter implies. The differences of the British Indians, their foreignness, then, does not permit the Cartesian viewer to attain any mastery over these peoples. Throwing the viewer off, the Bombay 'filmy' sequences, understood by Indian audiences as markers of the genre, nevertheless alter the melodramatic content significantly by actually using the melodrama to institute women's powers. While the Hindi film mode may glance back at a cultural value system inimical to women, the actions of the women in the diegesis gainsay that image.

As the women of the Saheli group get ready to go to Blackpool, the scandal of Jinder's divorce explodes. Typically, the older women are against Jinder for having left her husband and several unsavoury comments are made about how the young diasporic women are ignoring the old home customs. On the bus, Asha, whose own gender crisis is profound, is 'transported' into a Bombay Hindi film sequence sparked by a comment from an older woman who theatrically fears that Jinder's behaviour may kill her in-laws. The 'melos' is again signalled with bravura and we cut to Jinder's in-laws' home where Jinder comes dressed 'vampishly', smoking, and serves her mother-in-law food in an obviously brazen 'bad woman' mode. Mother-in-law gasps and stutters. Loving family pops pills in her mouth, in great amounts. Jinder cackles villainously. Jinder has the power here, she is not the victim and indeed, she controls the entire family by her deviation from the norm of the ideal daughter-in-law. On the one hand, the sequence mocks the codes that cast women as ideal in-laws, on the other it uses it not to exploit the women but to grant her some power. Within the code, the woman is of course villain now, not victim, but this dehumanisation of her for acquiring power is compensated for by the action of the film. By the conclusion, all the women cautiously subscribe to the 'new' version of femininity without the melodramatic vilification.

Interestingly the image of 'home' as a 'fallen woman' is introduced by the British actor Ambrose. Critics generally read the song and dance sequence that presents Asha with Ambrose, and later Asha with an 'Indianised' Ambrose, as indications of ineradicable difference between the two groups, or at least Asha's realisation of the same.[94] On the contrary, the introduction of the Westerner as Indian allows Asha to see how he would fit into a romance, certainly the role he is playing now. Culturally translated, the rendition of the romance scene in the Bombay mode then signals the insufficiency of romance and enables

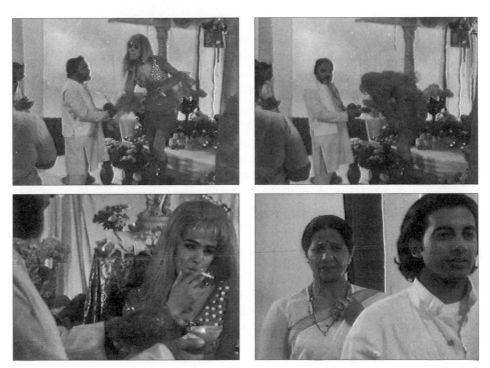

Fig. 13: *Bhaji on the Beach* – here, the Bombay 'filmy' sequence exaggerates the vampish 'Westernness' of the young woman, Hashida, breaking the traditional Indian taboo against smoking in temples

her to 'see' him as like any other Indian male. If a fallen woman is home for Ambrose, Asha certainly wants to distance herself from that particular imposition on women.

The trope of woman as fallen, as villain, envisioned by Asha in the Bombay film sequences, interrogate home and its values relentlessly. One sequence where Asha translates what one of the cronies says about Hashida, the young pre-med who is pregnant, specifically exaggerates Hindi film's lavish stereotypes of women. Asha sees Hashida smoking at the temple, hair untied, worn loose and coloured light, again laughing at her petrified parents who are trying to worship. The image of the wanton woman is very precisely Western. What is at stake for the Indian community is a sense of identity completely bound to an idea of home defined by a traditional and non-existent Indian woman. Indeed Rekha, the visitor from Bombay, challenges Asha when she holds forth on 'home'. Rekha asks: 'When have you been home? What women are you talking of? You, with the clothes you are wearing!' Asha wears saris. While Asha starts out as the victim of melodrama in having internalised societal gender values, in pinpointing her angst as relating to the younger women's changing values, she moves out of the victim class. Indeed, it is Asha who in a concluding scene rescues Jinder's son from a violent father and with some decision slaps him and then says, 'I don't want him to grow up to be like you.' Ranjit, Jinder's recently divorced husband, who had been beating her up because she had wanted to leave the in-laws and live with him on her own, falls into a heap and sobs. He had been afraid that his family with their values see him as 'soft' for not being able to get Jinder to toe the line. The community's investment in a separate identity has kept constant an 'image' of home that served to keep women tied to the family in highly codified restrictive ways.

The Bombay film sequences ultimately do not figure home itself as a negative or Indian culture as backward. Rather they provide a means by which Asha begins to understand the sacralisation of home. And indeed it is the very technique of the sequences, their distinct visual characteristics and their flashy verve that make such an understanding possible.

The community's resistance to Thatcherism and British racism apparently finds its expression in maintaining normative standards for women, failing any ability to impress its own agenda on the body politic. *Bhaji on the Beach* ends with the women's community rebonded on different terms but agreeing that it is time bhaji is sold on the beach.

Whether the bonding between the women at the end of the film is 'resignation'[95] or genuine change is an interesting question. Are the older women, such as Asha, merely giving in to the changing times? The stylised slap of Jinder's husband, based on the notion that a woman her age would be worthy of respect, seems to make a mockery of the Hindi movie formula, almost as though the extra-diegetic had slipped into the diegetic. Although quickly closed up, the transformation in Asha seems genuine because of her newly-found freedom to here express herself as herself rather than as an Indian woman. The theme is first introduced when Asha reminisces about how she enjoyed singing in India, and had aesthetic interests, outside of maintaining the corner shop, and the British stereotype of the Indian woman.

The film, however, does deal in stereotypes, but layers them in such a way that two things occur. Firstly, the layering permits the exposure of multiple stereotypes that are constructed about and by migrants that have such a long history with the British as the Indians do. *Indiastar*'s reviewer had a provocative comment to make about the stereotypes in the film. He claimed that 'it is stereotyping with a huge difference: it is brown stereotyping'.[96] The older women obviously think of the younger women as suffering from 'moral rot';[97] the older generation is riddled with prejudices about black people. The film also seems to follow suit in portraying the South Asian male as authoritative, but Chadha, like Kureishi, marks this portrayal with a touch of hysteria, unlike the rabidly stereotypical *East is East* (1999). Arguably, Chadha, in not presenting the positive image, seems to be challenging the British audience to accept Indians as full human beings, not the liberal ameliorative model that would be expected of the progressive filmmaker. Yet the film could be seen to be catering to stereotypical gender constructions of South Asian men, but with the difference that British, or European, men do not come off any better. Lastly, the brown women's stereotyping of the men of the community, as bullying, ineffectual and unreal in their demands, functions as a critique of the men (except for one younger brother), surely an important part of the film's critique of the Indian community. It is not accidental that the one father figure who is acceptable is black. All the other men uniformly leave a lot to be desired. Secondly, stereotyping with Chadha is almost a technique of psychological blocking, or shutting out of viewers from the interiority of the women, but of making their predicaments politically visible and comprehensible. Third world women, then, are not to be easily read with this opaque strategy.

The focus on political positionality rather than absolute differences of any kind from the British is also seen in Chadha's filming of the Blackpool sequence where, as Dimitris Eleftheriotis points out, we see the group as part of the larger crowd but still clearly visible:

> This sequence articulates the differences of the group as positional and relative, with the confusion of the point of view problematising any division of the world into two fields. This not only involves the playful rejection of the shot/reverse-shot pattern (which is essentially a division of narrative space in two worlds occupied by different characters and invested with different representational values) but also the systematic undermining of any position which supports as 'us/them' dichotomy.[98]

Establishing absolute difference then would be to reify difference, and make the women instantly readable. Insinuating the differences the women have with, on the one hand, the British and, on the other, the patriarchal portion of the Indian community ensures to some extent that they are not translated culturally by either group. Rather, the generic layerings of the text enable their positioning in the film to be read as nuanced and feminist.

The use of two discrete formats asks that the viewer, both Cartesian and subaltern, move between visual fields and understand that any representational practice that seeks to present the identity of the women must somehow negotiate the two. The women's ability to find points of articulation between the two ensures their authority in both visual fields. The choice of the two visual fields, and the rebuttal of the knowing look, presents us with an aesthetic entirely adequate to the construction of feminist authority for subaltern women in metropolitan centres.

In trying to work against the backdrop of problematic racial representations, the filmmakers discussed in this chapter screen the viewer's knowledge of the racial subject by refusing to place the racial subject in a knowable visual field. *Illusions* dramatically denies the viewer knowledge of racial identity, but succeeds in doing so without rendering the identity of the racial subject an imaginary construction. When Mignon's identity is 'uncovered' by the Lieutenant spy, it is important to notice that it is not through visual means, but through textual evidence. Mignon's historical identity is thus established in the historical, objective realm as is her lived identity as a black woman through her relationships with her mother and Ester, and her commitment to a particular kind of work in Hollywood. Issues of the representation of black women in film are given an added dimension through Dunye's meditation on black lesbian subjectivity both on-screen and behind the camera. Dunye's committed reclaiming of imaginative memory or fiction as black history both inserts black lesbians into film history, and invents genealogy. Mis-seeing becomes a way out of white seeing. Seeing is problematised by Duras in her avant-garde film; interestingly, here, the viewer's limited vision is never fleshed out, leaving a lacuna in our understanding of black subjectivity. *Chocolat* too plays with the decoy motif in setting up Protée as an African houseboy, and then miscuing the viewer in regard to his 'romantic' feeling for the white mistress. His inscrutability has the effect of Mignon's veil in *Illusions*. Nevertheless, the wedging of the colonial narrative between two ends of the post-colonial grant him an objective historical identity as his lived identity as a black man is established by his decisive inscription on the young France's palm. The 'knowable' servant emerges as the free Cameroonian. *Bhaji on the Beach* approaches the problem of racial representation by shifting the visual field. Including the 'Bombay' scenes disconcerts the viewer; indeed, it confronts the viewer's looking power by creating an elaborate set of visual motifs that cannot easily be decoded. Embedding typical stereotypes of Indian women within the Bombay visual field and in the diegesis prevents the viewer from having ready access to third world women, thus rendering the viewer's knowledge of the women's diasporic identity more complex while establishing their objective historical identity as black British women through the new community that emerges at the end of the film.

Reading the films as responding to the problematic of racial identity allows us to understand the valences of black/white looking power. The different cultural contexts of the films indicate different ways of approaching the dilemma, but each crucially modifies the insights of feminist film theory. Dash's film holds, in part, that for African American women, the desire is 'to be looked at' and Dunye's augments that insight with respect to lesbian identity. Duras' film, perhaps, exemplifies the deconstruction of visual authority, but constructs aural authorities that, while challenging the white viewer, do not constitute black female authority. Denis' film sustains the notion that the white female's look is hierarchically more compelling than the black man's but holds no truck with any universalistic notion of the female gaze. Rather, she notes that the haptic can overwrite white looking power, but uneasily keeps black women invisible.

Chadha also extends feminist understandings of melodrama by bringing visuality into the mix, and suggesting that for black British women the challenge is not to correct the stereotypical oriental construction of women for the male/white viewers but to understand how the women's experience of the stereotypes enables community building. For black British women, the task is to make the political visible, not necessarily to represent the fullness or humanity of the woman as envisioned by early European American feminist film theorists. By working only within different kinds of looking within the community of the black British, Chadha keeps the white viewer out. Duras also invokes the subaltern female subject, and implies that she has knowledge, but in aligning this to the white woman's knowledge, she constructs the authority of the white woman and renders the black less than powerful. She is most successful in undercutting the white male gaze through her experiments with sound. The other four films, while not underestimating the privilege of white vision, find a way of inserting the racial subject's knowledge.

3

GENRE COVERS

In confronting the viewer, we have explored one of the ways in which feminist filmmakers contested the visual configurations of black subjects, and observed the change effected to the scene of representation by the inclusion of race in the visual field. In approaching the subject of film genres, similar difficulties are posed by Western aesthetics' relationship to women and racial others. Affixed as the dominant genres of film are by their masculinity, they have been less than hospitable to feminist desires for female subjects in epic, history and myth.

The exclusion of black/third world women from the history of aesthetics is absorbed into the defining moments of aesthetic frameworks like genres. Although genres are not immutable, women's entrance into a range of genres has been less than ideal. Rick Altman has argued that in film, the genres have never remained stable and that no sooner did a studio establish a specific generic format than it tried to put a new spin on to it. The purity of genre, outside historical and production parameters, is mythical, and thus suits the critic's 'self-serving interest' in fixing noble antecedents for film genres. Altman addresses gender indirectly by referencing Hollywood's 'women's film' of the 1940s, and cites the grafting of melodrama on to 'women's film', and the feminist community's investment in the same as part of the cyclical, and impure nature of genre formation.[1] He maintains that the genre – family melodrama/women's film – did not have its staple conventions during its early period; later feminist critics including Ann Kaplan, Tanya Modleski and Annette Kuhn reconstituted it according to formal features of address that had at the best partial relevance to the historical examples of the melodrama, and the factors of film production. Two points emerge from this discussion. The first is that the search for genres seems to mimic the general feminist search for subjectivity in classical film, which is not to say that the feminist critical standpoint on melodrama as a boundary genre is not accurate.[2] Interestingly, the two are conflated with some deliberateness in feminist film criticism; however, as Mary Ann Doane's and Tanya Modleski's analyses showed, knowing female subjects, female subjects with authority and seeing female subjects (with glasses!) get their comeuppance in vicious ways. If all critics have the dream of the universality of a genre that speaks to human consciousness and myth rather than history, feminist critics confess to the desire to have non-universal, specifically feminist genres. Second, what remains astonishing to us is that even given the melée of mixed genres, and recyclings that Altman claims of westerns, musicals, narratives, dramas, film noir, war movies, road movies, buddy movies and avenger movies, very few films of whatever genre had the capacity to identify a female hero's journey, her struggle either with or for the community, or even present the female as having some aspirations outside the home space.[3] Robert Phillip Kolker speaks of 'woman as genre', whereby woman functions 'intragenerically' and 'transgenerically', in that the signifying elements are repetitive in the meanings about women that ensue, the generic frame not expanding sufficiently to alter some all-time stereotypical representations. The business of genre-crossing remains male business. History of course plays a part, and 'woman as genre' is not trans-historical. Kolker points out that after the advent of the feminist movement, films have been spectacularly physically destructive of women, and, as in the structure of fantasy, endlessly repetitive; what he, following in the footsteps of Gaye Tuchman calls, the 'annihilation of women'.[4] Although Kolker says some slight change is possible, his look at 1970s and 1980s film is not heartening.

Interestingly, during this time period, however, some changes were occurring in B films where women were not routinely being crushed as they were in mainstream films. Carol Clover identifies the 'rape-revenge' film in which women wreak vengeance on rapist men, and other men, 'on the grounds that all men are party to "rape culture" and hence corporately liable and fair game'.[5] The most visceral and recent expression of women's rage is *Baise-moi* (2000) where two young women kill many people – men and at least one woman; their wild desperate anger against their daily abuse in the urban world is chillingly rendered. Even genres that have had no relationship with women except through their bodies have been rewritten by directors with progressive leanings. Linda Williams, for instance, shows how female-oriented pornography plays with the 'come shot' to deflate the signification of the phallus, reveal it as the penis, by filming detumescence.[6]

The latter two examples amplify our sense of the dearth of inspiring models of female heroism in film genres. The issue of black/third world female subjects being represented as heroes is complicated by questions of genre and race. Citing Jacques Derrida, George Lipsitz, who views genre as a taxonomical system, argues that it assigns structural functions to race that foreclose possibilities for heroism:

> Race plays a crucial role in generic representation. Hollywood westerns, war movies, detective stories, melodramas and action-adventure films often rely on racial imagery, underscoring the heroism of white males by depicting them as defenders of women and children against predatory 'Indians', Asians, Mexicans and black people.[7]

Nicholas Mirzoeff's discussion on colonial visual taxonomies allows us to understand that these were the antecedents of cinematic genres' codification of raced subjects' positionalities.[8] The existence of taxonomies, and genres that support them, are important to supporting an imperialist politics of racial difference. Bringing genre in as a crucial factor that marks the representational terrain adds a vital dimension to our understanding of the visual complexities of representing race.

Recent scholarship has paid attention to the politics of address entertained in film, particularly the practice by which the Western viewer is acknowledged, and his/her colonial ideology reinforced by the film. Jacqueline Bobo and Valerie Smith, in their reception studies of black viewers and black feminist film, have shown how that racist view can be displaced, and 'black looks' brought in. Gwendolyn Audrey Foster situates her study of women filmmakers of the African and Asian diaspora in terms of issues of formal address and of representation, claiming that the filmmakers she studies 'decolonise the gaze, locate subjectivity'.[9] Implicit in Foster's readings is the assumption that new genres are being created to enable resistance to the 'persistence of white hegemonic Hollywood constructions of spectatorship, ownership, and the creative and distribution aspects of filmmaking'.[10]

In this chapter, I follow the efforts of four filmmakers to create genres that can accommodate women's heroism. While melodrama has been useful to post-colonial projects, such as Gurinder Chadha's, the family plot seems insufficient to the films discussed here. As the nineteenth-century slave narrative could not really follow the conventions of the sentimental novel, these films cannot traditionally follow the 'woman's film'; instead, they take recourse to other non-filmic forms, primarily the oral narrative. The accomplishment of these generic experiments is in their importation of elements to create specifically feminist genres. Julie Dash's *Daughters of the Dust* (1991), Assia Djebar's *La nouba des femmes du Mont-Chenoua* (1977), Sarah Maldoror's *Sambizanga* (1972) and Ingrid Sinclair's *Flame* (1996) come from different cultural and political traditions, but all are concerned with received history's misprisoning of women. None of the films is satisfied only with correcting the exclusion of women, but engages in foregrounding what is at stake for women in the narration of histories of migration, liberation and nation formation. How tradition is signified, modernity brought in and community built are important questions for all four films. The inclusion of oral genres creates an aesthetic that renders it possible to find female heroes, almost as though classical film narrative with its male plot would resist such appropriation. Of course, traditional oral genres have been at least as masculine in their orientation as classical narrative; however, their use in these films changes the significances of the visual in ways that reclaim the oral tradition for women in film. The authority of the oral tradition is then brought to the narration of the film, imbued with feminist resonances, and granted in all the films to the female speaking postion.

The contexts of the films make the issues of representation different. The avant-garde mode is vital to Dash's project of altering our perception of black women by locating the images in hitherto unseen contexts. Djebar's intervention in Western feminist film theory's tenet about women's 'to be looked at' status cautions us from applying these ideas universally. *Sambizanga* draws our attention to the heroism of ordinary women drawn into the business of revolution. The issue of whether authenticity in representation of third world subjects is possible in an imperial context is raised by *Flame*. The four together ask us to think of how the representation of women has been framed by imperialism, and the need for newer genres to house anti-imperialist practices of representation.

Tracking Black – Superimpositions on the Avant-garde: Julie Dash's *Daughters of the Dust*

Feminist filmmakers of colour have had to contend with a racist industry and apparatus quite as much as they have had to confront male mechanisms of enunciation. They have had to work with the 'Cinema of the Fathers', or the 'Cinema of the Sons', Hollywood or the avant-garde.[11] Some, like Euzhan Palcy, have chosen to work with the dominant genres: Hollywood and European narrative to graft women. Others have chosen to work outside the commercial channels of production and distribution: directors like Melvonna Ballenger, Ayoka Chenzira, Madeline Anderson, Connie Field and Julie Dash.[12] Women seeking change through film have had to decide whether to dismantle the master's house with his tools or to create a new woman's cinematic language, one that would not reinforce the old message by merely shifting the content but leaving the code intact. Within this debate many socialist women, black and white, who have adopted the alternative but not avant-garde route, have taken the position that the avant-garde films of Chantal Akerman and Laura Mulvey are accessible only to an elite audience. Grafting issues specific to black women on certain genres, especially the documentary, to effect social change has been high on black filmmakers' agendas.[13] The division between high avant-garde and 'talking heads' documentaries into white/black has inadvertently distorted the study of black women's films. This attribution of the desire for a clearer message and consequently the need for a carbon copy instead of a black feminist positive assumes that the films of black women do not change the way we see, only the way we see black people. Of course, when that happens, the phenomenology of vision/perception is radically altered. In other words, there is a process that can be called, following Michael Awkward, a 'negrification of genres'. Negrification exceeds the mere inclusion of blacks into the genre, but suggests that the defining framework is black.[14] Centering the black woman plays an important part in the radicalisation of vision. Many black women's films, then, do challenge the way we see, and do not necessarily have recourse to the conventions encrypted in the cinema of the sons. Among these kinds of films that are scripting a new sort of genre – one that there is as yet no name for – are Martina Attille's *Dreaming Rivers* (1988), Camille Billops's *Finding Christa* (1991) and, here discussed, Julie Dash's *Daughters of the Dust*.

The film is about a day in August 1902 when part of the Peazant family leave the Sea Islands for the mainland US. The conflicts that ensue because of this migration inform the bulk of the film. Eula and Ely face difficulties because Ely does not know who the father of Eula's unborn child is; Nana wants the family to stay behind; Viola and her photographer friend, both from the mainland, are captivated by the Gullah culture despite Viola's reservations; the younger cousins have their own issues; returning family members also bring their perspectives to this moment. While these conflicts are intra-familial, such as the decision of whether to go across into the mainland US and become assimilated or remain connected with the ancestors on the island, they touch on a number of key issues relevant to the larger black community such as its relationship to the dominant white culture, religion, and the role of black women in the community.

Dash's film makes good the avant-garde's most powerful claim: that it is about seeing and changing the way we see. Toni Cade Bambara argues that the film 'heals our imperialised eyes'.[15] Julia Erhart specifies the importance of vision and visuality to the film: 'its [the film's] point … is to articulate a new way of seeing both by refiguring formal, visual conventions and by reclaiming real, historical apparatuses of vision for a community's, specifically an African American community's, survival'.[16] Almost all the commentators of the film have registered its contribution in recording the history of the Gullah people. Julie Dash, in an interview with bell hooks, has said that she had difficulty finding a financier for the film because it was so outside Hollywood's New Jack syndrome. The financiers apparently did not think that there would be an audience for her film, ostensibly because black people were more used to seeing themselves in the ghettos, as though the community did not know that these images were oppressive.[17] Within the history of African American film, Dash falls into that group of film directors who lean more toward expressing vernacular culture, creating a black aesthetic; an idea that dates back to the Harlem Renaissance, rather than to those who seek to devise 'positive images'.[18] *Daughters of the Dust* did get financed. The film is a mythological rendition of black women of the diaspora that appropriates, but does not stop at, the phenomenology of the avant-garde. Dash stretches and transforms conventions of the avant-garde and deforms narrative technique to narrate a black feminist epic.

Hollywood has had, of course, its share of epic film, and even some that clearly pertained to African Americans, but these were based on a narrative of nationhood and a notional history that depended physically on the absence of African Americans on screen and narratively on what Toni Morrison might identify as 'whiteness' on screen.[19]

The film's extraordinary richness of imagery has come in for a great deal of comment, as has its departure from Hollywood and its differences from other African American films. It moves away from the work of Oscar Micheaux and Spencer Williams[20] thus setting itself a little outside of the visual parameters of the cinema of black fathers. Bambara regards the film as expressive of the independent black filmmakers' school that emerged out of LA: 'In its formal practices and thematics, *Daughters of the Dust* is the maturation of the LA rebellion agenda.'[21] Generally accurate as this formulation is, the film's epic narration, and Arthur Jafa Fielder's camera work subtly shifted some of the nuances of both theme and technique in the sense of superimposing the epic genre on to film, even when compared to such literary films as Charles Burnett's *Killer of Sheep* (1977). The film's resistance to a modernist look and recourse to the oral epic partly accounts for the quality of visual arrangement. Interestingly, after a totally convincing account of how the film belongs to a whole host of African and African American films, Bambara says, '*Daughters of the Dust* has a look of its own'.[22]

The traces of orature mark the film, however, belying the dominance of the visual. The origin of the soundtrack is instructive. Dash told interviewer Karen Alexander that she wanted the tale to unfold the way a griot would tell a family history, but had planned it as silent. However, American Playhouse, the financier, wanted dialogue and so she 'expanded the dialogue'.[23] In the final cut, if visual rhythm is important to the texture of the film, the auditory rhythms are equally important, and honour an oral tradition of history – the tradition of the griot – that as the transcriber of the *Sundiata*, D. T. Niane, points out, is dying out in Africa and is denigrated in the West because of its lack of written verifiability.[24] The Gullah dialect, presented in as accurate ethnographic detail as possible, resists easy translation, and draws attention to the oral. This new writing on celluloid which can retain the auditory rhythm becomes a way of recording history that is diasporic but with strong connections to African forms of filmmaking, many of which are engaged in the task of scrutinising the past. Oliver Barlet identifies Dash's movie as resisting nostalgia and the teleology of white civilisation's progress. He states that 'this film translates onto screen an oral tradition', and emphasises that it is 'an ethic of cultural resistance which the aesthetics of this crucial film presents – a film, which, without ever showing slaves, defines the issues around slavery for the present age'.[25]

I would only add that the 'translation' involves transforming the oral tradition to centre women as griots. Cultural resistance in the diegesis is symbolised by the unknown woman of the community who also has the power of the voice, of narration.

Daughters of the Dust begins with a woman's voice on-screen: 'I am the first and the last, I am the honoured one and the scorned.' The woman has the first word. The voice-over lends her authority, not just as narrator, but as narrator having the omniscience usually credited to the male voice-over in classical cinema. She enunciates her subject position. Additionally, she articulates the subject position of the whole community by invoking its history through her speech. Epic in its taking up of narrative space, she certainly breaks with patriarchal epic tradition in the way in which she accrues authority for herself as a woman. She does it, not through ancestry in the first instance, but through her own status. Further, as griot she does not use the third-person, but the first, enmeshing herself in the history, and naming herself as griot. In saying that she is the utterance of her name, but not naming herself according to lineage, the unknown woman differentiates her position as griot from the patriarchal tradition.

The specificity of the film's aesthetics, the creation of the epic able to identify women's history and heroism, is effected through the establishment of feminist authority in the film, the power given to the women to narrate history, to be authoritative guardians of the oral tradition.

The time is set both in the past and in the present allowing for significances to overlap. If the patriarchal epic achieved this temporal overlay through stasis in description, Dash also uses the present to unsettle what Mikhail Bakhtin discusses as the regressive impulse of the pastness of the epic, the 'absolute past', and brings in the dialogical, the challenge to that pastness.[26] The contradictions of the woman's claim also call into question the pristine legacy of the past, honoured maybe, but also scorned. The latter is important to understand the project as not being moored in nostalgia but as confronting the crisis of colonialism, slavery and its aftermath.

Time assumes a luminosity and also a significance at the narrative level because we are to witness the splitting of the Peazant family, but this event is definitely not the originary moment of the community. Nevertheless the moment of migration to the north is embedded in every image and every narrative turn of the film. The text is specific about fixing the date but it also emphasises a collective memory and is detailed about visualising the remnants of slavery. The strategy of both being specific about present time and evocative about past and future time locates the move to the mainland within the cartography and annals of the diaspora of black women. Yet both the day itself and the memory of the people's coming to the islands is not represented by using cinematic conventions of realism. It may be a day in their lives, but it is not a slice of life, certainly not newsreel footage or documentary footage. Rather the day involves 'a ritual in transfigured time'.[27] Flashbacks validate black women as subjects of history and add to the mythological core of the film. Ibo landing provides the *mise-en-scène* for this incursion into the history of the Africans who walked on water into the horizon rather than surrender to slavery. During the course of the day, Bilal, a West African Muslim, reconnects with his origin every time he calls on Allah. The woman who teaches the children words in West African languages underscores the conscious effort some in the community make to remember and to know who they are. Nana's scraps of memories, her jars and bottles, symbolise the connection across the Atlantic.[28]

Dash's rhythmic movement between images that do not get subsumed by the narrative to the stories of the women of the diaspora creates an overarching mythology. She succeeds

Fig. 14: *Daughters of the Dust* – framed posed still-life; yet overflowing with passion, stresses the connections between black women from Africa and its diaspora; here the women draw closer together physically and emotionally, despite very different personal and cultural histories

in remaining true to history and mythology. I disagree then with the notion that the film is a 'speculative fiction', and view it rather as an African form of epic storytelling that carries the ontological significance of history.[29] The revisionist aspect of the tale, the centering of the women as the epic warriors, the deliberate sidelining of the men, particularly Ely, is corrective, and very much in line with the model of the narrator of the *Sundiata*, Djeli Mamadou Kouyate, who says he speaks the truth as he has been told. The biggest component of the oral tradition, the authority based on what has been told, holds, and while Dash's sources may not have been oral, she operates within its parameters; her narrative does not question each facet of what has been received, but works using that framework, even if it is expanded. Certainly this does not mean that the film is claiming sole ownership of that truth; in the oral tradition whosoever has the training may narrate. Dash's dwelling on images serves history, her attention on the characters serves mythology. Her narrative line follows history, her framing constructs mythology. I prise history and mythology apart as though one were more true than another. Dash does not really make a distinction between the two, but I do, as a heuristic device to enable me to talk about those images that resist narrative and those images that transcend history. Whether mythological or historical, the images also remain records.

Avant-garde filmmakers generally insist that the context of the images is irrelevant and that the assault on the visual to challenge perception is the mission.[30] Dash's film lingers on images but each of them is imbued with a specific, contextual and even historical significance. The opening image of the hands with dust pouring out of the women's palms is an image we come back to in the narrative. Nana Peazant's memory wanders to the time when, as a young woman, she wondered if this dust would yield anything. This contextual link firmly places black women within an agrarian tradition and views them as cultivators rather than oppressed peasants. The image also suggests that their relationship to the land is not as mothers of the earth, but daughters of dust, invoking the history of black women in the south in general.

Jacquie Jones, like other viewers on the many rich images of the film, pauses on the film's 'preoccupation with beauty', one that she finds 'distracting'.[31] The movie's aesthetics breaks away from preconceived notions of how black films might handle Southern *mise-en-scènes*, and how it might articulate the relationship between screen and subject placement. Another way of classifying this difference historically might be Robert Farris Thompson's observation that the movie is moving away from 'the deficit model'.[32] Put simply, the deficit model explains black diaspora aesthetics as being what it is due to being forced into lack, whether the form is music, architecture or food. Thompson disputes this, arguing that the aesthetics of the film, like black aesthetics in general, draws from West African features, a point that the director emphasises through the film's *mise-en-scène*. Structurally, the distracting quality of the beauty is reminiscent of epic passages where narrative propulsion is retarded by scenes of description. Julia Erhart finds that these sequences confound the moralistic expectations confronting 'minority' filmmakers.[33] I would extend this argument slightly to say that not only are minority filmmakers expected to bring in the slice of poverty, but that they are not supposed to have access to aesthetics either in the diegesis, as B. Ruby Rich notes, or in the modes of representation.[34] Leaving aside the costumes and the looks of the women for a minute, consider the space itself that Manthia Diawara considers a 'character' in the film.[35] The long history of the filmic and literary rendition of foreign landscapes, or landscapes of the other, as threatening, hot and overpowering has been read as a figuration of the psyche of the white protagonist; namely projections of evil, in many cases a personification of feminine evil.[36] Dash's landscape images a different kind of relationship between subject and land, of work and more work; the work lending the women a heroic status in the powerful land filmed in red. The characters very often touch elements of the lands; Nana touches the red earth, two women husk corn. A native American man, St Julian Last Child, gathers moss from the oak tree; he is seated in the tree in another scene. Myown Peazant is lying on the sand in one scene, and Yellow Mary and Trula are sitting on a tree in another.

With reference to the representation of black women, and their aestheticisation, although the point is not new, it is worth reiterating that the film wants black women to be seen as aesthetic; witness the kind of specularisation that black women were subject to. Josephine Baker and the show that was organised around her is one kind of invitation to see black women;[37] similar but at the more extreme end of the semiotic chain is the 'Hottentot Venus', whose genitalia were exhibited in Paris.[38] It is important, if obvious, to note that female beauty is not being admired here, but black female aberrance; non-femaleness in other words. Thus, their status was not 'to be looked at' but 'to be gaped at', as curiosities. Recent studies of the American Natural History Museum show the kinds of constructions of Africans and African Americans that were afoot in the nineteenth and early twentieth centuries, both here and abroad, including photographs that showed African Americans with 'downcast eyes'.[39] Hollywood film's treatment of black women has been well documented: the entertainer syndrome exuding excess sexuality, or the Mammy ideal of race denial and non-femininity were the norm.[40] The ethnographic spectacle has been no less distorted, implying notions of the primitive body and making 'the native person (man or woman) into [an] unmediated referent'.[41] Therefore the nuanced notion of a family portrait, although showing awareness of the capture of black culture through black images, is restitutive in the most simple and clear of ways by being self-directed. None of the characters look away, but into the camera while the photograph is being taken. The photograph is after all the dramatic occasion of the film, and contextually situates the 'photographic' images of the film, and their staged quality. It is not taken by a member of the Gullah community itself, it is taken by someone who crosses over into it, thus crossing the seer/seen divide.

The record of the Gullah culture itself moves from an anthropological to an ethnographic register. Viola, from the mainland, brings in the photographer, Mr Snead, to record her family but neither Viola nor the photographer have any authority over the narrative or the record. The story of the Gullahs is told by black women of three generations. The 'unborn child' is the most inquiring of the three narrators and the one who comes closest to translating her community for the viewer while in the process of knowing and understanding her own identity and culture.

The three narrators – the unnamed woman, the unborn child and Nana – do not have any absolute authority over the history of the community. While being narrators of the community's story, they are not locked into the pastness of it, but comment on the present-ness of the occurrences and their own investment in wrenching the authority to present their interpretation. Their impressions are used for voice-over narrations, often bringing a tentative subjectivity into the epic storytelling mode, thereby using the generic format to assume a different kind of subjective place in the community, and a different kind of subjective authority in the tradition of the griot. When each of them speaks, she does not necessarily comment on the image we see on-screen, but she does specifically locate her narrative in that time, so that her negotiation with the community becomes history. For example, the unborn child's quest to be accepted by Ely also exposes the dilemma of the children born of women who have been raped by white men.[42] Nana's own indomitable need and will to impress the story of her foremothers on the succeeding generations, narrated through the whole text, interspersed with other voice-over narrations, also becomes a part of history. Nana's voice-over narrations may be tentative but in the diegesis her role as griot of community is foregrounded. And yet, because Nana is a woman of the diaspora, her authority is assailed by the next generation. Ely attacks her verbally when he taunts her by saying that her arsenal of bottles and charms did not keep Eula from being raped. Nana was not able to protect her family. Nana has to persuade the family that her accounts of their communal history are still valid, that these stories of the past are her legacy, their heritage. Unlike the African griot, Nana only has her scraps but among them is the lock of hair her mother gave her as remembrance when slavery separated the two. When Nana gives her family a lock of her own hair and demands, 'Take me with you', she asks that they take their history with them and her history, the one that she has told them all these years.

Nana and the unborn child play important roles as custodians and inheritors of the culture but they are not apart from their culture. They are not above it but under it, the child who seeks a family, the old woman who is about to lose her family. The unborn child is not more important than the mother who takes on the role of the griot as moral authority. Both reflective and challenging of the old tale of Sogolon Kedjou, Sundiata's mother, Eula's structural role in this latter-day epic is substantially differentiated from Sogolon's role. Firstly she speaks, secondly she fights, and in her own name without use of wraith or buffalo woman to shield her womanliness, virtue or femininity, and finally she fights for another woman, Yellow Mary. If Nana speaks for heritage, Eula speaks for justice in impassioned terms in a scene that shows her moving from being relegated to the side to the centre of the community; both past and present. When Eula's rape was first mentioned, we saw and felt Ely's pain, despite Nana's sharpness about Ely's not owning Eula, but Eula herself was also seen as suffering from the despair of Ely's pain in the storm sequence when Ely strikes out against the glass tree. The sequence where both Yellow Mary and Eula take charge begins with the three women in a huddle, and the rest of the sequence frames them in different postures. In this segment Eula puts herself in the centre of the fray when she says that she has been 'ruin't' like Yellow Mary has. The community is confronted with the choice of either accepting all black women, or rejecting Eula. Eula starts by hiding her face in Nana's bosom, and then breaks out, finally moving out. Almost as though possessed, Eula speaks, with other-worldly authority reflected in her body. She is filmed with some space around her in the beginning, followed by the children who watch her. Employing the same strategies she used earlier, Dash brings Ely into the frame. In the extended circle both men and women listen to Eula. The most powerful shots are the ones that are so extremely well arranged that without the low-angle effect Eula is framed with little space between her and the sky. She moves through the entire scene until she is surrounded by visibly moved people. The sequence ends the same way it began, this time the three women huddle, but it is Nana's face that is hidden. The three are in the left of the frame, earlier they had been to the right. The gist of Eula's message is that Yellow Mary is a part of the community, and that they are all 'daughters of the old dusty things Nana carries in her can'. Eula's statement is a definite bid for authority and respect. The cut back to the young Nana gives Eula a place of dignity in the community.

Visually, the cutting of the film, unlike either the jagged abrupt cuts of the *nouvelle vague*, or the hierarchies set up by Hollywood continuity editing, tries to connect the people to give the sense of a coherent, if conflicted, community. For instance, when Nana is visiting the Peazant cemetery and Ely is with her in the foreground, the hinterground shows the children playing in the beach. We then cut to the beach and come back to a shot which includes both foreground and background. Metaphoric cutting, emphasising political relationship rather than narrative continuity, invests the images with a social significance seldom directly lent them by the American avant-garde.[43] At the end of the sequence on the beach, Nana's palms, in recollection of the unknown woman's palms at the beginning of the film, go out and the children on the beach come between them. The political struggle to retain African identity has been won. That specific image has also mythologised the diaspora.

The absence of a strict match between visual and verbal, most strikingly signalled by the fact that the voice-over narration does not concentrate on the teller, overwrites both Hollywood and the American avant-garde to tell an afracentric story of women of the diaspora. Nana's reminiscences, in the context of the present and future, the unborn child's aspirations in the frame of past and present in the shot where Nana is at the cemetery, demonstrates the narrative direction. The technique of matching image and verbal through the grand narrative of the African woman's enslavement and migration results in a mythological and historical narrative, taking the discourse out of the space of the fictional and the factual. Other critics have suggested that the film's exploration of formal methods constitutes a 'feminist aesthetic',[44] or a clearing of the representational terrain for women's representation through non-Hollywood arrangements of space and time. Its authority lies, however, not in altering the syntagma to signify differently, but in the same mode; i.e., to make different meanings with different grammatical units but not alter the process of semiosis, but to alter the syntagma to signify in a different mode; i.e., the formal experiment with different grammatical units results in the narration of epic, not just the biography of the women. The grammar is then asked to bear a different weight, changing the texture of the film's aesthetic.

Julie Dash's strategy, her own position as griot of the diaspora, is suggested by the texture of the film which evades distinctions between diegetic and extra-diegetic dimensions. Many basic elements of the avant-garde, such as the presentness of imagery, are over-matched to the mythology of the diaspora and are consequently resymbolised. First, the making of the gumbo which goes on for the major portion of the film becomes a remembering of a distinct culture, a record, a memory of joy and community. It is perhaps the one event which is of importance in the diegesis for narrative momentum and yet it serves a more metaphoric function. Second, the staged quality of the film where characters seem to enter and exit the frame, combined with the slow pace of the editing, allows the characters to find a place for themselves on-screen and in history. The camera does not sneak up on them and indeed whether the photographer in the diegesis is present or not, the characters act as though they are ready to present themselves, rather than be represented photographically. Third, the repetition of images is not for symbolic accumulation but for historical placement. The two trees that Julian, the native American, and Yellow Mary perch on speak to the rootedness of the Gullah culture but also speak for different positionalities within it. Yellow Mary leaves the tree and comes back to it, Julian stays on it. It is also important to note that the trees themselves are different. Fourth, the psychoanalytic origins of images are completely irrelevant in this film that views psychic or psychological phenomena in non-individualised terms. Eula leaves a glass of water to communicate with her mother. We return to that glass later. Yet later Eula decides to stay on the Sea Islands after an emotional plea to the community not to make moral judgements on women. The strong voice of the newborn child and Nana's acceptance and tenderness to Yellow Mary validate Eula's gesture. The three permit the absent dead mother's voice a presence.

While the avant-garde juxtapositions images to jolt or disorient, and attempts to bury context as in the tradition of the films of the Sons (Buñuel), or repeats them with specific psychological connotations as in the work of Deren or Dulac, Dash uses images to celebrate the presence and complexity of black women. She once had occasion to refer to the film as a 'family album'.[45] As actors in their history, they make choices. And like the old Ibos on Ibo landing, they take their lives and histories into their own hands, they resist when there is no choice, and they make the dust yield. Dash does not glamourise these women, she enshrines them. They are ancestors in the African sense of the word, but not ancestors without flaws. Viola and Haagar both want to leave the island in the name of Christianity and progress. Neither Dash nor Nana condemns them. But while Dash does not reject them, she does privilege Nana and her scraps. This is Nana's history, Dash's history: the history of black women of the diaspora.

The presentation of the complexity of black women's lives and history, particularly the relationships between people, made a powerful impact on black women viewers. Jacqueline Bobo notes that their interest in the film made it viable for the distributors to keep it in commercial circulation after the art-house run had been completed.[46] Equally interesting, is the energy the women were prepared to put into being producers, instead of consumers of the text, in the Barthesian sense, because the film was seen as emerging from a black woman's 'sensibility'.[47] One viewer located the source of the authority in the text as lying in the film's 'represent[ing] all that goes on in the black community'.[48] Reclaiming the three women as heroes, their stories as history invests them and the film with feminist authority.

Feminist History in the Cinematic Age: Assia Djebar's *La nouba des femmes du Mont-Chenoua*

Feminist epics, such as Julie Dash's *Daughters of the Dust*, with their quasi-mythical historical status, have vitally restored the past for women. In the terrain of history, more generally, the challenge has been to listen to the silences and through a feminist method, what could be called 'excavation',[49] to place women in history. Feminist history undoes the slantings of prior historians; believing as it does that never again will the *grand récit* be recognised.[50]

And these stories that are told will not endanger women. Assia Djebar's *La nouba des femmes du Mont-Chenoua* ambitiously but very warily seeks to record a few of these stories.

In their discussion of what composes feminist historiography, Kumkum Sangari and Sudesh Vaid make a distinction between feminist historiography and women's history. Feminist historiography, they assert, scrutinises the constitution of modes of knowledges and their gendered premises. Cultural history would be ideal terrain for feminist historiography, which they describe in the following terms: 'A feminist historiography rethinks historiography as a whole and discards the idea of women as something to be *framed* by a context, in order to be able to think of gender difference as both structuring and structured by a wide set of social relations.'[51] In this sense, it is important to note that it is not sufficient to fill in gaps, to do the crucial elemental work of acknowledging women's existence and participation, but it is equally vital to relate patriarchal ideology to the contemporary lived conditions of women. Sangari and Vaid comment that the greatest difficulty of this project perhaps lies in being able to decipher how hegemonic notions of women that have attained exalted status affect, alter and impact the actions of women, and in trying to make sense of how those ideologies determine the women's social and economic status. Djebar's film follows the return of Leila, a combatant in the Algerian struggle for independence from France to the country, and her reflections on women and their participation in the war. Through the present condition of Leila, and the conditions present and past of the countrywomen, Djebar critiques the histories that disposition Leila. Djebar is both a feminist historiographer, and concerned with women's history, her own training being in history and much of her fiction being devoted to the purposes of feminist revisionist history.

Djebar's many commentators have returned obsessively to her techniques of composition, particularly in her fiction. That Djebar must work through alien tongues, texts and constructions has been reiterated,[52] that she seeks to speak for the voices that have been unheard despite the difficulties,[53] and finally that the former description of Djebar's project is a little too optimistic for her style which is revealed through veiling and unveiling.[54] In all these writings, Djebar's own self-presentation through autobiographical glimpses and quests in her work become important. Much of this critical work is fascinating, but does not resist the temptation to exoticise the third world woman herself, Djebar.[55] The presence of the third world author ruminating about the history of her people and of women, her strategies of concealment and revelation, given Djebar's autobiographical investment overshadows the author/filmmaker's contribution to both film and history. The critics do consider history, and even 'feminine history', but in emphasising the difficulties of Djebar's acknowledged project of rewriting history, the accent on Djebar as 'correcting' the *grand récit* prevails. It is important to recognise that regarding history, Djebar's many recorded troubles with colonial historiography have given rise to a model of 'peeling', or sifting through the layers, for instance, of colonial historiographer Fronteneau's writings, and do not perhaps clearly identify that Djebar has chosen to consider her subjects through a wide array of social relations such as tribal history, gender relations in the tribe and colonial intervention as structuring, but also structured by, the relations.[57]

Djebar's film *La nouba des femmes de Mont-Chenoua* responds to Julie Dash's character's question in *Illusions* about when and how film would serve the interests of subaltern history, and not represent history through the mystifying excesses of Hollywood. D.W. Griffith's *The Birth of a Nation* immediately comes to mind as an extraordinary example of the destructive power of the cinema to construct history 'written in lightning'. Fatimah Tobing Rony describes how Frantz Fanon sat cringing while watching the film, afraid as he waited for himself to appear in a guise that he could not recognise except as some horrible misprisoning of himself.[58] Djebar gives third world women a film outside what Rony dubs 'the ethnographic spectacle' of race. The reference is to the inevitable racial bracketing of the non-European.

Clarisse Zimra comments on the ethical centre of Djebar's film being fictional.[59] Narration is not Djebar's primary purpose in the film, although stories are told. As ethnography was important to Julie Dash even as she narrated the story of the Gullah Africans, the methods of feminist ethnography are instrumental to Djebar's recording of history. Djebar's hero Leila comes back home, but she is not seeking anything; she says that she merely wants to listen, and that she loves listening. Her return home is full of disquietude, the angles of the house are unrevealing, the interior as uncommunicative as the man in the wheelchair who neither touches her nor speaks to her.

The film itself is structured musically – Overture, Prologue, Adagio, Alle, Moderato, Fine – following, perhaps, the pace of an Algerian military band if the title of the film is any indication. The narrative breaks are musical, and the film, in some sections, is composed pictorially in that it follows the logic of the still camera rather than the moving camera. As in her novels, where Djebar finds the form insufficient for narrative voice and weight, here the conventions of either continuity editing, and the Hollywood studio code, or documentary filmmaking would be incoherent to the film's loose wrapping of women's stories, suffering and memories.

As Dash's *Daughters of the Dust* grafted the epic to cinema, through the oral, Djebar fixes the interior monologue to cinema through the pictorial. Using the resources of the medium, the techniques of the avant-garde, Djebar is able to avail of the method of feminist historiography and compose women's history. Her film allows us to understand that the burning theoretical issues at stake for Western feminist film critics/filmmakers are not entirely the ones that are compelling for third world feminist filmmakers. The significance placed upon the relationship between body and voice, and between subject and object of the look for the cultural construction of gender relations by Western feminists is shifted by Djebar's film which locates these significances differently.

The great avant-garde filmmaker Maya Deren is reported by Alexander Hammid as having disdained the techniques of documentary because 'It was more propaganda. It was as much a documentary as a TV spot, trying to sell you something. That's why she didn't like the word', and said to Miriam Arsham that it was 'false and pretentious'.[60] Djebar avoids the truth claims made by traditional documentaries by availing of a fictional framework, whilst borrowing documentary and ethnographic techniques. The documentary format had been used extensively by the feminists of the 1960s to listen to real women, as opposed to reel women, and Djebar continues in that tradition in a highly mediated way. The scrutiny of method and of ideological constructions of women favoured by feminist historiographers allows her to present the countrywomen who are one of the subjects of the film without the kinds of codings that would specularise them either racially or sexually.

Techniques reminiscent of the *nouvelles romans* of Alain Robbe-Grillet, Alain Resnais, Luis Buñuel and Maya Deren, particularly Resnais' *Last Year at Marienbad* (1961) but more crucially Deren's cutting techniques in *Meshes in the Afternoon* (1943), all are evoked by the avant-garde strategies *La nouba des femmes de Mont-Chenoua* uses to do the work of history even as it meditates on history.[61] Deren does differ very obviously from the male filmmakers in her treatment of women.

The experimental format in film suited Djebar well, already a great innovator of the novelistic genre. Employing the modernist technique of stream of consciousness for a female protagonist, without submitting to the standard formats for presenting consciousness, Djebar is able to examine ideology whilst not being subsumed by its code, or replaying it through her own apparatus. In other words, the technique facilitates her questioning the framing of ideology without overwriting it with undue optimism.

Leila, the female protagonist, routinely does not speak in the film, but we have access to her interiority. This gesture is significant in a film which because of the silence keeps the interlocutor's manipulation of the women of Mont-Chenoua as minimal as possible. Rather than have Leila question her intervention in any self-conscious way, Djebar shows that not only is the question of 'objectivity' the way traditional historians theorised it irrelevant, even not taking their practice into consideration, but that deeply attached desire impells the feminist historian. Leila does not think of herself as a historian, she is not even a voyager, a seeker or a seer; as she says, she is a listener. Her participation in these women's lives, her partiality towards them finally acknowledges their existence as country women who, like her, participated in the war for independence.

The film opens strikingly with an image of a white female figure crossing the white zebra tracks. Although the shot is ostensibly framed by the colonial French apparatus, Djebar's consideration of it through women's history diminishes its impact. The brief shot is composed almost classically with the figure arrested at the centre of the frame, offering the viewer a rectilinear perspective.[62] This archival insert, the shot of the figure crossing the lines, is repeated twice in the next minute, and both times the shot moves away from the earlier perspective subtly and disturbingly. The first shot pictorially represents a stable and powerful image despite the shocking adjustment to the vision demanded by the whiteness of the lines and the whiteness of the woman in hejab. Djebar avails of this archival shot, and uses it as punctuation, to introduce a sense of visual perspective that will be relocated by the interpositioning of her own footage. Further, through her 'overreading' impulse, whereby the auteur is able to reposition the French footage of the woman, the woman will emerge as heroic, and as related to the women who tell Djebar's protagonist Leila their stories.[63] We then cut to a medium shot of an armed woman in the middle of the field. Another rapid cut to a tree follows, and then a medium shot of a woman astride a tree hints at a compositional technique unbounded to a specific narrative.

Space is at stake, occupying space, in the reprisal of this archival shot. Black figures, armed, gendarmerie, from the left cross the space; the centre is marked by a white line that runs diagonally. One figure in white from the right does the same. The centre line has now shifted to the right as the figure in white crosses in from off-screen space to on-screen space. The centre of the frame does not actually dissolve although the movement of the female creates the impression of it having shifted. The movements of the woman figure in white in the frame are diagonal, the focus on the white line running diagonally blocking out the edges. This two-shot sequence of the gendarmerie crossing and the woman entering on-screen is repeated with a small but crucial difference. The first time the figure is shown crossing into the space, but the image is arrested just as she reaches the centre in a repetition of the opening image. The second time, the figure decisively crosses into off-screen space, definitely not crossing into the arena the soldiers had occupied. In just two shots, Djebar has situated her archival footage to alter on-screen space to accommodate two fields of action, with a changing centre, each crossing having its own centre. What Jonathan Crary calls the 'blickpunkt'[64] – the spot on the screen that the eye goes to because it identifies a centre based on the relationship between figure and ground – changes, creating not just separateness because of the division between the two movements caused by the shifting blickpunkt, but also vertiginiousness because of the sharpness of the line before the cut to the woman on the tree, the blickpunkt now being considerably higher, but still in the space occupied by the woman in white. These shots indicate the kind of visual restructurings Djebar will use in the film for what Crary loosely terms the modernist project of visual decenterings.[65] The shift in blickpunkt in this case will also be a shift in what we look at. The prior colonial framing is no longer instrumental as method.

The two-shot pattern of the gendarmerie and the woman crossing the marked space is intercut with shots of women walking in the fields, but this is usually a conventional left-to-right movement. Images of the woman on the tree, or of the tree itself are also interspersed connecting all three, bringing them together within a historical blickpunkt. The particular image of the woman on the tree is repeated and also fleshed out verbally by one of the women of Mont-Chenoua. The pattern of repetition of shots creates a choreography of movement that matches with the structure of the film which is musical and references tempo and rhythm, rather than the temporal sequencing and arrangement of events.

Djebar pauses on the tree in the field before she makes a clear scene change, but an unusual one to script on the screen, an accompaniment of the written to the oral voice-over of the woman describing the events that occurred in this region. A dramatic cut to a girl with her face to the wall takes us to the overture of the film. Combining the oral and pictorial, the director moulds the film form to write a connected history that traverses the generations. The image of the girl with her face to the wall, a contemporary one, is linked to the oral and written text that ostensibly separated the image from the opening moments of the film.

The overture of the film locates women's history in the crevices between war and peace, speech and silence, the past and the present. Leila meditates, 'I speak, I speak, I speak', but since sound here is strictly a voice-over of her reflective interiority, it produces the uncanny effect of silence. The man in the wheelchair, the child's father, does not hear her. Leila speaks, and does not speak.

The avant-garde techniques approximate the questioning of historical method, of gender placings, that entail feminist historiography. The interior landscape, rich both visually and aurally, unfurls itself, offset only by the bleak silence and watchful looks of both Leila and the man, Ali. The effect of the imprisonment of 'fate' that Leila talks about is total in these sequences that feature Leila's interiority in the space of the house in Ali's presence. The auditory impact of the silence is enhanced by the off-centre blickpunkts and the unconventional blocking. Neither Ali nor Leila are centred, visual perspective becomes difficult, and the viewer listens to the literary text for narrative mooring. One shot of Ali behind Leila is often followed by one of him in his wheelchair in a different spot with no suggestion of any kind of transition. Spatial dislocation is more discomfiting because the centre is emptied, as it were. Crary speaks of how Georges Seurat in his paintings used 'exchangeability' of signifiers, within limits of course, and while this makes signification viable, the 'floating' signifier destabilises its solidity.[66] While there is an exchange of signification brought about by spatial disruption, and by narratively uncued blickpunkts, there are new visual centerings in each new framing; however, it is disconcerting that the transcendental function of the centre is absorbed by the aural. Since the voices are always female voice-overs, the change of space and perspective has been initiated from another place, the place of feminist oral history and subjectivity.

A literary text, that even features a long opening written composition, the film might be expected to work with extra-visual elements in its design. Djebar's film, however, defies this category because of its insistence on working with the visual to effect change in the design and the spectator. Clarisse Zimra, using the authority of the auteur herself, makes a strong case for the 'phenomenological primacy of voice-over image'[67] and argues that Djebar's film makes its impact through the disjuncture between the soundtrack and screen. Réda Bensmaïa, however, argues that because the sound does not serve as the centre, the film is without any mooring in either voice or image.[68] Bensmaïa's notion of 'primordial atomisation'[69] is misplaced, as is Zimra's notion of the ascendancy of the voice-over image. The nuanced use of dislocating strategies of the visual call attention to the sound; the absence of a centre is crucial to visual aesthetics; the combination is vitally important to Djebar's sense of multiple blickpunkts, accretions to women's history. However, Zimra's idea remains appealing particularly because it shows us how to overcome the visual totalisation of women, specifically Algerian women during colonial rule. Equally important, as Mildred Mortimer has shown,[70] and Djebar has written,[71] has been to occupy visual space and to claim ownership of the visual, but not to deflect from it through the spoken. To signify through movement is a way of breaking out of the *ex nihilo* voice which is permitted to veiled women. Djebar's comments on the difficulties of Arab women coming to speech are well documented; I want rather to historicise/contextualise the whole notion of difficulty in speaking with reference to conventions of film form and the position of Algerian women. Given the considerable experiments that have been undertaken with voice manipulation in documentary to shake and problematise the authority of the viewer, it remains that the voice-over of the female bespeaks an authority not granted her in mainstream Hollywood. This particular taboo, then, is something that needs to be challenged by feminist filmmakers who are in dialogue with that tradition.[72] Women in hejab cannot be seen, but they can speak. Interestingly then, the classic thesis on the objectification of women, and the importance of sound cast in terms of that formulation, does not obtain in the case of Arab women filmmakers. In terms of a feminist film theory, the challenge is to represent women without the brokerage of Delacroix and Picasso, but also to represent them visually. The embodied voice is not problematic within this cultural nexus; the disembodied one is.

The conscious experimentation with the visual and aural in space enables Djebar to accord authority to women in both realms through her problematising of the voice-over by presenting Leila's interiority, and by visually stabilising the voice to the body when the women's voice-overs are interspersed through Leila's commentary, their continued use pointing to the consequences of prior gender interpellations that Djebar does not idealistically disperse.

The 'doubled voice-over', the voice-over processed by Leila's interiority, is germane to conferring authority on the visual. Here, the disarrayal of the visual is to allow for self-directed representation of the women through Leila's thoughts, expressed aurally. The voice-overs establish the importance of the women being seen, but as historical subjects rather than exotic colonial constructions.

Similarly, while acknowledging the importance of what Mortimer calls 'reappropriating the gaze',[73] I want to contextualise that whole notion of Algerian women not having the power of the gaze. For Western feminist documentary filmmakers the task was to present women as they were – in the famous slogan, 'real women, not reel women' – and to present their view of the world, while avoiding the objectification of the male gaze. For women in hejab, some part of the above is inevitably accurate, but lacking in understanding that while we may not be able to see the face of the woman in hejab, she is able to see us, what Djebar understands as the 'integrity of her gaze',[74] the authority of her gaze, and perspective. Indeed, Marnia Lazreg points out that the fetishisation of the veil in the colonial imaginary may have had much to do with colonial perceptions of the veiled woman who represented 'mystery, hidden beauty, but also an object of possession by aggression due to the frustration stemming from being seen by her but not seeing her'.[75] Thus, arguably, the woman in hejab has always had both the gaze and the female solidarity that Leila searches for in the film, and it is this legacy she comes to claim, not in its entirety, or even exclusively, but as part of a women's history pertaining to the women's community that is too easily slighted.

Leila also finds authoritative sources on the war for independence. Here, too, the film models authority slightly differently than the documentary modes prevalent in the 1960s. While retaining the importance of a non-hierarchical relationship between the interviewer and the subjects, the film is not necessarily invested in divesting or problematising the authority of the interviewer, a strategy in much documentary feminist filmmaking, nor in questioning the authority of the interviewees, an ubiquitous trope of the classical documentary. The film builds on the women's documentaries of the 1960s that sought to invest their subjects with authority. Here the base of authority is expanded because it includes not only the women's lives, but also the war; their lives encompassing the war. Consequently, the women's Rückblick, the backward glance, taking in the arching events of their time, bridges the caesura between the autobiographical and the historical. Giving these women authority to narrate outside of their own lives does actually accept their authority as historians. The colonial presence is located and examined by the women within the purview of their own long history as country women signified by the orature of the tribe and the identity that is interpellated by that culture also subject to feminist *sous rature*. Leila too is given authority because of her knowledge of some fragments of the women's history and her participation in their struggles. Mortimer notes that the camera serves Leila, and that we see through her eyes. An equivocal gift at best, point-of-view shots can easily be robbed of their significance outside the individual. We do periodically see through Leila's eyes, and the camera, as another critic has noted, picks up for Leila when she sleeps.[76] Nevertheless, her dream sequences and the general volatility of what she sees would curiously not be valid except as her expression, were it not for her vision's validation by the narratives of the other women.

Leila's seeing is so restricted, initially to the interior space of the house and then the interior psyche. Subjective, decomposed, it does verge on the anarchic. If the bonding with the woman is essential to her psychic health, it is also vital to an expanded vision, and to an authoritative vision.[77] Leila does not acquire the authority of vision, not at all equivalent to point of view, until she has processed the women's stories and interpreted her story through their words.

The *grand récit* is not restored in this process, nor is a corrective grand récit constructed. Yet a larger narrative composed of process, defining women's history as process, has been constituted defying both colonial and nationalist interpellations. Women's participation alone is not the issue here, but the exposures of ideology that restrained women under colonialism and through the nationalist struggle.[78] The film gives an account of their present subjugation evoked through the metaphor of visibility/invisibility in the song repudiating the need for the veil.

The pictorial techniques of the pre-cinematic age sustain the filmmaker as feminist historiographer. However, pictorialising this process through another medium, without the offices of the cinema, would have been impossible for they would have served to monumentalise history, not follow the process of its composition. Leila's authority is reinforced by the women's and vice-versa. This communal women's authority, composing women's history, clearly also constitutes the locus of feminist authority in the community. The man, Ali, is without authority and all other men are absent.

Having the gaze does not in fact imply liberation. One can be trapped and locked inside the gaze. Leila ends up looking at a much wider space in the end, that which the camera had earlier been able to apprehend in its shots of the field and the wide open spaces, the forests. Looking, forever looking, the gaze has been tortuous, a trope that feminist film exposes painfully; redirecting the gaze or taking over is not as pleasurable for the woman as it had been and continues to be for the male viewer. The softest shots of the film perversely are what Ali sees, Leila playing with the child, Leila bathing with the child, Leila sleeping with the child.

Leila wants the silence to be broken, she wishes Ali would speak. And she wonders if she has come back to speak about 'death and fire'. The memories she is 'fond' of are of the loss of her mother, father, uncle and the disappearance of her brother. Three strands related to the war are interposed here; the loss of family and imprisonment during the revolution, Ali's accident on the horse, and Leila's return now. The circle of interest is wider than these three events, as indicated by a shot of a circle of people playing music, and a woman almost noiselessly singing 'My Heart is Broken'. The music introduces themes that the thoughts of Leila do not. One song that follows after Leila is in the blue-tinged room looking at Ali is about being uprooted. The relationship of the diegetic music to Leila's thoughts is subtle in that the community is brought into her dilemma through their intuitive understanding of her psyche. While it does not provide the coherence that music often does,[79] it is not without narrative relevance to the themes of the film.

Fig. 15: *La nouba des femmes du Mont-Chenoua* – Algerian woman barred from French festivities, part of a countrywoman's narrative to Leila

The prologue takes Leila out to the community to Jamila's mother who tells her the story of the young woman, the seventh wife, who frees the doves from her saint husband's jars. Jean-Marie Clerc places special importance on the passage of these stories from the women to the next generation. He comments that because of colonialism, the Algerians had been rendered 'mute' and that women alone had been able to retain these stories in their '*patois fermes*' that recapitulated the glorious pre-colonial past.[80] His point about women keeping the tongue is well taken, but one is less certain about the assumptions of the glorious pre-colonial past. The film recognises continuities in resistance to colonial rule, but even this story questions the pre-colonial past. As Leila repeats the story to her child, the image of the woman from folk legend freeing the doves recurs at the end of the film. Curiously, the saint claims that the woman, the seventh wife, removed his blessings from him by freeing the doves. Mentioned only in the story, and not brought up again, the comment serves as a delicate indication of the rootedness of the patriarchal world view in the culture. Ali's watching of Leila, again presented without commentary, and a continuous motif through the various movements, speaks perhaps to the incommensurability of the relationships between women, men and war. Ali's impassive watching of Leila is fierce, containing some kind of implosive charge, but the female viewer does not fear that he will erupt violently. The sting of voyeurism is removed in one scene by the child pointing to his presence. The division of space in the bath scene serves as some kind of screen partly filtering his and our view of them. Sepia-tinged images of the gendarmerie superimposed on her sleeping face concludes this section.

Visual patterns are drawn linking conscious/self-reflection and unconscious/dream interiority. The relationship between the two is significant in understanding both past and present. The watching Ali bears a dream-like connection to Leila's unconscious in the design of the film. The oneiric pattern recalls the surrealist technique of attempting to visualise the dream state. Unlike Buñuel, closer to Deren, but still different, Djebar does not allow the dream to signify on its own, but assimilates it into history. The history of the community, the struggle during the war reported by the women, clarifies the unconscious as it does the folk legend of the Saint of Mont-Chenoua. If a dream is like a rebus that needs to be solved, history is the key to the riddle.

Through 'broken' memories, not necessarily Leila's own, and not necessarily 'broken' because the event has broken the person, the film connects the lives of the women of the community, Leila herself, and a mythical figure called Zuleikha. Each section then links a mythical figure to the protagonist and the community rendering feminist themes overtly. As a young child, Leila rides in her father's cart 'watching the world of men'. One of the pictorial images shows a man's oppressive behaviour to his horse making one wonder whether Ali were thrown from the horse or whether he was trying to control it. Zuleikha, who went to the forest at the age of forty and who became mother to the mujahideen and was tortured and executed, is kin to Leila not only through blood, but also history. Leila herself was imprisoned. A very stylised theatrical line-up of the women prisoners aligned neatly so as to bear visual inspection from left to right is redolent with an aura of madness. The pictorial quality is far from being documentary; rather, it is more avant-garde in the 'fictionalising' of the women's figures. The women's history of imprisonment, of watching the male world, also influences Leila's relationship with Ali. Difficult as it is for her to speak about her experiences, she does begin only to be asked to stop. In a rare gesture of revealed anger, Leila throws Ali's crutch away, but still does not speak. Instead, the voice-over picks up on her thoughts about the barriers between people – specifically walls; an aural repetition of the visual motif of her with her head against one. This is an obvious reference to Djebar's view that independence did not break down the walls between men and women, a theme highlighted in many of her works.[81]

In the formal movements of visual repetition, or of aural repetition and vice-versa, the continuity of the women's resistance is an important component of the history Djebar transcribes. In terms of the current moment, for instance, one of the women speaks of her daughter whom Leila had met when the girl was barely thirteen. Finally, history also connects to a community history of resistance where women participated actively in the battles. The struggle of 1871 led by Sidi Malek evokes the Cave of Dahra that shows still friezes of the women and children. This pictorial representation has the crude colours of the imagination, not the smoothness of narration.

Among the most powerful statements of the film about the country women's heroic participation in the revolution is made, as in the musical form adagio, with ease and grace. The story of the old woman who tells the tale of how for five years the partisans were housed in the farm and dependent on the labour of women evokes the notion of 'broken memory' in Leila, referring to a history not easily completed and sealed. The women worked, did laundry, hid the partisans, carried supplies. Pans of the land, its emptiness, contrast with the pictorial quality of other images. The insert of the French dancing in the village square while the Algerians are fenced out reveals the changes wrought on the land through the offices of French colonialism and 'culture', and brings in another theme of the film which accords the women their identity as peasant women, and notes their struggle to retain this identity by rejecting all city propositions, including of course the grand one of becoming subservient to the ruling classes by attempting to adopt their ways.[82]

Female double voice-overs, Leila's voice and the women's voices, link the women's stories to compose women's history in a terribly personal and intimate way. The moderato section features the women gathering together and clapping even as Leila reflects that 'all the women [become her] mother'. The finale spells out the political agenda through musical pieces. Uncovering one of the ends of feminist history as utopian, the song declares that 'women shall never return to the shadows'. That the processes of women's history can function as feminist critique is made apparent by the reiteration of the image of the seventh wife releasing the doves immediately after Djebar shows Leila looking through the gridles. A collage of women spliced together with wipes conveys both chronology and atemporality. Djebar disdains montage for collage, true to the still picture style of the film. Not a collapsing of time as in temporal montage, the motif is brought in, not even through rhythmic cutting, but as a repetitive musical note inevitable to the completion of the film as it was crucial to the middle.

Djebar reveals that women's history need not be exclusively a record of women's narration of their experiences, but can function as explicit feminist critique because of its relative unhingeing from the framings of colonial history. Thus we understand that the women's experiences are in part derived from their conscious apprehension of political events which in turn is instrumental in their resisting oppression. Transgenerational connections between the women are not effected in any trans-historical way. Leila shares in these experiences of the women despite her difference from them in age and education.

The film's conclusion connects visually and aurally the personal life of Leila to the communal life and song of Zuleikha, the embodiment of the fighting spirit of the women, who still lives in the mountains. The celebration of Zuleikha borders on the mythologising, raising the question of whether women's history can resist mythologising, and if indeed it should. Zuleikha, composed of all mothers as it were, takes the sting away from the dangerous mythologising of ideas of femininity. More importantly, a feminist mythology may not be such a bad thing, if it were to remain at the level of all women and be elevated. Djebar's earlier collage, the connections between stories, does strive to do that; nevertheless Zuleikha as a hero does stand out. The emphasis on Zuleikha's heroism is occasioned by her leadership, and raises the question of whether women's history should find and construct heroes. Problematic because the achievements of 'exceptional' women are held against the majority, one could perhaps consider the virtues of constructing female heroes to balance the legends of the great male freedom fighters. Yet this model lacks vision, in constructing a parallel system to one that does not actually serve male history well, and definitely does women's history a disservice. Zuleikha's extraordinariness is also a function of not having access to her interiority: through Leila whose ordinariness and extraordinariness are painfully apparent, we gain the measure of how heroes are sung and unsung.

Visually, the representation of the women who are the authenticators of women's history is intriguing. The veiled woman at the beginning of the film and the veiled hidden figure,

Zuleikha, distance us from them; in other words, no effort is made to construct visually a mythological presence as is done tendentiously in many genres of film with male heroes. After all, the veiled woman is one of the other women, seen through French eyes, whom we see anew. Nevertheless, the masking effect, the inscrutability, becomes perplexing, sets them apart, creating once again a hierarchy of heroes among women. The song perhaps has the last word on this issue when it contextualises the veil as being historically determined – 'during the occupation the veil had a reason' – thus suggesting that the women could not be known during the occupation for good reason; the occupation/history barring colonial knowledge of them. The singer asks, but why now? The veil should be removed, she says. Suffice to say, Zuleikha becomes the subject of a folk song, like the seventh wife of a folk tale, where neither is monumentalised.

Discomfiting, at another level, is the role of the inscrutable, unspeaking Ali. Father of Leila's child, his role seems to be to chide Leila without words, punish her for his hurt and hide behind those walls that Leila would make glass. Hurt, wounded, he seems to be failing; and yet, he desires human warmth. Most of the warm interchanges Leila has with her child are observed by him. Perhaps he is a symbol of powerlessness, but also helplessness. Leila heals because of the women; Ali remains wounded. There are signs that he improves because he begins to walk with crutches, and begins to work. It is not accidental that he is not wounded by war. Finally, his masculinity prevents his human need from showing through the walls that Leila has broken down through her claim and acceptance of all women as her mother.[83] Leila finds a way to live with history by going around him, not with him. And we learn that we too can get around men to find women's history.

The filming of Leila in open spaces at the conclusion, a trope favoured in feminist film,[84] seems to bring in a specifically utopian, characteristic feminist feature into this filmic exploration of the traumatic impact of war on women. Examining the impact of patriarchal ideology that resurges when independence is achieved, signalled through Leila's rejection of Ali and through the song of freedom from obscurity, the film succeeds in presenting women's history, rather than cultural history *per se*, as a strategy for the development of feminist critique.

The film's use of the pictorial technique, the development of the relationship between the aural and visual, its creation of the genre of women's history in film and the mixture of genres, suggests an approach to aesthetics similar to Julie Dash's in *Daughters of the Dust*. While the oral is important to both films, the insistence on the visual is crucial to the establishment of the feminist epic and history – a structural way of consolidating feminist authority.

Ingrid Sinclair's *Flame* explores different discursive modes, including the oral and the visual in terms of the photo, to follow the travails of two women soldiers during the Zimbabwean war of independence. Although based around revolutionary material, *Flame* does not have the format or aesthetics of 'third cinema' when compared, for instance, to *The Hour of the Furnaces* (1968), or Sarah Maldoror's *Sambizanga*, which focuses on women's involvement in the Angolan war of liberation. Shot before the Angolans had achieved their independence, *Sambizanga* was criticised for not dwelling on the brutality of the prison camps. Director Maldoror emphasised, however, her investment in educating the people, and raising consciousness, rather than making nationalist statements. She also maintained that she is interested in 'women who struggle'.[85] Shot entirely with a non-professional cast and crew, *Sambizanga* is about a woman, Maria, wife of a construction worker and member of the nascent resistance movement. When her husband is taken away, Maria, encouraged by the other women, straddles her son on her back, and walks to the capital in an exhausting search for her husband and the truth of his interrment. Maldoror's aim in the film was 'to show the aloneness of a woman and the time it takes to march'.[86] The film follows three different strands: the activities of the resistance cells, the interrogation of the prisoners, and the efforts of Maria to find her husband. Village life is disrupted by the imprisonment of Dominguez, Maria's husband. The sequence is shot to expose Maria's political naïveté, and her fierce courage; she hangs on to the truck, struggles with the police officers, even attempts to run behind the truck. When she decides to track Dominguez down in the vast colonial prison system, she does so with the greatest simplicity. Long shots of her walking in the countryside to Luanda stress her fragility and her determination, as medium close-ups reveal her wiping sweat off her brow, or adjusting the weight of the child on her back. Footage of her long journey is intercut with scenes of the men in the resistance finding out about Dominguez's imprisonmnent, and the prisoners themselves. Several shots of the prisoners intersperse Maria's journey; seemingly similar to the narrative design set up by the cross-cutting of *The Great Train Robbery* (1903) where the police movement is intercut with that of the robbers on top of the train. Similar suspense is not generated here in terms of whether Maria is going to make it to Dominguez in time despite the activity around the resistance fighters who are also engaged in enquiries about Dominguez. Three distinct examples of cross-cutting emerge. The first, when Maria is with many women at Madame Teke's house, is intercut with Dominguez standing isolated, against the prison walls; the second, when Maria, initially walking briskly, is then thrown unceremoniously out of the city police station, is intercut with the prisoners in jail scratching themselves and going about in circles; the third, when Maria and Miguel are shown getting closer to Dominguez intercut with the police brutally beating him. Maldoror's 'imperfect' use of cross-cutting unifies three fields of action: Maria's long walk and her struggle for answers, Dominguez and his comrades in prison, and the resistance fighters' attempts to find out if one of their comrades has kept faith with the cause. Following Jane Gaines' suggestion that 'third cinema' could alter the politics of cross-cutting which generally seems to unify disparate elements that cannot be unified, I would argue that Maldoror, through the establishment of the three fields and the sequence and temporality of presentation of events, is able to use cross-cutting for progressive feminist purposes, for drawing out 'incongruent knowledges'.[87] The problem/solution format of bourgeois cross-cutting that Eisenstein objects to is removed by our awareness of the largeness of the task she has undertaken and the possibility of its failure. Unlike the mounted police, she is not going to get there in time to save Dominguez. Maldoror takes care not to make a conventional individual bourgeois hero of Maria.[88] Her search is loosely linked to the resistance by a female neighbour telling her that her son had suggested that Maria go in search of Dominguez, but it is conducted solitarily, putting her in the position of the traditional hero. Unlike the women of Ousmene Sembene's *God's Bits of Wood* (1960) who support the Senegalese men's strike against the French colonial government, Maria walks alone, and even when accompanied by a small boy in Luanda, faces the colonial authorities on her own. Maria's actions occur temporally before those of the resistance fighters. Indeed, the fighters glean their information from her. The connection with the resistance might narratively imply that she is being 'observed', and therefore their 'operative'. Despite the cross-cutting with the resistance fighters, the speed with which Maria moves ensures that she is the initiator of action. For example, the boy takes action by going to the grandfather after Maria has started on her mission, and follows her as she goes to three different police stations. Consequently, she is 'leading' in this situation. Further, neither group of men, resistance or prisoners, plays any role at all in her experience of the journey, and finally in her cry for justice when she wails that the Portuguese have beaten her man to death. Maria fulfills her quest; she finds out what the Portuguese have done to her husband. The knowledges of the three groups do coincide roughly, but their experiences do not. In exploring Maria's experience, and in privileging her knowledge; of both resistance and prisoners, a position unique to her, Maldoror makes action secondary to the emerging political consciousness of her female protagonist. The scheme of inter-cutting suggests that she is now part of the resistance movement. Through the journey, Maria comes to knowledge, a classical structural positioning of the bourgeois hero, but also that of the hero coming to political consciousness. And as a woman, who had been in the dark about Dominguez's activities, her emergence to political conscious-ness critiques the male relegation of females, and suggests the emergence of a feminist con-sciousness. Maldoror, through the long journey that Maria survives, lends ordinary women the authority of feminist heroism. Third cinema aesthetic, of course, does not expand on individual heroes, and Maldoror does not over-film her as such, emphasising instead her utter ordinariness as a woman of village Africa. Ferrari points out that Maldoror came in for serious criticism because of her depiction of Maria as naïve and politically unawakened. He himself, however, feels that it is one of the film's strongest features.[89] By bringing her together with the other women at the end, Maldoror contextualises her actions, as well as the women's, as part of the resistance to colonialism.

Ingrid Sinclair's *Flame*, a film about Zimbabwe's war of independence, like *Sambi-zanga*, is invested in narrating the story of the participation of women soldiers, but unlike *Sambizanga*, uses mainstream film techniques.

The Scene of Photo-reportage on Revolution: Ingrid Sinclair's *Flame*

Within the framework of revisionist history, feminist filmmakers have worked with new formats to represent women in the 'imaginary community' of the nation constructed after revolutions achieved the new states. Assia Djebar, despite her many difficulties with the roles of women in the Algerian revolution, nevertheless saw them as having a presence that later grew more complicated as women were increasingly marginalised. Sinclair's *Flame* explores the participation of women in the imaginary construction of the post-colonial nation in Zimbabwe, and their place in the historical production of the state.

Discussions on colonialisms and third world nationalisms in the Western academy in the 1990s that critiqued the idea of the 'imagined community'[90] were given a new direction by the work of the subaltern scholars, who through a study of many different formations of nationalism offered a critique that was many-pronged, with nationalism's flaws highlighted through the collusion of national leaders with right-wing factions,[91] through the historicisation of communalism as a construct, and also by paying attention to gender and its occlusions in the history of nationalism.[92] In understanding these processes in representation, Homi Bhabha,[93] and Andrew Parker, Mary Russo, Doris Sommer and Patricia Yaeger[94] were influential in showing how narrative itself seemed engrossed in notions of nation. Yet nationalism has played a powerful role in the self-determination of third world peoples, including third world women, who were as invested in the emerging nation-state as women. Work authored and auteured by women, then, has been nuanced about an assessment of nationalism in relationship to its inclusions and exclusions of women. *Flame*, in dealing with the Zimbabwean struggle for independence, is one such effort, where the narrative subtly reveals the impetus for nationalism even as it ultimately suggests its incompleteness insofar as women are concerned.

Shot in a highly self-critical way, with more than a hint of the meta-reflexive, the film follows the lives of two young girls who participate initially in highly-coded gendered ways in the Chimurenga. Florence/Flame, bullied by her father and told not to join the militants because of her gender, as though she were trying to go to a risqué party, ultimately crosses into Mozambique with her friend, Nyasha, the narrator of the tale. Specifically-gendered issues follow the young girls in their efforts to become warriors for the Chimurenga. Realistically shot, the film challenges hagiographies of nationalistic rebellions, and avoids all invitations to the grand at the expense of the marginal. Instead, we see Florence raped by Ché, her commanding officer, and Nyasha's subsequent distrust of Florence. Unlike Lizzie Borden's *Born in Flames*, which is a wholesale rejection of nationalism, understandably so because of its first world context, or Gilles Pontecuervo's subsumption of women in the struggle for Algerian independence in his progressive film *The Battle of Algiers* (1966), Sinclair's *Flame* pinpoints the feminine as imbricated in the nationalist to the extent that she traces the mythologisation of the women as war heroes even as the new post-colonial government obviated their participation in the freedom struggle. The feminine becomes nationalism's residue, its shame in having to involve women, in this the ultimately macho struggle; yet the women were able to record their participation, and through that struggle enter history's playing field.[95]

Myth and history intersect frequently in the narrative on nation formation. Sinclair's film, although fictional, was originally conceived as a documentary project. The seven women, among the many who had participated in the struggle but who had been interviewed by Sinclair, were not willing to divulge their identities.[96] Documentary, even with a fictional heart, was not a possibility and therefore that history of women in the Chimurenga battle had to be told using different techniques, underlining the very real threats for women when they choose to speak out. The film was apparently dubbed 'pornographic and subversive';[97] Zimbabwe's *Sunday Mail* charged that producer Simon Bright's company was fabricating stories for publicity and viewed the making of the film to be a colonial piracy of Zimbabwe's history.[98] *California Newsreel* contextualises the divergent accounts:

> As a result, *Flame* became one of the most controversial films ever made on the African continent. To understand why we must remember that film has played an important role in nation-building – providing a counter-history to that of the colonisers and a unifying vision of the country's origins and purposes.[99]

Interestingly, the *Sunday Mail* review dichotomises the stakes for black women's history by positing a tired old formulation: black women's history is being captured by white women and thus has to be inauthentic or white, while the male nationalist struggle is both black and authentic. This move puts black women outside of the historical arena and denies them any kind of existential ability to form alliances or make judgements for themselves. The specific witnessing of black women, their own testimony, is at the very least completely set aside as unimportant,[100] and as one critic noted, the real story is about the grand defeat of Ian Smith's minority regime to the exclusion of other strands of history.[101] The film certainly initiated an interesting discussion, as *Screen Africa* noted, on 'to whom history belongs, how it must be told, and who has the right to tell it'.[102]

Although many of the *Sunday Mail*'s extremely masculinist formulations are worthy of dismissal, in the theatre of the West the consumption of third world images that are imperialistic and orientalist is so current that the other valid excuse of women who are critical becomes a way for Western audiences to enjoy the spectacle, secure in hegemonic difference. *Flame*'s director's British birth also gave rise to questions of authenticity. Issues of third world subjectivity emerge from the dense set of factors at play here.

Representations in the West that are deeply injurious to third world women are those in mainstream Hollywood that use one strand to define the entire civilisation, and films that do not have any layerings within them to situate occurrences. Female representations in James Bond movies or Vietnam movies come to mind instantly. As one reviewer points out, *Flame* is also an advance on how women in war are usually presented as 'passive victims of the horror that men do'.[103] Viewers of the film come out, however problematically, commending the strength of the female characters and noting that these representations indicated a rich context of interplay between characters developed in a fully developed world. Speaking specifically of male representations, male behaviour is viewed within a feminist framework and analysed, some might say problematically, to the point that patriarchal violence is overly contextualised. The genre of the film too, with its ethnographic overlay, does not seek to replicate colonial history with post-colonial history that falls into the same parameters of 'official discourse'. The film uses what Martin Mhando calls the discourse of the 'bushman (sic)/woman':

> The discourse of the 'bushman' is that of those who do not speak but are spoken about. In this there is a perverted sense of authority. The director of the film avails not only of the 'civilised's' discursive power and authority of the genre but the authority of knowledge as well.[104]

Neither the filmmaker nor the cast can take responsibility for the appropriations of the film to suit liberal Western agendas. The charge that the film feeds into the liberal Western worldview begs the question of whether the women would benefit from the practice of these values.[105]

The journal format of the film allows complexity of perspective by indicating the biases of the narrator, Nyasha, who essentially records the story of her participation with Florence in the struggle to free Zimbabwe. While 'the inflected intentions of the filmmaker' do not subvert Nyasha's commentary,[106] hers is not the only locus of authority. Told from the present, the story also carries the traces of Nyasha's post-independence understanding of the war. The fabricated sepia footage of the Chimurenga that opens the film is also self-conscious about the film's presentation of history as definitely mythic in the present context, but also evocative of the 'real' through the techniques that jostle the dominant pseudo photo-journalistic mode. The range of strategies used by the film is partly characteristic of African film which is in continuous dialogue with colonial genres and seeks to 'africanise' the form.[107]

The ethnographic impulse of the film is apparent largely in Nyasha's voice-over. Curiously, because the voice-over offers its interpretation of events in the voice of the classical memoir style, and is also unknowing about a large part of the war, its voice does not dominate, but serves as a more grounded perspective than the style of the filming itself.[108] Not exactly newsreel footage but alive with colour, not exactly documentary but presumably historical, the series of sequences that compose the film paradoxically becomes more mythical, despite the photo-reportage technique and its own commentary on the construction of myth in the war. This mythical footage of the woman is absolutely essential to the director's project of recording the women's war heroism and to its ironic commentary, the male nationalist mythologising of women soldiers at the expense of the women's participation in real nation-building.

Nyasha's voice-over is interestingly not one that emerges from any kind of recognisable feminist framework, whether youthful or acquired since the war. Rather her vision of life is dictated by a desire to be independent through education, probably inspired by the missionary school and certainly espousing colonial ideology. In the long run her adherence to the law of the colonial order is profoundly challenged by the war, as is her mimicry of those values.

Despite the fact that the film is not interested in the epic dimension and its 'narrative evolves in a realistic rather than dramatic fashion',[109] its use of the transparent realist mode allows it easily to glide into a discursive mode that is free-floating, partly photo-reportage, that is not independent but follows the journalistic storyline and matches it, even if it does know more. The most powerful gestures toward the real in the visual diegesis are when Nyasha and Florence discuss their roles, actions and what their positions are. These work towards abridging the mythic nation-building project by interposing the difficulties and thoughts of women who are being interpellated by the war as *women*.

The disjuncture between women and soldiers is fundamental to the marginalisation of women from the nation-building project of the revolution's male heirs. This is why Sinclair diverges from the quality of the realist mode with some mythic framing of both landscape and character. Purportedly essayistic, the footage is still saturated with the dream of the nation and women's participation in it.

The film's investment in showing the women's battle for their own independence through the war has been recognised by auteur and reviewers alike.[110] As important as the rendition of heroism is the interpellation of their subjectivity, what has been called in the case of many African films auteured by women, the 'reconstitution of the woman's image into a new identity'.[111]

The photograph of the two comrades Flame and Liberty, taken before their separation, images the soldiers. The photograph itself begins the movie and reminds both friends of their friendship and the war. Stuck on Nyasha's door, it is a testament to the real, yet an

Fig. 16: *Flame* – Comrade Flame's total investment in the struggle for liberation; realistic as the shot is, it carries a mythical resonance and becomes more than documentary record

empty signifier in terms of its cultural and historical resonances. When the photograph is taken, the auteur's camera shows a level angle, then the photographer takes a low-angle shot that is more imposing. And that composition is not a lie, but does not tell the whole truth that the combination of journal and photo-essay do about the women's participation and struggle.

Most of the footage is supposedly realistic, but perhaps romantically tinged by Nyasha's perspective and Sinclair's own penchant for the landscape. For the most part, the visual is not really filtered through either woman's point of view. The moment of crossing the river into Mozambique is mythical, and for the voice-over narrator, entry into the military camp also is. Yet difficulties confront them. These too are registered by the voice-over narrator, rather than the camera itself. While Nyasha's visual perspective may be romantically in-clined, her voice-over directly maintains that the women were shabbily treated.

The Mozambiquan male soldier who drops the women off at the training camp cracks a sexist joke, diminishing the stature of the soldier recruits, even though they do not notice it too obviously. Tests of loyalty further delay their joining the training camp, and still later they languish without food in the heat. The rhetoric of the hardships of war and the injunc-tion to prove themselves soldiers brings them to the brink of leaving camp and returning home. Men are severely beaten to ensure that they will not break down under enemy pres-sure. The women have yet to be asked to start training. A delegation, led by Florence, confronts the commander Ché who tells them training will begin in a week. Sinclair presents the women's conditions as partly a condition of war, but also partly a condition of the commanders' delay in training them.

The disclosure of the male soldiers' sexual abuse and rape of the women soldiers is presented without any melodramatic flourishes.[112] The scene remains chilling, however, because of its overall low-key matter of factness signifying routine instances. The women are woken up when they are sleeping and taken to a party. Ché takes Florence back to his tent and grabs her. Slow-motion shots screen Florence's shame and despair from us, but prolong very painfully the moments of sexual violence. The sequence begins with his saying, 'Why do you hate me? I love you.' The camera pans to the gun, hides Florence's face and then shows her empty bed in the tent. In an obvious parallelism, we cut to a male soldier with a bottle in his hand pulling Nyasha by the hand. She bites it to escape, and he slaps her. We then cut to medium-shot/reverse shots of Ché and Flame to the slow-motion shots of her going heavily backward to the sound of 'no, no, please, don't'. The heaviness of her movement backward carries the pain of nightmares that are impossible to escape. In terms of an aesthetic strategy, the difference in shooting techniques and *mise-en-scène* mark the scene's departure from the transparent real/mythical into the historical real.

The presentation of Nyasha biting the man and escaping followed by a shot of Florence's empty bed raises difficult questions about agency and choice. Florence indicates that she had no choice: 'Do you think I enjoyed it?' to Nyasha's stinging 'You stayed.' The question followed by Nyasha's own escape, given comments about Florence's own interest in men, foregrounds the kind of erroneous assumption about rape that prevail, as the footage of the rape unambiguously reveals. Despite her initial implicit accusations and conflation of Florence's interest in romance with the violence inflicted on her by Ché, Nyasha comments that Flame had become 'afraid'. This is poignant for the soldierwoman identity. Here is a woman who is not afraid to walk from Zimbabwe to Mozambique, join a training camp and go out on missions if need be, who then becomes afraid.[113]

Ché continues to watch her, but Flame is not presented as vulnerable in this scene as she is in an earlier one when he was shown watching her before he raped her. This time Flame is armed.

Sinclair also deals with the difficult issue of the rape victim becoming involved with the rapist. In a scene that is as emotionally manipulative as the earlier rape scene was physically an assault, Ché calls Flame into the tent. She does not have the right of refusal because of the order issued. He tells her about the strains of war and how it has been three years since he has seen his wife and child. Flame has just found out that her father has died in prison, but clearly she believes the rigours of war are onerous on men, not women; an ironic prophecy of how hard it really will be for women in general, and for Flame in particular. Flame falls into the role of 'comfort woman' when she puts her gun down and walks across and sits next to him. One reviewer calls her choice 'improbable'. Ché offers an apology: 'Sometimes we forget that we're human beings', and tells her she can leave. Perhaps she consents to be with him because she now has the luxury of 'consent',[114] or perhaps she still believes contradictorily and inconsistently that she could be happy with him, or fulfill a need.[115] Equally, Flame could be acquiring a protector. Regardless, when Ché later offers to take her and her child with him, she does not jump at the prospect of being taken care of, but has her own ideas of what she wants to see accomplished. Nyasha, both in the diegesis and in the voice-over, is silent about Flame's decision to spend time with Ché.

The film continues with its programme of showing how the women develop into heroes. Because Nyasha is the narrator, she does not make much of her own persistence in fulfilling her own education. Shots of the platoon burying a young female comrade caught full on the chest, like the footage of the razed camp they see on the way to Mozambique, give an indication of the brutality of the colonial oppressors, and the women's own growth through the war. A key moment in this development is when Flame is confronted with the choice of killing the man who turned her father in, Chihuara, the store-owner. The use of fire imagery here also ascribes her development to her new identity as a soldier. She sees the fire of a match when she decides to pick Flame as her *nom de guerre*. The sequence where she sets fire to the shop fulfills the promise of the new identity, the glow of the flame is metaphoric of Flame's own fighting spirit. Flame does not kill Chihuara who says he sold her father down because he did not have a choice. 'You always have a choice', says Flame as she lets him go.

Flame's comment appears to be one of the most disturbing things for her to say in the context of her own rape. Surely she must know, given the power relations between captains and foot soldier trainees, that the latter have little choice. Is the belief in choice the auteur's 'liberal' feminist/existential comment? A facile, but still not overly problematic, reading would be that Flame, now a soldier, knows that she has choices that she did not have earlier, which would then be consistent with the notion that she definitely did not have a choice when she was raped. Notwithstanding her newfound sense of control, Flame is traditionally submissive to Danger when she marries him at the end of the war, but finds the courage to leave him when he starts to drink alcohol routinely, beats her, and asserts his masculine superiority over her.

The soldier identity is built through other earlier shots of Flame bursting through the jungle to attack a whole jeep full of soldiers massacring a village. Nyasha comments in this instance on her bravery and then later confirms Flame's legendary status. Flame loses a son born to her in an attack on the camp; again we have quasi-mythical footage of Ché and his young son. It seems that war, very disturbingly for female viewers, has wiped over the shame of the rape. Ché's gun is given to Flame, and in a severe irony, she asks if she is worthy despite her later success, in part because of the rank she acquires at this point and the faith placed in her to carry the torch for a dead comrade whom she calls a 'good friend'. The condition of being a woman soldier alone can possibly explain that chilling statement, showing what low expectations of fellow soldiers the female soldiers have in particular, and what little women are prepared to settle for in general. That Flame has contradictions, and that a fighting soldier is not necessarily a woman free from the constraints of patriarchal ideology is definitely demystifying and exhilarating; noting as it does heroisms of a kind that are not as facile as to grant hero status automatically to a female fighter in simple terms that are ultimately limiting of the more complete heroism of the *female* soldier.

'We are heroes': the comment is tossed back and forth ironically. Flame is left behind, as are the peasantry. When Flame first comes back to her village, she seems thrilled to be Danger's wife. Her 'folding back' into the traditional role is expressive of the expectations of women after the war. The beating scene is shot in a grammar that makes it comparable to the rape sequence, but with one very crisp, powerful difference. Flame talks back, and makes a connection between Danger and her father, who had also put up traditional barriers. Barlet points out that Flame is 'alienated' on her return from the war;[116] she does not actually become alienated until after she has lived the life of the peasant woman for a few years. Nyasha too is alienated, and her alienation is because of her gender. Arguably, part of Flame's alienation has the same root; she finds herself in the same place despite having fought a war, and helped to win it.

The mythologising of the women that helped insert them into the filmic national narrative, the footage of the soldiers on thin wire bridges high above land; Flame in a medium-shot slowly divesting herself of ammunition, framed by the land; the music, the narrative of their heroism; men and women, serves as counterpoint to that other story of how the women warriors were exploited during combat, and left out of post-colonial nation building. Inserting women into the history of independence struggles is incomplete without ensuring their status in the future of the nation. *Flame*, through its combined aesthetic of photo-reportage and myth, ensures women the authority of both historical participation in the war and their heroic roles in it. If *Sambizanga*, shot before Angola gained its independence, raised issues of sexual politics in the resistance movement, *Flame*, shot after Zimbabwe achieved its independence, develops these issues in the theatre of war itself.

The filmmakers discussed in this chapter approach the difficulty of the absence of genres for women filmmakers by refusing to accept the option of merely changing the content of genre. Each filmmaker works with the concept of the existing genre but radically alters it. The format that each filmmaker uses raises questions about the existing genre's relationship to women, so that it can never again be impervious to the claims of women. Dash effects this transformation with a specific kind of avant-garde film, Djebar through the traditional historical documentary, Sinclair with the war film.

In each case, the genre invoked is crucial in teasing out the truth about women's condition, in light of their customary representation. Dash struggles with both mainstream and alternative film's uneven representation of black women, and their detachment in both genres from one another and a larger history of diaspora that connects them. For Djebar, history and the place of Algerian women in that history is at issue in her exploration of the documentary and the ethnographic formats. Like Dash, it is important for Djebar to effect a shift in visuality which she foregrounds through a deconstruction of Orientalist visuality and its antecedents in Western aesthetics, just as Dash confronted white supremacist visuality and its hoary heritage in Western aesthetics. Maldoror uses the 'imperfect cinema' to rewrite the hero motif in terms of the revolutionary female. For Sinclair, the impulse, like Djebar's, is to interrogate the writing of history, even post-colonial writing on nation formation. Sinclair quarrels with the latter's version, even as she attempts to give women their due through her combination of genres that self-consciously questions the position afforded women in each version.

The assault on the conceptual apparatus of existing genres in order to narrate the condition of women permits the filmmakers to create feminist genres in epic, history and photo-reportage.

4

AURAL SUBJECTIVITIES

The insistence on the visual as the singular path to the conferral of subjectivity in film is challenged in this chapter. The philosophical proclivity to privilege the visual as productive of knowledge subtends the persistence of this theme in mainstream Hollywood film. Sound too has been pressed to the service of the visual, which has typically accentuated the divestiture of female authority in film.[1] Genres that have favoured performance accompanied by music have specifically constructed a spectacular scene to dwell on the female figure. Here I seek to shift the scene from the visual to the auditory to open up possibilities for understanding female subjectivities constituted within the aural field. As we will discover, women filmmakers have been particularly successful in exploring the auditory, although due to constraints of space I will refrain from discussing other modalities they have explored such as the haptic, the tactile and the supra-visual.

Auditory subjectivity for women in mainstream film is problematic, considering the insistence on the 'fantasmatic' body, or the unity of sound and body in the diegesis.[2] The wholeness of voice and body, perhaps a tribute to the theatrical tradition, and also the invocation of 'presence' in the Derridean sense, has specific implications for women in the diegesis.[3] The space the female voice fills in classical film is definitely secondary to the fullness of the female body, particularly its movements during the song and dance sequences, where the body would call attention to the song. If the song were extra-diegetic it might be narratively significant; if the woman were to sing the song, it might signify almost excessively. The female singing voice would fill the space of male desire, if accompanied by bodily movement.[4] Further, certain types of film music itself is associated with dangerous female sexuality whereby visual expressions of female sexuality are signalled and developed through the score, the soundtrack conspiring with the visual apparatus in the representation of women.[5] In the so-called 'women's films', 'melodramas' that discussed female desire, expression was possible for women through other means: song and dance.[6] Expression may have been possible through song, but not without being in one of the two positions melodrama offers women: that of the object of desire or the hysterical subject of desire.[7] Such objectification would also be conclusively visual.

For feminists the whole issue of 'giving women voice' has been crucial, especially giving marginalised women voice. Confronted with the 'zones'[8] of silence, women filmmakers have had to constitute the female viewer as auditory spectator, an awkward but necessary term, to be able to understand women's voices.[9] The woman as listener has been as important to speaking as the trope of woman as speaker.

Empowering women to speak in a medium that is mainly visual, which moreover places women as the ultimately pleasurable supplement, would seem difficult if only because of the medium's denigration of the auditory. The primacy of the visual in Western epistemologies, what Luce Irigaray calls the scopic economy, conspires to institute its centrality in film, and to marginalise other ways of knowing.[10] Yet the importance of the invocatory drive, the privileged place of the maternal voice, has been stressed by feminist theorists. Irigaray describes the fetishisation of the scopic, suggesting that subject formation might occur through other senses, such as touch, and other kinds of conversation, rather than hingeing around the 'what does one see' modality as informative of knowledge.[11] For Julia Kristeva, the semiotic chora, the voice or speech of the pre-Symbolic, could speak a truth outside patriarchy, which is not at all the same as Irigaray's conception of language, which remains discursive and within patriarchal parameters.[12] Carol Flynn points out that although other theorists give primacy to the voice in subject formation, music too in the Western tradition is considered pre-discursive and 'becomes the object – static, meaningless, enigmatic and feminine – and scientific enquiry, in a sense, is the masculinised subject that penetrates it'.[13] Consequently, despite the play given to the voice, particularly the maternal voice, the pre-eminence of the visual as informing the discursive knowable is not challenged in this line of thought.

These received understandings of the role of woman and voice in the diegesis, and her relationship to the extra-diegetic is problematised by feminist films which seek ultimately to offer a feminist cultural critique thus having to work their way out of these seemingly immutable masculine histories of aesthetic codes.

In looking at films from diverse cultural contexts, and in different discursive modes, I follow the attempt to subvert the visual within not just a pre-eminently visual mode, but also genres that specifically raid the female figure at the site of performance. Maria Novaro's *Danzón* (1992) works with the 'cabaretera', a genre built around the female dancer; Dana Rotberg's *Angel of Fire* (1992) revolves around the 'show' of a child woman's fire-eating performances in a circus and offers a subaltern context to Novaro's film; Moufida Tlatli's *The Silences of the Palace* (1994) is organised around various 'performances' of two generations of women including dancing and singing; and Aparna Sen's *Sati* (1989) dramatises the visual by featuring a mute woman as protagonist. The scene of 'performance' in this film is of the woman undergoing sati. In *Danzón* the emphasis is on extra-diegetic sound, in *Angel of Fire*, on unheard speech, in *The Silences of the Palace* on diegetic sound and its relationship to seeing, in *Sati* on female speechlessness and seeing.

The films alter our received understandings of the articulation between extra-diegetic sound and diegetic speech. While the relationship between music and femininity is important to Novaro, silence is the informing discourse in the other two films. Linda Dittmar understands the importance of reading sound/silence as relevant to contextualising the woman's multiple-layered position in terms of class, race and imperialism: 'Clearly at issue here is not the absence of sound, but a value-laden relationship between articulation and presence, notably as it bears on women's position within society.'[14] This insight is particularly germane for an understanding of the aural subjectivity of the young Alma in *Angel of Fire*. All four films ask us to listen to the obliquity of women's speech, and demand that we 'read' their silences/speech. While gender is the controlling element on the discourse of sound in *Danzón*, colonialism, class and gender as interlocking systems of oppression locate the woman's silence/speech in *The Silences of the Palace*, and the latter, combined with specific cultural systems, situate the discourse of the woman and the film in *Sati*.

Visual control and knowledge that had been denied women in filmic representations is wrested back through a deliberate development of the relationship between image, sound and narrative frame.

Auditory Subjectivities: Maria Novaro's *Danzón*

Feminist appropriation of genres has greatly facilitated the attempts of feminist filmmakers to explore women's desires, women's lived experiences and women's fantasies. The inability of existing genres to be adequate to any one of the three categories has demanded that women filmmakers cross generic boundaries to invent new genres,[15] or at least to appropriate and transform older genres to enable their bearing the weight of women's desires, lived experiences and fantasies. As a genre, melodrama has facilitated the exploration of women's roles in society,[16] and women filmmakers have had occasion to use elements of the genre to test the limits of femininity within a culture, as in Gurinder Chadha's *Bhaji on the Beach*. Like Chadha, Novaro uses melodramatic elements in *Danzón* to question the role of women in Mexican society, a move made by Golden Age filmmakers and modern progressive filmmakers interested in the relationship between family, women and nation.[17]

The plot of the film follows Julia, a dancer's, in her journey to find her dance partner and bring him home. Danzón, a dance with Cuban and Haitian roots, is extremely popular in Mexico, and has such specific conventions that the dance is metaphoric of the social regulations, including patriarchy, that Julia adheres to. One reviewer notes the 'pleasing reversal of convention ... in a warming woman's voyage of self-discovery'.[18] Focusing specifically on the melodrama genre, Dolores Tierney has successfully argued that Novaro rewrites the cabaretera, dancehall films from Mexico's Golden Age in the 1940s, in order to represent a female subject.[19] While Tierney's analysis works with the trope of the female as the dancer, Novaro's extensive use of music in this film, specifically to suture the visual and to lend narrative coherence, asks that we reconsider the role of the relationship of the female in the cabaretera to the music. Indeed, the term 'bricolage' has been applied to Novaro's work with reference to its abundant use of music and its plundering of popular forms of entertainment,[20] including music. Because of the cabaretera's emphasis on the visual, on the specularisation of the female, little attention has been paid to sexual difference in the other arenas of that space. Jacqueline Rose's comments on how sexuality operates in the field of vision are relevant here: 'One of the things that strikes me about these images ... is their curious desexualisation, or rather the way that this absorbing of sexuality into the visual field closes off the question of sexual difference.'[21] Novaro draws attention to the other sites of sexual difference in the cabaretera: the space of the singer, and more generally the role of sound in constituting the female subject. Novaro takes on a genre so radically suited for both melodrama, and the cabaretera, but shifts the focus to create a new genre that challenges the Latin American family romance by using the cover of the feminist cabaretera. Through her technique of using the visual to pictorialise the music, she succeeds in questioning the power of the master narrative of the quest romance to explain the lives of working-class women. Latin America's 'foundational fiction',[22] a 'family romance'[23] that imbricates the erotic in the historical, makes narrative compulsory for history and invokes the whole idea of the quintessential journey as family history is retained by Novaro but in terms that questions the master narrative of the heterosexual family.[24]

As Novaro uses the Golden Era's genre *par excellence*, so does she appropriate Latin America's modernist mode of magical realism to consider women's desires, lived experiences and fantasies. Although Tierney calls the film an affectionate tribute to *Salón Mexico* (1949), the film also deforms the melodrama genre, not just in terms of its shift in plotting female desire, but in its use of spectacle and music so that it comes to create a wholly new genre in Mexican film history, the female quest, or in more modern nomenclature, the female road film.[25] Melodrama's female adventurer is now recast as the epic voyager.[26]

Novaro's work has customarily been associated with the 1980s New Wave Cinema, and as such belonging to a mixed category that is neither art-house nor pure entertainment. Working within the 'perfect cinema', Novaro nevertheless seeks to address the complexities not just of the role of women in melodrama, but also their articulation of the domestic role with the public role.[27] Her point of departure is the culmination point of 1940s cabareteras: where they offer women the space of the club, and exploit her status as a Malinche or a 'chingada/vendida',[28] she begins by using the space of the dance hall as quasi-domestic in that the danzón dancer Julia very much plays the role of the demure woman for whom dance is a form of graceful art, far from the steamy excesses of sexuality referenced by the cabareteras. Where this space would have been the public space of the 'fallen woman', here it is the space of the working-class women and men who perhaps are aspiring to a certain elegance that the danzón conjures. The opening song, 'Lagrimas Negras', a composition of 1930s Cuban composer Miguel Matamoros, brings in the trope of the melodrama, 'tu me quieres dejar, yo no quiero sufrir' ('you want me to stay, I don't wish to suffer'), which also seems redolent of a certain order in which the man does not want to stay. Predictably, the man in the diegesis of the film, Carmelo Benitez, Julia's long-time dance partner, does not stay, but we abandon him to follow the woman who actually leaves and for whom the music could apply in terms of plot movement, but appears otherwise to be discursively incoherent. Movement from Mexico City to Vera Cruz puts her in spaces that are far more expansive than the ones afforded her inside the dancehall.

Julia ostensibly leaves Mexico City to 'rescue' Carmelo and bring him back to the dance floor. Her departure signals the advent of the epic journey. Filmically, Vera Cruz is shot very differently than Mexico City and is reminiscent of those films where the male hero voyages into the underworld in order to understand the truth about himself, his sexuality and the world;[29] essential information if he is to triumph over his enemies and regain his prizes.[30] The open spaces, the colours of both Vera Cruz and protagonist, the night-time sequences are imbued with a magic, even as its realism is not questioned. Novaro uses both the registers of classical realism and magical realism as an entrance to accommodating women's desires and experiences.[31]

While the inadequacies of the melodrama in sustaining female desire are rendered apparent, the genre of the romantic epic and the mode of magical realism do delineate a female desire within the specific working-class Mexican context with reference to another community, the community of marginals, or even the rejects of society, in Vera Cruz. A complex negotiation between pleasure as commodity, and pleasure as desiring subject is effected between the two modes of melodrama/classical realism and magical realism that Novaro shows. Female desire, then, does not follow the course that male desire does of mediation, condensation and fulfillment, but of registration, recognition and acknowledgment. Visuality is opaque in communicating knowledge in this trajectory.

In also using magical realism, Novaro's cinema marks a shift from 'imperfect cinema', but still tries to stay away from the 'image commodification' of the mainstream cinema.[32] Letting the image float freely without a context, a narrative significance or a framework epitomises the newer versions of the dominant commercial film.

The opening sequence of Danzón uses tightly-framed shots to show Julia's foot in a shoe, and then slowly pans to show the dancer's feet in what would appear to be almost a textbook case of commodity fetishism, uninhibited by any kind of narrative trapping. Indeed, Cladiua Schaeffer views these shots in this light.[33] Fredric Jameson's definition of 'magical realism', as distinct from what he calls the nostalgia film, also emphasises the ontology of the image, which alters the conventional mechanisms of the gaze; even the image remains a symbol of the 'articulated superposition of whole layers of the past within the present'.[34] The credits sequence then impose the commodification of desire on an older art form, the danzón, a move emphasised by the diegetic music of the 1930s, thus presenting layers of time and locating two contradictory impulses in the images: packaging of pleasure as female, and the reference to female desire through marking its absence, and hence contradictorily registering its presence in time, if not in the ontology of the image of the foot, or the dance. Jameson's additional notion that narrative mechanisms are reduced because of the primacy of the image is an argument that is indeed brought up with the role of star female performance in film. The woman, too closely identified with the image, impedes the smooth flow of the narrative.[35] Calling those sequences that are story stoppers in the Hollywood code, the song and dance sequences that specularise the female, 'para-narrative', Ravi Vasudevan argues that these sequences are denoted as (male) fantasies and that they threaten 'to float free of the business of narrative'.[36] These assertions are consonant with Laura Mulvey's observation that the diegesis is congealed during such 'para-narrative' performances.[37] However, Tierney notes that the importance of diegetic music as a signifier in Mexican film defies an easy application of this model.[38] Novaro uses the diegetic and extra-diegetic music in this film to act as a corrective to the 'para-narrative', and hence does not disable the narrative by use of the female image. Using the extra layer of authority granted by the extra-diegetic music,[39] the narrative functions of diegetic music, she rewraps the melodrama to create a female romance quest, deftly shifting the earlier melodramatic role of the female as implicating desire rather than desiring. Both functions of music in the film contrive to confer the authority of the romance tradition to the woman. Carefully-staged visual backdrops to the music position the female as hero of the quest romance.

The gendered implications of the shift in genre are significant. As Ginette Vincendeau has noted in the context of women's films from the 1930s in France, melodrama, even in the criticism, has been seen as 'excess, femininity, a-historicity', compared to the more elite form of realism which is identified as 'soberness, masculinity and historicity'.[40] The use of a realistic mode, albeit complicated, and a genre that is associated with the archetypical male, lends Danzón the authority of master narratives. The female hero acquires voice in the quest tradition; the female quest narrative itself acquires authority as a consequence of the use of modes associated with the realistic. However, unlike quest romances and epics, the film does not seek universal [male and] female hero status for Julia.

Danzón, as many reviewers have noted, is motivated by Julia's desire to find her dance partner who has disappeared without explanation.[41] Like the traditional hero of the quest romance whose affection is also ostensibly platonic, Julia sets forth in defence of the wrong-ly-accused Carmelo. The opening sequences, however, do not posit even a platonic desire on the part of Julia who seems uninvolved in romantic liaisons, compared to her friend who is having an affair with a married man. Carmelo, in contrast, is termed a regular gen-tleman. Whether the danzón is site of the displaced eroticism of these men and women is secondary to their recourse to the dance-hall as a refuge for their alienation from work. The dance-hall is explicitly divested of the excessive displays of femininity endemic to the genre of the 1940s. Julia is no siren waiting to lure men with her sexuality. A shot of the women changing their dance footwear for their regular shoddy work shoes reveals that the earlier glamourous visions were part of a process of fabrication, or the fraud of feminin-ity that Novaro exposes. As though to emphasise the price paid for that fabrication, one sequence shows Julia massaging her friend's feet. The deglamourisation of the woman is matched schematically by the sequence in which Julia 'makes herself up', or glamourises herself. Marilyn Frye argues that all women are in drag, or mark themselves in some way to specify femininity, a point brought home when the drag queen Suzy feminises Julia by dressing her up.[42]

Carmelo's departure is disappointing to Julia who watches the dancers wistfully, placed in the privileged position of being the spectator, albeit a reluctant one.[43] Novaro here in-troduces female desire through the mechanism of the gaze, a trope she develops later to identify the object of Julia's desire, the young and handsome tug-boat sailor Ruben in Vera Cruz. While the traditional para-narrative may arrest the advancement of the narrative, the danzón that Julia watches introduces a desire, perhaps transgressive through her watching of the dance. The dance itself seems to shift in meaning rather quickly once female desire is introduced. Presented earlier as the site for working-class recreation, it is now suffused with Julia's desire. The third song in the film, and the second in the para-narrative mode, starts with a flourish. The camera moves to the dance and then cuts to Julia standing at a higher plane, watching the dance. So perfect in its presentation of patriarchal order, the dance nevertheless sublimates male desire quite as effectively as it suppresses female desire. Ironically, because the floor is in the field of Julia's desiring look, the dance now becomes an expression of Julia's troublingly unacknowledged desire for some continuous erotic sup-plement to her working-class existence as a telephone operator. The iterative cross-cutting between the hall and Julia establishes the dance-hall as theatre of her desire. Thus the para-narrative does not impede narrative progression when the female is the voyager; rather, it facilitates it precisely because neither the traditional patriarchal plot nor the melodrama can accommodate it.

Julia's look is not that of the spectator; she does not specularise, she wishes to partici-pate, to be part of their event; not apart from it in any voyeuristic way. The importance of the para-narrative elements – the performance – is further diminished once Julia's desire is recognised. Indeed, recognition and misrecognition are tropes that are developed in the film. The music takes over and the dance sequences are serrated while the narrative goal, the departure of Julia from Mexico City to Vera Cruz, is contextualised.

Primary among motivational devices is the commentary on Julia's interiority, invested with an overlay of narrative authority, and in the register of the aural rather than the visual point-of-view access. A cut from daughter Pilar and friend discussing Julia's dissatisfaction takes us to a woman dancing on her own, now not metonymic of Julia's desires, but metaphoric. Expression of Julia's desires then subverts her earlier submission to the commodification of desire. The incredible longing expressed in the motion of the older woman's right arm is enhanced by the diegetic sound. Because we do not see the source of sound until after the club employee brings a record, its effect is authoritative. As the male singer begins his plaintive song, 'Traveller, moving through sea and sky/you leave hearts behind/that beat with passion/and vibrate with song',[44] Julia enters from off-screen space on the right side of the frame while we still see the woman dancing. Three fields of action are entertained here: the spatial source of the music, the dais, the woman dancing in the privileged centre left, and Julia entering from the right. Purportedly, this is Julia's song – misplaced, or obliquely transpositioned through the male – a necessary ventriloquism in a medium that does not usually allow the female the authority of the voice-over.[45] Novaro does not just articulate the emotion of the hero through the song: through a delayed reaction the song begins to also be about her, for she will soon travel. In taking up the position of the romantic hero, as opposed to the female aventurera, or adventuress, Julia begins to be the traveller. As the song continues about the 'thousand deceptions/I too/I loved you … You'll get tired of travelling/and finally want to stay/What will I do without you?/What will my future bring?', Julia climbs up to the dais, describes Carmelo to the employee, walks back down, proceeds to walk fast as the song goes, 'I might die without you/My moon and my sun will/go with you.' Here the technique used is similar to that associated with silent cinema which uses extra-visual elements to make the narrative coherent. The lyrics, then, provide motivation, centre her as voyager, a desiring subject, and, most importantly, if in a displaced way, lend her the authority of the romance tradition, of a sentiment that affords escape from the quotidian, for without that, there might be no moon and sun. Through a reciprocity of logic between the movement of Julia and the lyrics of the song, women's traditional relationship to romance is challenged.

Jean Franco's thesis on romance in Mexican pop culture forms is instructive here.[46] She argues that the patriarchal romance plot is pleasurable for women because it establishes their value as commodities. In Julia's case, the seeming lack of valuation of her commodity status releases her from the obligation of further consolidation of that role, and hence frees her to play the more active role of the seeker of romance, a model that varies from both characteristics in the male romance plot where the woman accepts deferment of pleasure because of her ultimate valuation as a commodity, and the male pursues success and sexual pleasure. If the poignancy in the depiction of female desire in the films of the 1940s was poised on the woman's troubled question of whether she was loved or desired, Novaro's Julia is very far from asking either question. Interestingly, here the narrative betrays its 'inchoateness', despite Novaro's attempt to stitch it to the regularity of the everyday, and indeed to the order of the everyday. The songs speak to the excess of desire, uncontainable by the ordered danzón, but unlike the melodrama where 'vertiginious displacements' result

Fig. 17: *Danzón* – Maria Novaro uses magical realism to show Julia's transformation in Vera Cruz; the brightly-coloured dress, her flashing a smile at the man in drag, then enjoying the sensual pleasure of water on her feet

in recuperation, the move to the romance quest genre enlarges female desire to that quest for the self, to that existential identity quest.[47] Such narrative 'incoherence', explained ultimately as 'menopause' by a couple of Julia's friends, is presumably occasioned by the illogic of female desire, or the inadequacy of the traditional narrative to channel the desire. The lyric then bears the burden of that desire.

As the genre is reformatted, so is the mode. Since realism would not be an adequate mode in which to depict Julia's adventures in Vera Cruz, Novaro uses magical realism, or the mode by which the marvellous is real, not merely perceived as such.[48] Taking on Latin America's preferred mode, Novaro shows us how inadequate even this model must be for the realisation of female desire, and ultimately returns to narrative to conclude, if not resolve, Julia's unspecified, and perhaps unnameable, desires.

The difference in visual effect between the Mexico City scenes and the Vera Cruz scenes is remarkable. Indeed, the use of colour singled out in Jameson's discussion of magical realism is pertinent to the protagonist and her presentation.[49] Dressed in whites, blues and muted colours in Mexico City, she is now a vision in red, particularly that in her hair. Novaro satirically indicates the process by which she becomes valuable: through the fabrication of a femininity which is then both marvellous and real.[50] Predictably, Julia enjoys the cross-over from her place in the patriarchal order to a more fluid, negotiable position in the economy of commodities. Paradoxically, the colour that suffuses Vera Cruz is *real* in that the articulation of male desire through obvious relays of looks that target Julia, and through the subsequent production of femininity staged marvellously by Suzy in her show, is expressive of Julia's sensuality, and not repressive of it. It might be naïve to read this 'realness' in a unitary way considering the play on 'tropicality' and 'exoticism',[51] and the deflation of these tropes that Novaro effects by the brief but violent scene between prostitute and pimp that Julia witnesses to the strains of the diegetic 'Warm and Silent Night of Vera Cruz' sung by the woman proprietor of the hotel. So, while magical realism is sufficient to articulate these libidinal tensions and brings to the surface the process by which femininity is manufactured, it is incomplete in terms of the real desires of a woman Julia's age, the scenes with young Ruben being almost staged, as much a part of the danzón ritual, not a whit more real. The two worlds of Mexico City and Vera Cruz are contiguous: if Julia's friend is seeing a married man in Mexico City, the woman proprietor here has been abandoned, not once, but six times. Motherhood too appears to be without rewards, for she has six children. Desiring love and admiration, the wonderful Suzy, called 'artiste', transforms himself for the gaze, commodifies desire. Vera Cruz may not be ordered patriarchally,[52] but it answers to the commodity economy. The prostitutes have to work every day, not so different it would seem than Julia. Julia may not have discovered romance, but like the romantic heroine, she has figured out the value of the commodity.

Arguably, Julia goes back to Mexico City and to the dance-hall because she puts herself outside the commodity market. Yet Carmelo shows up and the film ends with the ubiquitous shot/reverse-shot suturing of classical Hollywood. The narrative ostensibly signals her triumph: like the quest hero she comes back to the Penelope who has been awaiting her, like Orpheus she has reclaimed Eurydice.[53] The rub is not that she does not find him and rescue him, but perhaps that even the feminist quest romance is insufficient to women's desires and that Novaro refused to lie about it. Alternately, the reprise to the realistic mode may suggest that the female survives, does not die, does not get cast away, does not get married! Narrative inchoateness on female desire notwithstanding, the family romance prevails as narrative motivation as the story returns her to family and danzón. Here Schaeffer's argument that there are continuous reminders of family in Vera Cruz which make the return to the danzón inevitable is more plausible than Tierney's claim that Julia is liberated through dance.[54] Indeed, a moment of great freedom appears to be when she removes her high heels and dances on the shore. Schaeffer views both the Vera Cruz sequences and the return to Carmelo as redolent with a nostalgia for homes of various kinds: Vera Cruz as the home of the danzón, Mexico City as home and Carmelo as auratic of home.[55] While thematically nostalgic, the film does not discuss history or period in formal terms that are nostalgic, and thus avoids the pitfalls of presenting history statically. Further, it is important to note that Julia recognises the commodification of all women, an insight that presents the danzón on the return home as performance, much like Suzy's show of *Salón Mexico*'s song in the 'Coconut Water' number, rather than as the impermeable authentic Schaeffer would have it signify.

Knowledge of the commodification of women tears at the fabric of the master narrative of family. The return to its construction is problematic, but does not necessarily mean that the narrative has remained intact. Indeed, Novaro has shown almost no heterosexual family unit through the film. The big family party at Vera Cruz depicts an old grandmother dancing with her granddaughter, and another danzón sequence ironically shows young children being trained in the dance; the maintenance of patriarchal order. Both in Mexico City and Vera Cruz the men serve as hangars, or dance partners/sex partners but do not seem to be essential to the business of female living. A community of women supports Julia in Mexico City, a community of women sustains her in Vera Cruz. The community of women prostitutes and the hotel proprietor help serve as her family. Her friends are the artistes, or the men who dress in drag and perform, who clearly have something in common with her. These women completely dismiss the heterosexual compact, made more startling by the fact that Suzy is not dressed as a female when Julia teaches her the danzón. That sequence, when Suzy insists that Julia plays the lead, puts femininity and its masquerade up for erasure. Julia appears to cherish these women, but says goodbye to no one except the hotel proprietor. Is she afraid that she might never leave? She says she is going back to her daughter and her memories, and perhaps a story in which she knows all the dancing parts.

All the women in the film are working class, and completely outside the master narrative, a point brought home sharply by the status of the dancer: a single mother. Her story about the father of her child is fabulous, but it is clear that he too has disappeared.[56] Family is radically different from the patriarchal order, a reminder that serves to foreground the situation of Mexican working-class women.

Schaeffer's argument that the feminist dimensions of the journey are curtailed sharply by the conclusion, and that Julia's return to Mexico City signifies a resolution of the contradictions of modernity by recourse to nostalgia bears discussion. Schaeffer's comments are a propos the thematic of modernity as loss of the authentic culture, and consequently she sees the return to the danzón as the nostalgia for the authentic.[57] Novaro herself has commented, 'It's a world of things as you would like them to be, I don't think that's primitive; I think it's essential … In the middle of all these cynical, sceptical, post-modern Mexicans, I think there's a Mexico that shouldn't be allowed to get lost'.[58] Further, the danzón can be seen as a sign of 'authentic' culture in a global economy where cultures are reduced to a frightening sameness. While Schaeffer is convincing in this respect, the specific thematic of a feminism returning to the archaic is less convincing because of the change Julia undergoes, the rebirth in the journey to the underworld.[59] Unlike the epic hero, she is not reaffirmed, but her convictions are called on.

The journey itself has been viewed as Julia's recapturing of lost innocence, of childhood itself, where the return home is viewed as the return to the father.[60] Such a view is problematic in that it infantilises Julia, and puts Vera Cruz itself in another space, almost the space of the Kristevan chora,[61] and places those people of Vera Cruz in a time that would be 'primitive', thereby ignoring the techniques Novaro uses to show contiguity between the two places.

The other solution, leaving Julia in Vera Cruz, would place her with the marginal, again problematic for feminism. Bearing an identity as a sexual being within the family narrative, and retaining sexual autonomy does suggest a tacit, if cautious modernity for women.[62] Maria Rojo, who plays Julia, is definitive about the film's feminism. Elissa Rashkin, however, found that there was considerable difference in the way men and women worked their way through the film. Initially, women generally viewed it as both having a feminine sensibility and being feminist, and became more critical if aesthetic issues were brought up; men were initially distant from the film, and later became more involved when issues of representation of men arose. The men regarded the film as 'feminine' rather than feminist, a move that Rashkin finds to be conservative considering that this ethos runs through the work of other feminist novelists in Mexico. Accordingly, she states: 'The displacement of the term [feminist] by a more conciliatory euphemism [is] a strategy of containment that serves to negate what is powerful and empowering in the film text, making it into an affirmation of the status quo.'[63]

Curiously enough, the discussants did not bring up the idea that the feminism itself might have been packaged, although implied in Rashkin's discussion is the proposition that feminism of any kind in the culture stands to intimidate some segment of the audience. While the feminism itself may be commodified and not threatening, its specific use value in popular culture needs to be taken into consideration. In her study of popular artifacts in Mexico, Jean Franco observes that the narrative might often be more progressive than the moral attached to it.[64] The conclusion of *Danzón* would seem to imply that the return home is essential if the woman is to retain her status as the good woman, not Malinche.

Here, the moral seems to defy the narrative logic, or be inconsistent with it. Not only does the conclusion show the inadequacy of magical realism in handling modern working-class women whose choices are restricted, but it also disregards the kind of epistemic shift Julia has made in self-definition. Because of the narrative mode's serious investment in the marginal communities she encounters in Vera Cruz, and because of Julia's own abandonment of the old ideal to the water in the bottle tossed into the ocean, the narrative belies the moral of the good woman going home. Julia now will not hang on to that family/heterosexual idyll that had held her in thrall, and is now aware of herself as a sexual being who can nevertheless participate in the national narrative on family. Note her amusement about her daughter's change of boyfriend when earlier she would have tried to keep her closer to home, also her sense of enjoyment with her friends who do not tie her down to the Julia who would not be modern. She even refused to dance with younger men. In discussing Julia's journey and her return home, Mario Valdes states that Novaro opens up new possibilities for the representation of women.[65] Whether she embarks on a romance with Carmelo or not, she is no longer tied to the role of the chaste woman, and absolutely not obliged into the fallen woman role. That dichotomous conception of femininity has been ruptured by her return home to the family as a sexual being.

Regardless of the breakthrough in the final sequence of the film when Julia looks directly at Carmelo,[66] and in the camera shooting the characters instead of the shoes, the ending remains to remind us of the theatre of femininity, not the resolution of its discontents. Nevertheless, recourse to the extra-diegetic music has enabled the director to re-place the female protagonist's subjectivity outside of the cultural parameters indicated by Mexican film's placement of the female hero.

The film's sound aesthetics eloquently explains the difficulties of women's ability to speak within the conventions of romance, and the even greater difficulty of 'articulating'[67] the self within the specific cultural parameters invoked by the danzón, Mexico's plotting of romance. Using sound as an entrance to constraining the genre of melodrama, Novaro's aesthetics confer the authority of romantic discourse to the female.

Confronting Silences: Dana Rotberg's *Angel of Fire*

Another Mexican film, also about visual excess and tenor, that was released the same year as *Danzòn* would be useful to contextualise the moment when Julia glides into the danzòn with a feminist step. Dana Rotberg's *Angel of Fire* questions the idea that a feminist quest is possible in Mexico at all. Rotberg brings in the material conditions of her characters through the visual, thus showing the difficulties of urban poverty in the 1990s in Mexico for the underclass.[68] Rotberg shifts the terrain from the middle class to the working poor, from the dance-hall to the circus. When auditory subjectivity is conferred on Julia in the sequence that shows the beginning of her voyage as romantic hero, Julia's consciousness regarding her quest is not as fully developed as it might be. Novaro suggests a gap between authorial consciousness and the female protagonist's, rendering the auditory essential in the audience's understanding of Julia's subjectivity. Alma, the 13-year-old protagonist of Rotberg's film, is shown as following a different path. The film is about a young girl who experiences abuse at the hands of her father and finds herself pregnant with his child which she wishes to keep. The two are members of a circus troupe; the father is a clown, and Alma is the fire-eating angel. The visual – the presentation of the protagonist, the *mise-en-scènes* of her journeyings, the visualisation of the characters she meets and the shows performed, the meta-diegetic element – suffocates the young protagonist who seeks over and over to speak. Her stifling by the visual serves as Rotberg's commentary on the effect of the spectacle of urban poverty and popular culture on the young female child.

Criticised for its 'surreal' qualities that seemed to exoticise third world garbage for the first, the film traverses what Rashkin refers to as 'heterotopias'.[69] Unlike the heterogenous spaces that Julia travels in *Danzón*, these do not add to the protagonist's knowledge. Alma's journey into the underworld, to follow the metaphysical theme implied by names of the characters – Alma, Sacramento and Refugio – does not armour her for her journey back to the living; it just crushes her completely. Where Novaro makes distinctions between Mexico City and Vera Cruz, but shows them as contiguous, Rotberg does not comfort the viewer by constructing semblances of reality.

Every sequence in the film is saturated with a sense of apocalypse that Rotberg attributes to her own mixed perceptions of Jewishness, the Old Testament and the vastness of urban Mexico City. While the metaphysical strain in the film is sustained, its meanings, being questioned, mock the shell, or medium, in which the message is carried: the visual itself. Framed by skies, open roads, vast spaces and contrasted with extremely small spaces, such as the caravans in which Alma lives, this sense of a shattering because of divine wrath, or even the child's understanding of the sacred, is wrecked by the complexity with which the child's desire to speak, love and express herself is snuffed out by the film. The reds that overpower the film, signifying fire,[70] while seemingly surreal, are what Alejo Carpentier famously described as the 'magical real', where the incredible *reality* of Latin America was a challenge to a European perception of reality. Within these reds that represent the real, the appearance of Alma, in a red sequined dress, performing to a largely silent 'audience' would display Rotberg's strategy of revealing the visual style as essentially exposing the 'imperfection', the fabrication, or the falsehood of the construction of femininity. The trope of 'erring', invoked by Djelal Kadir to account for Latin America's *mestizaje* history, and the suggestion by a Chilean feminist critic allows us to read Rotberg's situating of Alma in these diverse performance roles, where we see her up on the ropes as problematising womanhood. As Nelly Richard puts it, 'the images also operate as a simile of the errata of womanhood: imperfection operating as style in order to upset the control of a master image'.[71] Alma is not seen through the diegetic audience's eyes. We too are invited to see another errant figure, Alma's mother. Her very presence causes the clown, with whom Alma has shared an intimate gesture, to collapse and then continue with the show in such an extremely paralytic style that the panache of postmodern spectacle is completely absent. The later sequence where Alma waits outside while another woman takes care of her father, Renato, is profoundly disturbing. Renato is afraid that Alma's mother, his ex-lover/wife has come to take Alma away from him. Alma stands at the edge of the room, waiting to catch his look. He sits up, she undresses and then kisses him while the extra-diegetic music plays, 'Without love/there is no hope', a piteous commentary on this horrendous sexual violation of the young girl. Alma's affection for her father and her desire to keep the baby are both presented as being human, ordinary. Alma's affection and desire for her father are shown as

Fig. 18: *Angel of Fire* – the mother, hiding behind dark glasses, tries to watch Alma's act; the daughter's eyes are riveted on the father as she comes on stage – note the absence of a controlling eye on her

aberrant only through the violence of the contrast between the sick, blood-spitting old man and the young, pregnant girl; not because of its unnaturalness, but because of the tenderness. Rotberg describes the scenario as 'conceptual violence'.[72] The mastery of the 'controlling eye' is subverted by the substitution of tenderness for desire in such a forbidden, taboo relationship. Regardless of feminist sensibilities, it is difficult to deny that the father and daughter have a relationship even if one were to argue that the girl may have had no choice in the matter. The lack of the controlling eye, however, does not make for a feminist reading of this scene nor this film which seemingly shuns the mother for the father. Indeed, Rashkin notes that the film does not raise issues pertaining to feminist representation when she compares it to other films such as Novaro's *Danzón*.

The very relegation of the maternal figures would argue a different point; namely that the auteur is critiquing their 'corruption' within a specific paradigm of Latin American identity where 'the feminine is related to that which was *repressed-censored* by the Spanish Conquest, representing the original (maternal) corporeality that the conquistador attempted to annex to his domain'.[73] Signifying both the chingada, and the virginal, she has evoked complex feelings. The 'imperfection' of Alma is reinforced by the absence of her biological mother and the cruelty of her chosen mother, Refugio. Yet the scene in the caravan is not of the mother, but of the daughter. Alma's initial and primary identity is as daughter. And it is not the mother who is being raped by the conquistador if the daughter's story is being told. It is the daughter who is being sexually exploited by her father and wanting to start a new family out of this beginning. Therefore Rotberg, while not being able to underwrite the possibility of quests, has been able to account for her refusal by showing that the old family romance does not hold. That paradigm has shifted, and the new one is of the daughter and the father: no conquistadors, no mothers. And Alma does try to tell that story, but is completely unheard until she acts.

Alma's straightforwardness about her father's abuse, despite the fact that she does not identify it as such, is important. She does not feel shame, she does not hide it, and most importantly, she does not blame herself. In other words, she moves on, trying to survive, and does not act as a victim. Her embracing of the child, her wish that the child would look like her father, might strike some (feminist) and other viewers as repulsive, but this is to ignore the paradigm her story sets for the new urban life. She is thrown out of the circus when she will not prostitute herself, and she ends up in street corners blowing fire. Perhaps her refusal to return to her mother later when she is with Refugio, Sacramento and the little boy is because she has found a new family, and this one has not begun to abuse her yet; after all, her mother does not stand up for her. It is incredible, then, that this girl should come through such a claustrophobic relationship with the circus and her father without killing herself, or resorting to abortion, which would have been the decision of choice, regardless of who the father of the baby was.

Alma's speech is flattened by the new wandering puppeteers with whom she throws in her lot. There is laughter and joy and talk of starting a new family with the little boy being uncle when they are alone, but when Sacramento and Refugio are there, the silence is deafening. Interestingly, the only time Sacramento speaks is to tell Refugio sternly that she should 'take in' Alma because Refugio herself had been in the same situation; thus offering some kind of explanation for Refugio's intense apocalyptic religiosity and her sexual repression projected on Sacramento but in the more understandable vein of a clenched control over desire, and its channelling into aggression. The virtuous mother is less appealing than the absent one, who presumably is more sexually promiscuous.

Alma's physical abuse at the hands of Refugio is horrific in its implications. Her body is violated by both father/chosen mother. Made to sleep naked in the cold, go without food, told she has sinned, Alma's own honesty, her speech, is completely taken over by both circus and wandering religious troupe. Caught between the two, Alma makes her way with dignity and compassion.

Thrown out as refuse, taken in as garbage, Alma is still not ashamed of her story, and she is extraordinary in not internalising the ideas of shame that are imposed on her. She may be naïve in believing in dispensations through writing in the book, or her initial trust in the boss and her ability to intervene directly with God, but she refuses to be silenced. She understands that the kind of pain that she experiences cannot be a sacrifice. An earlier enactment of Abraham's sacrifice of Isaac makes sense to her only because God saves Isaac. Indeed, she speaks the words that allow Isaac to be saved. But no one saves her, not Sacramento, nor the child. In another disturbing vignette, one of the old circus friends takes her to her father's old woman friend. Indeed, it is never clear what this woman's relationship to her father is, but it appears that they may have been close, if not intimate.

When Alma recovers from the miscarriage, and physically composes herself after the brutality of Refugio, she deliberately goes back, tricks the kid into letting her in, and se-

Fig. 19: *Angel of Fire* – the concluding sequence takes us back to the beginning; the vividness of the *mise-en-scène*, the blaze of colour renders the visual spectacular – Alma is 'on show', and can be seen, but not heard

duces Sacramento. In personifying the female role of seductress, Alma manages to prove that Sacramento is not divine, and therefore that religion had abused her too. That she cannot go on seems to suggest a loss of will. The burning of the tent is Alma's answer to the society of spectacle. Ironically, she wears her costume and swings on the bars before she douses the place as though to burn out the role, and perhaps at this point, because of the loss, an inchoate pain that tells her that she has been had by all of them.

Even with this immensely powerful narrative move, the specular casting of Alma's speech act muffles her speech once again as though Rotberg is all too chillingly aware that in Mexico at this point no one wants to hear Alma. Her plight is interesting only if seen. Rotberg's achievement is in giving us a film painted in such lurid colours that the visual ceases to signify except as the obstacle to speech. Showing Alma die in the same visual haze lets us know that although she has spoken, she has not been heard.

While the aesthetics of the film can be considered feminist because of its unravelling of femininity, the issue of authority seems more difficult to ascertain, considering the child-woman's marginalisation. Yet within those restraints, she challenges the lies, and questions the morals of those around her. David R. Maciel and Joanne Hershfield's point that Alma herself is decimated even though she avenges herself on the circus troupe and the puppeteers is well taken. Comparing Rotberg's film with several others, they argue that *Angel of Fire* 'offers no hope for its female audience'.[74] No hope of redemption, certainly; but by exposing the difficult circumstances that Alma handles, and inviting the audience not to judge her, including Alma's voice, asserting her claim to life, certainly offers some kind of hope for women. Rotberg commented that although she had not expected people to identify with Alma, she had wanted them to understand the processes of her life almost as 'a theoretical elaboration'[75] on how sacrifices become inevitable when laws are broken. Rotberg implies that all of them – father, surrogate mother, son, daughter – are sacrificed. Finally, She insists that Alma not be judged; and that her sacrifice is the sacrifice of the 'innocent'.[76] The notion of Alma's innocence is important to establish her agency later when she seduces Sacramento, for she is aware for the first time of the powers of the erotic.

Alma speaks, but is confronted with silence. Silence of a different sort, enforced silence, structures a narrative on sexual violence from Tunisia, Moufida Tlatli's *The Silences of the Palace*.

Memory in the Aural Field: Moufida Tlatli's *The Silences of the Palace*

Gender is the informing discourse in *Danzón's* rearticulation of the aesthetics of music. Gender, class and the imperial context contextualise the study of a speaking female self in Tlatli's *The Silences of the Palace*. Gwendolyn Mae Henderson's comment on women 'speaking in other tongues'; that is, signifying otherwise,[77] resonates in this context as does Linda Dittmar's observation that the silence of women in film is not necessarily a sign of powerlessness but of anger and resistance to exclusion, and a way of using difference to resist the social world.[78] The women in *The Silences of the Palace* could be said to avail of all these modalities, silence being enjoined on them for multiple reasons. Set in Tunisia in the throes of its nationalist struggle against France, the film focuses on the lives of the women in the beys', the ruling class's, harem. The story is told through the stylised flashback of a young girl who had been raised in these sequestered quarters, Alia, on her return to the palace after the death of the bey. In many ways, the film is about Alia trying to understand the palace women, and to come to terms with her own life in the beys' palace. The women are subject to physical and sexual servitude to the beys, have been brought to the palace in extreme youth, do not know their biological families, and are not allowed to step outside the palace grounds. Over and above this class/gender subordination, they are completely 'invisible' to the colonial elite except in their dancing roles. They have no existence at all in the civil/ juridical sense, and thus are triply bound to the beys. Tlatli explores the relationship between the aural and visual against this highly-charged historical backdrop.

The scopic certainly went into overdrive during the French colonial regime, particularly the voyeuristic impulse to view into the harem, famously painted by Delacroix and later by Picasso. In this particular North African context, what was not seeable was music, specifically music that women sang which kept a certain indigenous tradition alive. Music is central to Tlatli's film and the Tunisian culture it comes from. Viola Shafik notes that music was the basis of the development of Arab film, and that film had to learn its way around music; thus in the history of Arab film, music was never subservient to the visual.[79] Long associated with cultural discourses, and used as a site to discuss politics, music was important to the nationalist discourse. Naguib Mahfouz, for instance, punctuates *Miramar* (1978) with characters' references to Umm Khulthum songs. *The Silences of the Palace* remains very much in the discursive field, and is able to respond to patriarchal language in a recognisable mode, albeit not within the same visual paradigm. Despite the difficulties inherent in dramatising silence in a visual medium, Tlatli is successful in constructing an aural field that enables her to contextualise the lives of the women in the palace.

Feminist-auteured film has experimented with the technical properties of the complexity of sound as expressive of women, or representing women's relationship to expression, as in the cinema of Trinh T. Minh-Ha[80] and Marguerite Duras. Moufida Tlatli's film would rewrite the view of the 'colonial harem'[81] current in late nineteenth-century visualisation of Arab women. It has received some positive attention for its use of silence to structure the film,[82] its deployment of female bodies,[83] and its presentation of women within the confines of a palace shortly before Tunisian independence.[84] One reviewer specifically praises its move away from 'the category of the traditional oriental tale into a doubled significance: political and personal, historical and contemporary'.[85] Tlatli's film diverts melodramatic mores to explore the relationship between mother and daughter, and deflects the superscription of the paternal in the constitution of the daughter's identity. In placing the young Alia firmly in modern Tunisia, Tlatli plots memory and time outside generic codes. The use of the aural field in positioning women's bodies and contextualising women's expressions serves to place women in history, and finally outside the theatre of male desire.

The film depicts the lives of the palace women, or the bey's staff, drawing a studied parallel between the women's enclosure and Tunisia's plight, and focuses more closely on Khadija and her daughter, Alia.[86] The film would easily lend itself to the most blatant kinds of exploitation on account of the sensationalistic Western discourses on the notional 'harem'[87] and could be exploitative of Arab women in delivering images of the Arab, and the third world female that suit the West's crisis style of reportage on the third world. In this context, it must be remembered that the fantasy of the rescued female[88] has not only gendered connotations in the first instance, but also imperial ones. Where the nineteenth-century version of the fantasy refers to the European's impulse to save the 'other' woman, in more contemporary terms the urge might be on the part of first world women (including those from the third world or that origin) to rescue, or at least 'deplore' the plight of these women.[89] The *mise-en-scène* and the locution of the film pose these unsettling questions,[90] particularly that of whether first world spectators are being addressed.[91] Whether in the mode of 'romanticised nostalgia',[92] or apologia, Tlatli has to find a way of discussing the epoch of the beys just before Tunisian independence without falling into either mode.

The story of the women who wait on the beys' needs by day and serve them by night, their roles as entertainers, lends itself to orientalising. Tlatli's narrative aesthetic, structured around silences, refrains from exoticising the women of the palace. The film cuts between the spaces of the women – downstairs, and the spaces of the beys – upstairs, carefully contrasting the class differences between the two while also showing how the events outside of the palace, the struggle for Tunisian independence, and inside the beys' quarters affect the lives of the women.[93]

The film's narrative impulse is the return of Alia to the palace on the event of the last bey's death. Her memories of the palace and past have been repressed, and resurface through Khalti Hadda's narration of the past. Umm Hadda's story sets the context for the film; her narration validates Alia's memory and her trauma emphasises the importance of the women's lives, becoming a conduit for Alia's exploration of her relationship with her mother. Paradoxically, then, the key to the visual flashbacks is auditory.

The long takes of the film, particularly in the kitchen showing the women working, gossiping, singing and mourning, are intercut with sequences in the palace grounds, or the beys' personal quarters. That rhythm of the women's bodies subject to servitude, and that sense of repetitiveness of their lives that follow the carnal – cooking, reproduction and death, and their gestural understanding of rape, fear of incest, abortion, death – would signify a women's language that could overpass patriarchal syntax. Moufida Tlatli shows the women circumventing the taboo of silence:

> For me, the women's silence is a silence through the inability to speak. Their mouths are closed. Human beings want to speak, to express themselves. If the mouth is closed then the eyes speak. I wanted to make their eyes speak – and say a great deal. All the women are within the tradition of taboo, of silence, but the power of their look is extraordinary. They have had to get used to expressing themselves through their eyes.[94]

The film, however, does not stop at this form of expression which is, after all, as indicative of subjugation as of subversion.

The sequestration of space, the cultural connotations of the harem, all could combine to make this female territory, the kitchen, a space outside time and linear history. The gestural language, the repeated motions and the completeness of communication between the women could actually imply a separate world, a women's world caught in hysterical time, or in the experience of the plenitude of the maternal body, as discussed by Julia Kristeva. The repeated image of spinning round and round until she falls – running in circles – is perfectly metaphoric of this Kristevan conception of time. Regardless of some convivial moments in the kitchen, for Tlatli such insistence on repetition is discomfitting, if compelling, because of the repetitions that problematise both mother's and daughter's sense of identity.

A major structuring device of *The Silences of the Palace*, the flashback, is put to feminist use. Where the melodramas and film noirs of 1940s and 1950s 'bind flashback structure to the psyche', and both seek to find out the secrets, melodramas more often use flashbacks as part of the solution. However, this difference is rather negligible, considering the genres' 'fascin[ation] with the psyche as an agent of evil, causing the destruction of self and others'.[95] In melodrama, the action is around a female. Despite using the standard cue of a voice-over, Tlatli's exploration, while unearthing a secret, and offering a cure, refuses to psychologise the female's subjectivity, offering instead a political analysis for the necessity of secrecy. Further, 'evil' is not invoked; rather, power relations embedded in sexual relations are insistently exposed. Finally, the power of knowledge is granted both to the women in the flashback and in the diegesis.

The insistent motions of the women in the flashbacks would make the plot unreadable because of its presentness through repetition had Alia made the long journey back only through her visual memory. The flashbacks, which very often function as cinematic memory,[96] would be without context and would render the past unreadable were it not for the auditory cue that directs our reading of them. The auditory in the diegesis is narratively mismatched slightly with the visual in the diegesis; while hardly going in two completely different directions, this does offer a more complex interpretation than one based exclusively on the audio or the visual.[97] Alia sees, the old woman Hadda speaks. Hadda, who says she took care of the bey as if he were a child, renders the past readable, and puts it into a less exotic context. The story is told, the silence is broken, and what is told is more significant than what is not.[98] Ultimately, Alia listens.

Alia is traumatised in youth by not knowing who her father was, but finds out in adult-hood who her mother was, which she acknowledges as being more important. Her ultimate understanding of her mother's life, not acceptance, renders the secrecy of the palace far less foundational than it might have been. The history of that time, her childhood, scarred by the lack of knowledge of the father and loss of concomitant privilege compared to the other palace age-mate Sarra, is surmounted by Alia's newfound softness toward her mother. The younger Alia misplaced the responsibility of the voyeuristic paramountcy of the men's licence with women and their restitution of patriarchal power on the women, particularly her mother.

As a young girl, Alia had desperately wanted a way out of the palace for her mother, and had been bitter about her mother's quiescence to palace rules. The experience of feminin-ity in patriarchy, particularly the distressing kinds of disavowals of femininity enforced by patriarchy that are paradoxically necessary if patriarchal structures are to be challenged, is written by the mother/daughter relationship developed in the film. Determining the social relationships in the diegesis, the *mise-en-scène* pointedly locates these distresses in terms of the female sexual function.[99] Were Alia to assimilate, to grow up female, and be like her mother, she would, the film cruelly insists, not just become like her mother, that is, a woman who performs a similar sexual function, but would become her mother, thereby undertaking the same function with the same men, hence incest.[100]

The women's serf status, the men's unlimited latitude, reshape the conflicts the girls face. A girl child moves to maturity by reproducing her mother's values; however, autono-my and self-identity might demand that she reject the mother viciously to avoid her fate. Alia seemingly faces the prospect of either living in servitude, including sexual work, or of a glorious freedom, confusingly symbolised by the freedom of the country from French colonialism.

The protagonist's rejection of the maternal body and the desire for paternal approval all seem to consistently defy the considerably different cultural context of the harem in relation to the sacrosanct Western nuclear family; and yet, the pattern crops up, coming ambiguously close to inferring the desire for the father.

The overt parallelism between the imprisonment of the women and the subjugation of Tunisia confuses the problematic of female identification further. Alia's 'father' is allied with the women and is presented as linking the 'downstairs' commoners on more than one occasion, and as quasi-sympathetic to the independence movement. His eroticism and sensuality are perversely attributed to his association with them, rather than with the self-indulgence of his class.

Tlatli's symbolisation of the nation is careful not to focus too closely on the female and thus symbolise the female form, or visualise the female herself as Tunisia. While it may el-evate the women's struggle, or lift it up, 'Aufhebung',[101] it would once again diminish their struggle, render it indecipherable because it symbolises women, rather than locating them in history. Commentators are persuaded by this rhetoric of symbolisation, more especially, Alia's song at the end which is taken to be the defiant speech of the new Tunisia. This view obtains in that it follows a long tradition of Arab music, such as the Umm Khulthum songs that Alia sings, as progressive; however, the more general origin of Arab film in music that would make Arab viewers 'an audience of listeners before becoming an audience of spectators'[102] would indicate that Tlatli's development of the tropes of silence and speech in the context of the political is legible only though her representation of aurality within the sexual field. The insistence of sexuality in the aural field curtails the impulse to symbolise and overdetermines the meanings of the singer and the song on liberated Tunisia.

The aural as completely evocative of the same savage voyeurism as the visual, emphatically as primary and distinct in the sexual field, is crucial to fixing and resolving the desire of the daughter and naming the desire of the father.

The relevance of starting the film in present time, indeed to Alia's music, is germane to the connections between the aural, memory and male desire.

Umm Hadda's story takes the viewer back to the labour cries of her mother and, in effect, fills in the function of memory, of events Alia should have known to have her own 'memory' but does not. In contextualising the women's lives, including Khadijah's, Umm Hadda offers Khadijah's life, particularly Khadijah's fierce defence of Alia, and more problematically, this time on Hadda's own cognisance, the father's love as a real treasure. The shots of the prince pacing outside Khadijah's door during Alia's birth frame these sequences that curiously are not Khadijah's, but Umm Hadda's, thus making this story a communal one with the stamp of history.

The auditory framing becomes clearly secondary to the visual retelling of the story; the images narrating in consonance on occasion, counter to the aural on other key auditory claims. The aural plays its own significant part in the space of Hadda's memories which become Alia's; a birthright denied to her because of the code of silence in the palace. Unlike childhood memories that are ratified by the present, Alia's 'memories' are given to her through an interpretive layer that seeks to interpellate her as one of them, an inmate of the palace, long after she has actually rejected it. The power of the story is such that Alia does acknowledge the humanity of her mother's life, and her mother's courage, without accepting Hadda's spoken view of the bey's affection. The visual perspective that unfolds alongside the aural is Alia's, leaving memory itself ambiguously perched between Hadda's aural and Alia's visual.

The visual belies the paternal myth by introducing the theme of incest. Presumably Hadda speaks, but Alia sees, if the convention of Alia walking through the doors to see the past is viewed as the fairly routine contrivance of the existential search of a past denied. This visual story that Alia has access to suggestively implies a scarcely-veiled predatory sexual abuse punctuated by the seemingly innocent space of the kitchen, replete with song. In marked contrast, the scenes in the courtyard that hint at incest are marked by silence, or stifled sounds.

The ululations in the kitchen, the songs and even the radio, while seemingly permitted are also censored. The cosiness of the circle, the warmth of the food in the kitchen are deliberately shown as being insufficient. One woman talks of how her cousin was turned out, another of how she feels suffocated, another shows rage, yet another is on the verge of madness. Like other films that show women together serving men, such as Lizzie Borden's *Working Girls*, the conviviality of women is not celebrated simple-mindedly. The imprisonment and spatial enclosure is stressed. Nostalgia does not work this time at all; every apparent warm memory being tainted by the exclusion of the women from society, and their active repulsion from any kind of human endeavour that is not servitude.

Memory, in these sequences, is unravelled through the visual. The continued silence about the women's lives is exposed by the visual. Neither Hadda nor Alia controls the visualisation of memory. Hadda functions as revealer and teller, but also as interpreter while Alia serves as listener and interpreter. This embeddedness of both dimensions – visual and aural – in the two women composes the truth of the narrative without any Aufhebung. The narrative mode then rescues the visual for women as capable of telling the truth but through the aural that breaks the silence that allows the visual to be envisioned.

We are never allowed to forget that Khadijah is not speaking directly. Khadijah's exploitation is explicitly set up as sexual; the visual and the performance aspect are part of the sexual exploitation, the visual does not create it. The camera lingers on touch, not to show the scenes of molestation, but of the erotic surplus the princes enjoy. The skin itself becomes translucent, not because of the camera's invasiveness but because of the men's invasiveness. When the other prince uncle sees Alia lying on the ground, the gestures are controlled but erotic, and when he picks her up and takes her to the room, then raping Khadijah, the incestuous desire for the niece is obvious. Again, the visual complements the sensory but serves the interests in uncovering the violent. The touching of the mother is a tearing open, apart; with some uncanny frightful semblance to the restrained, but forceful touching of the sleeping girl by the bey. The visual in the film, therefore, is revelatory of endemic structural exploitation, not the form of exploitation itself.

The time shared by the women downstairs is seldom inviolable. Interruptions cause the laughter and song to be stilled abruptly. Performance in public is work for Alia's mother Khadijah, and work that she does not particularly care for. Her relaxed mood changes and she becomes upset when she is told she has to go upstairs. She definitely does not participate in any rivalry over the men, or make any claims for herself through her connection with the prince upstairs. She neither desires the attention, nor enjoys the performance in any artistic way. Alia does, however, aspire to be a singer, as the start of the film references. She can actually separate the art from the bodily slavery, another subtle, if unknowing, homage to her mother.

The sequences that show Khadijah bellydancing upstairs for the beys and their guests are filtered for the audience through the curiosity and later, pain-laden mistrust, of Alia's eyes. Mirrors reflect the women when they are upstairs; Alia watches them through the mirror – both her mother and another woman silently arousing the younger bey at his command. We watch the girl watching her mother, who is being watched by the man; a bitter brokering of the male gaze.

The silence of the watching pervades another sequence through which the aural/visual notes the incestuous. Alia sings, entirely for herself, and is watched by her father, the bey, who looks at her through the mirror. The bey's complicity in grooming Alia for sexual slavery is apparent in his imperiousness with Khadijah and his certain assumption that Alia would be successful, coveted. That Khadijah could only aspire that her daughter please these men is so unquestioned that she is not even permitted to express unhappiness about the requests for Alia upstairs. The story that Umm Hadda tells is reassuring to Alia in its focus on Khadijah's love and concern for Alia that extended to her defying the younger bey by not sending Alia to him, something only Hadda could have told her. The story itself reveals episodes that Hadda could not have witnessed, that Alia did not know of.

The story visually represents the extent of Alia's vulnerability and the inordinate difficulties that Khadijah faces in trying to protect her from the beys. The metaphor of watching is expressive in this context. The mirror itself acts as a dangerous surface partly because gazes are not caught and held, and because of the silence during the looking. An exchange of looks implies some measure of acknowledgement of an 'other'; looking without the returned look is empty in its absoluteness, whether of power or powerlessness. Predictably, the bey draws attention to himself after Alia's song is over through clapping, and Alia then returns his look, thus conferring his previous look with presence, authority and validity; however his earlier look had the mastery of the unseen.

Alia's own looking silences her literally. Having run in ever dizzyingly expanding circles, a compacted kind of eroticism in her running, she falls down on the grass and dozes. For the female viewer, Alia away from the women is in danger. Even before the younger bey devours her with his touch, the servant, less powerful, had tried to touch her. The circling conveys a certain kind of hysterical sexuality, repeated cyclically because of the impossibility and futility of expressing that desire outside the circle. Alia's female 'cousin', her age-mate, was getting married. Clearly there were no such options open to Alia. The predatoriness of the men is even more troublesome, damning as it does the natural expression of female desire, by owning it to service their own sexual interest.

The younger bey picks up the young Alia and takes her to her room, and in among the most complex of scenes, the female viewer moves from relief on seeing Khadijah as if she ensured Alia's safety to watching Khadijah herself anally raped, and then raped again. The sounds are stifled. Alia sees her mother's humiliation and is silenced; a silence that she emerges from only with the gift of the lute that she then cherishes.

Alia finally leaves the palace on a night of another stifled note; the death cry of her beloved mother who bleeds to death while trying to abort the younger bey's child. Khadijah's decision may have been influenced by her consideration of what the exposure might be construed as: licence to be sexual with the ruling classes in the palace. There is more than a hint of resistance in Khadijah's refusal to bear a child conceived by a brutal rape. Alia's own decision to keep the child she had considered aborting is a sign of hope.[103] Curiously, Alia, unlike Khadijah, is not shown as having a female community. That Alia leaves the palace speaks to the strength of this new post-colonial generation. Hadda's comment about how the bey, rendered helpless and taken care of by Hadda, loved Alia is not as comforting as Khadijah's unswerving love and ultimate defiance. The episode of the photo reminds Alia of how hollow the nostalgia that Hadda seems to be experiencing is. Refused a place in the family photo, Alia had later been included in a photo with the bey, her 'father' and his niece, Sarra. A treasured item, she rips it later, presaging her understanding of Khadijah's cry that she is both mother and father to Alia.

The song that Alia sings, intercut with her mother's voice dying down, is less significant for its political rebellion than for the fact that Alia transforms the audience's pleasure in the aural to displeasure, taking control of both aural and visual. This is witnessed by her refusal to marry Lotfi and her decision to pursue her own path. In deflecting the excess of sexual pleasure derived from the aural/visual, through the aural, Alia lays claim to the visual.

The *kan zamana* song redolent of nostalgia, and evocative of a past time in the palace, is cut by the song of Tunisian independence, that defiantly looks into the future. The aural field does not function as a positive scene of instruction in *The Silences of the Palace*, despite the song of independence. Yet the aural becomes key to the visual because the film brings aural and visual memories together to tell a communal story that finally enables the female protagonist to claim communal memory, and with that, both voice and subjectivity. Alia goes back to the palace and through memory is able to come out of circular time and to look forward to the generations, understanding Khadijah's gift as the future of resistance.

Time in the palace, colonial/feudal time, is no longer static. Alia's move into the future is one where there will not be the insistence on repetition. Khadijah has halted that decisively by her refusal to carry the baby, and to 'groom' Alia for a position in the harem. The aesthetics of the film, the introduction of the visual through the aural, the positive feminist use of the flashback, gives the women narrative authority to break the silence, despite the silences in the story. Decisively breaking that silence about rape/fear of possible incest, enables Alia to claim a future.

Auditory Absence: Aparna Sen's *Sati*

Maria Novaro and Moufida Tlatli conceived of auditory subjectivity with specific reference to the conjuncture of traditions of representations of femininity, and the post-colonial moment in those cultural contexts. This focus has been made apparent by their varied modes of structuring the relationship between women on-screen and sound. Auditory presence for women in some feminist film from the third world is wrested through very different stratagems that arise from the specificity of the historical moment detailed. For Moufida Tlatli, the resounding of the female voice was a fraught attempt to understand the silences of a previous generation. The continuities and discontinuities between generations is important to Tlatli's construction of auditory post-colonial subjectivity.

Like Tlatli, who is very much engaged in making films of the current moment, Aparna Sen has also offered us many filmic texts on post-colonial subjectivity.[104] In *Sati*, she explores the the limits of the voice/body problematic for women by featuring a mute female protagonist during the 1820s in West Bengal in India when the 'modern' first emerged for women.[105]

The film details the life a young orphaned woman called Umi who lives with her uncle's family, a rural poor Brahmin family comprised of two sons, one daughter, grandchildren and Umi herself. Umi is exploited by the family, which is presented as harsh and brutal; yet, in a radically different manner from the kind of female exploitation that Nelly Kaplan pictures for us in *A Very Curious Girl*.

The choice of a mute hero can be seen as expressive of the thematic of the film, given the tremendous difficulties of eliciting any kind of direct discourse from the woman herself[106] who has undergone sati, widow immolation.[107] Any suggestion that the woman has not been given a voice within any discourse is problematic.[108] Viewing Umi's muteness as a plot function, and thus very literally instead of metaphorically, enables us to evaluate the silence of the protagonist in terms of its knowability within the film and its significance for a representation of the woman undergoing sati.[109]

The voicelessness of Umi is painfully apparent from the beginning of the film when her aunt abuses her both verbally and physically almost continuously, and Umi has little recourse except to stare back, stiffen her body and tolerate the abuse. Her increased resistance to the aunt's physical assaults are very strong indications of a person struggling to resist subjugation with no framework within which to do so. Literal muteness, then, does not imply blankness, or lack of intelligence.

Umi's muteness has another sub-text to it that needs to be teased out. While Bollywood films are modelled after the studio system, the art/parallel cinema mode that Sen works in is not dependent on dialogue for its effects and uses camera work quite plentifully outside the Bollywood format. In this parallel genre, considered the progressive one in India, it is not completely shocking that subordinated women do not speak. *Ankur* (1974) for instance, features the same female actor, Shabana Azmi, as a tribal woman who, if she speaks at all, speaks seldom. That said, one must also assert that Bollywood does not offer women great speaking roles; the younger female heroes are usually confined to tittering and commonplaces, and the reactions of women are often signalled by facial gestures, movement of the sari pallu, a smile, with older women being allowed more dialogue.[110] Noted as a comment on the general 'to be looked at' quality of both Bollywood and the parallel cinema female hero, Sen's casting of her protagonist as mute works contrarily to impose her presence in the diegetic space as other than female.

Were Umi to be read as metaphoric of other women in society, either the woman who underwent sati, or the women who have no choice about whether their husbands will remarry,[111] as is the case with Savitri, the first daughter-in-law of the house, the critique of the construction of her as other than female, as bestial, would be considerably weakened. More relevant is the proposition that the speechlessness of Umi becomes the site for an interpellation of a different order and kind. The chain of semiosis linking women's representations is interrupted by the construction as bestial. Here, the work of feminist anthropologists in suggesting that women have been linked with the natural because of their closeness to nature's cycle comes to mind, but this plays no part in the film where the other women are plotted minutely according to their spaces in the class system. Umi's muteness, then, is more than a limit case for femininity here, it actually places her with the bestial, or at best with the non-human animate. Auditory absence becomes a way for society to place her outside. Sen, however, by communicating the knowledge that Umi has of society, reveals that auditory absence is the site of the visual knowing seldom given to women in film, and at the narrative level becomes a way of giving voice to the woman undergoing sati who can not testify to her experience.

Granted the kinds of associations made between women and animals because of women's bodily functions and their closeness to the natural cycle, similarities are drawn between the women and animals through cross-cutting of daughter-in-law and the cow giving birth. Umi is put outside the range of humanity, and, to all intents and purposes, of femininity as understood by the culture. When Umi's pregnancy gives proof of her humanity and femininity, she is excluded from the human family.

In placing Umi so far out of the human community, by not articulating her thoughts, and by not giving us access to her interiority, Sen could be charged with mystifying the woman at the very least, or, in an equally loaded criticism, with casting her as victim; thus condescending from a superior position in a repetition of the colonial move in the past, or the Western move in the present.[112]

Umi's muteness cannot be read as a nullification of subjectivity, nor can it be as a silencing. Rather, a visual medium that seeks to unravel powerful mythologies such as the inarticulacy of pain experienced by the woman undergoing sati can do so only by *working over* the silence; that is, acknowledging the inability to experience that pain in actuality, but bringing it forth as pain that can actually be responded to sympathetically, at the human level. Rajeswari Sunder Rajan contends that the body in pain can lay claim to female subjectivity.[113] The muteness of Umi in the film is not an effort to victimise her, but to signify the abridged status awarded her as a human being which then rationalises the ultimate instances of cruelty against her. In other words, Umi's silence does not occasion her oppression but diminishes her market value and allows her to be more exploited without moral recourse. The plot of the film follows the paths of these ascending levels of psychological, spiritual and physical assault on Umi.

If we were to set aside the whole issue of women as the ground of representation for discursive conflict between seemingly competing patriarchal investments then we can insist on the literal. Insisting on the literal at a plot level suggests that Umi's muteness becomes pathologised so that she is constructed as bestial and then disposed of. In this scenario, her muteness becomes the reason for having accepted societal construction; thus freeing her of the passivity attributed to the inability to speak. Obviously Umi has language, even Bengali, because she can hear perfectly well. Her muteness is the positive signifier, connoting as it does, the depth of the resistance but also the extent of alienation from the societal world.

In this visual medium, the mute woman can see. What she sees is very different from the mythologising of sati that is advanced by the Hindu fundamentalist camp. Opening shots of the byre of an old man set up the material conditions the film elaborates. The paucity of recent satis is discussed in a cynical callous way.[114] The sati itself is cast in sunset hues and shot in such clichéd terms that were it not for what is to come later one would be inclined to believe that sati fulfils some kind of intense romantic obligation, the woman herself in silhouette, the whole in medium shots, almost like an aestheticised picture-postcard view of sati. Toni Morrison raises the question of whether pain should be aestheticised through the sycamore trees in the plantation in *Beloved* and the chokecherry trees on Sethe's back that mark the body in pain. It is a difficulty with the film which, like Morrison, Sen never resolves.

Fig. 20: *Sati* – the beauty of the landscape, the woman in silhouette are common images signifying romance; medium shots present an aestheticised view of sati; however, the woman is drooping, but visually very pleasurable

Fig. 21: *Sati* – Umi looks at the sati procession; medium-long, moderately low-angle shots of the priests make them appear menacing, contrasting with the earlier sequence

When Umi looks at the sati, we no longer see the same softly-focused scene. A shot that recurs in the film, we see Umi behind a tree, gazing spellbound at the procession. This sequence contrasts with the earlier one because the shot of the officiating priest, Guruji, is now in a low angle, rendering him threatening. The scene of the procession is intercut with her watching them. There are other times when Umi watches scenes from behind trees or other hiding places, but never do we see such a clear point-of-view sequence again. The contrast, put simply, is between the 'cultural seeing' and hers.

The silky appearance of the sati sequence is raised again in a scene of equal horror, the rape of Umi. The medium shots of the drugged but beautiful young woman are also recalled during Umi's 'wedding' when Umi herself looks half-conscious. The silhouetted shots of the sati sequence, in their length and enormity, are predictably a presaging of Umi's own status as sati at the end of the film.

Much of what Umi sees is not remarkable, most of the footage is not shot through her perspective, but the omniscient auteur's. The seeing that Umi undertakes, in the context of her muteness, establishes her intelligence, her intelligibility, and secures the audience's identification. Her seeing, most importantly, establishes her knowability.

Knowing and understanding Umi is central to Sen's film. Knowing her and the material circumstances, the mythologies that undergirded people's relationships to her demystifies both fundamentalist and liberal constructions of the woman, de facto radically other than us, as unknowable because of divine sanction in the case of sati, or of the extremity of pain that would be presumptuous for us to identify with for fear of appropriation.[115]

Through Umi's muteness, Sen signifies the attempt on the part of society to constitute Umi's sati as bestial;[116] and through Umi's vision, Sen guarantees her humanity and femininity. The auditory, or lack thereof, is thus a pre-condition for the visual, or the knowable. The absent signifier invests the present signifier excessively.

The film itself follows the circumstances of Umi's life as an inset to the cultural narrative/discursive conflict over sati initiated by the opening. The specularisation of sati in the popular media, one that conflates the fire imagery with that of the goddess herself, shot in a style that is pictorial and owes much to India's temple art and the calendar art of the goddesses that proliferate in India, is problematic. The conventions of a borrowed neorealistic technique that Sen, like many of her other contemporaries, uses, at least does not celebrate it unequivocally, despite my earlier difficulties with sati's aestheticisation. In the context of Indian Hindu representations, Sen's is definitely materialistic rather than mythological. The latter has become increasingly more aggressively presented in Bollywood.[117]

The conditions of Umi's life, then, are relevant to the project of knowing Umi. Left orphaned in the care of her uncle, she clearly serves the family as an indentured female labourer would. The economy of the family partly determines the course of her life; her wishes, or her desires, although revealed through her gestures of theft and escape, are considered insubordinate. The family is in the marriage market for the daughter of the family, Sashi. Custom apparently demands that Umi, probably older than Shashi, be married earlier. The groom dies before the marriage, bringing forth the pronouncement from the aunt that had the groom died after his marriage to Umi, the family could have won the glory and status of being a sati family. Later, when the aunt's husband dies, the notion, of course, does not come up. The aunt sees it as a solution to the dilemma: the family would be rid of the woman in a noble, socially sanctioned way. Having this revealed right at the beginning does away with the whole question of the agency of the woman who undergoes sati that Sunder Rajan worries about.[118] The issue of voluntarism, as in Umi's case, is totally set aside by the locution of Umi's narrative which models the making of a mythology for us through semiotic excess; that is, by symbols that in the diegesis function at the plot level, where these exorbitant things did happen the way they have been narrated. The historical real is crucial to indicate the mythology being spun; curiously the historical real is forgotten by received history, and the mythological, through a glide, becomes the real. The symbol functions literally in its diegesis, and becomes *symbolic* in the space of history that will follow it.

Umi must be married so she is asked to marry a tree, and thus divest herself of the unacceptable single status that prevents her cousin Sashi from being married. An added heuristic element is that she should marry the tree she spends time around. The tree, a real physical tree, that Umi actually 'marries' remains the tree in Sen's film, but through over-investment in the diegesis in the construction of mythology, begins to signify the male husband in the feminist unravelling of the mythology of sati. The tree that Umi dies by is also the tree that stands in for a husband during Umi's 'marriage' ceremony. When the tree is split apart by the storm, and Umi is found lying there, the pundits and the community regard her as a holy sati. The tree is initially metonymic for the husband. If the tree is examined paradigmatically, that is, among ranges of possibilities of shots of trees, its significance is more than indexical, more than that of a tree; and viewed syntagmatically, within the shots that precede it, it is replete with the significances of the funeral bier that Umi sees early in the film when she is wedged into the tree. Thus, the final scene casts its meaning on the open scene: as futile as the loss of Umi's life ostensibly 'for a tree', so was the loss of the other young woman's life for a man. By this accretion of meaning to the tree, Sen suggests the following in the truth-telling project of *Sati*: if the tree is the man, the man is a substitute for the tree or a tree-like entity.

Similarly the flame imagery, in contrasting with the darkness that describes the funeral of the man and the subsequent sati, is overladen even within the diegesis of the film, both literal for the other unknown widowed woman in the film but symbolic for the cultural narrative on sati.[119] The rape sequence is shot through in these colours, the flickering lamp and its flames signifying more than the rape. In terms of film convention, due to the censorship code, the rape would not have been visualised, and neither for that matter sex that included copulation, but would have been signalled through ubiquitous images. Indeed, more detailing of rape would have been permitted because its narrative significance would have made it artistically essential.[120] This is clearly problematic in its representation of women, showing as it does the fierce power of the male and the helplessness of the female, including semi-nudity, which can be perceived as titillating. With regard to these scenes, the rectitude of the parallel cinema was supposedly by comparison more progressive for women. The symbolisation of something that is not a stand-in for a sexually-explicit scene does mark a difference in using symbol to visualise concretely the oppression of women through its connection to sati rather than fulfillment of an element of the plot.

The sequence itself, disappointingly, is uncomfortable for the female viewer. Throughout most of the film, the camera as it dwells on Umi is fairly non-hierarchic, filming her in a similar manner to the others, following her movement and often showing her watching when she is not moving. Now we suddenly see her through the male teacher, Nabin's, eyes, and the camera marks the difference dramatically. As long as he has not noticed her, but continues to chat as though to an idiot, the scene is not tense. He is looking downward and she is, as usual, taking in the scene. When he begins to look at her, his gaze is horrifying. She looks terribly afraid, and her utter powerlessness, the result of being unable to cry out loudly (although she can utter sounds and cries) is very affecting for the female viewer. The scene finds its resolution in the silhouetted framing which identified the sati scene subsequent to the funeral. On deeper reading, the second sequence could also work as the funeral for Umi herself.

Strategies used to represent rape are indicative of the way subject positions are constituted by a culture, argues Juliane Burton-Carvajal with reference to Mexican and Cuban films. Her comment perhaps allows us to understand the representation of rape in this film as subjectively evoking the disastrous consequences for women, as opposed to the mainstream cinema where it often functions structurally as a lynchpin for the narrative and as productive of the kind of male sexual pleasure that is deeply subtended by intense inequality between male and female.[121] Burton-Carvajal states: 'Textual rape arguably represents for the female character that same liminal moment that death conventionally represents for the (textual) male.'[122] If mainstream films can produce subjective viewing positions for women through the rape sequence, its conflation with sati/death here forcibly reminds us of the material female body, not the dematerialised body of the woman undergoing sati. In this context, then, the pain induced by the sequence is necessary as a strategy, as a way of making sure that the body of the woman undergoing sati is not othered.

The visual connection being made between the rape of a mute woman and a woman who is undergoing sati would perhaps be a problematic connection for women, sliding too easily from sati to rape and not perhaps paying attention to the different modalities that achieve this.[123] Deification seems to be the cover for sati, and showing that the woman is subject to rape also calls into question powerful cultural imperatives on purity and impurity.

Cutting across many cultures, the characterisation of the madonna/whore, Holy Virgin/Malinche is able, as one of its primary functions, to police women's sexuality. Interestingly, the culture in question here does not actually entertain this particular dichotomy in any mythological way, yet bizarrely works in similar terms by precluding the possibilities of sexuality for the *mortal* woman who is deified. The woman undergoing sati is forswearing life itself as the ultimate ascetic gesture, the woman widow abjuring any kind of sexuality. The rape survivor is impure,[124] and the woman undergoing sati is pure.[125] In filming the rape with the same codes used to film the sati, Sen indicates a couple of different factors that structure this parsing of purity and sexuality. First, no woman is held sacred in patriarchal culture.

Second, with Umi having become 'impure' and yet still being the woman undergoing sati, this covers the aggressive and predatory actions of the man in the diegesis, and the men in the culture at large. Forcing a woman into committing sati becomes a definite way of ensuring that she is no longer sexual,[126] and never sought to be sexual outside her relationship with her now dead husband.[127] The deification of the woman is a way of preventing her from having sex.[128] In the film, Umi's being forced into 'sati' exposes many cover-ups. Firstly, the deification serves male interests because it obscures Umi's rape. Secondly, it masks the male sexual predatoriness and projects it onto Umi who would now no longer be a 'lure' to the men. Finally, the perpetrator of rape is now completely free, as are other members of the community, because neither the men nor the women wished to find out how Umi had got pregnant.

In presenting both the woman undergoing sati and the rape survivor in the figure of Umi, Sen is uncovering the motivation behind deification; a simultaneous avoidance of predatory male sexuality, a wilful ignoring of women's sexuality.[129] Tracing the history of the woman undergoing sati to male sexual pillaging is the most devastating kind of debunking of the deification of sati. To reinforce the visual similitude brought up by the shooting of the sati and rape sequences, Sen has the schoolteacher say, 'Don't tell anyone – oh! that's right, you can't speak. I like it that way.' Given the way the woman Umi is silenced, and kept from revealing who has raped her, these are chilling words pointing back to the possible prior history as the unknown woman undergoing sati. If the rape sequence invites a reading through the sati sequence, the reverse is also true. If the schoolteacher's sexual abuse in the fire-lit scene is read backward, the sati can be viewed as sexual exploitation. The specificity of the woman's gender is of course important, and if one considers that the killing of a woman to prohibit the slightest possibility of her being sexual,[130] as widowhood pretty much forbids it anyway, then certainly sati is highly sexually motivated, no less than a sexual crime masquerading under religious abuse. The link of the rape with sati further suggests that violent excitement of rape is comparable to the arousal experienced by the killing of a woman.

The course of Umi's life follows this pattern as the ultimate punishment for the sexual abuse that cannot be revealed as such because of the constraints of silence. Although the woman who provides the medicine for the abortion assumes it to be so, and comments contemptuously that one would not expect these men to take responsibility, and more damagingly that the women probably did not want to find out for fear of the identity of the male. Further, she says that this happens in many high caste families.

Here, the silence works both literally and symbolically in an obvious sense by touching upon the shame brought to women who speak up against sexual violence. Had Umi been able to speak, it is not clear that she could have confided in anyone. She is beaten for saving a few guavas for herself and responds with a cry followed by tears in the sanctuary of the tree. Umi works, the women work, while the men, it seems, participate in helping the family finances by the dowries they can bring in. The older brother remarries because his wife has had yet another daughter whose dowry would need to be taken care of. Umi's marriage to the tree makes it possible for Sashi, Umi's female cousin, to be married, but Hari needs to remarry to raise the revenue for the marriage.

Umi appears drugged or least unknowing when she is being married off to the tree. We see no point-of-view shots, but a complete marriage ceremony. The narrative follows the social construction of her as less than human. It also shows that Umi deeply seeks the human that she is excluded from. Later she is shown searching for some kind of response from the tree. This shot is quite different gesturally than the earlier ones that show her sheltering there. Brutal beating and humiliation heaped on by the family, combined with the new status of the tree as bridegroom, renders her attachment to the tree comprehensible in completely human terms. Sen discusses this part of Umi's attachment to the tree: 'The relationship between her and the tree which forms the core of the narrative, though not an obviously sexed one, does have sensual overtones ... In fact there is a scene where once again this is only suggested – the girl seems to be masturbating under the tree. But the people may miss it, which is fine.'[131] In the sexual scene that Sen describes, Umi actually looks like she is masturbating with the tree, which while showing the girl's sensuality, accentuates the tree's roughness, particularly of skin, and immovability, suggesting desire unfulfilled. A more enigmatic, less easily decipherable, moment in the text is Umi's visit to the teacher Nabeen shortly after being beaten for eavesdropping on his wife and the family. The teacher smiles at her and asks her to come in. We do not know whether she does. The next shot is of her vomiting in an easily recognisable symptom of pregnancy. While the image of the woman vomiting is a common enough cliché in film, its placement immediately after Umi is standing outside the window is arresting but remains ambiguous, perhaps deliberately so.

After visiting the tree, Umi goes to the teacher either because he is human, and that is the only human touch she has known, or to show herself that she knows something the gossiping women surrounding Nabeen's wife do not, or to try and tell him about her pregnancy. We do know that if she is seeking human contact with the schoolteacher, she is really clutching at straws. She is despairingly distraught after the rape, but he throws her out of the house so that his friend will not discover her there.

In an intriguing reversal, Nabeen cowers in the shadows while he overhears the women planning the abortion. Umi is forced to take the medicine, and is told not to enter the kitchen. Among the most disturbing of scenes in the film is the one where Umi throws up continuously on the tree. And falls asleep. When she wakes up and goes back 'home', she is 'outside', 'excluded'. The cowshed does not provide any shelter in the lashing rain.

The morning finds the tree felled and Umi dead. The conclusion is a sharp reminder of how this 'sati' was forced by the inhumanity shown her, and how the cover-up process takes the form of the deification of the woman, punished for having been raped, for impurity.

Fig. 22: Sati – the tree that Umi seeks sanctuary in, and 'marries', and is now a sati for the felled 'tree'

And a reminder of the mythmaking of sati.

In commenting on Sen's aims in her filmmaking, Brinda Bose emphasises the challenge to basic notions of gender in the culture: 'Sen's particular dilemma, therefore, is not just to make sexuality an acceptable criterion for discussing gender relationships, but to raise basic questions about gendered assumptions within Indian social structures.'[132] The film's chilling insight that sexuality is controlled by death and rape certainly challenges cherished ideas of the purity of the female, and the culture's self-image of itself as revering women, particularly women deities. Bose follows her observation with a quotation from Sen on the link between her films: 'There is another link, perhaps, and that's for the benefit of the feminists – the "woman" in all three films emerges with strength.'[133] It is hard to see how Umi emerges with strength. The quotation marks around 'woman' perhaps refers to the female spectator; a stretch since the reference is to all three films. The 'perhaps' modifies the assertion which could leave *Sati* out of this formulation about strength and maintains the comparison of the loneliness of the three female protagonists. I dwell on this throwaway comment only because it raises disturbing questions about the directoral ideal of 'strength' of women. Umi certainly decided to face fate alone when she refused to seek help from the family that stormy night, but to celebrate it as strength would be to romanticise Umi's oppression and her very limited choices. If strength implies dignity, then Umi did retain her dignity. Given the film's strong critique of sati, Sen's comment can only be taken as an attempt to preempt Umi's being perceived as a victim, and to insist on her subjectivity. Finally, in *Sati*, the absence of speech as the positive, the auditory as negative signifier, transforms the visual into the positive, guaranteeing the mute woman's subjectivity, not agency, and her history at the site of 'performance', whether of sati or in the cinematic field, by establishing her humanity through her vision, which functions as language, or speech.

The aesthetics of the film – the play between the auditory and the visual, the importance of the former in the plot, the latter in the discursive – is successful paradoxically in granting the mute female hero the authority of vision, and through it, speech.

In working against the taboo of authoritative female speech in mainstream film, the filmmakers in this chapter explore the relationship between sound and the visual as understood through the narrative of the film, and through the cultural narrative the films address.

Their account of aurality is not meant to celebrate women's voices, or women's speech on screen, but rather to assess and ascertain the role the auditory has played in representations of women in this visual medium. Unlike its historical cousins, painting and the plastic arts, cinema did come to sound; presumably, then, women could be expected to have a different speaking presence in this medium and yet that was not the case. While the directors have different approaches to this dilemma, each first acknowledges the collusion of sound to speech in the repression of female subjectivity, even as each explores a fairly extreme case of the auditory for the female in the diegesis, in terms of sound or lack thereof being primary in framing the female's relationship to the social.

Nevertheless, the auditory scene in the four films discussed above has been substantially different. In *Danzón*, recourse to extra-diegetic music allows the director to re-position the female protagonist's subjectivity outside of the cultural parameters indicated by Mexican film's traditional placement of the female hero. The auditory enables the female's subjectivity in this film. Whether the forgotten can claim auditory subjectivity, even when they insistently seek it, is the question raised by Rotberg's film. Yet we are in no doubt that Alma speaks when she sets fire to the circus. The aural field does not function as a positive scene of instruction in *The Silences of the Palace*. Yet the aural becomes the key to the visual in this film which brings the aural and visual memories together to tell a communal story that finally enables the female protagonist to claim communal memory, and with that, both voice and subjectivity. Finally, in *Sati*, the absence of speech, the auditory as negative signifier, transforms the visual into the positive, guaranteeing the mute woman's subjectivity, and her history at the site of 'performance', whether of sati or in the cinematic field, by establishing her humanity through her vision, which functions as language, or speech.

Caught in the vicissitudes of a visual medium unarguably hostile to women, these women filmmakers have been able to work within and outside the visual, confronting the notion that the visual alone directs knowledge, proving that the auditory could indeed be instrumental in the path to knowledge and subjectivity.

5
DESIRE AND FEMALE SUBJECTIVITY

The preceding discussion on auditory subjectivity inevitably included the trope of female desire. Historically, the imposition of male desire in film has left little room for female desires to be articulated. Female desire, whether authorial, diegetic or spectatorial, has been articulated either as fantasms of the male imaginary, or is underwritten by a male desire which conflates the image of women with desire itself. The cinematic apparatus colludes to institutionalise male trajectories of desire. We saw, however, that feminist genre crossings entertain the possibilities of registering female desire, even genres so steeped in patriarchal cultural norms as the melodrama, as in *Bhaji on the Beach*, or the cabaretera, as in *Danzón*. In feminist film, reworking the relationship between the acoustic and visual could also inscribe new learned desires outside the heterosexual enclosure.

In an early discussion on the possibilities of female desire being articulated, Mary Ann Doane made the expansive move of considering the female spectator's desires in relation to the female in the diegesis. Reviewing feminist psychoanalytic work, Doane, in an analysis of the female spectator's lack of distance from the screen, or from the character in the diegesis, finds that this inhibited the female's ability to desire as this specific identification mechanism does not posit lack, a necessary condition of desire. The woman's place, then, is a 'nonplace', 'the position allotted to the female "subject" both by psychoanalytic scenarios and by the cinema'.[1] Denied the authority granted the spectator, the female spectator and her diegetic stand-in cannot have the pleasure of being desiring subjects in this framework that curtails female desiring subjectivity. Linda Williams summarises the complex relationship between female spectator, and female in the diegesis, looking and desire: 'In the classical narrative cinema, to see is to desire.'[2] She adds that good female heroes in the classical cinema were often blind. Indeed, the desire of the female in the text and the female spectator are all severely punished in classical cinema. Julia Kristeva's assessment on the omnipresence of the paternal signifier and its impact on desire *per se* – 'to love is to survive paternal meaning'[3] – speaks to the difficulty of female desire plotting, or motivating narrative.

At the risk of being repetitive, one notes that the double dismissal of women, as seeing and desiring subjects, is embedded in those masculine structures of looking and positioning that value seeing and desiring in that specifically masculine context, or semiotic network. This chapter intervenes in those accounts of desire in film that assume a representational terrain that excludes the inscription of female desire. When that specifically masculine world of desire is not foregrounded, even if patriarchy is still firmly in place, the terms of women's relationship to desire changes, including the film's spectatorial address, and the film's presumed rejection of female subjectivity. In this chapter, I seek to show how renditions of female desire that shift the accent of the discussion from the psychic to the social are vital to the discursive representation of female subjectivity in the social. I do not doubt the importance of the debates on the psychic and sexual that feminist study inspired for women and feminism, nor do I question their intimate relevance to the social, but note that women filmmakers dealing with the theatre of male desire do not stand transfixed in that space, but shift the theatre itself.

In looking at female desire in films authored by women, I have chosen texts from different time periods, modalities and cultures. Germaine Dulac's *The Smiling Madame Beudet* (1922), a silent film employing some of the practices of the French avant-garde, takes a step towards historicising female desire by placing it in the social register. Dulac also opens the way for spectatorial subjectivity in this text which shows the woman as reader/viewer and patriarchy as art/film/text. The emphasis on the context is important to Suzana Amaral's *Hour of the Star* (1985), which considers what female desires are in an underdeveloped economy. Played out against the backdrop of male desire, Amaral emphasises a young woman's journey towards understanding the conflicts between male and female desire. The visual is not crucial to the female's desiring subjectivity. Finally, Kathleen Collins' *Losing Ground* (1982) explores what ecstasy might mean for women, and shows, as the two earlier films were not able to, that desiring subjectivity is a complex matter for the woman in the diegesis, and the spectator, occupying as they do the shifting postions of artist, model and actor. All three films acknowledge the authority of the women's desires in the narrative in that they motivate narrative movement and resolution.

In thematising female desire, all of the films problematise the contexts of the sexual for women, replay traditional visual trajectories and challenge the knowledges these have produced. Subjectivity, however compromised or fragile, is a possiblility only if received understandings of female desire posited by visual paradigms are questioned. For Dulac, the real interposes and challenges the visual; for Amaral, it is the tactile and for Collins, the supra-visual. All three ask us to look at vision in connection with other senses if we are to understand the relationship between desire and female subjectivity from a feminist place.

Discourses of Desire: Germaine Dulac's *The Smiling Madame Beudet*

In addition to the nuanced feminist critique on the place of women's desires in psychoanalytic scenarios, male fantasies and mainstream film, feminist theorists have considered the specificity and context of women's desires important, and the relationship of desire to power.

Teresa de Lauretis has written about the urgency to 'historicise' desire – certainly an important move when one considers that more often than not woman is viewed as desire itself[4] or as the 'site of desire'.[5] The trope of woman as aesthetics works as a sublation of the thematic of woman, not as object of desire, but as desire itself. The conditions of woman's representability have so deeply attached to her *signification* that contradictorily the female form in cinema 'speaks castration for the male viewer'. In what Laura Mulvey calls 'the second avenue', however, her persona on screen exudes an aestheticism that signifies differently, or more viscerally, as desire; an invitation to desire, or what Hal Foster has called 'a perfect misrecognition of feminine beauty as phallic plenitude'.[6]

Mary Ann Doane, Teresa de Lauretis and Sandy Flitterman-Lewis have all bravely attempted to sketch a way out of the theoretical impasse which Foucault discusses with specific reference to the relationship of desire with power. He indicates that one's conception of power governs one's notion of desire; that is, there is 'the promise of a "liberation" if power is seen as having only an external hold on desire, or, if it is constitutive of desire itself, to the affirmation you are always-already trapped'.[7]

How is a girl to get out of this impasse? Flitterman-Lewis takes recourse in the notion of the 'enunciative apparatus' to maintain that female desire has been articulated in the history of film in a variety of ways: by Dulac in her version of interiority, i.e. female subjectivity; by Marie Epstein in her restructuring of the looks that 'suture' cinematic practice and by foregrounding the relationship between mother and daughter; and by Agnès Varda in her meta-reflexive meditations on how cinematic discourses are brought together. Flitterman-Lewis's foray into the topic bears the supposition that informs much feminist work today: that women have always spoken, have always articulated their desire but have not been understood in these terms because of androcentric modes of intervention and interpretation.[8]

Flitterman-Lewis suggests that feminists would be well rewarded if they searched for the traces of desire in places other than the trajectories hitherto outlined because female desire is spoken from another place. This allows one to take oneself, briefly but crucially, away from those theories of desire which insist that female desire must be recognised within male frames of signification. The representation of woman itself is inextricably connected to the dominance of male desire on screen so that many filmmakers have avoided, for instance, any kind of generic presentations of the female body for fear that it would inevitably signify either aesthetics or desire.[9] Following that, one could maintain that attempts to convert the terms by which woman as aesthetics and woman as desire subtend film must then challenge the conditions of women's representability.

The early French avant-garde's (particularly the surrealists') visual innovativeness and emphasis on imagery, brought an aesthetic model that inhibited discursivity, and provided filmmakers with an opportunity to screen women outside prior narrative framings. Although the efforts of the male surrealists did not venture in this direction, Dulac's pioneering *The Smiling Madame Beudet* is an attempt to undo the conditions of women's representability by dividing the trope of woman as aesthetics from woman as desire. Her definition of 'pure cinema' describes a new kind of cinema which arguably could also be said to speak to the detachment of women from the desiring apparatuses of mainstream narrative film. It was the era of pure cinema which, rejecting all other action, wanted to cling only to that which emerged directly from the image, 'in the attempt to give a strictly personal expression of the universe'. Pure cinema did not reject sensitivity or drama, but it tried to attain them through purely sensitive elements.[10] The emphasis on the image might appear more than problematic considering the capture of the diegesis effected by the female image. Attaching the image to the purely personal, however, delimits its representative potential; indeed, this kind of cinema tried to stay away from the representative. *The Smiling Madame Beudet* does not fit into this hypothetical scenario; in shuffling the conditions of representability, Dulac represented some aspects of women, albeit not women of her own time. The subjective presentation of the chief character of the film was visionary and had resonances for women of the future, as witnessed by the many films drawn from one aspect of this early work.[11]

Memory's building up of desire was acknowledged by the surrealists. If one's desires had never been fulfilled, how could one know the pleasure or the power of that desire? Because of this lack of knowledge of desire fulfilled, anamorphosis, a feature that Katherine Conley believes is 'emblematic of the surrealist worldview' is rendered unbearably complex in the film. Conley's description is of relevance to the diegetic and extra-diegetic sequences of *The Smiling Madame Beudet*. Her contention is that 'surrealist work attempt[s] to convey the co-existence of two apparently mutually exclusive worlds – that of conscious reality together with that of unconscious dream reality'.[12] Where the two worlds meet would then indicate surreality. In the film, the point of convergence of the two worlds returns to the *mise-en-scène*, which emphasises the wall enclosing the protagonist, and the role the woman protagonist plays in the male theatre of desire. In the case of women, then, the two discourses inevitably are the received/male and the other which may of course assume any form such as received/alternative or received feminist in the sense of proffering a coherent ideology. In the film, the 'authentic' or the 'emotional' is expressed in the real, pressed in the 'dream'. Were this received discourse the sole one, we would have to confront a mimicry we know all too well, the discourse would only serve to gain our consent in the participation of the discourse. The other discourse, in the register of the 'real' in the diegesis, and firmly placed within the narrative symbolic, traces a desire for power, deliberately differentiated from the erotic and stunningly removed from the notion of recovery or recuperation of that which is lost. Female desire is discursively presented as utopian in urgency rather than retrospective in impulse in this other discourse. Old desires, such as the desire for the lost maternal object, were never completely fulfilled for women because the girl has to be lack rather than see lack and become the mother rather than have desire for the mother substitute. The utopian drive seems the only possible way to conjecture on female desire, for the woman clearly does not have the pleasurable memory that would spark desire activated by memory. Within the diegesis, this other discourse is not foregrounded but is nevertheless the lure for the female spectator; it specifically positions her in relation to discursive power relations, which enables her to understand this desire as both alternative and revolutionary. Participation in this discourse thereby becomes the pre-condition of a dialogue between the authorial voice as manifested in the desire of the text and the feminist spectator, if she is to stop watching the spectacle. For that is precisely what she does, watch, when she understands female desire as the sum of received discourse. Acceptance or despair, but in neither case moving away from the position of spectator. *The Smiling Madame Beudet* thus locates two discourses on desire at the narrative level, and shows the female spectator what it would take to move from her position as spectator to that of actor, or desiring subject.

The film worked within the avant-garde framework to record the 'unconscious' of the young woman. Yet the code of the surreal had been insufficient to the desires of the woman, and in order to register these in the social, Dulac noted that the desires of the woman articulated in the symbolic or the space of the real were diegetically more crucial to the narrative that had overtaken the surreal expressiveness of the unconscious. Perhaps the 'unconscious' itself is propped up by the conscious in this rendition, for very good reason. Within the surrealist Weltanschauung, the liberation of the unconscious was so intimately saturated by the dream of woman that the unconscious itself had become feminised, even feminine. Being tied to the conditions of the pure expression of the unconscious would entail the appropriation of a subject position that released the desires of the unconscious only because of its security in the conscious.[13] Even as Dulac insists on the desire of the female, she shows the insufficiency of her mode of address in its inability to speak to the complexity of female desire, or female desires that are not single, or univocal, or even female desire that is not symmetrical to male desire in that the named desire is the desire that drives the plot, the unnamed submerged, similar to the male narrative mechanisms already familiar to us.

Strategically, Dulac sidesteps the question of sexual desire; interesting given that the surrealists explored male desire and fantasy exhaustively in their painting and film. Hal Foster's question about fantasy resounds: 'Indeed all the primary fantasies according to Freud (seduction, castration, the primal scene or the witnessing of parental sex, as well as intrauterine existence) are active in surrealist reflections concerning subjectivity and art. And whenever we encounter such reflections certain questions will recur: are these fantasies defined in terms of heterosexual masculinity?'[14] One can only conjecture that the reticence to explore female desire sexually in visual mediums is partly because of the fear of the appropriation of images, but also partly because female heterosexual desire has been scripted so many times as male fantasy.[15] Foster acknowledges the insight of feminist theory in recognising the male gaze effect in the work of surrealist artists, but suggests the possibility of a 'returned' look or doubled-look that paradoxically questions the earlier figuration of woman as threat of castration. However, he fails to note that once again the terms of reference by which the imaging of woman is read as being progressive, a practice in much modernist critique, are astoundingly male.[16] Within such a framing, the promise of a surreal cinema, outside the mainstream narrative one, can hardly be encouraging for women. If the woman figures as 'unconscious',[17] the fantasy unmoored to the social, after the model of the surrealists, would seem to be punishing, unless of course the male position were taken. In other examples of women's investments in fantasy, outside of the surreal model and in mass culture – comic books, films, soap operas, romances – women's fantasies are usually *socially* rewarded.[18] I am hardly suggesting that women do not have an unconscious, but that their unconscious is perhaps not quite to be understood as that which is repressed *socially* but expressed in the unconscious. Since women are oppressed socially in such clear ways, their sexual repression may signify by means other than those connected with power. So the road to fantasy may not necessarily or exclusively be through the unconscious, and obviously does not exclude the conscious.

The film deliberately moves the issue of female desire from the obviously erotic or sexual arena to the space of the real or historically situated in the diegesis; otherwise the arenas problematise the notion of the female erotic within the diegesis. I use the concept of 'real' space to designate that area which has been repressed or covered but misrecognised and which bears the imprint of female desire. The real is also the locus of the connection between female desire and power and the only discourse in the text which considers the relation of desire to power for the female. Further, it distances itself from the subjective and works to place female desire within, rather than outside, the narrative, thus moving towards historicising it. Plotting desire *in* the narrative gives it an authority in the social register that points to the power desire could conceivably exert in the social sphere.

Before I highlight the textual spaces in which female desire is located, it is useful to talk about the spaces in which it is not present, and why this may be the case. Desire in *The Smiling Madame Beudet* is not located as a primary propelling motivating device of the narrative, nor is the spectator to be satisfied by the clear delineation of desire and its fulfilment in the attainment of the goal. The withholding of pleasure by the creation of absence and its consequent fulfilment, or the meta-play around withholding and fulfilment, are not the defining features of a discussion of desire in women's texts. Most importantly, female desire within the textual space is not imprinted only in those markings of the text now routinely linked with the thematics of the constitution of female subjectivity, nor in the unconscious register of dreams, fantasies or subjective visualisations of desire. Certainly, there is a kind of desire inscribed in these apparatuses but I would argue that they fall in the received register of playing a relay on the male unconscious and demonstrate rather that manner by which these discourses demark the boundaries of desire remarkably precisely.[19]

The film is about a draper and his wife, Madame Beudet. The draper mockingly threatens to kill himself each time Madame Beudet will not go along with his wishes. The pistol he puts to his head is not loaded. Monsieur Beudet keeps the bullets in a drawer separate from the gun. Madame Beudet loads the gun one day and then loses her nerve. Ironically, Monsieur Beudet shoots the gun at her, shattering the glass behind her instead. After this interlude life returns to its regular monotony.

The Smiling Madame Beudet's theme traces the relationship between Monsieur and Madame Beudet in a French province where the 'horizons stay the same'. A range of devices establish that Madame Beudet is the subject of enunciation; both story and discourse are told from her point of view and inset with scenes of her interiority: dreams, fantasies, day dreams, imaginings and thoughts.[20] The plot as such is not motivated directly by either Monsieur Beudet's desire or Madame's. The action works around their struggle for control over space, a space that very specifically traverses both the physical and the imaginative. The *mise-en-scène* captures the issues succinctly with a series of shots that show Madame and Monsieur shifting a vase on the table. Madame wants it off-centre, Monsieur dead-centre. During the course of the short, Monsieur wants Madame to accompany him to the opera *Faust*. Madame refuses to go. He locks the piano, which is a source of her pleasure, signifying his desire to control her imaginative life. In some dim way he is aware that her passion for art – poetry and music – cuts her loose from him. We seldom see a neutral or realistic shot of him. He is exaggerated, very much the object of enunciation. Consequently the filmic narrative offers us a nuanced notion of the differences between the discursive interpellation of female subjectivity and the articulation of female desire.

The contrast between the husband and wife is revealed in the opening shots of the interior where we see female hands playing the piano. In the right-hand portion of the frame a close-up reveals masculine hands rhythmically tossing, and presumably counting, coins. The compactness of the imagery here shows the persistence of the surrealist influence in its high contrast of masculinity and femininity, and later the violence of the gestures that the film captures. A striking instance of this is when Monsieur Beudet pans the row of dolls on top of a shelf, picks one up, and unwittingly crushes it in his hands. Dulac successfully condenses the violence into a symbology, but the violence remains explosive, uncontained by either narrative or symbology.

The distance between the husband and wife is further marked by the 'smile' that refers to the title of the film, and perhaps to the enigmatic smile of the Mona Lisa.[21] The smile seems to signify a retreat into interiority, and recurs at the conclusion of each episode when Madame turns to art. The smile of indefinable victory, however, seems more than a little ambiguous, each of Madame's tournées into the fine arts as either reflective of the trope of artist as male, or desire as female.[22] The Faust sequence shows the young woman stifled by multiple echoes of male desire structured by the voices of the five men crowding her,[23] the Baudelaire poem about the lovers and their subsequent end is more amorous if equally disastrous for women. The distinction between the classical construction of women and the modern one is well done; both perhaps subject women to the 'imprisonment of dependency or the violence of meaning'.[24] Flitterman-Lewis notes that Madame's rejection of these produces a creative entrance into her psyche,[25] and I would only add that the emphasis of the film in following through on these staged male desires uncovers the paucity of both male art and an imaginary influenced by it. Madame, typically, does not figure in this fantasy at all; she is watching it. Definitely an alienated viewer, Madame Beudet refutes Doane's sense of the female spectator in classical cinema as being consumed by the images it offers. Madame's distance gives her some sense of perspective, control and authority over male images of females.

As female spectator, Madame sorts out the aesthetic valence attached to the female. We are led to understand that the male artist/female model underwrites this teleology of woman as aesthetics/desire. Madame is aesthetically unpackaged, she is not presented through other diegetic eyes except the director's contemplative intellectual view, or her own self-reflexive gaze in the mirror sequence where we see Madame through three mirror imagings. The presentation then refutes the aesthetic framing of women, not just through visual structurings, but also through the studied underplaying of Madame's physical presentation. She is dressed in a loose robe through the entire film. The smile could thus imply intellectual knowledge, or awareness of that hoax by which female matter becomes beauty and women are violently restrained from creating beauty.

This is confirmed by Monsieur's locking of the piano as a punishment for not coming to watch *Faust*. He also shuts her book early in the film. Dulac's rhythmic return to the trope of Madame's attempts to imagine, arrange, create a world introduce the sequence where the tennis player figures.

The two major non-diegetic sequences feature Monsieur Beudet prominently. In the first, he is receiving mail and gives Madame a magazine which is a departure point for her imagining of the floating car and tennis player. The second sequence with the phantom lover carries the weight of a fantasy for Flitterman-Lewis who maintains that Madame's double experiences the fantasy.

The non-narrative shots of the car floating in the room and the tennis player flying across the space interrupt Monsieur Beudet's harangue of Madame. These, we assume from the expression on both characters' faces, are routine. Monsieur bangs his fists on the table, raises his hands to his temple. Madame is shown in close-up, and has a particularly grim look to her, adding new meaning to the earlier complaisant smile. The tennis player moves, floats very slowly across the frame, the background is completely empty. The shot of the tennis player is not sutured to Madame's look and is totally unlike any kind of surreal dreamscape. Madame's back is to him, and she laughs manically as though triumphing over Beudet's relentless presence.

The music changes when the opera party leaves. Madame moves around the space and begins to read Baudelaire. When the maid leaves, she shifts the vase again, away from the centre to the edge. A medium-shot shows us the clock, symbol of her imprisonment, reinforced by the view of the prison, defined restriction of her horizons. She sits down in the chair and appears to doze. Although this is conventionally a mechanism with which to signal the entrance of the double, I hesitate to concur with Flitterman-Lewis that the whole sequence is experienced by the double. A sensuous, ill-defined figure comes to her; she raises her arms and smiles. This imaging is certainly surreal in its ambiguity and in its finessing of the two co-existing worlds of sleep and wakefulness. The former reading places Madame outside the register of the real, the latter allows for a relationship between the two. In any event, Madame raises her hands in a welcoming gesture, and smiles in certain sexual satisfaction. The director, however, pauses, for the whole sequence is completely saturated by Monsieur's insufferable constant presence. He floats in through the window, he is behind her, plays the suicide joke again, grimaces wildly. Shot 5 of this sequence is just a pair of eyes, enigmatic, suggesting perhaps some indication of visual primacy or freedom. In the narrative break-down of shots, shot 2 is of the phantom lover, and shot 4 has brought us back to shot 1 which is of Madame sleeping in her chair. Therefore we could expect shot 6 to be of the phantom lover again, but it is not. It is of Monsieur Beudet. Shot 7 takes us to her hands, and her playing with her rings, removing them and putting them back on, in direct reference to his hands on the pistol. Other images of Monsieur Beudet, coming in through the window, sitting at the table, glumly moving the vase to dead-centre, make Madame even more distraught. That none of these shots are sutured to her look gives them perceptual validity that seems to insist on the social.

Madame Beudet's subjectivity is guaranteed by her ability to read and interpret her own specific life and life more generally. Madame Beudet's fantasy of the tennis player, a matinee idol coming to her space, is drastically foreclosed by Monsieur Beudet's entrance into the space of fantasy. Her received images of desire mark the boundaries of erotic desire and stay within the conventional register but nevertheless allow us to interpret her desire within the realistic register of the diegesis more sharply. Madame Beudet desires to kill her husband. Where the earlier fantasies and daydreams had positioned her as a female spectator in a male theatre where the lawful husband curtails the flow of a socially sanctioned fantasy, when she places the bullets in Beudet's gun the rules of the game change. The narrative is no longer controlled by Monsieur Beudet although it will eventually be. Rather, it is controlled by Madame in a visible register but the caesura in the surreal representation of Madame's interiority emphasises the utopian without marking the move as either fantastic or phantasmic.

Madame Beudet's desires in the text that are not mimicries of male versions of female desire are played out in the social matrix, not the imaginary register. She does not eventually shoot her husband, but suffers remorse and wishes to unload the gun which is apiece with her earlier dreams. This is a complex rendition of female desire in its ambiguity and its foreclosure, particularly in its naming of the intervention of desire by the received discourse of desire which positions the female subject as receiving pleasure but remaining a spectator

Fig. 23: *The Smiling Madame Beudet* – Madame Beudet's dream-like state is interrupted by the insistence of the real on the unconscious; Monsieur Beudet makes repeated entrances, parodying the suicide joke – the close-ups of the hands draw our attention to Beudet's violence, and her sharp consciousness of her married status

of the show. The blockage of the desire to do away with Monsieur Beudet is self-imposed through the earlier register of received fantasy. Madame Beudet's execution of her plan, foolproof as it might be because of Monsieur Beudet's daily grotesque parody of suicide, would have carried her to violence. Within the terms of the text, the violence may well have lifted her act out of the range of desire into the register of social praxis or revolutionary protest. Ironically, Monsieur Beudet while replaying his daily joke lifts the gun and fires it in the air, believing that it is not loaded. The irony reaches a hysterical pitch for he concludes that she had intended to shoot herself. Madame Beudet is once again the spectator; the play she orchestrated has taken her back to spectating. Through the narrative, Monsieur Beudet threatens to kill himself and forces Madame Beudet to plead with him, to cringe from his violence. In both instances we are privy to the male desire to stage female desire.

Madame does introduce a new theme, but Monsieur Beudet's belief that she wished to commit suicide lends her the masochistic position and places her as the object of enunciation for the first time in the film's enunciative apparatus. However, the punishment for the transgression out of the space of received desire does not cancel out both the narrative and epistemological significance of Madame Beudet's desire. Dulac has presented two very different discourses on desire without privileging either, without making either dependent on the other, but establishing connections between the two that produce narrative resolution. The last shot shows us the unchanging horizon of the province even as the curtain goes down in their room marking the conclusion of the 'theatre'.

The self-conscious female subject, capable of interpreting her narrative, need not own her narrative but can own her desire while being inundated by the debris of the male desiring imaginary and be able to negotiate the two without resorting to madness or hysteria. Madame Beudet offers us an exemplary allegory of the mis-placing and mis-appropriation of female desire by the male interpreter. Not coincidentally, it offers us a theory of female spectatorship that is trans-coded in that it shows us that the female subject and the feminist spectator understand that the fantasy in the text was the desire to vanquish Monsieur Beudet, and that the meta-filmic text was the fantasy with the phantom lover. Our reading of the meta-filmic in the text alters with our placing of the 'real' as the space of desire in the text. The Smiling Madame Beudet's negotiation of desire within filmic narrative creates a space for female desire to be theorised by presenting two discourses, the diegetic (social) and the extra-diegetic (fantasy). The desire that emerges is not mixed in with the male erotic, nor with the moral, but with the purely daring, in not knowing what will happen when one completes the desire.

By refusing to prop up the female figure as desire in the diegesis through recourse to the extra-diegetic which underlines the construction, and by coding aesthetics in gendered terms whereby the artist is male, and the aesthetic supposedly female – a formulation that she shows the protagonist resisting – Dulac was able to open up film for renditions of female desire that had as yet not been conceived. The textual scene presented in the film, and the constitution of spectatorial subjectivity, challenges classical film's rendition of the female spectator as losing her ontological status through her submersion in the image. Dulac's protagonist sees the image, and resists it; Dulac herself does not give us an image we can sink into – rather she gives us a resisting reader who mockingly watches even herself as she plays along with a patriarchal script. The female spectator is thus not asked just to imagine a changed world, as Madame Beudet has, but to change it herself. As spectator, she has the authority.

Underdevelopment and Female Desire: Suzana Amaral's *Hour of the Star*

'The desire to desire'[26] in an art form that is predicated on the aestheticisation of male desire is difficult to frame within knowable models. Without specifying sexual and visual objectification of the female as the only possible visible form of subordination, and without articulating female desire as singular, or as only fantastic, Suzana Amaral explores the articulation between underdevelopment and female desire and subjectivity in her first feature film, *Hour of the Star* (*Hora de Estrela*, 1985).

The film bears out Mary Ann Doane's contention that the female's over-identification with the image is destructive, but with a twist. The underdevelopment of the female hero, her ethnic and national status, makes the desire for the image an act of subject formation. Her distance from the image is so great that bridging the distance would actually make her visible; indeed, exist. Having the authority to spectate thus does not guarantee subject status. The implausibility of the authority of vision is here challenged to suggest that the desires of the senses might be more instrumental in the constitution of female subjectivity. Visuality holds the promise of failure in this context, all the images already having been bought by North American metropolitan culture rendering identification with the image difficult for the subaltern woman who is the hero of the film.

Hour of the Star, about a northern 19-year-old retirante in the metropolitan south of Brazil, has been acknowledged for the subtlety of its portrayal of the migrant female and has been considered a breakthrough in that it specifically opened up new territory for women. Indeed, B. Ruby Rich regards it as a 'key' film in the 1980s films made by women, that constitutes an 'alternate formal engagement' with 'interiority'.[27] Nelson Perreira dos Santos's earlier film *Vidas secas* (1963), which was very much a part of the tradition of Cinema Novo, had been brutal in its exposure of the northerners' plight in the industrial south.[28] Amaral accomplished a similar feat for women workers and the film has been ana-lysed for its acute exploration of the gendered and ethnic subordination that the lead char-acter, Macabea, experiences. The film's portrayal of femininity and feminism is extremely different from other more popular constructions such as Carlos Diegues' *Xica* (1976), also a film about a female's desires, which has been critiqued by feminists for its representation of the lead black woman character. Amaral's film, set in contemporary times, is uninter-ested in the kind of history/nostalgia of black resistance that Diegues offers, and is quite distinct from popular Brazilian film for not using music.[29] Amaral's contribution in bring-ing to the cinema the lives of these retirantes, and more generally in the film, the lives of the working underclass, is all the more startling because the film does not render Macabea as an object of study, or as prey to her environment. In an interview with Michael Martin, the director discusses her sense of the lead character as subject.[30] Despite the almost un-nameable odds, Macabea is depicted wresting a new contemporary subjectivity for herself and other retirantes.

Critical discussions of Macabea's role in the film acknowledge the 'interior' dimension, or the exploration of the self, but largely view the film within the allegorical frameworks instituted by Cinema Novo. Ismael Xavier maintains that allegory had been central to Cinema Novo, and that 'tropicalismo' continued to work with allegorical questions.[31] Even as critics still view the films of the 1980s within this dominant paradigm, they also register the many differences; cynicism, parody and 'tropicalismo'. In noting that the big differ-ence between dictatorship and post-dictatorship is the difference between 'revolution' and 'revelation', B. Ruby Rich emphasises the role of women filmmakers in the new shift.[32] Her point of view is that 'interiority in this sense is not a retreat from society, but an altered formal engagement'.[33] Rich speaks of how the self itself that makes an impression on the national allegory has become characteristic of 1980s films and the textual relationship between self and state: 'Her [Macabea's] inchoate self becomes both a metaphor and a concrete representation of Brazil.'[34]

The reformatted national allegory sustained by the self but stamped by the mockery of 'tropicalismo' is the thematic of José Carlos Avellar's commentary on 1980s Brazilian film. Avellar considers Macabea the new Brazil, and interestingly also sees her as the image of the Brazilian cinema: 'Macabea is really much more than the sum of other strange characters. She is the image of the Brazilian, and of Brazilian cinema between the bye-bye and the hope for better days.'[35]

Notwithstanding these powerful claims to symbolisation of Macabea, the most compelling coming from the director herself, the emphasis in the film is on the tension between Macabea's allegorical role and her role as female subject. The cracks in the national allegory are significant, considering the very thematic of the north-easterner entering the urban south, which of course would be transposed to a Brazilian entering urban North America. In regarding Macabea as the 'image', 'symbol' or 'metaphor' of Brazil the notion of woman as the embodiment of nationhood is invoked, of woman as personifying the country, an old and hoary trope.[36] What is at stake in the Amaral film are the allegorical cracks. Macabea is not shown as bearing the burden of representation; she is shown as unable to represent herself. Perhaps her difficulty stems from the problems of having to create images without a self-image. In a very general way, this could fit Brazil, but then once again the female is left out of the historical space and does not have the opportunity to enter either history or cinema. As an anti-hero, someone who is acted upon, Macabea is as much female as she is retirante Brazilian and the sum of her desires exceeds both the realistic and the allegorical.

That Amaral portrays Macabea as representative of a large group of retirantes is unproblematic, but whether they are indeed metaphoric of the nation-state is highly questionable. Arguably, Amaral's distant camera lends Macabea signifying features, for instance that the meaning accrued is greater than her actions and gestures. However, these realistic sequences testify to the central thematic of the film which is Macabea's migration, her poverty and her desires. In exploring Macabea's desires, Amaral could well be exploring Brazil's, but the depth and diversity of her expression of Macabea's desires leads me to suggest that while the two may seem to intersect, it is the specificity and the excess of the retirante's desires that the film deliberately does not contain, but articulates in the registers of the realistic and the allegorical.

Amaral's style of filmmaking allows for a representation of the retirante woman without mythologising her or taking away from the possibilities of 'realistic' subjectivity for her. Cinema Novo of the 1960s had used a mixture of genres, and employed allegorical modes to retain a certain indigenous quality, and primarily to advance the cause of the people's liberation. A nationalist sentiment that was many times specifically invested in the marginal people, such as the north-easterners, certainly coloured the movement.[37] Working in the 1980s, Amaral displays a very different sensibility, despite its initial departure point in Cinema Novo. In the post-dictatorship period of 1984–85[38] movies again worked with the allegorical, but the allegorical was very often the butt of parody.[39] Allegory and non-realist filmmaking frequently came to mock both the state and the people. Although Amaral, in fact, uses some non-realistic techniques, for the most part she uses a realistic style, one that seems to challenge some of the nationalist aspirations of the 1960s cultural allegories. Certainly, the allegorical films, both during the dictatorship and after it, opted to present these models: of the people, of the left, of the populist, of the dictator.[40] Although *Hora de*

Hour of the Star is neither a nationalist allegory or a cultural one, Amaral has made a gesture toward symbolisation and allegory in her discussion of the protagonist Macabea:

> They [Brazilians] are anti-heroes in the sense that heroes are those who make history, and Brazilians don't make history. Brazilians suffer history … The film tells about Macabea, north-easterners, Brazilians and Brazil. Because Macabea is a great metaphor for Brazil. Macabea is Brazil.[41]

Curiously, in invoking history, Amaral brings up the subject, and in speaking of Macabea's larger significance in the national narrative, she claims that Macabea is Brazil, but does cast her in the film in realistic terms that problematise Macabea's metaphoricity and indeed represent her as definitively as a subject in history, whether maker or sufferer.

Amaral does not cast Macabea's experience in simplistic terms of the pure young woman worker's confrontation with the big, bad, corrupt city. The novel that Amaral based her film on, Clarice Lispector's *Hora de estrela*, does not in fact politicise Macabea's situation in the city to the extent that the film does, nor does it articulate her subjectivity in any overt way, for it is the subjectivity of the narrator that is at stake in the novel, and Macabea comes dangerously close to being both the object of his pity and his knowledge.[42]

Amaral, while not necessarily presenting Macabea's point of view, creates a context within which we can understand Macabea. Using her considerable experience as a documentary filmmaker, Amaral does produce a history of the *retirante* and in so doing also produces a desiring subject. In showing Macabea as a woman who has desires and in exploring these in their social context, Amaral creates a singular exploration of the relationship between female desire and Western capitalist commodity underdevelopment. Cileine I. De Lourenco notes that the film 'places the displaced protagonist on the margins of the industrialised modern south-eastern city'.[43] The film works through the notions of what female desire is in underdeveloped contexts, and again, how the production of this desire creates a new urban subject; indeed, how desire defines the new urban subject.

Metropolitan underdevelopment, in the sense of socio-political, industrial, cultural and Western capitalist, provides the context of Macabea's difference from the urban workers. The director uses a distant, even realistic, camera to show Macabea's living and working conditions. And as Amaral is exterior to the diegesis in recording Macabea's living conditions, so is she exterior to Macabea's experience of the city. She does not presume to intuit Macabea's 'alienation' or 'discomfiture'. Interestingly, except for one poignant entrance into Macabea's interiority, we do not have access to it. With this move, Amaral watches her and registers her response and interprets it, but by placing herself as mediator, she leaves open the possibility of a truth incompletely told, or yet to be told. Amaral does not confer subjectivity on Macabea: instead, she records Macabea's increased understanding of how her subjectivity is being constituted in the city, how it is being challenged, and how it is being reconfigured.

Combined with the puzzlement of geographic displacement that Macabea experiences, the sense of desire, terribly undernourished and directed by urban culture, mixed in with a sensuality that is again redirected by urban culture, begins to frame Macabea's urban experience. The underdevelopment of the north has meant that both Macabea and Olimpico, the male retirante that she meets, have been very poor and had no exposure to metropolitan culture but some exposure to consumer goods. Amaral links that sense of underdevelopment with Macabea's early introduction to desire.

An early sequence of Macabea arriving at her new quarters marks the gap between her and her fellow workers. A woman at the rooming house comments that Macabea does not have much stuff, to which Macabea replies that since she has now got a job, she will be able to buy things. The buying of things, yet to be mentioned, broaches the subject of the underdevelopment of desire. Even as Macabea tries to figure out what things she wants to buy, her physicality and its demands are noted by the director. The volatile mix of what she wants and what she consumes shows the radical nature of her desires – desires that evolve rapidly, and meaningfully, but without the knowledge of desire that allows desire to be named, fulfilled and culturally acknowledged as legitimate. The opening sequence shows Macabea wiping her nose on her blouse repeatedly; a follow-up sequence shows her frontally alternately wolfing and biting away at a sandwich whose fillings are around her mouth. A shot of the cat urgently insistent about her demands seems to link Macabea's appetite for the burger to the cat's. Macabea has clearly not eaten too well in her life; her boss, Mr Raimundo is in the background of the frame watching her eat. While he does not express his distaste through facial gesture, the camera's pause on Macabea in a medium close-up notes the otherness of Macabea. Mr Raimundo's request that Macabea wash her hands points to the urban code that Macabea does not recognise. Peeing in the slop jar and simultaneously eating, not showering, gorging herself on food, over-creaming her coffee are all indices of her dislocation, and her relative indifference or lack of perception of the cultural code.

Moving almost rhythmically between the desires that Macabea physically expresses and the desires that she begins to experience, Amaral follows Macabea's journey in the city towards claiming an identity. Amaral builds this theme by using the trope of reflection and punctuates Macabea's urban development through a focus on her mirror image.[44]

The first reflection we see of her is in a dirty, smudged mirror after Mr Raimundo has asked her to wash her hands. The filthy bathroom is as much a comment on the retirante's life as is the almost distorted reflection. In her quarters, we see her reflected in a clean mirror, but in double reflections, wearing a sheet, masquerading as a bride. Both first and second reflections are crucial in her construction of her identity, but both are images that 'other' her, and paradoxically in othering her, they give her a sense that she would like to be seen. It would be too facile to say that the first reflection, among the first she has in the city, is solely instrumental in crafting a self-consciousness, or even providing a clue as to its genesis, but following as the reflection does Macabea's tracking of desire, it works to bring her into the world of public or cultural desire. Unlike other feminist films, such as *The Smiling Madame Beudet*, where the mirror images serve to underline the woman's self-consciousness, and hence her subjectivity, in *Hour of the Star* the reflections serve to accentuate the woman's otherness and her awareness of public culture.

The mirror images do, however, also serve as a more direct entry into Macabea's increasingly urgent sense of urban self-consciousness. Amaral's technique of filming Macabea makes the use of the mirror trope crucial. In showing Macabea's responses to the urban stimuli, Amaral uses an almost static camera that does not immediately interpret Macabea's emotions. Macabea's face is almost uniformly uninformative about her reactions; yet it is also unbearably expressive in showing no social response, and in showing an almost intolerable inability to reveal her interiority. Critics have viewed this strategy as a commentary on Macabea's lack of intelligence, but Amaral's restraint in showing Macabea's emotion is complicated by her expressivity when she is on her own. Those sequences, when Macabea is on her own, of which there are many, approximate moments of recognition of her newly emerging urban self.

An early sequence that sparks Macabea's sexual identity illustrates Amaral's success in figuring Macabea's urban consciousness without recourse to social expressivity. Macabea's co-worker, Gloria, gives a male sexual partner news of her pregnancy and asks him for money for an abortion. Amaral shoots this sequence with Macabea in the centre of the frame, observing Gloria and listening to the conversations. Macabea's face shows more interest when she is eavesdropping than when Gloria actually speaks to her. When Gloria asks Macabea if she has had an abortion and tells her that she herself has had five, and been sexually active since she was been fifteen, Amaral's camera holds on Macabea's face which shows intensity, but a very diffuse intensity that marks her as an intent observer rather than as an emotion-filled interlocutor. In a later sequence when Macabea is on her own, she twirls a sheet around her head, laughs, dances and when interrupted twice, answers deadpan. But to the mirror she says, 'I am a virgin, a typist, and like coca-cola' – her status in order of sexuality, profession and participation in the urban consumer culture. A brilliant rapid cut from the mirror image to a black mannequin in a wedding dress with a rapt Macabea looking at the window links her awareness of the self to the urban. Regarded as quintessentially modern, the moment of window-shopping here shows the moment of identification and distance. The rapidity of the cut from the Macabea to the mannequin would seem to indicate absorption in the image, but the shot of Macabea looking returns to the thematic of Macabea learning to look, to spectate and hence build some semblance of an urban identity.

The sequence in her living quarters is full of animation, shot just a little faster than the otherwise slow rhythm the film is shot in, and dwells on Macabea's face as the other sequences do, but this sequence shows control of physicality, grace and a liveliness that the others lack. The doubled images of Macabea in the reflection are the focus of the shot. The camera pulls back from focusing first on Macabea's double image, and then on a single reflection, and then on Macabea's face, before we come back to the realistic space of her living quarters. The mannequin, interestingly black, is not interposed in these shots; the doubled images of Macabea indicating a self-consciousness, comparable to that of Madame Beudet's in the fantasy sequences in the Dulac film. Typically, in other sequences that show Macabea on her own, without a sense of her own otherness (or her urbanness), Macabea appears to be controlled by her physicality. Although Amaral does not equate physicality with the rural north, it is hardly coincidental that scenes where Macabea is in control are also sequences which are conscious of urban values, in the glory of being able to participate in them. Amaral certainly does not suggest that either Macabea or Olimpico are naively nostalgic about the rural north, and she herself is not; however, control of physicality is linked with urban mores. Amaral does not reverse the clichéd connection of physicality with the rural; rather, she shows how the physical is a conduit to the urban.

The trope of physicality is reconfigured in urban spaces and intersects with the director's presentation of Macabea as observer, as with Macabea's own perception of herself as an observer. In her outings with Gloria, we see Macabea noting Gloria's feminine physical address to men, her call and their response. These sequences are shot in the manner of the office sequences, in settings without too much detail, and with a non-expressive, observant Macabea centred in the frame.

The director calls attention to Macabea's newly understood concept of being looked at.[45] The sequence opens with Macabea sitting at a coffee counter. A clever, symmetrical shot of the classical shot/reverse-shot trajectory opens with Macabea's glance falling on a man in a coffee counter. He appears to return the look and Macabea's face bears a semblance to Gloria's face when she is being looked at – pleased, conscious. The next cut shows the man walking toward her, but the shot/reverse-shot trajectory has been neatly parodied; the man is blind. This is followed by yet another complex parody of the male gaze trajectory that underlies classical mainstream filmmaking.

One central sequence, much discussed because of its rendition of Macabea's sensuality, illustrates the remapping of her physicality. Macabea is at the train station, and like Gloria who had been sighted by men, wants to be looked at. A clever point-of-view shot of the station guard lures the viewer into believing that she is going to be approached by the guard. A slow cut to the guard, and the camera follows him in the film's customary measured rhythm. The guard approaches Macabea only to tell her that she should stand behind the yellow line. She pauses, and then abruptly moves backward. On the train, however, she is in control of her physicality and relatively rapid cuts show her enjoying the press of bodies in the train. Here, her face is suffused with pleasure and satisfaction; she has told her co-workers that she likes to ride the metro.

The camera shows Macabea flush between two men, her head close to their upper arms. It cuts from left to right, repeats the shot, pauses on the fourth shot, and then focuses on the underarm hair. As the camera moves to and fro between the men, Macabea's head moves with it, richly enjoying the sensations produced by her physical proximity to them. Her face makes it clear that her senses have mingled to give her pleasure; smell, touch, sight, hearing. She is, of course, silent. That night, Macabea masturbates and then makes the sign of the cross. The sensuality of the experience is underlined by a lingering last shot of the males' underarm hair.

Macabea's desire 'to be looked at' has been produced by the city, redirecting her sensuality. The city has also created other desires in her, the most important being the need to know and to connect with this new world. The diegetic voice-over from Time Radio that opens the film attests to her demand for a newer, different cognisance of the world.

While the 'looks' register the protagonist's investment in being looked at, the auteur follows another trope crucial to Macabea's exploration of the city and the constitution of urban subjectivity. Giuliana Bruno's insight about flânerie, the trope of walking and observing which gives the subject a sense of urban pleasure and a stake in public space through looking, is relevant here. When females practiced flânerie, they were of course considered prostitutes, hence the question about the taboo of women walking in modern spaces: 'Is the mobile gaze male?'[46] Bruno's discussion on the moveable, as opposed to fixed, spectator of film theory is also provocative in terms of conceiving of Macabea as the mobile spectator breaking taboos. Macabea takes over the mobile gaze when she steps out into the city and casts a roving eye on everyone and everything, even as she herself wants masculine attention. Interestingly, she grabs it; what she enjoys is terribly sensuous and to be had in the city, the press and touch of bodies, what Bruno calls 'wandering through erotic geographies'.[47]

Amaral contextualises Macabea's specificity by introducing and developing the character of the male retirante, Olimpico. Olimpico, who is also from the north, has aspirations that are tragically absurd: really making an impact in the urban south and of becoming rich. Macabea's desires are simultaneously greater than his, in being diverse and unnamed, and paradoxically nonexistent in being unnamed. Macabea's chief source of conversation is to refer to the snippets she gets from Time Radio. Olimpico's responses to her conversation are initially to express bewilderment, but finally to condemn her for asking too many questions. Two of his most telling comments are clearly meant to intimidate her, although they do not succeed. Olimpico's definition of algebra is that it is for faggots. The whorehouse, he says at another juncture, is full of women who ask questions. Olimpico knows what he wants from the city and proudly proclaims the sense of grandeur he has achieved, at least in part, because of the city.

The seeming guilelessness, and the expansiveness of Macabea's desire, provides a perfect cover for her to challenge normative male migrant behaviour and the received wisdom of assimilation in the city. More specifically, in a bizarre way, Macabea challenges Olimpico, and exceeds the conventional female role. We have already had an inkling of the retirante's resistance when she opts to go riding in the subway rather than to the zoo. Macabea's questions, prompted by Time Radio, cross seamlessly into questions of assimilation and identity. In a banal exchange with Olimpico, she says, 'I am not much of a person ... I am not used to it.' Quite clearly, identity is something one gets used to, and Macabea herself is aware of being interpellated. Her later 'Am I what I am?' seems to echo a more modernist sense of alienation which nevertheless has been given a history as that of the female retirante. Macabea's 'craziness', as Olimpico would have it, combined with her status as an 'observer', or a nonparticipant, enables her to see beyond the simple consumer dream that Olimpico has, but of course does not give her much leverage in a world that she does want to grab and to have. And in terms of her gender, she wants the look returned; indeed, wants to give up her observer position, but can do so only in one wild moment when Olimpico picks her up and she flies. But we see his face, and it is not a pretty sight.

The auteur does give Macabea one other moment of transcendence in the film, the final moment when she is filmed as the movie star she wants to be. And she is shot in total mimicry of the female hero, hair blowing in the wind, running into the arms of a blond, blue-eyed hero/saviour. The sequence can only be read parodically, given the manner in which the rest of the film is shot.

The most enigmatic sequences of the film are those which are fabricated, that are setups rather than realistic registers of Macabea's life. The fortune-teller sequences and the concluding sequence are shot in a different mode. The former uses expressionistic lighting to set it apart, the latter golden, obviously recognisable cinematic lighting to indicate its special status as 'film'. Granted Cinema Novo of the 1960s had never balked from the magical or the mythical in its attempts to stay connected to indigenous cultural roots. Amaral's

Fig. 24: *Hour of the Star* – the fabular conclusion to the film, mocking the idea of the poor Brazilian woman finding the handsome gringo prince; the shot itself is clichéd and shows Macabea rising from the dead to float into her North American lover's arms

rendition of the sequence is scarcely romantic or empowering, but is nevertheless ambiguous because it is not clearly parodic. The older woman does make contact with the younger one, but her message is clearly urban, and overwhelmingly romantic. In some profound sense, the fortune-teller is Macabea's urban guide – telling her what she wants, and telling her that what she gets will far exceed whatever her initial hopes with Olimpico had been. While not parodying Macabea, Amaral does seem to be making a cynical commentary about how the message of the 'people' had changed from cultural nationalism to rampant market capitalism. Interestingly, the 1960s Cinema Novo group – Glauber Rocha, Carlos Diegues *et al.* – would have condemned the capitalism as colonialism and argued for an indigenous, as opposed to a market, culture to strengthen a political and cultural nationalism, but Amaral is reticent about critiquing Macabea in these terms. Rather, she seems to point to the failure of nationalism to deliver to the north-east, particularly the women, for whom the nationalist message may have been a matter of indifference. In this context it is important to note that despite the message of liberation of the peasantry and the 'people', with some notable exceptions Cinema Novo did little with the roles of women.[48]

In terms of the diegesis itself, at one level, the fortune teller promises Macabea love and fortune and happiness;[49] a prediction shabby in its triteness, but at another level, the fortune teller tells Macabea that she, Macabea, has a pretty name, and would marry a gringo. The cross-cutting between the gringo and Macabea, straight after Macabea is run over, is cynical in its complete parody of such a possibility for a very poor retirante women. Amaral herself comments on the concluding sequence: 'So the end is deliberately styled on advertising. It's intentional that the end has nothing to do with the film.'[50] By the same token, the 'realistic' ending of Macabea dying while crossing the street is equally inadequate to the plot except that like the fairytale ending, it too shows that her earlier urban desires have been remapped by longings that are both fantastical and cynical.

The 'death' at the end of the film can be read very much as a postmodern moment, leaving the text open rather than closed. The stylised hit and run is the obverse of the fairytale ending in its dark note, but an equally unrealistic counterpoint, suggesting that identification with the image can only be disastrous. According to this reading, Macabea is free to ride the subway again. The stylised conclusion, inset in the aesthetics of Cinema Novo, provides a way out of her impasse, suggesting an alienated condition, but one that certainly registers a sense of self, which is unavailable to the retirante before her acknowledgement of urban desires.

The Female Intellectual and the Sexual Mountain: Kathleen Collins' *Losing Ground*

Given that women's desires have been difficult to present in non-schematic ways, women directors have found highly codified ways of making women's desires apparent. Specifying these desires out of the realm of the fantastic, but still with reference to fantasy, Dulac and Amaral have been successful in naming women's desires, and have plotted them within androcentric frames of reference, partly to acknowledge the audacity of these desires and their place in the social. Kathleen Collins' *Losing Ground* (1982) moves towards recording women's desires with reference to male articulation of desire, but not in connection with their fulfilment; the discourse of desire being cast in terms of the creative endeavour. The pursuit of any kind of creative venture by the characters we meet, almost every last one of them an artist, is framed by seemingly bracketed comments on the relationship between the black artist and his/her art. Collins has been considered a literary filmmaker, and indeed is regarded as the first black woman filmmaker in recent history to work with narrative in *The Cruz Brothers and Miss Malloy* (1980).[51] *Losing Ground* is both literary and painterly, and brings in the black social subject in the role of the artist. The film explores the process by which women come to identify their desires, and how these might be overdetermined by both race and gender.

The authority of the female spectator, considered crucial to the construction of female subjectivity, is never at issue in this film which positions the protagonist as an authority capable of great detachment from the image. The film departs company from both Dulac and Amaral's acknowledgement of the destructiveness of the image, and over-identification with it. The film's insight is that identification, or over-identification, need not necessarily be problematic; rather the loss of the ego's boundaries in the merger with the woman/image may result in richer understandings of the self through understanding other women.

The film revolves around Sara, a teacher of philosophy, and her relationship to her intellectual life. Her husband, Victor, an artist, has just won an award for painting, and is now set to go to Riverview, New York for the summer to develop his art through portraiture and landscape in a remarkable shift from his previous commitment to abstract art. Sara, during this time, questions her desires and reviews her life and her own sense of self.

Fig. 25: *Losing Ground* – Sara plays the role of both intellectual and artist; equally passionate in both roles

The opening of the film establishes Sara's intellectual authority and passion. Medium shots show her discoursing fluently on Existentialism while her students listen intently, none more so than the young man who comes to her after class, discusses Jean Genet, and disconcerts Sara by telling her that he hopes her husband appreciates her. The comment, followed by a similar one later by a female student who also finds the professor inspirational would seem to initiate a line of questioning in the professor who teaches the 'absurd' world view of some of the Existentialists. While the questions of the students may enable the professor to understand the personal, and even gendered, appeal of her teaching of philosophy and experience, in privileging 'the husband and his appreciation' of her, the students replicate fairly stereotypical norms in implying, however vaguely, that the splendour of Sara's achievements would somehow not be complete without the husband's valuation of her. Equally subtly, their gratitude for her enthusiasm also conspires to devalue her intellectually.

Collins' painterly style, and her compositions which resemble paintings, offer an uneasy reflection on women intellectuals. Sara tells the young man that Genet is a marginal playwright/philosopher who understands the marginal experience, a comment that has resonance for Sara as a black intellectual woman, and for the student, as for most of the characters in the film. Almost no one supports her intellectual life, and indeed the painterly attributes of Collins' visual style, too, seem to militate against the 'abstract', a concept that both Sara, and her artist husband, Victor, struggle with, particularly regarding representational issues. Sara, of course, deals with the abstract, being a professor of philosophy. The artistic world created by Collins in the loft apartment with its abstract paintings, in Riverview shot through Victor's point of view as dream paintings and the picture postcard framings of the quaint, the coloured and the local, diminish Sara. That setting disempowers her, unlike the classroom setting, the fairly restricted space of her office, the small arch around her mother's dining table, and even the perfectly Renaissance perspective of her in the library, all of which give her some authority. Granted that these compositions too are centred, and that the effect of the still life dominates, the sound of Sara's voice speaking influences each of the latter sequences and removes her from having to be the painting or the aesthetic object to be viewed. If the film were to be seen as a quarrel between the painterly and the oral discursive, it is clear that the discursive permits Sara to express herself, not the artistic, which, as defined by Victor, would leave Sara out of the loop, except as one of Victor's artistic object choices.

In a conversation between the couple, Collins pinpoints the manner in which art is defined by both Sara and Victor as what Victor does. What emerges from the conversation is the explicit admission that Sara's intellectual work is not as important as Victor's artistic work. Sara, annoyed with Victor's plans for them to spend the summer outside New York City, asks if she would merit consideration if she were an artist. Interestingly, her resentment of Victor is first mumbled to the mirror in the bedroom, and then yelled out to Victor who is not in the bedroom. She is not in the same space as he when she puts her question about the library, but first off-screen, and then away from him when she protests his lack of consideration, an indication of her lack of assurance, and her acceptance of his values. Indeed, she had already asked him about the library when the plan had first come up, before Victor had even visited Riverview, and had been brushed aside. Dishearteningly, even her mother tells her later, when they are celebrating 'the genuine Negro success', to give up her abstractions and write a play about her, the mother. Sara's intellectual life is devalued in very obvious ways.

Among Sara's intellectual projects is a paper she is writing on ecstasy. The research she is undertaking for the paper makes her question her own lack of intimate knowledge of ecstasy, and compels her to begin her search to understand ecstasy, if not to find it. Her intellectual quest is presented in the context of a group of visual and performing artists who surround her. Her mother is an actor, and one of the students in her class is a would-be-filmmaker. He compares her to Pearl McCormick and wants her to star in his film. Initially amused, she is later intrigued, and later irritated, we assume, by Victor's singular and individualistic pursuit of ecstasy, and decides to give it a try. Duke, the man she meets in the library who brings her out of her raptness, once interested in philosophy/theology, is now an out-of-work actor. He comments that he had given up a secure living, perhaps to find himself, or to lose himself. At any rate, he too is a performer. Carlos, a minor character, and Victor's mentor in abstract art, is a painter, and Celia dances, if not professionally. Frankie and Johnny in the film within the film are of course vaudeville artists, and also dancers.

The film makes subtle distinctions between art forms and associates painting, as presented in the film, with the masculine; ironically directing with the masculine, and acting with both the masculine and feminine.

Two women pose for the male artist, Victor. The thematic of the aesthetic as woman is replayed without any great conviction except to reconfirm the role of the artist as male and the role of the aesthetic object as female.[52] Both Sara and Celia are painterly objects, and moreover shot through the painter's eyes. However, the very presence of the female in the scene of painting appears to disrupt the pure form of the artistic as conceived by Carlos and Victor. Women's presence in the painting begins 'to represent', to move away from art, the purity of the form, line, colour and the artist's imagination, or what is in his 'head'. Victor's shift away from the abstract to the representational, to portraiture of the concrete, women and houses signals the move to referencing the representational, apparently a conflicted move for Carlos in terms of its impurity, and its search of narrative. In the midst of the classic discussion on the relative virtues of abstraction versus mimesis, Victor stops and points to Celia walking up the street in a perfectly painterly composition; he laughs and challenges Carlos to find 'that' in his head. Victor's ecstatic glow, the feeling of being born again, seeing through new eyes is impelled by his *seeing*; by the representational. The composition is arranged perfectly. Victor paints Sara, slightly elevated and partly framed against the window. The depth and richness of colour, the self-conscious blocking and the shadows that lend Sara translucent glow are overtly presented as constructed. The painterly sequences are presented from Victor's point of view and make no claim to any kind of realism. Victor sees painting, not reality. The eye is the conduit for the ecstasy that Sara craves. Victor says more than once that he feels like he is walking in a dream. His eye offers him pleasure, not knowledge. Collins' technique of the incandescent lighting, the comment on it – 'Are you pretty, or is it just the light' – and the response – 'you want a murder the first week in this house?' – and the taking over of nature by art, questions the acquisition of knowledge through vision. Victor sees, but what he sees is another matter.

Celia is also painted in carefully posed framing; in the outdoors in another obviously arranged scenario, a medium close-up of Celia is again shown from Victor's point of view. Both subjects object to the stillness; Sara threatens murder because of Victor's comments, and Celia complains about how she's never going to be able to move again. The portraits clearly pause the animation of the women, rendering them into beautiful still lives, or in the French 'nature morte', fixed by the male artist. An amusing interchange between Sara and Victor that takes place in bed touches on Victor's sense of his own creativity and Sara's response to it. Victor returns to the hoary myth of man fashioning woman:

Victor: There's a place in the Bible where they talk about woman fashioned from the rib of man… (Sara looks up at him) That's how you sleep… (pointing) right against my rib cage….

Sara: And that makes you feel exceptionally creative, like you fashioned me…

Victor: I notice it.[53]

The comment shows Sara's awareness of, and understated bitterness at, Victor's ego. Victor's observation about how 'right' Sara is standing by the window adds value to Sara in Victor's eyes because she is now an artistic or aesthetic object.

The portrait as an art form isolates the woman from the group,[54] takes her out of a social context[55] and renders her vulnerable to the creative fantasy, a difficulty unacknowledged in much traditional visual critique. The insistence on painting the painterly scenes through point-of-view shots is certainly not accidental, but calls into question the long-standing Western belief that knowledge is revealed through vision. Collins, however, does seem to make a distinction between kinds of vision; the vision of modernity, the moving camera conscious of its attempt to construct reality and the older tradition that presented 'truth'. The young male film student seems to be able to capture a semblance of reality through illusion, through film. The self-consciousness of the filmmaker offers an implied contrast to Victor and the concept of the artist's vision as unmediated. The technological apparatus and its mediation is in that sense more enriching, in being able to convey the truth of what is *seen*, rather than what *one* sees. Without claiming ontological completeness for the object the cinematic apparatus records, one can argue that the 'objectness' of the object, that is, representability, can come through in a way high modernism refused. It is important to note that the response to high modernism is not through a reprisal of classical realism or neorealism but through folklore and performance, through the student's filming of the Frankie and Johnny vaudeville routine.

Quite often, Sara is shot through male eyes, the artist first, the monocular vision of George, and then of course the camera of the film within the film. Jonathan Crary's comment, 'Vision is always multiple, adjacent to and overlapping with other objects, desires and vectors', throws light on how the complex and multiple mechanisms of each item employed overdetermines the visual presentation of Sara.[56] The film within the film obviously contests the realist claims of the camera in general by focusing on performance, gestural movement and emotion in the Frankie and Johnny sequences, by the instructions of the director which then interrupt the seamlessness of the visual, the truth value of what has been filmed, but which nevertheless elevates the film within the film as carrying a truth hitherto undiscovered and unrepresented.

Victor's rapture when he comes back from Riverview is almost offensive to Sara in its exclusion of her. She says that it is like being with a horn player blowing his horn all day, clearly wrapped up in his own 'private vision', almost in a 'trance'. The search for this kind of experience becomes important to Sara because she is led to believe that the intellectual experience is insufficient, even though she herself says confidently that she does feel that 'tremendous leap', but then concludes that it is too abstract.

Sara's research on ecstatic experience is intense, and personal. We hear her words on ecstasy spoken with such concentration that we could perhaps understand that such loss of oneself in other material is ecstasy. She observes too that the ecstatic moment is after the fact. The voice-over and Sara's absorption in her work lend her the same authority as the first sequences showing her in her classroom and office did. The scene ends with the shot held on her until the gentle fade. The cuts in film work much like scene breaks, particularly in the extensive use of off-screen sound and voice-overs which tend to undercut the dominance of the visual apparatus and recall the effect of the drama where sound and human form were as important as the visual, and signified more, the visual pictorialising the sound.

Another key use of off-screen sound occurs as a motivational device in the Riverview sequences. Sara overhears Victor and Celia in off-screen space quarrelling about Celia's lack of stillness for the portrait. Collins catches the atmosphere through a combination of Sara's half-annoyed, half-tense face and the noisy clamour of the absorbed exchange between the other two. The next scene beautifully elucidates the distance that has sprung up between them.

The camera pans rhythmically from Sara at one end of the table, past the wine, dish, candle, butter, flower, candle and wine, to Victor. The camera pauses on each item before it stops, suspended over the flowers in the middle. Their distance is due to their conversation on Celia, who is Puerto Rican, masked in terms of whether Puerto Ricans are of African heritage.

Sara's decision to make the film for the student, George, takes her away from Riverview into a fictional world of art and passion. The gentleman who plays the role of Johnny to Sara's Frankie, Duke, is attentive to her intellectual comments, and they share an easy rapport. Sara claims that she does not understand what the film is about, but says that it is a 'tragic mulatto' part, a reminder to us of Victor's tart comment to her: 'Put the mulatto crisis on hold.' Sara is framed by skyscrapers in this film within a film, and is either dancing, talking or watching Johnny. In the film, she does seem to lose herself, absorbed as she is in identifying with Frankie without commenting on it.

The trope of acting, as empathising with another, the Stanislavsky-like school of acting, is important to Collins' depiction of what is at stake for Sara in her search for ecstasy. Early in the film, after Sara, annoyed by Victor's indifference to her intellectual needs, says that she could have been another Dorothy Dandridge, the significance of the art form is registered. George compares her to the earlier black actor, Pearl McCormick, which obliquely inspires Sara's comment. Sara as Frankie watches Johnny go through the same moves with the other woman that he does with her. Slowly she loses herself completely in the role, experiences the anguish, the rage, the sorrow, the passion of Frankie, understands that Frankie will not be a toy to be picked up and put out when she blows Johnny, played by Duke, away. Ecstasy does not need to be solitary, egotistic or without connection to other people. Through identification, Sara experiences an artistic and emotional ecstasy, an intellectual experience that is both abstract and personal.

Clearly the film is meta-referential of Sara's own relationship with Victor who gets into a sleeping bag with a protesting Celia in Sara's presence. Sara's mood shifts from politeness to sheer anger. In her icy fury, she makes a connection, a leap; she comes to an understanding of his ecstasy when she says that for Victor art is sexualised, and visible:

> Don't fuck around then… don't take that giant dick of yours out and fling it willy-nilly here and there like it was *artistic*… pointing it at trees, and lakes, and women… like it was some artsy-craftsy *paintbrush*… I got nothing to take out, god damn it… that's what's uneven, that I got nothing to take out![57]

Sara's apprehension that for Victor art is the use of an instrument to capture the artistic object is presented in gendered terms, with the landscape itself being feminised because of the artist's attempt to mould it with his instrument.

When Sara finds ecstasy, it will be through an empathy with other women. The other woman in the Frankie/Johnny routine imitates Frankie, wants to be Frankie, not only because of Johnny, but because of Frankie. In the diegesis, while Celia does not make the same moves as Sara, because of the other woman's imitation of Frankie, her subsumption of herself in Frankie, the distance between Sara and Celia is abridged. Note that there is no question of Frankie blowing the other woman away. Sara, Frankie and the other woman share common ground.

Identification, the loss of oneself in the character on stage, in the ego ideal, has been regarded as coercive in reconfirming the ideological status quo, or assimilating the Other as oneself. Yet for women this scenario might play itself out differently. While Mary Ann Doane's formulation points to the difficulties of retaining a sense of female self because of over-identification with the image, the film offers another reading of the process of merger of the self. Because women in patriarchal societies are encouraged to view other women literally as Other women, as competitors for men, empathy may in fact, by abridging distance, affect social change. Sara is not like either Frankie or Celia, so her identification with them, with Celia through the role of Frankie, may seem stretched if one assumes that the Other has to be assimilated, or that identification has to follow the Aristotelean model of identifying that results in sameness. Kaja Silverman, in her discussion of the Brechtian alienation model that challenged the Aristotelean so decisively, suggests that heteropathic identification can ensue in change because of bodily loss, a possibility that Brecht refuses by keeping the stage so separate from the audience.[58] In Sara's case, she is of course acting the role, not watching it, but her experience does result in the boundaries of the body being challenged. Silverman, in her discussion on political ecstasy, is convinced that such radical alterity allows the subject to love, without subsumption of the Other.[59] The film, through Sara's acting, challenges that gendered model of distance between artist and subject favoured by Victor as authentic art and offers a different model that allows for ecstasy.

Victor does eventually watch Sara being filmed, but not through his eyes. He finds that art is suffused with emotion, not just the need for narrative he has so recently begun to feel; and in narrative, Victor replays the story of the male artist and the female model.

The role of the black artist is imbricated in this decisive shift from the abstract to the representational. The first sequence in Sara's and Victor's apartment, completely dominated by Victor's abstract paintings, colour and lighting, rather than direct narrative/cultural reference is supplemented by a voice articulating a manifesto on the black artist and his freedom to paint what he wishes. Clearly the racial burden is a serious factor even if the characters do not openly discuss it, except to mock the pressures put on them to fit mainstream views of the black artist's function. Victor's success is celebrated mockingly as a 'genuine Negro success', Sara's mother complains about not being able to do realistic roles; they all make fun of the 'shuffle along' roles given to blacks in musicals and other productions. Even Sara wants to mock the stereotype by saying 'blimp' at a department meeting. Duke notes that when he first got into film, there were no Negro films, that the artist was primary, not his race. Each person resists the expectations placed on a black artist to represent the race, or to represent what ought to be spoken about by blacks. Yet Collins comes back to the cultural and the representational through Sara who moves from the 'boys' – Hegel and Kierkegaard – to the African American version of Frankie and Johnny in a stylised black avant-garde film before she can experience that ecstasy she craves.

The African American expressive arts, the vaudeville tradition, are here being memorialised, a tribute on the part of both Collins and George, the filmmaker within the film. The filming of the artistic performance, not the first in the film, given that Celia dances watched by Victor, expresses perhaps the suppliancy of the filmic itself, the visuality promised by the filmic apparatus, to the other senses, including the auditory and tactile. Given that there is no dialogue, or only punctuating dialogue in the Celia dance movement and the Frankie and Johnny dance routine, the filming is self-consciously reminiscent of primitive cinema with its anxieties about being unable to fold in the human voice and the inadequacy of the visual. Yet the sequence seems finally to come to a complementary understanding of how the mechanical reproduction can actually preserve the authentic work of art, the performance, and keep the folkloric alive in the most urgent living way by which it helps people make sense of their lives.

Acting is foregrounded as an art form that can bring one to ecstasy. That women have to find their sense of selves in other women, or fantasise as in *The Smiling Madame Beudet*, to realise their wishes and to come to themselves would seem disturbing if one were to follow the model of the male 'I', abridged by its own ego boundaries. However, if one conceived of the dissolution of the ego as a way to become oneself, Sara's identification with Frankie and subsequent expression would nevertheless take us to ecstasy without implicating the dominance/subservience model of much male art history. Considering that Sara (Frankie) does blow Duke (Johnny) away, the very violence might not preclude the dominance/subservience model. Yet the violence is extra-diegetic, explosive as it is, and is used to show the limits of experience and the annihilation that results, the extreme danger of art itself; not the conquest of the artistic object. The film concludes by holding on Sara in medium close-up, leaving us to wonder if she has found herself as artist and intellectual.

We do know that she will not cover old ground. Staying in New York for five days she has staked a claim to her own space. While *The Smiling Madame Beudet* concludes with Madame's sense that she has exchanged a frightful life sentence for another by not killing her husband, Sara's (Frankie's) killing of Duke (Johnny) in the performative piece releases her to understand what letting go of Victor might mean. After killing Duke, Sara expresses the grief she would feel under the circumstances and hence finds herself through art which suffuses her in a way that it could not for Madame Beudet. Madame Beudet seeks to escape her husband, Sara seeks to find ecstasy and discovers that the male artistic ego curbs female venturing, and that the male model is insufficient for her. While Kathleen Collins does not explicitly connect the intellectual with the artistic, the tradition of empathy, identification and loss of oneself would seem to point in that direction. Moreover, in the terms of the rapture Sara experiences while reading and writing, comparable to her acting, the intellectual is bound to the artistic. Unlike the unmediated visual which is seen as controlling and masculine, for women, the ecstatic is understood as the folding of the intellectual, artistic and emotional.

Through art, the woman has found the spectatorial position inadequate, rather than authorising, and has found a new authority in taking action. It does seem disconcerting that her authority should not be based on the intellectual; however, that can be read as a critique of masculine intellectual traditions, now enriched by Sara's altered understanding of empathy and ecstasy. Control, especially over the artistic object, cannot be a positive intellectual trait, especially when the pleasure of vision is used to control, as Sara accuses Victor of doing. Sara can thus become a whole intellectual only when she acknowledges the authority of emotion and vacates the spectator spot to act herself.

The three films discussed in this chapter ask us to consider desires outside the domain of the masculine. Dulac articulates the desire of a woman to be both artistic and independent, to claim the creative and the social. The aesthetics of the film, radical for its time, projects the female's desires both in the fantastic and the social, thus asserting the female's authority over her worldview. Madame Beudet's desire to be rid of her husband is effortlessly authorised by the director who shows the female's dismal acknowledgement and awareness of the role she has been assigned when the curtain comes down on what was essentially Goethe's play, Beudet's theatre. Using the fantastic, or the extra-diegetic, Amaral too is able to convey a doubled understanding of female desire in an underdeveloped context by showing the woman's simultaneous attraction to and repulsion of consumer culture. The insertion of fantasy into the realism of the film creates an aesthetic that emphasises the importance of the urban, and of female desire, in the construction of rural women's subjectivities in a capitalist world economy. Although the lead character is left unfulfilled, her understanding of her desires gives her the power to act, and the authority to search for both urban pleasures and herself. Interestingly, the intellectually sophisticated professor in *Losing Ground* comes to an understanding of her desires only when she exchanges subjectivity, or shifts to the fantastic. The mixture of diegetic and extra-diegetic are imperative to this film's understanding of a woman's relationship to the intellectual and the emotional. Ultimately, she secures the authority of the self when she vacates a specifically masculine visual tradition.

6

FEMINIST NARRATIVE AESTHETICS

In this chapter, I turn from the plotting of desiring female subjectivities in narrative to narrative design. I seek to map out how specific aesthetic and narrative strategies enable the creation of feminist narrative. My analyses are meant neither as paradigmatic nor as comprehensive, but exemplary of some feminist interventions in film narrative; the history of mainstream film has seldom been commensurate to the task of creating feminist narratives. The narrative aesthetics of the films discussed here – Jeannine Meerapfel's *Malou* (1980), Marleen Gorris' *Antonia's Line* (1995), Prema Karanth's *Phaniyamma* (1981) and Leontine Sagan's *Mädchen in Uniform* (1931) – cover very different time periods and cultures. The specificity of each intervention is marked by a movement away from traditional filmic narrative by challenges issued to the classical paradigm.

Meerapfel frames the discussion on what feminist narrative might look like by raising the question of the role of the body in the woman's acquisition of authority. Given classical patriarchal ideology's refusal of authority to women on the grounds of the female body, such feminist attention to the body is vital to any project that seeks to grant women narrative authority. By introducing the body, Meerapfel is able to rewrite one of the paradigmatic narratives of patriarchy, the mother/daughter plot. A specifically feminist mythology is important for women for future generations of women to believe in the authority of their voices and stories. Gorris' *Antonia's Line* offers us a feminist modernist myth, shifting the male modern bases of subjectivity from the authorisation of the self to the authorisation of other women, both in history and in the present. Seeking narrative subjectivity in the recesses of history, Karanth's film delineates a space outside both past and present visual interdictions, a third space for the invisible woman of traditional myth and history. The early film classic, *Mädchen in Uniform*, foregrounds a narrative model for women in its narrative topography that is a substantive departure from the classical male narrative.

The spaces women inhabit and traverse are important to the films mentioned above. They ask us to understand how women, having access to so little space, have been moved to change the course of everyday life from that place, and with it the course of history itself. Finding that third space from which women's narratives can be authorised determines the narrative aesthetics of the films that demand we recognise the authority of other women in the human narrative.

Rewriting Narratives of Maternity: Jeannine Meerapfel's *Malou*

The story of the relationship between a woman's identity and her mother's, *Malou* also deals with how the mother's subjectivity is constituted. Feminist psychoanalysts have convincingly shown how male theories of subjectivity divest the maternal voice/gaze of authority and autonomy in a manoeuvre which privileges the subject's gaze on the maternal body. The subject's gaze thus becomes the pre-condition of the subject's perception of his ego-ideal during the mirror stage.[1] The subject's sense of loss or exile from the maternal body structures this constitutive moment. The theory posits implicitly that the subject loses an anterior self during this phase which marks the rest of his life as an exile driven to desire by this lack. Consequently, the anterior self and the maternal body are elided which effaces the materiality of the maternal as a signifier and postulates it as a signified of the subject's exile from the anterior self. Commenting on filmic practice which 'like the fetishistic ritual, is an inscription of the look on the body of the mother', Constance Penley alerted us to 'begin to consider the possibilities and consequences of the mother returning the look'.[2] The challenge for feminist film practice organised around the female subject's and the mother's look is to recast the narrative of female subjectivity in terms where the exile from the maternal body does not efface the corporeality of the maternal signifier, but allows it a space whether bound or unbound to the female child's gaze, and assuredly outside a phallic scopic regimen.[3] *Malou* is a direct exploration of the mother's corporeality and a rather more complex negotiation of how the daughter deals with the insistence on the corporeal.

The film resorts to a startlingly simple narrative device: the Jewish daughter, caught in cultural borderlands in Germany, having been raised in Argentina[4] tries to find out who her mother was.[5] Hannah, the protagonist, says that she will not know who she is without knowledge of the mother. The narrative seems to be structured around the classic feminist quest motif whereby the daughter finds herself when she finds her mother. How do you present the mother as independent when the narrative structure, albeit a feminist one, is organised around the daughter's search? When the daughter is the seeker, she also becomes the knower, and the mother would remain unspoken. The film succeeds in transcending a narrative structure which posits the mother as object of knowledge by playing with the narrative structure in a variety of ways and by introducing the thematics of exile, the metaphysics of exile.

Malou deliberately locates the quest for the mother and the consequent self-knowledge of the female child as a pre-condition to a self-conscious positioning of the adult in society. More than a startling inversion of the phallic economy, the film suggests that knowledge of the mother (rather than the father as in the Ur quest of Telemachus in the *Odyssey*) allows the female to traverse the path from girlhood to adulthood by establishing difference from the mother, rather than similarity. The voyage is marked by a genuine uncovering of the mother's life and does not thematise lineage connections. When the protagonist of the film confronts her mother's life, she discovers that she too had played out the patriarchal theme of overloading the maternal signified, viewed her mother through other eyes, viewed herself through other eyes; both had become symbolic absences. The introduction of the sociological, the attempt to understand both their lives in terms of their historical contexts provides the daughter with a way of grasping both lives outside of the pathology that marked the patriarchal construction of their lives.

Subtly the film plays with the theme of the difficulties of accommodating heterosexuality. The mother Malou's life, and its markers, could well be said to function as object lessons for women who do not assimilate into wife/mother roles. The pathologisation starts with the story of origins; Malou is an orphan and as such has no estate. The setting of the cabaret already sets her apart as the 'bad' girl; or if not, at least the 'other' woman whose femininity signifies exclusively and rather stereotypically. Although shot through the daughter's eyes, these sequences are broadly framed and meant to extract the surplus pleasure of the aesthetic qualities of the female despite artifices to register the unease with the patriarchal exteriority of presentation. The sensuous, the depths of alcohol and the losing of oneself in it, dance and its ecstasy, music and its hypnotic appeal are all projected on Malou. The surface quality of the presentation is developed by more extreme variations of the loss of the self, through promiscuity, through depression and ultimately severe alcoholism. Malou's final blindness serves as a symptom of her extreme 'hysteria', or blockage of patriarchy. Blockage refers to female resistance to severe patriarchal edicts. Of course resistance can be articulated more directly, but here we are speaking of an orphan woman who in the narrative is presented as without female allies until Hannah is born. Malou says to her mother-in-law that she feels so 'allein', alone, on one of the occasions that Paul Kahn, her husband, is away.

The emphasis on the corporeal recalls the trope of hypostasisation of female as body. Malou is all body and this immaterial body, the female body pinned on her, modulates her subjectivity and partially determines her alienation from all the spaces she inhabits. Elizabeth Grosz's distinction between the cultural body and the 'lived body' enables us to understand how living through the body, insisting on its materiality, allows Malou to find a 'home' in her exile.[6]

That surface presentation of the female body, complicated by its fetish object here, the voice, raises the question of how the lived female body as opposed to the abstraction of the anterior self affects the life of the daughter in a patriarchal culture.

The dangers of associating with the mother, and identifying with the mother, are both made apparent in this film which seems strangely reminiscent of the discursive ambiguities of Dorothy Arzner's *Christopher Strong* (1933). Can a film that thematises femininity in overtly pathological terms be considered feminist according to a negative thesis that holds that the revelation of the pathology produced by patriarchal cultures is essential to understanding the mediations in the mother/daughter relationship; that is, the mother eliciting the same response of horror from the daughter that the male child experiences? Of course, the horror is supposed to be of the lack; however, I have long suspected that it must be of the excess, of the surfeit of femininity.[7] In the daughter's case, the latter obtains. So, no, the film probably cannot be considered feminist, when the female character accords with the patriarchal thesis on femininity. Does the film, however, show a feminist consciousness in sketching the pathology even if the intervention is not as crisp as one might like? Probably. Does the task of authorising such an ambivalent text become more dangerous, more difficult? Definitely. Yet authorising such a text becomes important for a trans-subjective mother/daughter acknowledgement of patriarchal pathologisation of difference specifically with reference to the body. Elizabeth Grosz sums up the pathologisation broadly in the following way:

> Instead of granting women an autonomous and active form of corporeal specificity, at best women's bodies are judged in terms of a 'natural inequality', as if there were a standard or

measure for the value of bodies independent of sex … The coding of femininity with corpo-reality in effect leaves men free to inhabit what they (falsely) believe is a purely conceptual order while at the same time enabling them to satisfy their (sometimes disavowed) need for corporeal contact through their access to women's bodies and services.[8]

Whether either mother or daughter is able to act on the realisation is another matter. The limits of the psychological discourse are far out of the heterosexual frame of reference, considering that the logical end point of the recognition is the exit from heterosexuality. Whether the exit is to lesbian sexuality,[9] celibacy or other non-heterosexual options neither character can actually confront the pathologisation of their bodies.

The whole issue of the authorisation of Malou's life is further complicated by the narra-tive strategies of the film. The first two segments, her tenure as a maidservant and her work at the cabaret where she sang, are introduced by the voice-over narrator who is the daugh-ter. The veracity, or Real Effect, of what we are about to see is qualified by Hannah's com-ment that Malou sometimes spoke of having worked as a cabaret artiste, and sometimes as a domestic servant. The transition from one segment to the other is provided by Hannah, thus questioning the historical accuracy of the narrative that will unfold. We are, however, aware that even with a little invention, the lives that Malou led were because of her migrant status. The many that Hannah pulls out to show her husband, Martin, in the diegesis of the film are factual testaments to her wandering. The disconcertion about Malou's life lacking verifiability is pertinent because it suggests that the pathologisation of Malou, the charge of lack of credibility, is also imposed on her by her daughter who has understood Malou's story according to what we might call a male model of interpretation. Authorising Malou's narrative in terms other than through the daughter's apprehension becomes crucial to the project of claiming maternal subjectivity and of parsing the notion of maternal sacrifice. The film does eventually authorise Malou's story; as the *subject who is spoken* but also as the *speaking subject* through the corporeal signifier. Distinguishing the mother's subjectivity allows the daughter to establish a separate identity.

Hannah, the daughter in *Malou*, makes her motive for the search of the mother explicit when she tells her husband that she 'may find out something about herself'. Although the conversation between Hannah and her husband is the verbal starting point of the narrative which fixes on the quest as a reference point, the visual has already spoken a different story. The film opens on a slow panning movement which pauses briefly and undifferentiatedly at Malou's personal effects before the title of the film, named after the mother Malou, comes up. The introduction of Malou, signified by the objects which serve partly as narrative mnemonic device, has been presented as independent of the daughter's life. We also hear Malou's voice outside the diegesis, while her objects lay claim to the diegetic space. As Kaja Silverman states, the voice of a female unattached to the narrative carries a certain authority with it.[10] Of course, the fact that Malou is singing a song, a conventional filmic placement for a woman, gives us pause. And yet, we do not see her, suggesting the ambiguity of the presentation.

The voice of Malou singing functions as extra-diegetic voice-over in this crucial open-ing sequence. Hannah, of course, cannot hear it, but we can. The significance of the mater-nal voice is worthy of discussion. Although extra-diegetic, it seems to create a link between its narrative and the objects strewn around the room; a physicalisation of the presence as Derrida has argued the voice is in Western metaphysics,[11] and functioning here as a traditional invoking of presence. Such an unambiguous reading comes into conflict with the physicality of the artifacts, some of which are writings, letters. Hannah cannot hear her. The voice then signals absence, and in the lyrics of the song itself that poignantly asks who the singer is, the very absence of the self. In his discussion on the history of the voice in Western metaphysics, Mladen Dolar makes a case for the voice as being ambiguous and challenging the authority of the patriarchal *ex nihilo* voice that Derrida established. Dolar maintains that the voice without word is considerably destabilising, and further that the female singing voice carries the very force of the devil with it according to this hoary tradition of metaphysics.[12] In the film itself, the conventional narrative role of Malou as female cabaret singer is challenged by the voice-over song which we will later recognise to be Malou's. Most importantly, because of its feminine quality the voice is no longer the voice of patriarchal authority but the disruptive voice laying claim to a sensuous authority, to be linked to the discursive corporeal. While Derrida's reading of the relationship between voice and authoritative presence may be substantially correct for a male tradition, and Dolar may be substantially correct about the female voice being ambiguous, threatening and absent in the same tradition, it does not speak to the many experimental uses of the voice in feminist film,[13] and the uses of the female voice made by this film. Here the song is both disruptive and authoritative; disruptive of patriarchal preserves, authoritative about the female corporeal. That opening song lays Malou's story out and by presenting it as voice-over, Meerapfel makes the opening gesture of authorising the story through elements other than the look. Malou cannot return the look; she does not want to, but can signify differently about the body and interrupt the patriarchal chain of either maternal or pathological signification on it.

The disembodied male voice, authoritarian intrusion, locates Hannah's desire as transgressive. The space in the room, the voice suggests, has become chaotic. The voice is of course the husband's, Martin's. Likewise, Hannah's desire to find herself through her mother is disruptive of the heterosexual contract. Martin suggests that Hannah go to a psychoanalyst to solve her problems rather than on a pilgrimage of her mother's life. The next sequence nevertheless still seems to place Malou's life as an inset in Hannah's. In these sequences, Hannah is the subject, Malou the object of knowledge, for we see Malou in her deathbed and singing in the cabaret through the readily familiar ubiquitous flashback stitched to Hannah's look. The female viewer is aligned to Hannah's perspective. At the cemetery where this sequence takes place, Hannah's quest changes from finding a solution to her problems through her mother to attempting merely to listen to Malou's story which is shrouded in mystery. Was she a cabaret artiste, was she a Dienstmädchen? The narrative then takes a different turn here for Malou's story is no longer cinematically sutured to Hannah's look but assumes its own narrative force. Malou's story is presented by a seemingly omniscient narrator. Hannah is no longer prime interpreter of her mother's narrative, nor does she retain the earlier posture of voyeur.

The female subject as voyeur, in this instance, finds that she cannot retain the gaze for the look she casts turns against her as she is unable to maintain the distance between subject and object. At the narrative level, the story outside Hannah, the one she reads stands in danger of being the one inside her, the one she writes. Cinematically, this is signalled by the fact that Hannah is as much the object of knowledge of the narrative/technological apparatus as the subject of knowledge as the sinuous cutting with no temporal transitions is evidence of. Hannah is standing at a hotel bar, asking about Malou, when with no editing cue whatsoever, we see Malou there singing. A more obvious connection between mother and daughter is forged in the sequence during which Hannah drives through the tunnel. On the other side of the tunnel Malou emerges.

This shift in the narratological convention marks an epistemological move, which serves to link the lives of mother and daughter at the visual level, and distinguish their lives at the narrative level, renders the question of exile poignant and almost unbearably complex for the female viewer. The relative freedom of the mother's story from the daughter's reveals a certain interest in the mother's life on her own terms. While the narrative may not neces-sarily be told from Malou's point of view, Hannah's loss of authority as prime interpreter ensures that Malou's story is told away from the space of Hannah's exile from the maternal that the film started with. Hannah's repetition of Malou's actions at the corporeal level is significant in establishing her identity as a woman with a recognisable body, a pleasure-yielding body of her own. The maternal body does not contain the anterior self in any placid way; indeed there is no elision of the maternal body and the anterior self of the subject, Hannah. Rather, her insistence on her body's pleasures affirm her always-already existing self, independent of the maternal body. Indeed, because Hannah does not know the history of Malou's life, Meerapfel wilfully steps in and takes control so that we are inside Malou's narrative and do not rely on Hannah. The female viewer loses her reference point when Hannah's look ceases to be interpretive and becomes receptive. At the same time, the female viewer is not rendered passive but has moved from outside both Hannah's story and Malou's story where neither woman can distance herself from the experience of exile. The removal of the voyeuristic gaze reclaims the time of Malou's life and the trope of exile resurfaces in the context of her life.

The lack of separateness between the female viewer and what she is seeing, famously theorised by Andreas Huyssen[14] and Judith Mayne[15] in the feminist film context, testifies to what Constance Penley explains in her account of Lacan on the scopic drive as 'the functioning of lack at the level of the scopic drive which renders the subject not an objec-tive subject, nor the one of reflecting consciousness'.[16] One would have to counter the last proposition by arguing that subjectivity may be constituted outside the scopic field. The voice, or touch – the aural and haptic instead of the scopic – can function effectively for women. Indeed the boundaries that are erased between subject and object allow the daughter eventually to acknowledge her lived body, similar to the mother's, but definitely not an extension of hers.

I would contend that while the simple inversion of the female as bearer of the gaze does not topple the phallic economy, the narrative framework of the film does indeed posit an answer to the constitution of female subjectivity at the level of the scopic which does not rest exclusively on the realisation of the self through the acknowledgement of the Other. Because the narrative of the film moves from outside to the inside and liberates the female viewer from the voyeuristic perspective of Hannah to take us inside the narrative of Malou, the woman-as-subject, Hannah's status as a speaking subject is posited in terms outside the opposition between subject and object of knowledge. That replacement at the visual level is in concert with the inner purview on Malou's life suggests that the female viewer and the would-be female subject Hannah do not see as much as experience likeness so that the boundary between the subject and Other far from defined by the act of seeing is erased by the act of experiencing.

The church sequence shows that Malou had exiled herself from her home because of her Jewish husband, an exile doubly severe because of loss of contact with language, music, voice and self. Interestingly, Malou's home is not established in any stable way at all. Meerapfel makes the point that women live in the borderlands. Malou lives and works on the French/German border and is equally at home in both languages but because of World War Two lands up in Argentina with Paul. Her estrangement from her land begins with her marriage. Hannah too is exiled from her native Argentina and from her mother who is not allowed to live with or care for her after a point. The film suggests that Malou turns to liquor and men to stay the sorrows of exile, and implies that Hannah does the same. Again, of course, her condition as woman already exiles her.

Such an analysis is rendered possible only by the narrative context of exile. The opening sequence indicates that the mother's exile seriously misdirects the male desire that views exile for the subject as exile from the maternal body. Malou's lyrics signify at the literal level that Malou is a stranger in a strange land, has given up language, land, heritage and religion. At the metaphorical level, the literal exile from a nativity also signifies, not exile from the mother but an exile from the self because of complicity with men in the individual instance, collusion with patriarchy in a more global frame. The enunciative apparatus links Malou's literal exile with her exile from subjectivity by positioning her as the object of the male gaze *par excellence*, professional giver of visual pleasure in her role as cabaret singer. This insight is clarified narratologically by Hannah's exile which blurs the difference between her story and her mother's. Unlike Malou, Hannah does rage at Martin; notwithstanding that she plays the roles of actor and audience rather than narrator. Finally, we are not given single narratives from either her or Malou. The subjectivities of the two women then are predicated on a shifting, if specific, knowledge of exile which guarantees that each woman looks through the other woman's eyes in a trans-subjective frame.

Mimicry as a trope is relevant to the film's authorisation of maternal subjectivity.[17] A sequence in the opening sections of the film features the young Malou singing in the cabaret. The set-up positions her across a mirror so that she is singing while looking at herself. The act of self-looking here is a sign of imitation, of a mimicking of herself, for the cabaret viewers and specifically Paul Kahn. Yet the self-specularisation is less important than the pleasure of the senses; Malou wants to dance, and does. The estrangement from the place of her upbringing and her successive migrations exaggerate the mimicry and through excess collapse the signifier of visual femininity to reveal the corporeal maternal. This is to be distinguished from the maternal body as described by psychoanalysts. The corporeal maternal is the body *soi-meme*, the body for herself, not the child; the body and its experiences, not the body as the object of the child's gaze. The film's narrative discourse makes it very clear that Malou's body is hers; indeed, the only entity over which she has any authority.[18]

Each milieu we see Malou in seems unnatural, not home, at any rate: the house where she is in domestic service, the cabaret, and later the Jewish extended family. Here Malou's distance and difference from the community becomes patent; desperately afraid, she does not have the same compelling need to show courage that the Jewish do. She does however. Placed in the 'doll's cottage', alone and constantly waiting for Paul to come back, Malou is narratively clearly displaced. The picture of a woman who is waiting for a man to fulfil her is disturbed by the sequence when she goes out gambling with Paul. Right in the middle of the evening, she sees the woman, herself, singing of exile and the loss of self. The film has a couple of mirror images that are so prominent that they seem to border on the narcissistic. The narcissistic, however, is predicated on the gaze being returned.[19] Both times, the gaze in the mirror image does not lock into the viewing subject. Paul catches it the first time when Malou is singing looking into the mirror, and the second time, the mirror is not present, if there as an inferred entity by the nature of the image. In the gambling salon, the image makes clear the gap between the surface and the 'real'.

Self-looking reveals the imitation for its surface quality. Self-seeing again questions that boundary between subject and object. Herself and not herself, she is both the viewer and the image, but unlike the male viewer who in recognition feels disconcerted, Malou's recognition of the image itself is wanting, in part because the image encases the material that incorporates the recognisable self. While this may not be true for all women, the rarefaction of the material into the image gives Malou pause, as noted by the unseeing look in her eye although she has 'seen' the singing figure.

As Elizabeth Grosz has argued, the subject's body becomes representative material for her, that is, material that will represent her, stand for her; this material is articulated both psychically and socially.[20] Malou's body type, the abstract immaterial body that has the stamp of stereotypical femininity, has no place outside the cabaret because it has been constituted only for that place. Each new venue that Malou goes to, she looks less and less like the women there. Nothing like the Jewish family, bizarrely doll-like when she goes through the ritual religious conversion. She is contrasted to Lotte, her blonde looks standing out almost obscenely against the dark-haired young Jewish woman who crossed Europe on foot to escape the Nazis. When Malou is in Latin America, her body type is even more exaggeratedly marked by difference; her colouring is noticeably different from those of the indigenous women. This visible bodily difference manifests itself on the social and the psychic. If there is no material body, or at least no fixed material body, *living the body out*, or intervening into the cultural construction of the self would have to be effected at the level of the body. Thus Malou's living the body out causes the daughter to be ashamed of her. Far from the controlled maternal body, or the controlling, or the compactly sexualised one, it becomes demanding. The desire to sink into forgetfulness is achieved through the pleasures of the body. Malou sucks one last gulp of wine in before she is rushed to the hospital. In this context, her blindness accentuates the senses that readily give tactile pleasure, or pleasure at the level of the skin. Self-looking is implicated in this process of living the body out. Exploration of the mimicry involved in composing the body shows the composition being deliberately unravelled by Malou. Shortly after Paul has taken in the young Jewish woman, and Malou has had Hannah, Malou would have been abandoned to the spectacle of femininity, would have begun to bore holes through the spectacle.

En route to Argentina, Malou drinks, dances and drops on the dance floor. With the loss of the self, oblivion is perhaps one way of resisting assimilation into wifehood and motherhood. Hannah too imitates Malou in her drinking, her sensuousness and her insistence on the body. While Kahn, Malou's husband, is not domineering, he is certainly upper class and holds the cards in the relationship. Malou's resistance is reconfirmed for us by the fact that Hannah's lover Martin's demand for 'assimilation' is presented in comprehensible terms because of Hannah's class position as relative to Malou's.

Hannah is pathologised as the foreign female; figured as having more body and less intellect than the native-born architect. Her physicality and his rejection of it is emphasised. Twice, she is shown wanting to initiate sex with him; he exhibits distaste for this excess. At one point she is undressed and steals his bath; in this instance, he is less irritated because she has given up her independent journeying and therefore her body would be confined. When she comes back drunk, he says with deep revulsion, 'And you've eaten garlic too.' As she says to him during one of their frequent quarrels, 'When I am around there is cat hair, and when I cook, it smells of food.' At a bar, a man speculates on which foreign port Hannah belongs to. This contemporary pathologisation of the foreign female body reminds us that the female as body, which is one of the dominant cultural perceptions of women, is still in exile. The female's body has still not been accepted. Albeit the emphasis on Hannah's foreignness, its imposition on her body comments on the pathologisation of the foreign female. Consequently, Hannah is really insecure in Germany. Malou's refusal to conform, while self-destructive, gives her a certain freedom. In Argentina, Malou asks Paul to come back to her once. Perhaps this indicates her decision or her wish to assimilate both to Argentina and the marriage and motherhood. But she is not a Jewish émigré, merely the wife of one.

Malou's behaviour can be pathologised as Paul does, suggesting that she is an unfit mother or understood as responses to the migrant situation. The repetition of the lyrics of the song lend coherence to the notion that both mother and daughter understand their lives as conditioned by this migrant identity which cannot compose a self, or even a notional self in any concrete way. The body's pleasures alone are real.

The daughter refuses to understand the body's place in the mother's life; that is why Hannah takes the memorabilia and puts it away. Or maybe she understands it too well.

The daughter's complex feelings about understanding exile and its limits, despite her quest, are signalled when she shuts her ears as her mother tells her about the father and his displeasure with the mother. He wants to correct the influence Malou has on Hannah by sending her to a European boarding school. This scene in her early youth speaks to Hannah's difficulty both with Malou's exile and Paul's pathologisation of her. Malou knows that she has paid a price in not assimilating to marriage and Paul; she tells Hannah to find someone like him. Yet Hannah cannot understand it. The resistance Malou offers through enjoying the pleasures of the body does not come without a sense of self-loathing. Malou clearly never condemns Paul in the diegesis; further, she seems to claim responsibility or show awareness of her actions in her comment to her daughter. And so Malou endlessly imitates the one role she knows – cabaret-artiste/singer – and in the meanwhile satisfies the demands of the body. Malou's daughter perhaps just does not want to hear that heterosexual protection comes with a demand for the erasure of identity. After all, Martin is building an integration centre and tells her to forget about her past.

Malou's eventual blindness, caused, according to the pathological narrative, by her excessive drinking or sex or dancing, seems to function as a determined desire not to see. Looking at oneself, though, that imitation is not over because she asks her daughter to show her a mirror shortly before she dies. Yet she does not care to see any more; she sits in the dark but asks her old-time companion to drink a vermouth with her. Malou does not care to see because she cannot bear to see. At her most seeing, she only saw an imitation, a surface; a mimic image in the mirror, not a reflection of herself, nor even the Other. While Hannah cannot embrace Malou's life, Meerapfel authorises it through the narrative apparatus as resisting patriarchy even as it constitutes the female subject. For the daughter, the mother's life, falling outside patriarchal norms, is too threatening. To remain within the heterosexual compact, she must ignore both her mother and herself.

The film concludes, however, with Hannah going round and round in circles while Martin her boyfriend does the same. The pathologisation of the female corporeal in the female, the female's response to it, has foreclosed the possibility of unambiguous heterosexual closure; the surfeit of body has not been sealed yet.

Despite the difficulty of authorising a narrative where the protagonist seems riddled with a woman's internalisation of patriarchal edicts, Meerapfel's contextualisation of the pathologisation of the female/migrant body, and her strategy of using the voice as opposed to the gaze as an entrance into the story, has foregrounded the corporeal as essential to female subjectivity and hence as another female character, Antonia would think on the day of her death (in Marleen Gorris' *Antonia's Line*) 'there would be nothing to be ashamed of' for the auteur and the female viewer. The daughter is still out there.

Narrating Modernist Myth: Marleen Gorris' *Antonia's Line*

Meerapfel's *Malou* challenges dominant classical male narrative paradigms by its insistence on the maternal corporeal signifier. By authorising maternal subjectivity, the film's narrative delineates a plausible feminist narrative aesthetic scheme, one that does not scorn the female body, and does not abandon the maternal. If undoing received mythologies of motherhood is important for feminism, so is the creation of feminist myths.

Creating a way of telling stories through lineage and through knowledge of one's female forebears has been important to women filmmakers as they have struggled to tell these stories while also leaving the space of storytelling open to others. Part of the struggle has been to narrate the experiences of women as myth/legend/history without universalising the experience. Specific and local histories, however, when shot through realist filters achieve only realist goals, which for film feminisms is crucially relevant; however, realism does not impart that sense of how stories are told *for others to tell* that a mythical apparatus hooked to lineage can. While unhingeing the mythologies about women that are part of the 'trans-itional'[21] material that enables the smooth chain of male generational storytelling, the lure of mythologising is also an essential part of feminist filmmaking ventures. Utopias and imagining these,[22] foundations and inventing these,[23] are as necessary as the realist project of truth-telling if spaces are to be created for claiming stories that enable women to name themselves.

One possibility that has been explored quite successfully has been the rewriting of genres, or what I like to call the overwriting of genres, for the original genre that is overwritten is still visible in its new format. Many genres specific to film have thus been rewritten including horror, pornography, melodrama, documentary and history. Myth has been difficult to rewrite because of the kind of canvas early cinema captured to achieve full literary status.[24] A realist *mise-en-scène* would curtail possibilities of formulating a mythology, even leaving aside the problem for women inherent in constructing mythologies. Mythologising women, whether in epic or film, has not served women well, robbing them of historical agency and indeed historical identity. Is screening myth for women even a possibility then? Is modernist feminist myth a contradiction in terms?

Modernism is a dubious context for women despite the promise of progressiveness. Its radical innovativeness in literature and film did not endure the subject positions of females at all. This is readily apparent in the canon of progressive male European modern drama where despite the openness of the form, the Barthesian quality of inviting the reader to produce rather than consume the text, the female is again hypostasised as the Other.[25] In art, surrealism and modernism in general did little better by women as Rosalind Krauss has shown.[26] In film, Joan Mellen has discussed the depiction of sexuality in the 'new' film.[27] Women seem no better off than in the old films. Without labouring the point on the representations of women offered by the modernist pantheon, one can suggest difficulties with the very innovativeness of the techniques in literary and filmic arts, that feminist film critics have appreciated. The singularity of subjectivity is perhaps hardest for women. While the individual woman's experience is valorised, that speaking space does not authorise other enunciations. As a mode of narration, the speaking space of modernism, while rebellious, is not expansive. The partiality and subjectivity of the narrator is another case in point. While this certainly helps in dismantling patriarchal authority, it is not helpful to the project of consolidating feminist authority. The use of specific film techniques such as the jump cut may actually be irrelevant. If the female spectator is already alienated by the construction of femininity, dispositioning her need not be a progressive move. Gorris, in a previous film, *A Question of Silence* (1982), uses modernist editing, not to disrupt continuity, but to establish contiguity among the women who are narratively unrelated to each other.

The film is about a woman, Antonia, who returns to her village after the war and raises her daughter there. The plot is fairly strictly organised around her setting up an alternative family with children, grandchildren and other villagers. The film loosely follows the lives of those in the community that Antonia builds; her daughter, her granddaughter, her great-granddaughter, her companion, and those men and women who seek and find shelter in this alternative community.

Similarly, Gorris uses modernism to feminist ends in *Antonia's Line*. Even if modernist myth seems a contradiction in terms, *Antonia's Line* works towards such a possibility. The 'I' of subjective modernism is necessarily mediated through complex mediums if spaces are to remain open for other voices. The telling of the 'I' so important to subjective enunciation, and so problematic for women, is made even more difficult because of the modernist 'I's uniqueness, individuality and complexity. Gorris succeeds in making modernism usable for women by expanding notions of subjectivity to include community. Certainly subjective first-person renditions by their modalities can offer themselves as models; my point here is that in and of themselves they do not contain the space for those other enunciations. By using a third-person child narrator, the film invests the legatee with authority, while keeping the protagonist relatively inscrutable. Although she is inscrutable, a female viewer can identify with her. Although an outsider in the modernist tradition, her outsider status invites the identification of other women. *Antonia's Line* points to a modernist way of constructing myth for women that would not be destructive to self-image as identity. As B. Ruby Rich has pointed out, modernist strategies have not been particularly empowering for women, particularly in the case of male auteurs. However, she maintains that there is a modernist 'female line' that is 'non-controlling'.[28] That feminist modernism must necessarily be non-controlling, or that it should not follow the hierarchical processes of male modernist narration, seems a little polemical. The processes by which authority is accrued and the self-questioning that it entails probably best serve those in power, not those who are seeking the power. Examination of these processes allows those in power to question the self and to revert to a modernist self-reflexivity without sustained reference to the outside world. The modernist 'non-controlling line' does not necessarily help the project of women gaining authority, but merely reconfirms the old modernist project of women's diffusion of authority, this time initiated by women themselves. Traditional patriarchal authority and hierarchy are unambiguously destructive. Shared authority, not consensual authority, in which each member in the group has the authority of both group and individual, does not deconstruct authority, it recomposes it. The family structure that the film builds veers in a direction which is both feminist-modernist and mythical. The film makes a powerful move away from the notion that the act of writing is implicitly to authorise one's voice to the notion that it is to authorise another woman's voice.[29] The film begins with various ways of signing the authority of Antonia and Danielle to conclude with authorising the young child narrator. The older women's 'writing' enables hers.

A tricky 'flashback' unfolds the story of five generations of women. Antonia is looking out of the window in an opening sequence. We cut to a younger Antonia with Danielle returning to the village. Right at the end of the 'chronicle', the great-granddaughter claims the story and its authorship. The folded perspective of the narrative is an indication of a space being created for another both to claim and tell a story.

The film has been regarded as a fairytale.[30] It has also been compared to *Like Water for Chocolate* (1992), largely because of its focus on women and its magical realist qualities.[31] The issues of historical agency and historical subjectivity are murkier in the film, caught as the film is in the flight from mimesis. If, as Paula Rabinowitz maintains, feminism's politics of personal subjectivity is pressed into the service of the nation to construct the modern, the female heroes of *Antonia's Line* do make a measured impact on the nation-to-be. Rabinowitz's other proposition regarding the modern American nations and women's dependence on them for their modern identities also holds in the mythology of the film which presents the women as wrestling with the intractable even while the modern accommodates them. That 'feminism itself is part of a modern nationalist identity'[32] and is itself mythologised through its incursion into the temporal in the mythical mode speaks to women's desires for such a mythology.

As a mode, magical realism too seems relatively inadequate to the demands of women, embalmed as they are as phantasms and obsessions in the male imaginary. Archetypal figuration is the fullest role for women in that mode. Again, the magical component of realism seems to extinguish historical separateness for women, putting them out of time. Julia

Kristeva has spoken of men's time and women's time: men's time being cursive, linear and, according to Nietzsche, fitting into a sequence, while women's time fits a more anarchic, less teleological project, tied to the cyclical which, of course, is the narrative hanger for the mythical. As a notion, women's time has arguably been part of the mystification of women.

Antonia's Line explores a concept of women and time that fits neither paradigm of cursive or anarchic time, and what this other concept outside of this dichotomous formulation might mean for a mythology *for* women. Starting with mortality and ending with mortality enables the corporealisation of women as bookends and gives the film a circular structure without necessarily implying the cyclical. History, the end of the war, is noted; but so is the mother's death that brings Antonia home. A notable instance of a time that is natural is Mad Madonna barking and braying at the moon because she cannot be with her lover. She dies of a broken heart; her protestant lover follows suit. In myth, cause, an element of the proairetic code, is magisterial, not immediate or emotional. Emotion is often disregarded.[33] In magical realism, on the other hand, emotion, reverie, contemplation and speech are highly effective in motivating action. The attempt to grasp a time that is neither male, nor 'women's' à la Kristeva, could be said to be reminiscent of the time of magical realism where years can be like days, days years. Inevitably, then, repetitions bring even magical realism closer to a Kristevan concept of women's time than any the film deploys. More nuanced, the film is about the slow, even passage of time, despite one comment from the narrator about how time sometimes seemed to rush, at others to swoop down. When asked about how she handled time in the film, Gorris noted:

> You can show the passage of time in very many things, but in the end we decided that it would probably be best in all respects – art direction, costume and make-up – to show it as casually as possible, like the passage of time which, especially in the country, goes quite slowly. You don't see abrupt changes in time. I think within the film that works very well. Suddenly you think, if you think about it all, 'Well, I was in 1948 there, and now I'm possibly in 1967, but it doesn't really matter whether it's '67 or '68 or what have you', and suddenly you think, 'Maybe I'm possibly halfway through the 1970s now.' But somehow it doesn't seem to matter all that much. You see people and things change and you see people grow up, but almost off hand, and I think that's a good thing.[34]

Although critics view the film as magical realist, and in an interesting interpretation the magical realist dimension as contesting the male gaze, Gorris, in this film, shifts to recording interiority and imaginative apprehension.[35] This is to be distinguished from magical realism where the ontological validity of the magical events that occur are crucial to that worldview which can be seen as the triumph of myth, but a myth disrobed to reveal the patriarchal spine and bone. Magical realism has ontological substance in the diegesis and the real; the glimpses we have in the film are firmly modernist, part of a way of signalling that subjective perception has greater validity and can make larger truth claims than objective reality. Point-of-view footage has achieved relatively little for women except in the most facile of ways as a more politically correct way of relegating difference as absolute. Subjective perception firmly foregrounds the subject, telling one more about the subject than what is seen. Those extra-real occurrences in the film, none felt or experienced by Antonia who is an opaque character, establish their truth claims through recourse to the painterly, the static, the hieratic, the monumental. No vestige of the eccentric/excentric is allowed to disturb these visions, on which the entire range of the discourse of the Dutch/ Flemish artistic tradition is brought to bear.[36] The truth in 'seeing', or the perspective of the Flemish painters transposed to the visionary female authorises the vision. Teresa Brennan formulates this concept in a fascinating manner in her essay on contextualising vision. In discussing the differences between the passive viewer of positivism, and the cultural viewer, Brennan suggests that the notion of the receptive viewer would allow for us to understand vision that is not passive, not constructed, but not purely subjective either. She states that when the cultural grids through which we view the world are shaken, 'suspended', 'we have an experience of the "supersensible", a perspective that is not confined to a personal standpoint'.[37] Danielle's visions can be seen as both subjective and following a tradition of 'seeing' where what is seen is neither wholly constructed nor wholly psychically driven. Dubbing it the 'magical look',[38] as one reviewer does, assumes that Danielle's visions then are not entirely driven by a 'subject-centred position'.[39]

The social commentary provided by the film's painterly perspectives is only one component of the film, and while it jostles with the villagers' worldview, it appears to emerge from the crucible of a similar ideology, if only because it emerges from similar discursive techniques. A scene that occurs in the real is of Antonia's old mother spewing curses at Antonia's father; an imagining is Therese's mother seeing Therese's teacher naked and beautiful. The former is pictured crudely and energetically, the latter dreamily and mystically.

Karen Jaehne argues that these images, particularly the visions that appear to Danielle, the painter, speak to 'the power of art to elicit from the material world its potential for change'.[40] I would add, however, that the stability of these paintings is questioned by the discursive real that precedes and follows it; that is, the temporal arts of narrative interrogate the plastic arts of painting. The volatility of the images removes the temporal stasis of the painterly image, and arrests the temporal flow of the narrative. These two contradictory discursive moves in the film complicate both its aesthetic and political strategies. The qualification of stasis by the discursive real in the temporal, and the arrest of temporality by the painterly image enables the possibility of a feminist lineage in mythical terms that is critical about the very conditions of myth even as it asserts its necessity for women.

The challenge of feminism to the old patriarchal master painters is of a different order. Consider the image of Antonia's old mother at her burial in the church. A beautiful static image of the woman in the composition introduces the sequence. Completely in keeping with it, Allegonda raises her hand evoking a visual memory, but in narrative contrast to the earlier raising of her hand from her death bed, she starts singing. A second later the drooping head of Jesus on the cross rights itself. The seers are to the right in the deathbed scene, to the left in church. A medium-shot of Allegonda rising in church is a rough match to the deathbed shot. Allegonda overcomes the composition with joy and rigour in church, animatedly singing, while the singer watches open-mouthed. In the first the seers are respectful and distant, in the second they are not part of the scene. In the first they are addressees, interpellated as it were, if resistant; in the second they do not figure, the visionary mythical being self-enclosed. With these movements, Gorris emphasises the desire for myth and the significance of the discursive real. Literally, the service is speaking of everlasting life. Danielle's pictorialisation of it rubs against the villagers' complaisant view of the miracles of life and death. Antonia's comment after Danielle's imagining about how it is all 'a load of rubbish' interprets both the metaphysical and visionary. The authority of the visionary understands the metaphysical in rich terms that the church and village do not. That vision is more hospitable to the humanist feminist because it does not accept the bitterness of the female's life, Antonia's mother's life, as her only life. Danielle's vision suggests the mystical, however improbably. Antonia's 'load of rubbish' in the discursive spoken interrogates both, and questions the facility and desire with which myths are constructed. Through Danielle's desire for myth, Gorris acknowledges women's desires for the mythical. For feminists this is manifested by 'a powerful need to name an originary yet thoroughly modern mother',[41] which is the film's project, made more subtle by the conversation on the traditional metaphysical and the female visonary.

Gotthold Ephraim Lessing claimed that painting arrested time and poetry advanced it.[42] Myth repeats time or is cyclical and hence not really useful for either utopian or realistic ends. Yet it provides familial authority, the authority of lineage and descent, creating a space for telling stories. Telling the same stories will not do for women, part of the problematic of myth as patriarchal renditions have assembled it.

The pictorial interventions of the diegesis have the effect of re-marking the past and commenting on the present. These interventions are humourous and serve to note the superiority of the visionary over the traditional. One such example is when we see a grown Danielle walking through the village churchyard in the company of her mother, Antonia. Antonia reminisces about a friend who had supported the Resistance by housing a Jewish family. Unobtrusively but visibly we see the back of a stone angel. Antonia continues with the story of how the friend had been turned in, shot by the Germans. She raises her voice as the priest passes by, so that he can hear what she has to say: that the resisting friend had been denied his last rites by the priest. As Danielle looks at the statue, the wing which had moved tentatively earlier moves decisively now and hits the priest sharply. He falls to the ground. We see Danielle looking at the priest through the frame provided by the wing. He is shamefaced. Danielle smiles. Some pictorial interventions are more telling, if less overt.

Another instance is of Danielle looking at the statue of the Virgin Mary for a whole minute who then smiles very imperceptibly and subtly in approval of Danielle's actions. While not interested in a heterosexual relationship, she had sought a man out and become pregnant. After having sex with the young man, Danielle had fled. The Madonna's eyes appear to touch Danielle, not literally, but physically, since their looks are not sutured through eye contact. The gaze of the Madonna on Danielle follows European traditions of iconography. Janet Soskice notes: 'The icon is furthermore not passive to the gaze. If anything, and explicitly with the icons of the Virgin and Child, it is the worshipper who is looked upon.'[43] This approval by Mary reclaims an existing Western tradition of painting and art of the Madonna that is ambiguous and expresses male difficulty with the feminine by coding the Madonna as both 'pure' and 'carnal'. In terms of a joke, it seems that the joke is on the church. Danielle the visionary has taken the creed of Mary; that is, of her purity second only to Jesus, literally, if within a secular framework.[44] The certitude of the

Fig. 26: *Antonia's Line* – the eyes of the Madonna touch Danielle approvingly

past is disturbed by the painterly: the earlier envisioning of Allegonda's diatribes in present time as opposed to her static silence. The certitude of the present is disturbed by the painterly interposed present perspective that denies the mythical continuity of the past to the present. Breaking that continuity of past to present through the painterly present (Danielle as Mary) intervenes in the reaffirmation of male myth.

Replacing male myth with feminist myth is not the ultimate consequence of the film despite some obvious gestures towards the same. Antonia sowing seeds in the field against the sky, seemingly monumentalising time, and the pictorial quality of the film itself seems to arrest narrative pressure for movement. Here, the film is at odds with male mythical texts such as the *Odyssey*; regardless of the lack of narrative suspense common to myth, the text has a clear goal: the return home which the story inexorably follows both in the movement of the hero and the narration of the tale. Antonia settles in the place and lives here; not much actually occurs by way of trial, challenge or even compulsion. An opaque character whom we never really know, her role seems to be as feminist outside observer, commentator and perhaps educator of her daughter, who is also as much her confidante as her pupil. Despite her mythical framing that punctuates the film, she does not act in any obvious heroic way; a thematic important to feminism that encourages us to view heroism in diverse ways.

The narrative mechanism restricts the heroic scope opened up by the landscape/external framing of Antonia, so infrequent in mainstream film for women that it appears mythical, coming from land and elements, larger than the social or symbolic. The voice-over narrator who at first seems omniscient and hence consonant with the notion of a mythical storyteller is not at all a communal authoritative narrator, but a little child. If some of the characters appear larger than life, the child narrator's desire would account for it. Yet the project of creating a space in a lineage with which to identify oneself without the imposition of a larger universal narrative has been finessed, if with some mythical material that can be shared by others not directly in the family.

The film begins with the return of Antonia and her daughter Danielle to the village to bury Antonia's mother and is effected without any realist narrative pressure. No suspense about any narrative outcome is maintained. The voice-over narrator who lends ironic distance[45] from the story complicates the whole temporal movement by discussing the passage of time in organic, pre-modern terms. Yet this time is not imposed on the female herself and her life cycle, but on time itself. In this passage of time, a notion that is outside human awareness seems to prevail, particularly the idea that time seems to be hunting to conquer or finish itself. Distancing both male and female subject from time thus gives neither a privileged place in history. But the women, by breaking every social rule, maintain complicity with that organic notion of time that bypasses a historical notion more inimical to them.

The village itself seems lost in time or forgotten, much like Macondo before Ursula found a way to the sea in Gabriel García Márquez's *One Hundred Years of Solitude*. The reappearance of Antonia to the village has been viewed as disarraying the village's desire to retain its 'pre-war hegemonic past'.[46] This lost quality of the village, Gorris shows, is a function of the way village values prevail over all else. The phrase, 'everyone in the village knew about it', is eerily and troublingly repeated. Here is where Gorris's hardcore sense of what women do and do not do is revealed; the women actually do not alter this code. The women can force the truth out into the open, but silently. When Antonia's daughter, Danielle, finds DeeDee being raped by Pitte, and has the courage to rescue her, Antonia and Danielle take her to church with them. The gauntlet is flung down fairly decisively; that is, a discursive space is taken by the mother/daughter in a public arena. The force of these actions extend beyond traditional feminist concerns. Antonia hangs the boy who torments Loony on the crook of the tree, earning Loony's devotion. When the priest starts berating Antonia and daughter about promiscuity and immorality, it is Farmer Bos who quietly blackmails the priest. Ultimately the priest becomes a member of Antonia's extended community. The vision of Antonia is firmly materialist; anti-metaphysical or spiritual, making the perspectival vision of her daughter all the more enigmatic.

Antonia eventually speaks, and when she does, it is speech as murder. Having created a discursive space for herself, and even 'accommodated' village concerns by her discretion and her silent, rather than loud, refusal to participate in their ideology, she speaks in public after the traumatic rape of her granddaughter.

The rape by Pitte, who has also raped DeeDee his sister, still a child, is not shown but recorded by the voice-over narrator. Antonia takes the gun from her daughter, in a move reminiscent of a warrior arming himself/herself before the epic battle, and goes to Pitte's house in search of him. When she does not find him there, she goes to the pub and asks him to get up. When he does not, she shoots the glass on the table, whereupon he comes out. The scale of the filming invests the sequence with heroic overtones. Long shots outline Antonia in the landscape, as she approaches the bar, and finally reaches the middle of the street. Here Antonia delivers a speech that has the efficacy of murder. She curses Pitte with the mythic overtones of a Draupadi who speaks from her place as a woman. The silence is broken here as she names what he has done: raped a child. With that statement, Antonia challenges the village. Her response to his act does have the fabular effect of holding women to that standard of both courage and dignity. Hiding the act would have allowed the young grandchild to experience shame. Confronting Pitte and the village means that only speech would address the situation effectively; and while DeeDee was publically protected earlier, here Antonia lets the village know that nobody in the village ever dare hurt a child in this way.

As powerful, in a reversal of the famous scene from Gorris's *A Question of Silence*, the men come out, jostle and hurtle and beat Pitte. Pitte is killed by his brother immediately after, as though in incredible magical dark response to Antonia's curse, although the narrator comments that Pitte's brother wanted to retain his inheritance. The colours used to depict the separate space governed by the family are idyllic. However, the villagers' participation in the demise of Pitte arguably indicates that the discursive space the women have been able to carve out cannot be a separate space.

Far from being idealised then, the film thoroughly covers the difficulties of women living in patriarchal systems at the narrative level. Two of the women are raped, one a child, the other, perhaps not fully mentally competent, by her own brother. Family values are certainly exploded here. In the case of DeeDee, the village is complicit with the family insofar as they do not challenge DeeDee's living with Antonia. Because she serves as a serf in the other family, the loss of her services would be damaging for Farmer Dan's family. On the other hand, they do not demand justice for DeeDee. Antonia, Danielle and DeeDee face the family in church. The daughter DeeDee is rescued by Danielle, the mother remains in the brutal masculine family, but not complicit at all in the patriarchal tyranny. She approves of her daughter's flight, and smiles and blesses her. Antonia's daughter's father is never mentioned. These trials, the backwash of patriarchy and the institutions that support it, are stayed – kept at arm's length but never fully conquered. Gorris certainly does not suggest that the feminist struggles have been won by all women, or even by these women, simply that they have been able to take over a discursive space without being burnt in the process. We know that the child prodigy, Therese, never forgets the rape, never gets over it.

The difficulties that women experience are not confined to their interactions with the villagers and the external world. Danielle reacts badly to her daughter's distance, her daughter's difference from others. Danielle herself seems a little outside of even this female space, suggesting difficulties with maternal spaces itself.

The patterns of changing maternity are in and of themselves striking but not, I believe, intended to convey any extraordinary significance except to insist that maternity is not archaic and mythical. Antonia's mother died saying Antonia was late as usual. She also condemns the absent father. The absent father is completely out of the picture for Danielle. Therese has a father who is redundant in this particular set-up, and Sarah has a very present father. Each woman deals with men differently. Antonia herself accepts Farmer Bos. Heterosexuality as pleasure, without conferring power on the male, can apparently be rewarding for both. Therese opts for the nurturing male for her daughter, and keeps her distance.

Even as the film fulfils the desire for that originary modern mother, it also more importantly fulfils the dream of female creativity, of the extraordinary. As Marli Feldvoss points out, each member of Antonia's immediate family is an artist in his/her own right.[47] She also notes Antonia's high degree of consciousness about her life that extends to knowledge of the time of her death, which I would argue would be indicative of Antonia's creativity. Antonia's constitution of her family is innovative, and extraordinarily creative in its inclusiveness of those who are 'not normal', a term that fits the philosophically pessimistic Crooked Finger, DeeDee and Loony Lips, the woman who wants to stay constantly pregnant, the child prodigy, and so on. Each of the persons of the family has an element that exceeds the normal in some way.

Antonia's own extraordinariness is signalled right at the end of the film when she knows not only that she is going to die, but what is going to happen to her. Her great-granddaughter Sarah, who is the narrator of the film, 'sees' all the characters coming towards her as she sits high up in the loft with her scribbling pad in front of her. The great-grandmother predictably rises from her supine posture yet again. Her seeing of these characters realises them for the mythical fiction the film composes.

Ultimately, the mythical modality of the film is to lend the *real* the power of *imagining*. Antonia's confronting Pitte, Danielle's running away with DeeDee, ordinary acts of solidarity, are by virtue of the violence of patriarchy, extraordinarily courageous acts identifying and acknowledging heroism without foreclosing the possibility of yet unnamed acts of courage by women for women and the community yet to be built. Antonia dies, her legacy the possibility for women in her family to identify lineage outside the violence of patriarchy, within the matrix of a changing, changeable women's community; with men, but always with women's values. For women then, both time and space need to be redefined, a time that is neither cursive nor cyclical, but can move forward with attention to female lineage, and a space that is neither masculine nor feminine, but where women can both occupy male space and create female spaces.

A 'Third Space' in Feminist Narrative: Prema Karanth's *Phaniyamma*

Feminist modernist myth has revealed the importance of women occupying male space to make demands that would entitle them to claim and retain female space. A study of a film set during the British colonial period in India reveals the difficulties for third world women in defining spaces for themselves. Interestingly, both Gorris and Prema Karanth look back into history; but unlike the female characters of Gorris's *Antonia's Line*, the characters in *Phaniyamma* must expand female spaces to retain self-identity.

Phaniyamma is the story of a child-widow from an upper-caste Brahmin family in India, and the social strictures that confine her. The film follows her life as she attempts to understand her existence as a woman, and subsequently begins to challenge the roles of women in orthodox Brahmin society. The film is based on a novel of the same title by M. K. Indira, written in the original Kannada and translated into English by Tejaswani Niranjana, which enjoys a fine literary reputation both for the text and translation which won awards. Published by Kali for Women, a feminist press of foremost repute, Prema Karanth had a formidable task when translating the acclaimed feminist text for the screen.[48] Both text and film discuss the social problem of child-widowhood prevalent in the nineteenth century but continuing well into the twentieth. The novel and film are both organised around the life of one such woman, Phaniyamma, born in 1840, died in 1952.

In terms of a third world feminist aesthetics, inhabiting the space of the frame, or stamping one's ownership of the frame, is not without ambiguity. From a historical perspective, cinematically and otherwise, such a move cannot be regarded as unequivocally positive. Madan Gopal Singh, in his brilliant and complex discussion on the issue of third world filmmakers and their aesthetic/political choices regarding what kind of cinema to produce, considers the historical position of the third world filmmaker. He cites one third cinema filmmaker as wanting to 'build a living room out of the layers of politics, cinema and theory'.[49] In analysing the impulse that would seem to articulate the place of the third world filmmaker outside the cinematic frame/screen, Singh discusses the ways in which filmmakers have thematically worked with homelessness to enable ontological reflection on the cinema. Singh's sustained analysis of V. Damle's and S. Fatehlal's *Sant Tukaram* (1936) offers us a provocative theoretical framework for considerations of third world aesthetics.

Singh discusses a specific third world aesthetic context as one that has tried to evade the grand colonial narrative. Using Deleuze's notion of 'durative' as encompassing both time and space, or in my own understanding, as having stilled time and space by the withdrawal of the camera and the dissolution of the image, Singh argues that *Sant Tukaram* inaugurates a new image that is placed outside of narrativity. The durative forces one to consider the cinema's ontological status and by extension its implication in historical processes. The historical dimension of the image's placement outside narrative/realism is of paramount significance to the history of the colonised subject. The 'epistemic subject', as opposed to the 'practical subject', is folded into the 'semiotics of silence'.[50] Singh suggests that even as the 'practical subject' marches forward in the formation of the nation, the 'epistemic subject' reserves judgement. Singh reads the evasion of narrativity as the resistance to the grand colonial narrative of progress.

This powerful reading of realist narrative as reflective of the external world and, as I take it, as mimicking colonial models in the colonial subject's cinema, has relevance to any discussion of third world aesthetics. Would the colonised woman's epistemic integrity lie in an aesthetics outside of narrative? Interestingly enough, Singh himself points out that the role of Jijai, the woman in *Sant Tukaram*, is very much within narrative, particularly with regard to her different positionality vis à vis the male characters. Chidananda Das Gupta's ideas on comparative aesthetics allows us to critique the resistance to narrativity also as a hiding away from history. Das Gupta brings up the notion in the context of pioneer filmmaker Dadasaheb Phalke's fixation on a mythology outside history and Hindi film's subsequent obsession with such a manipulative history. Certainly any cinema oblivious to history would mythologise women.[51] It is important to add that most realistic Hindi films also mythologise women because of readily available frames of reference.[52]

The feminist filmmaker has to contend with historicity in absolutely relentless terms if she is not to place woman in an ahistorical space where her signification would derive from male taxonomies. Indeed, realism has been the most readily available form within which to achieve some tangible recognisable historical specificity.[53]

Phaniyamma confronts the dual challenge of both undertaking the task of 'uncovering' as opposed to 'concealing' an epistemic self and showing the 'coverings', including that most intransingent of covers – history. The story of Phaniyamma is not known to anyone in any great detail – no authentication exists of that narrative. It becomes all the more important to historicise such a narrative before one uncovers an 'epistemic self' that hides itself strategically from colonial eyes, but one that has purposefully been obscured, rendered invisible, by the bearers of history. In other words, the task cannot be conceived only in terms of maintaining an inviolate epistemic self but of finding the female subject.[54]

In the historical, even modern, context of widows providing selfless service to the family and community, the historicisation of the figure becomes important to an understanding of the roles women were assigned in this period of history – the mid-nineteenth century and early twentieth century. Although realism has historically been the most accessible mode within which to unravel the coverings of the self, Karanth uses a mode that is not classical realist, neorealist or Hindi cine-realist, but poetically realist.

Given the importance of 'history', poetic realism would seem to offer problems in that the reflection of reality would not be an immediate congruent, or at least a simulated congruent. When dominant realism is not used, transparency is ruled out;[55] poetic realism has the edge as far as showing the construction of reality.[56] The seemingly 'poetic' quality of the reality being represented is difficult to extract from history because of the eternal qualities of poetry. Poetry also bears the burden of over-aestheticisation, taking pleasure in the beauty of a social evil, or in its representation. Notwithstanding these objections to the tone, the emplacement of Phaniyamma's self in the colonial and historical narrative would seem to demand that a 'third space' be set aside for self-introspection thus preventing the necessity to embed her narrative in the *grand récit*, colonial and indigenous patriarchal.[57] The third space, despite the insistent narrativisation of space within the historical mode, becomes a way for the auteur to introduce considerations of an epistemic self, formulated in that third space even as it is constituted by history and narrativised space. It is to Karanth's credit that this third space is not mysticised or sacralised, or Hindu fundamentalised, but set in the community – ultimately a historic function but possible only through a third space.

Space is narrativised as time and history by Karanth. Historicising space becomes the raison d'être for putting space in the narrative grinder. It also serves as defence for the poetic realism that makes it possible to show the coverings of an epistemic self – but without showing the self. Revealing the self is an impossibility; in the recesses, not deliberately hidden, but concealed by a history shown through the camera – showing the insidious, symbolic and poetic, the traditional wrappings with which the covering up of the self is done.

What makes *Phaniyamma*'s spacings free of narrative subserviency is not that they do not have narrative significance, but that they do not have diegetic narrative significance. The space is not pulled into the plot to serve the functions of advancing the narrative or retarding the plot. The significance of the space is extra-diegetic and not reflective of space outside but of a time outside it; a history being played out in its space.

Karanth sketches out a feminist aesthetics through a cinematic meditation on space and the self that moves towards discovering, rather than recovering, an 'epistemic self'. Spatial configurations work discursively; the frame's arrangement of space becomes the discourse of the film. Reading *Phaniyamma* as a film that changes the cinematic codes because of women's fraught relationship with these codes and what these codes signal about women's places in society invites us to undertake a reading of the film's aesthetics.

Phaniyamma as a film belongs to the increasing canon of 'parallel' Indian films, films that are socially progressive and that do not aggressively follow the Bombay Hindi film's formulaic placement of the female as narratively insignificant but visually demanding of the male gaze.[58] Rather, these films, including *Phaniyamma*, allow for women to play narratively significant roles and mark them as important in the social register, not merely because of the generic exigencies of the melodramatic genre as in mainstream film.

From the beginning the film refers obliquely to spaces, and starts out showing the viewer the spatial arrangements of the grandest house in Malnad in Karnataka. Karanth uses the 'big house' as a metaphor for the Brahmin orthodoxy. The camera tracks past the portal to the main entrance behind which there are spacious verandahs. The camera quickly pans to show us how many thinnas, or pillars, there are and how wide they are before it returns abruptly to the portal. We pause at the portal that leads to the inner courtyard where feasts are held, the camera a mute archivist of the time, before the female voice-over narration begins. Her tone is that of an informant. Even after her commentary starts, the director spends time on intimating the various spaces of the house. We are shown the wooden staircase and the three steps that lead to Thimmayya's room. The spatial grandeur becomes a metaphor for Thimmayya's high office as Postal Clerk. The camera pulls up to the door, pauses, and when the voice-over announces that we can now see Thimmayya's room, we are taken in. This deliberate attention to the space, the camera's insistent horizontal and vertical panning of the windows, indicate the extraordinary dual power of the family, derived from the British and from their own wealth and eminence in the community. Even as the voice-over establishes that no one dare question ancient customs and norms, the camera takes us to other spaces in the house. Everything apparently has a place. During the times the film is set, women by and large would not have had free access to all the space of the house and custom demanded that widows would make themselves as invisible as possible. We are taken to the bottom where there is the black room. The camera stays a moment to show us the darkness and the bars on a window but we do not really see the dimensions of the room too well; and the narrator does not know what use the dark room serves. The camera then moves to the outer courtyard, to the well, back to the sheds and to the exterior. The sequence is almost like an overture, a separate act as the camera takes us out to the fields before the theatre of action shifts in a disturbing way from the big house to the thatched hut.

It is all the more dramatic that the film begins, not with the child-widow proper, but with three women: a woman in labour, her mother and the midwife. Three faces of pain comment silently on the ordeal of childbirth. Later we cut to the shot of the labouring woman who shakes her head back and forth synchronised to the ritual beating of drums.

The first shot of Phaniyamma is a powerful one, a close-up of her lying down. While not an extreme close-up, the medium close-up of her face gives her a certain screen space and a power. Her room is bare and she is lying on the floor on a mat. Curiously, the bareness of the room conspires to lend her greater screen presence. The context – she is woken up to help a woman give birth – demands that Phaniyamma is lying down. Phaniyamma decides to go. The significance of her decision is underlined by a subtle framing, a quartering off of her section of space. When she steps out of that space, she is also stepping out of tradition. One of the women in Phaniyamma's household comments that she has become senile to visit the untouchables after her pilgrimages. Phaniyamma breaks every rule in the brahmin book to help one woman in labour.

Karanth lends her hero luminosity and a tremendous strength by shooting the sequence before the birthing lit only by a hurricane lamp and contrasting the darkness –both outside in the fields and in the birthroom – by showing us Phaniyamma's face extraordinarily well-lit and mostly in medium or extreme close-ups. Yet her face is not highlighted in the way the studio star's is. Phaniyamma's face is lit but not in its 'to be looked at' modality. In no shot is she looked at. That she cannot be looked at frees her and gives her her own space; it also narratively emphasises that she is not worthy of being looked at and that she is not to be looked at. Tradition has covered her up. Karanth does her best to uncover her without causing her any indignity, sensitively and subtly through evocation of the 'third space'.

Karanth does not let the viewer into the intimacy of the birthing scene. We see it through an aperture. The scene carries the richness of a drama because of the stillness of the three faces that create the effect of a tableau. She alternates between long shots and close-ups that draw attention to background and foreground. We see Phaniyamma's horrified face. The cry of the woman is contrasted with the cry of the child and we are immediately taken away from the scene. Karanth moves from distance to closeness, from system to person, from space to enclosures. This movement allows her to locate the story within a larger context and becomes the means by which she critiques the position of child-widows/widows in Hindu society. The tableau effect, the alternating rhythm of the shots, implies a viewer standing outside the aperture; either the archival camera, or the recording woman who has heard of Phaniyamma's story from her own mother.

When Phaniyamma returns from the birthing, she is lit in darkness. We witness her then, working, giving life, not just to the child but the other woman who would have died had it not been for her help.

The narration is not restricted to the voice-over or the archival camera. The narrative is spliced with Phaniyamma's searching look throughout. At the dialogic level, her question-ing begins early. When she returns, we are privy to her thoughts on the difficulties of child-birth. Phaniyamma wonders why women continue to have children when it is such a trial. Karanth introduces the motif of sexuality delicately but complete with the social resonances it has for women. As Phaniyamma ritually cleanses herself in the river after the 'pollution', she sees a male relative changing his poonal, his sacred thread. On her return home, she finds out that he too is covering up, but that he is keeping up observances well – he has just had sex with an untouchable woman because of his wife's pregnancy. Phani Athe is the only one who is not aware of this man's doings. Phaniyamma's address to the off-screen viewer about how these purity norms are set up to protect the hypocritical miscreants enables us to understand the story as her story. We have a strong sense of Phaniyamma's presence in her own story because we see both the old and young Phani in the same frame.

The notion of the recording woman re-telling, rather than telling, the story is empha-sised. Karanth shows Phaniyamma stepping back into the enclosure after her address to the off-screen viewer. One shot, for instance, shows us her eyes and then pulls back to rest on Phaniyamma's whole face. Karanth shows us Phaniyamma stepping into the landing that functions as an enclosure. The camera follows her climbing up the stairs, crouching in front of the window, and then frames her with her face flush against the window bars. Her posture implies a shrinking of the self, ambivalently registered as a troubled contemplation on both the self and sexuality.

The shifting of the camera from behind Phaniyamma to a space outside the house underscores Phaniyamma's enforced retreat. Phaniyamma smiles. A straight cut to a softer focused scene takes us to a girl swinging and then running. The spatial contrast is rich. We cut back to Phaniyamma behind bars to establish the rhythm of the spatial contrast. Another cut brings us to Phaniyamma walking down the same space. Space becomes a thematic narrative transitional marker – an envisioning of life as defined and delimited by spaces. The presence of the child raises the question of whether the story is of the life of a child, of a woman, of a childwoman or of a widow. What estates can Phaniyamma claim?

Karanth cuts back and forth between the old and the young Phaniyamma. There is some sense in which the child Phani becomes the 'epistemic self'. Only Phaniyamma looks at her, and in looking at her, the whole process of self-reflection becomes intense, and becomes the motivation of the narration, or how the story comes to be told. Visual self-reflexivity becomes important for the film's feminist narrative aesthetic in that the image reflects the woman in the story as opposed to the narrative apparatus reflecting for the male protagonist.

While the narration does not make it clear who the storyteller is, the events that formed Phaniyamma's life are clearly rendered. The past and the present, although separate, are related in uneasy ways that the protagonist tries to fathom. Karanth cuts Phaniyamma's face in a contemplative register between episodes. In the triggering sequence mentioned above, for instance, the viewer is asked to focus on a desk that Phani is also looking at; at the far end of the frame, the furthest edge of the space, a girl, the young Phani, is sweeping. The presumed physical or spatial distance between the viewer, Phaniyamma and the young girl hints at the difficulty the older Phaniyamma has in finding that young girl. That this particular episode comes out of Phaniyamma's rebellion and that sex surrounds the incident, both the childbirth and the infraction of the male relative, gives us pause. Phaniyamma is well into middle age and yet unaware. One shot of total darkness in the frame, of dark space where the space is relieved by a voice asking why she is imprisoned makes the logic of the narrative apparent. This scene ends with Phani looking at her bangles.

A flashback ostensibly provides us with a reason for Phani's incarceration in dark space. Through some extraordinarily poetic editing that conveys a 'Hindu' sense of the inevitability of certain events when certain symbolic acts have occurred, Karanth does a montage of the knife on the young Phani's hair, cuts to a shot of the hair on the ground and then to a shot of the scissors on the hair. Next is a shot of the blade moving faster in keeping with the music, a poignant medium close-up of the barber in tears and then there is the ultimate cut to Phaniyamma in white cloth, in widow's garb. That this scene is placed after the scene when Phani's pretty colourful bangles are broken brutally by her mother indicates that Phani's incarceration was due to the great superstitious dread of widowhood. The thief who cut her hair, instead presumably of her jewellery, apparently jeopardises her happiness even before her husband dies because of what the omen betokens. Phani is kept in the enclosure so that her in-laws do not find out about her mishap at the festival. Karanth shows us Phaniyamma looking at her bare hands. The young Phani had registered the events surrounding her husband's death only by her blank bewilderment at the loss of the bangles. The young and old woman both look at their hands successively in mute questioning of what has occurred. Karanth conveys quite exquisitely the child's total unawareness of the separate and blighted fate that awaits her as a widow. Her lack of awareness formulates the most powerful critique of the system that sets her aside, presented as the story is in an autobiographical modality – the child's grief is combined with the older Phaniyamma's retrospective exploration of her past.

The immediate circumstances that place the young Phani in an enclosure are not readily understandable without the symbology around hair, its auspiciousness and lack thereof.

At the festival that Phani and family attend, we see one shot of her braided hair. Phani has asked for the golden tresses, or the hair plaited with ornamental material. She has apparently strayed from the family or got lost in the crowd. If there are any implications to her having strayed and consequently run into trouble, they are not foregrounded. Phani realises that her hair has been cut as she rejoins her family. She is urgently dragged back into the house and pushed into the doorway, almost as though to extricate her from the world. The door is then slammed shut, very decisively. The next long sequence moves between Phani either in dark space (two spaced shots) or Phani behind the bars (several shots with cuts and one shot of some duration) and the Yakshagana dancer from the troupe. Phani is clearly out of that kind of public space. That is poignantly and touchingly shown by the fact that her mother is outside the nellapadi, Phani inside. She cannot cross the threshhold and go outside.

Narratively, Phani's imprisonment as a young girl is not the greatest confinement of her life. What is more limiting, what restricts Phaniyamma for the rest of her natural life, are the stringent madi rules, rules of pollution and contamination, that govern her life as a widow and that form the basis for the roles of widows more generally. Phani's new routine is of constant and total work. She is not permitted to eat if someone touches her and therefore has to bathe again if she is polluted in any way. Phani's purity depends on her not being touched. There is, of course, no question of her being touched by men, or of remarriage since the Shankaracharya had ruled that although Phani was a virgin widow, she would not be permitted to remarry. More pragmatically, one of the numerous male relatives in Phani's family maintains that the family – read: the community – needs madi women like Phani.

This argument raises its ugly head again. When Dakshayini, a young woman, loses her husband, the community wants to have her head shaven and to join the ranks of madi women. During the course of the discussion, one of the men asks Phaniyamma for her opinion. Phaniyamma considers that the times have changed and that Dakshayini need not follow the old, barbaric customs. Curiously, the other women, sumangalis, the married women, disagree with Phaniyamma and maintain that she has not upheld madi; after all, she has gone to see a dance/drama/romance.

Karanth uses the same ritual of haircutting to show both the entrenched nature of the orthodoxy and the change in women. Dakshayini, not a child-widow, chases the barber out. In the film's most rebellious moment, Dakshayini actually drags her mother-in-law to the barber. He exits, horrified. A close-up of Dakshayini's dead husband, a fantastic framed shot of her coming out at the portal with long hair, and a later cameo frame of her slowly and deliberately putting kumkum on her forehead, shows that her rebellion has not been stamped out brutally. Phaniyamma's support of Dakshayini, despite an entire life spent in following orthodoxy, speaks of her compassion for other women and is virtually the only sign that she, Phani, sees the difficulties of her hard life.

Widows are joined by childless women in this life of continuous toil, ritual purification and servitude to others. Their work, not least its codification because of purification rituals and fear of pollution becomes an impassable, unbreakable enclosure. The body is the primary instrument of maintaining this physical isolation. Karanth films Phaniyamma with space around her to show her physical distance from others. At one juncture, a young boy touches Phaniyamma inadvertently; because she has to take a bath again before she can eat, the mother of the boy slaps him hard. Phaniyamma seems to realise the divisiveness of the madi ritual, but decides to give up the meal she would have had. From that time onwards, she has only one snack. Madi has forced a privation on the body that far exceeds the taboos of touching. Not coincidentally, all the taboos of touching are connected with forbidding eating if in an 'impure' state.

The taboo against touching, madi, of course is not exclusive to widows. Orthodox Brahmin women followed it. Yet in the case of widows, the taboo is clearly meant to prohibit and discourage physical contact. Phaniyamma does bathe small children in the house, but otherwise all her physical contacts are outside the big house.

Phaniyamma's moment of greatest intimacy is when she helps the woman give birth, also the moment of greatest rebellion. Later, Phaniyamma is friendly with a young midwife. One long sequence cut to a slow-moving extra-diegetic song shows Phaniyamma walking through the village and in and out of villagers' houses. The orbit of her contact is outside the house, not inside. The space inside is sacred, outside profane. From the barred interior she perceives intimate scenes outside the house, for instance the sexual encounter between two inmates in the house. Outside is also the space of the carnival or the Yakshagana. Outside is the sexualised space of contact, even if painful and terrible, one that Phaniyamma is barred from when she is first put inside that enclosure.

Karanth draws the sexual resonances out by not sacralising the woman as martyr, but showing her as a female with submerged desires that society buries. By initiating the self-exploration through the birthing scene, Karanth makes a comment about the role of sexuality in prompting Phaniyamma's questioning.

If Karanth shows the distance forced on the female hero by filming her with space around her, she shows her obsequiousness, a traditionally ingrained belief that she does not even deserve to live, by the shots of her covering herself tightly over her head with the sari palu and holding herself away from people. Combined with the fact that Phaniyamma uses a mixture to make sure that her hair does not grow, with her wearing the same widow's garb, her upkeep cost nothing.

Phaniyamma's status as a child-widow subtly puts her out of the cycle of women's lives as established in her community. One sequence is poignant in showing Phaniyamma's first awareness of sex. Phaniyamma is lying down. She overhears a man and a woman. She looks through a barred window and sees the lovers from afar. Once again, we have the tableau effect. We cut back to Phani's eyes looking at them only a second later. Phaniyamma's disturbance over sex, indeed her late awareness of sex, and only the vestiges of a hint of her own sexuality are painful in their muffled origins and are smothered by the work load that Phaniyamma carries. Not that she does not mull over the topic: one of the women she is close to asks her why she is so pensive. Phaniyamma wonders what the place of sexuality in women's lives is, and indeed what would be better, the life she leads, seemingly unimpinged by sexual motivations, or one where (male) sexuality governed women's lives. Phaniyamma cracks the acorn, spreads the paste, and ensures that her hair will never grow again after this episode. The renunciation of sex does not seem willing at all, rather, it seems angry and disturbed. She glares at the barber, tells him to come the next day, and dismisses him permanently when he does come.

We see evidence of her scepticism about the 'rightness' of the life she leads when she comes out in favour of marriages that are not based on horoscopes. Hers was, and indeed the astrologers had said that the match was perfect. Phaniyamma does not accord with the belief system in its important aspects even as she abides by it – a strong portrayal of women caught in systems that are hostile to their well-being.

Ashish Rajadhyaksha and Paul Willemen, quoting from Susie Tharu's and K. Lalitha's general comment, state that the film 'resurrects a stereotype from reformist fiction', and that its emotional capital derives from 'powerful and deeply embedded cultural formations and is emblematic of the way Swadeshi formulations of gender, nation and indeed feminism have reappeared and are renotated in the literature of the 1970s and 1980s'.[59] Karanth's text is much more informed by the local than this statement takes into account. Indeed, the emergence of the trope marks its difference from Swadeshi formulations strikingly in its mode of narration, in the role it gives the to-be-reformed subject. The film's 'imaginary community' would to some extent coincide with the nationalist imaginary, and in that sense the timeframe Karanth works with does not permit her to overtly offer directions for feminism that stretch beyond the reformist impulse. Yet the trope's recurrence in the 1970s and 1980s more obviously speaks to the troubled sense by which feminism is once more viewed as engaging in the battle between tradition and modernity.

The film, it seems, does accommodate tradition in an almost unseemly way in its elevation of Phaniyamma, despite her measured resistance. Rajadhyaksha and Willemen comment that the film offers 'not a radical critique of orthodox society but a purification of tradition adapted to modern condition'.[60] The song that eulogises her also subscribes to the 'transcending' model in that Phani is commended for having retained some beauty regardless of the thorny circumstances. T. G. Vaidyanathan points out that despite such accommodation, the film is, from his perspective, tiresomely anti-tradition. He finds that the staunch sharp anti-tradition stance of the female hero is imbricated in her rejection of the natural or instinctual life. As one of his examples, he uses the sequence where Phaniyamma, sexually disturbed after spying on an illicit pair in the family having sex, refuses to let the barber shave her, or rather, touch her. In contrast, according to Vaidyanathan, Dakshayini is shown as 'triumphantly' returning to tradition. He considers Dakshayini's remarriage, and her wearing the sindoori as a sign of her participation, where I would consider them as signs of altering tradition. The framed mirror image of Dakshayini, with the camera drawing ever more close to her and concluding in a tight close-up, emphasises her assertion of her self, her control over her appearance, a recurring motif in the film which with some justification associates the changes wrought on the exterior of the woman to her visible status in society and its complex relationship to her sense of self.

Vaidyanathan's serious charge that the anti-traditionalism of the film is at the cost of the natural is a serious one that deserves some deliberation. Although he does not say it, the insinuation is that it is because Phaniyamma is unable, either socially or psychologically, to participate in the seemingly natural order of life in the big house that she rejects tradition. It follows that the critique of tradition cannot have as much weight as it might if the critique were to emanate from one who did enjoy the traditional life. Vaidyanathan's merging of nature and tradition, a combination that the film deliberately splits, dangerously assumes that what is social is in fact natural.[61] Indeed, his one example of the natural is tied to sexual mores and practices. Karanth in fact shows the harnessing of female sexuality as one of the blockages of traditional life. The rhythm that runs Phaniyamma's life is the rhythm of relentless work and continuous observance of traditional rites. Tradition is shown as being dry and dessicated, sucking up the natural. Had it been left to tradition, the young untouchable woman in labour would have died. Tradition halters nature, it does not harmonise with it.

Another figure, familiar in reformist literature, around whom the conflicts around tradition and modernity coalesce is Subhi. Subhi has been sent back by her in-laws. The sequence is an interesting example of Karanth's style. The stillness of the big house is shattered by Subhi's unexpected arrival and the reserved welcome she receives from the doyenne of the big house. Even the sudden movement of Subhi from one side of the frame to another seems excessive in the quietness of the space. Her anguished protestations stand out as exclamations, as aberrations, as excessive in the tenor of the big house: 'They beat me like an animal. I will kill myself if you send me back.' Subhi has not borne her spouse children. Again, Subhi's resistance against tradition is, of necessity, restricted; she has already been sent back by the in-laws.

The space of tradition – the big house – is not obliterated in the film. The closing shots of *Phaniyamma* dwell on these pillars that seem as staunch as ever. The voice-over too asks if tradition will prevail or if it will break down. Yet the spaces of women have stretched, and through this expansion, a new subjectivity, not possible in the grand narratives, is glimpsed. The epistemic self is discovered, incredibly enough through the feminist authority granted by the expansion of women's spaces.

Another Narrative Paradigm: Leontine Sagan's *Mädchen in Uniform*

The discussion of the preceding films has emphasised the ways in which subjectivity for women in different cultural contexts is authorised through narrative processes. *Malou* inscribes maternal subjectivity, *Antonia's Line* narrates modernist myth, and *Phaniyamma* explores the discovery of the 'epistemic self'. Each text challenges the contours of male narrational modes. Leontine Sagan's *Mädchen in Uniform* represents a challenge of a different order to patriarchal narrative. The film allows us to conceive feminist narrative aesthetics outside the hegemonic/subversive model, although that model cannot but obtain, and think of how cultural narratives might be altered, not merely inverted, when narrative paradigms are shifted by not allowing the woman to signify excessively – or by not allowing the woman to signify-as-woman.

In an essay on the Oedipal myth, Laura Mulvey argues that there may be some benefit for women in understanding the central idea of the Sophoclean text as being about the process of telling, of acquiring self-knowledge through telling which then becomes important as the culture's story about itself.[62] To discuss the actual significations by which Oedipus has been culturally 'read' Mulvey uses Barthes and Propp. The codes used to discuss the narrative aesthetic of the myth, the proairetic and the hermeneutic, I would maintain, are insufficient to discuss feminist narrative aesthetics.

The proairetic code that follows cause and action is relatively insignificant for women for whom many actions are already dictated by the cultural imaginary and imperative.

While this is of course true for men as well, one of the injunctions on men is that they should act, so that the proairetic code is able to describe the events.[63] Cause and effect then are plotted; that is, the larger cultural narrative is described differently to enable the latter.

A similar fate befalls the hermeneutic code. The hero is confronted with the enigma which then, in relationship to the proairetic, becomes the story. If one were to look even cursorily at some of the major myths, including the Oedipal, the enigma in these narratives is women. Although it is true that the Oedipal myth is not about women, and the mother figures only as absence, her identity is the one that recalls Oedipus to himself, as Pasolini shows in the film where Oedipus talks about what he has seen, the taboo mother's body, a wonderfully telling metaphor for what mainstream cinema represses: the fear that the body will be maternal. Another founding myth/epic of Western culture, that of Odysseus, bears out the proposition that women are the enigmas, ultimately resolved more neatly by the epic, as obstacles.

An examination of an early women's film that has received much attention, Sagan's *Mädchen in Uniform*, might suggest less linear patterns that are not yet settled because the stories being told have not yet become embedded in story/discourse. Notions of story/discourse may be remapped by the cultural memory being coded differently than the founding patriarchal myths.

It is instructive to arrive at some provisional narrative codings for a filmic text by looking at what replaces the proairetic and hermeneutic codes, and how these affect the larger significance of the cultural narrative. Laura Mulvey herself discusses the difficulties of a 'negative aesthetic',[64] an endless chain of signification dependent on the dominant system to lend its aesthetic meaning. Certainly, the avenue has been productive for students, not just of film, but of culture in general. Worth repeating is the notion that feminist aesthetics do not have immediately accessible reference points that will become available only through women's history, women's literature and women's culture.

Mädchen in Uniform has invited some superlative analyses where cultural meanings signify otherwise; differently than the patriarchal narrative code, and where the codes have not necessarily been placed in the highly specific narrative semiosis specified by Mulvey regarding Oedipus.

The first condition of the existence of young Manuela of the film is predicated upon her gender, not her class position, or her desire for knowledge. And this function serves as both proairetic and hermeneutic codes for this film. Had she been a young boy she might actually have gone to the military academy. In general, the women on screen are not lacking knowledge and seeking it as the action plot-driven films are, they have knowledge and certainty that they are assured of, and the journey is to try to persuade the world thereof. The paradigm is radically other than that the Bildungsroman project of the young man trying to find his place in the world,[65] or the female marriage plot, the outcome seldom apparent.

Manuela, once she falls in love with her teacher, is persuaded that she should be permitted to continue the relationship, and that the public should accept it. Thus she announces her affections to the public. The knowledge that she has is further regarded as 'secret',[66] and taboos are broken when the world is told. Finally, the fear of the maternal body, maintained in the Oedipal trajectory, is removed, restoring the eroticism and attractiveness of the maternal. These meanings will signify elsewhere; their meanings will challenge the dominant *récit* but uncover its repressed desires, and reveal its supplement, not just its 'transitional material', as Mulvey refers to it,[67] that inhibits the form from being unified, but also what cannot be slotted into the proairetic and hermeneutic codes.[68]

The film is about lesbian sexuality, and also reveals the patriarchal imaginary. The idea of the film signifying doubly is not startling; presumably works of art work at more than one level. The issue here is with the narrativising of sexuality that results in its being 'produced' if Fredric Jameson's thesis maintaining this has any credence. Further, he speculates on whether 'sexuality as an overt theme always bears an ideological message of a secondary kind that concerns anything but sexuality'.[69] The reception of the film seems to bear witness to these anxieties. The first group of critics insisted on the anti-totalitarian interpretation; the feminist recuperation drew out the lesbian resonances and discussed its relevance as a social model. The film thus does 'produce' subjectivity through sexuality. However, the ideology of sexuality that emerges, which could hypothetically be read as a response to the tyrannical practise of the boarding school, is not primarily presented as such by Sagan, who is more invested in insisting on the presence of the erotic relationship between women,[70] the unshowable lesbian affection as an 'essential' rather than as a constructed category. Sagan's studied essentialism preserves for women the anarchic, presents lesbian sexuality as 'natural', however constructed that concept is. Sexuality produces subjectivity because sexuality is.

Manuela's falling in love with the teacher crosses barriers because she refuses to accept her hierarchical place as one of the many who will love Fräulein von Bernburg. Von Bernburg's actions towards Manuela have been interpreted as maternal. The erotic component of the maternal has proved threatening for classical psychoanalytic theory, suggesting as it does for the male child the possibility of not having any legitimacy in the symbolic/literally public. The suggestion of lesbian relationships through the mother/daughter bond in mainstream film has been mixed for lesbian women as it seems to deny the physical relationship between women and reinforce the unrepresentability of lesbian sexuality. One of the ways of both being able to maintain the code of invisibility and to suggest lesbian sexuality was by portraying surrogate mothers and their daughters: 'The mother/daughter relation in question is most often a *surrogate* relation and the gratification achieved by a lesbian interpretation is inversely proportional to the strength of that surrogacy.'[71] In the case of the film, Fräulein von Bernburg serves as a weak surrogate mother to more than one child, which of course complicates viewer identification regarding the mother/daughter relationship.

The surrogate maternal role projected on von Bernburg is further complicated by the presentation of the other women as phallic mothers,[72] or at the very least, women who are enforcers of patriarchal strictures, which of course carries a different valence. Both roles, however, seem to be at cross-purposes with the maternal role presented by von Bernburg.[73] Von Bernburg's playing the feminine role versus the masculine role within the structural design of the film adds a layer to the exposure of the enforcement of patriarchal structures by two kinds of women, femme and butch, or perhaps more contextually, lenient and authoritarian.

The deliberate use of the erotic to command obedience is stressed in the famous sequence where the girls kneel on their bed, awaiting their teacher's kiss. The power to command through the erotic is not restricted to demanding and absorbing the children's affection and devotion but also, very obviously, as B. Ruby Rich pointed out, to ensure their obedience to school regulations, and consequently, national imperatives. When challenged, von Bernburg says she gets the best results because of her methods. Rich refers to her acting as the 'focus of dissident energies', what I would call, erotic energy.[74] The erotic energy that von Bernburg invests in the young women is a mode of controlling their erotic energy, channelling it to suit the purposes of the institution, and by extension, nation. The clearest indication of von Bernburg's direct control over the young women and the use she makes of it to defend the school's authoritarian interests and its humanitarian facade, is when she brings the runaway back into the field with a thump on the rump.

This system of control is, however, questioned from our first glimpse of von Bernburg. Particularly interesting is the comment that she is almost uncomfortably kind. All the references to her place her in ambiguous light, suggesting that she may in fact be aligned with the excessive. Her appearance is stage-managed rather classically. Like the classical hero who is spoken of but does not make an appearance until the middle, Fräulein von Bernburg is mentioned more than once by the young girls to Manuela. Each of these references carries erotic connotations. Manuela is asked not to fall in love with von Bernburg because everyone is in love with her; or 'sleeping with her' is mentioned, as is the goodnight kiss.[75] A more concrete erotic insignia is the name EvB (not Fräulein von Bernburg) marked on the dress that Manuela is given as a hand-me-down. The seamstress laughingly explains that the girl must have been in love with von Bernburg.

A cut to a figure walking towards the centre of the frame is our first introduction to von Bernburg. The image is not immediately beguiling. The uniform, or costuming, plays a part in the severity of the figure. She walks through and up the stairs – we follow her, but from behind. The figure has the same gravitas Manuela's aunt's figure had, but that the other teacher, lower in the hierarchical rung, does not. Von Bernburg's figure imposes a presence, or a relationship to space that is authoritative and commanding. The concealment of her face, the delay in showing it, makes the first clear view of it arresting in its disjuncture between the figure and the face; the figure carrying the aura of a dark, definitely repressive persona, while the face, lighted, carries the radiant aura of complete satisfaction. Fräulein von Bernburg is almost replete with what she is seeing. Manuela is aglow in the composition, at a higher level, and very much a study in absorbed beauty. Manuela has descended the staircase, and stumbled on one, turning to find herself face to face with von Bernburg. Her face is tremulous. Von Bernburg further inspects her; her eyes do a scan from feet to hand while she smiles with pleasure, apparently moving easily without caesura from intensity of contemplative desire to surveillance. Her face is spellbound at the object of its gaze. Another shot of the close-up of her face reveals the same suffusion of tenderness.[76]

This visual overture is remarkable for its lucidity in specifying a moment of modernity for women. Maternal subjectivity does not figure in Western culture until the advent of modernity when female subjectivity is articulated, in however triangulated a fashion; that is, the desire of the mother, or mother-figure, is spoken in this case by her, through this joy and desire that leaps into Elisabeth von Bernburg's eyes on looking at Manuela. No controversial shot/reverse-shot sutures this scene: Manuela's gaze is averted, underlining the reticence of the camera, having already accentuated the desire of the female teacher.

The emphasis in readings of the film has centred on the initiation of a lesbian relationship by the young Manuela, and has perhaps overlooked the insistence with which the director imposes the desire of the teacher/mother surrogate. As B. Ruby Rich has noted, she kisses Manuela on the lips.[77] In the classroom sequence, when a student behind Manuela is reciting her lessons, von Bernburg sees Manuela's face, almost occupying all the screen space and blocking out the voice. The blocking out of the voice is crucial in making von Bernburg conscious of her desire. In this classroom sequence, when we first see Manuela's face before Hildegard's, we are not sure whether it is through von Bernburg's look or the camera's. Interestingly, we see Manuela looking at von Bernburg, but not in a tight shot/reverse-shot exchange. The girl behind Manuela is standing, reciting, so she is at eye level with von Bernburg, and the exchange of looks should have been with the girl. Thus Manuela's interposition of her desire is unknowing, von Bernburg's knowing, in the instant the camera dissolves from von Bernburg's face to Manuela's in the same space, and then shows von Bernburg slightly to the left, looking dazed and shaken up. Von Bernburg's ambiguity or naïveté about what the maternal role entails is revealed here.

The narrative opening insinuates the presence of girls/women desiring women/girls.[78] Causality of any strict kind is not posited, no external factor directs any action; instead the opening dwells on a complex channelling of desires between women. The conditions of this institution do not really permit any action as might be expected of the proairetic code. The students are definitely in jail. The hermeneutic code, the presentation of the enigma to be solved, is not enigmatic. Indeed, barring the authorities everyone else in the school – the girls, and the employees – accept the girls' crush on von Bernburg and its more powerful corollary: that women have crushes on each other.

Filmically, the director does not allow us to see things through Manuela's point of view, indicating that Manuela's desire is only one component of the complex network of desires that already exist in the school. Although this is Manuela's first day and we are exposed to all the interdictions and her responses, we do not have access to her subjectivity. By and large, she submits to all the demands made of her without too much of a fuss.

The director uses parallel editing to make connections between the three worlds of the school: the administration, the students and the staff. The principal is usually filmed with a lot of space around her, her authority being reinforced by the cowering posture of the staff. One of the other teachers is initially shown as an advocate for the girls but she is quickly co-opted to agree that soldiers' daughters who will be soldiers' mothers have no business being hungry. The girls crowd around each other, leaving virtually no space between them. This creates compositions that are relaxing to the eye, the centre of authority being diffuse. As in Fritz Lang's *M* (1931), it is the domestic staff who are critical of both groups. Again the filming here is not tight, as it is in the presence of the administrators. The obligatory courtesy is another gesture that emphasises the forced distance between student and authority figure, and between Frau Oberin and her staff. Predictably, Fräulein von Bernburg is drawn both ways; sometimes, as when she catches the letter writers, she is in the group with the students; at others, she is distant and then drawn closer.

That all three spheres of influence register lesbian desire, and that this already existing knowledge needs to be acknowledged, are rendered transparent by the director and function as a narrative impetus insofar as *emotion* motivates the action. Lesbian female desire itself does not impel the action in this particular narrative trajectory; its fulfillment being almost secondary to public sanctioning of its truth value.

The extra-diegetic sequence that prophetically features the military authority of Germany is offset by the classical statues of male nudes wrestling. As the military framing presages the set-up in the boarding schools, announced by a cut to a matching composition of the girls marching, so it is hard to believe that the images of the men wrestling do not intuitively declare the compress of single-sex erotic entanglements the film covers. Softer images of the girls hugging, engaged in intimate scenes, as distinguishable from intimate spaces, such as dorm room and bathroom, are narratively insignificant yet litter the film. What recurs is the dispersal of that intimacy by the authority figure in question. Some of these softer images also circulate in public. The girl who welcomes Manuela puts her arm around her. Other images group girls together, in such close proximity that the centre does not prevail. The entrance of the authority figure normally restores the centre. There are four or five sequences of this nature. Some are compositions of dyads. A long shot of two of the students with their arms around each other classically framed by the window spells out their intimacy and claims aesthetic beauty for them; another long shot of Manuela and a friend on the bed also reinforces this impression of beauty, harmony and closeness in less than ideal circumstances. When Manuela is dressed as Don Carlos, what Richard Dyer calls the Hosenrolle,[79] which he thinks is crucial to the film's ultimate modernity and lesbianism, one of the girls backstage, with both hands on Manuela's leg, says 'What beautiful legs you have.' This crucial cross-dressing sequence gives the young women permission to express their erotic feelings for other women.

The character of Ilse can be regarded as a desiring lesbian subject. Chris Straayer argues that 'Ilse, although narratively heterosexualised, has the conventional markings of a baby butch (for example, dark hair, physical activity, body posture, tomboyishness)'.[80] Indeed, Straayer considers Ilse crucial to the film's signification of physical lesbian desire.

The 'crush' on Fräulein von Bernburg is only one of many possibilities in the all-girls establishment. When Manuela as Don Carlos says she cares for 'her', the school wants to know who she is in love with. Von Bernburg is clearly one among many love objects in the school. Indeed, von Bernburg intercepts a *billet-doux* between two girls who are planning some sort of assignation. Without the enforcement of compulsory heterosexuality, many of these young women would clearly not become the wives and mothers of 'soldiers'. The faculty have no difficulty identifying or registering the existence of lesbian affection. They merely consider it wrong. One of the teachers tells Hildegard that it is 'perverse', and that she should not worry about Manuela when Manuela is isolated in the infirmary.

Manuela is separated from the other girls because her identity as lesbian is confirmed by her public 'outing' of Fräulein von Bernburg. The focus on discipline is to curtail the erotic energy, or channel it for national purposes. Von Bernburg herself makes a powerful observation when she comments on different kinds of love to Frau Oberin, and seeks to 'set Manuela straight', not about lesbian love, but about the conventional impossibility of its being fulfilled.

The domestic staff also recognise the existence of affection between women; this through the figure of Fräulein von Bernburg. The seamstress tells Manuela that the dress she has been assigned is from a student who probably had been in love with Fräulein von Bernburg. Indeed, von Bernburg is the charge, or locus, for this energy and this is in part because of the mystique of authority. Von Bernburg enjoys exalted status with the girls because of the power she has. Part of the attraction is her ability to make a difficult situation easier, but part of the attraction appears to be that among authority figures, she alone through the erotic, offers the promise of authority being jarred or jostled a little, though paradoxically the attractiveness lies in her retaining that authority. The situation plays itself out differently for Manuela than for the other students. Manuela's revelation about Fräulein von Bernburg at the concert initially disconcerts them not just because von Bernburg would become less attractive because of a commitment, much in the manner of a rock star, but also because her reciprocity makes her equal and hence no longer the idealised object of affection. For Manuela, the ideal is too cold; hence she 'outs' von Bernburg, hoping to fuse intimacy with adoration.

The play within the film, Schiller's *Don Carlos*, brings up important issues, not least of which is the notion, not just of forbidden love, but of incestuous love. Due to the play's Romantic reference, the incestuous theme is woven in with awareness of its taboo nature and with the desire to break the taboo. The Oedipal returns with a vengeance, but this particular enigma is a decoy; there is no secretiveness about the object of Manuela's affection, and its taboo nature, not just because of its lesbian affection, but because of the inflection of the romantic bond of the mother/daughter relationship. Manuela's love for Fräulein von Bernburg is because they are two people of the same sex, but the discomfiture over the reciprocity touches on deeply buried cultural beliefs about the maternal, the maternal body and the maternal erotic.

The maternal melodrama, a mainstream Hollywood film genre that has received considerable attention from feminist film critics, also creates the 'conditions' of lesbian 'representability' through the luminous presence of the mother/daughter relationship; the possibilities of a lesbian relationship are presaged by the strength of the mother/daughter bond, and the codes that represent it.[81] *Mädchen in Uniform*'s exploration is radically different because it follows the possible meanings for *maternity* of a lesbian relationship, not the other way around.

The 'femininity' of Fräulein von Bernburg emphasises for Richard Dyer the film's insinuation of the continuity between femininity and lesbianism itself; the mother/daughter bond of course is imbricated in this cultural understanding of lesbianism: 'In the context of the gynaeceum tale and contemporary ideas about Schwärmerei and lesbianism, the mother/daughter quality of the relationship only makes it more lesbian, not less.'[82]

The trope of the phallic mother is brought into the mix of mother/lover/daughter/phallic mother. The fear of the phallic mother is of her overpowering the child, specifically the male child.[83] The absent mother, Manuela's dead mother, characterised as very devout, leaves a gap that is mystifying and problematic on the one hand, but on the other seems to insinuate the erotic affections of the mother, borne and welcomed by the daughters, that are insupportable to both patriarchal institution and the patriarchal surrogates that run the boarding school. The relationship between the two kinds of 'mothers', or two signifiers of

Fig 27: *Mädchen in Uniform* –
the centre is insignificant in this
composition where the girls group
together, signifying erotic closeness

maternity, is rendered more complex by the absence of the patriarchal real. Do Frau Oberin and her staff stand in for that kind of patriarchal authority as can be readily understood, or do they in fact signify the ultimate failure of patriarchy – its own worst fears realised – men manque or castratos; men without the power of the symbolic? These phallic women operate in the name of the symbolic, they do not *act*. Men, on the other hand, do. In imaging authority as lacking its real force, transparency or the right to be natural in the symbolic, Sagan brilliantly undoes the planes of the composition of power. All depends on appearance; hence the students wish to make their situation public when royalty visits. In projecting patriarchal fear on Frau Oberin, Sagan also decomposes the patriarchal narratives that would have it that the phallic mother is the dangerous one; indeed, it is the other, who represents that space of plenitude, that is ultimately more threatening because in the patriarchal imaginary she is inaccessible, not being able to be brought into the patriarchal empire of signs. Sagan's narrative aesthetic superimposed on the patriarchal imaginary suggests how new patterns of narrative can emerge that work within the shifting significance of women as represented and women as representing themselves.

The ouster of the principal, descending the stairs slowly through silent students, is certainly a triumph for the students, and for a less coercive school situation. Whether the story ends as a lesbian fairytale is another matter. In that sense, the film is open-ended; stressing the community of girls coming together. After Fräulein von Bernburg gives Frau Oberin a ticking off in her role as the students' advocate, we see neither her nor Manuela. Even given censorship constraints, the acceptance of lesbian love as part of the community is stressed, not necessarily the union of the couple, Manuela and Fräulein von Bernburg. That the community has accepted the worldview, and that this has been achieved with the help of the mother acting for the daughter, not the father, and that the mother's desire is acknowledged, concludes the film without bringing it to closure. The discourse of the film obviously does not imply that mothers sleep with their daughters in some wretchedly obverse version of the Oedipus tale, but that feminist narrations are able to discuss maternal desire and subjectivity without articulating distaste for either.

In this fetishised text of feminist film studies, we see a narrative design that articulates female desire without foreclosing maternal desire. The articulation of female desire is not blocked, and is not merely expressed, but also realised in the social world. The design of the impress of female desire is embedded in the larger pattern of the community who are also seen to articulate it both forcefully and effectively. The hero is thus able to transform society, and raise consciousness about issues hitherto neglected. The wider world of the school is more aware of self, sexuality, politics and culture as a consequence. This trajectory is quite different from the Oedipal hero's coming to self-knowledge. Another story altogether, another way of telling it.

Arguably, feminist film studies gained impetus from Laura Mulvey's formulation on narrative in cinema, particularly the pointed comment on 'woman as bearer of meaning', not 'maker of meaning'. Semiotic readings would infer from her interpretation that women were signs exchanged between men in the diegesis, audience and behind the camera. Woman as sign, as myth, began to be contested, and although the initial impulse towards verisimilitude was heavily critiqued, it did not really hold much sway except to persuade women that there were realities that competed with the dominant Hollywood construction of women. Despite the availability of so many sources of alternative media, and of multiple voices in mainstream film, cultural narratives of women that map different stories such as the ones described in the last chapter remain rare. Feminism itself is understood in terms of 'strong women', without reference to the lived realities of other women. Credos of individualism that are particularly harmful to constructions of third world women have emerged with confused perceptions of how we have it better out here. The cult of celebrity is a case in point of the problematic emphasis on individual strong women. A recent show on women athletes talked, for instance, of how empowering it is for these young women to command the cultural show by stripping. In a difficult tough world, who dares to question these young women's sense of empowerment? Yet it has to give one pause if the culture so confines these terrifically talented young women athletes that to retain sponsorship, and advertisement contracts, they have to show hard bodies, and like showing them in order to prove that they can be both women and athletes. The story has much in common with the kinds of stories discussed throughout this book: of acquiring authority against all odds. This final chapter on narrative aesthetics has demonstrated that cultural narratives can be decentred by reconsidering some central stories, such as that of the mother and daughter. While the mother's maternity had hitherto given her authority in society, Jeannine Meerapfel envisions a different model, based on corporeality. Marleen Gorris succeeds in structuring a feminist narrative frame, in understanding that it is not enough for the woman to tell the story; for the story to have authoritative resonance, a woman must hear it. Prema Karanth restores a story of resistance to all kinds of cultural hegemonies, when she takes on the task of telling the story of Phani's child-widowhood and her final role as feminist authority in her circle. In all four films, women crucially find themselves as authorities.

Afterword

This book has sought to locate feminist authority and identify feminist aesthetics in films auteured by women.

Exploring films from diverse cultural traditions, it has become apparent that women filmmakers have confronted similar problems in the representation of women that has assumed different forms. Their approach to the questions of women's representation has differed, as have their responses. In finding strategies to overcome the suppression of female authority on screen, the films define a feminist aesthetic. This aesthetic, while locating feminist authority, articulates positionalities for women in aspects of representation that had hitherto been codified in highly confining ways.

Feminist authority in the readings in this book devolves around the modalities filmmakers use to circumvent problems in the representation of women. Authority is not exclusively the property of the auteur herself, but represents her understanding of how women can acquire authority. Thematic solutions are not adequate to this dilemma. Consequently authority cannot be located unless the filmmakers address issues of representation. The aesthetics that emerge as a result of negotiating hostile terrain successfully enable the positioning of feminist authority in the film, thus marking the auteur's signature and acknowledging the central importance of other women's actions in the construction of female authority.

The first chapter that brings Borden, Sen, Kaplan and Varda together confronts the problem of the visual in a medium that is predominantly visual and counts on the female for its pleasure. Deaestheticising the feminine serves all four well, but authority itself is handled differently. Varda alone refrains from consolidating her female hero's authority, a chilling warning to us of the assaults on women's acquisition of authority. The chapter shows how differently the 'aesthetic' feminine is viewed by each director: as 'show' in *Working Girls*, as desirable because of *class* and then undesirable because of loss of authority in *Parama*, as 'profitable' in *A Very Curious Girl* and finally as the patriarchal version of the *feminine* itself in *Vagabond*.

Women filmmakers have also handled the uneven representation of subjects of colour in relationship to white women. Confronting the white viewer provides the basis for the films' aesthetics, and barring *India Song* and *Chocolat*, *Illusions*, *The Watermelon Woman* and *Bhaji on the Beach* give female black subjects their authority through the dual modality of blocking the viewer, and privileging black female visuality. Duras and Denis, both inside and outside the traditions they film, use the aural and haptic. Duras fortifies the white female's authority, Denis the black male's.

Consideration has also been made of the attempts of women filmmakers to create genres adequate to women's heroism. The discrepancy between women's participation, and the representation of this participation is addressed in the African American and African historical/cultural contexts. How does one bring women from margin to centre in the dominant genres of culture through film? Situating the women as heroes – lending them the authority of leadership in thematic terms – connects the four films studied in this chapter. The meaning of feminist epic, history, reportage and myth become clear in these efforts to centre women as participants of history, as contenders in the community, the emerging nation, the colonised nation and the nation-state. The conversion of genre to include African visuality, orature, imperfect cinema and bush narrative can be seen in *Daughters of the Dust*, *La nouba des femmes du Mont-Chenoua*, *Sambizanga* and *Flame* respectively.

Sound too had also been an impediment to women's authority on screen. The diminishment of voice to enhance visuality further curtailed women's authority on screen. However, women filmmakers like Novaro, Rotberg, Tlatli and Sen find ways of foregrounding the aural as the positive, enabling a critique of the visual and a construction of feminist authority through the interplay between the visual and the auditory. Interestingly, silence becomes a positive signifier; thus revealing techniques of subversion through exaggeration. Each film grants the female authority through revealing the female protagonist's powerful speech through modalities of song, speech and silence that contest both visual and aural objectification.

Considering matters of narrative, women filmmakers have rewritten them by introducing discourses of desire and establishing them as powerful motivating devices. This thread connects *The Smiling Madame Beudet*, *Hour of the Star* and *Losing Ground*. Female desire is differentiated from patriarchal views of it in these films. While female desire is historically specific, for freedom in Dulac, urban pleasure in Amaral and for ecstasy in Collins, the directors are similar in their efforts to attribute authority to female desire. By using fantasy and the real contrapuntally, the films expand the range of allowable female desire.

Finally, cultural narratives themselves are rewritten by the films discussed in the last chapter: *Malou*, *Antonia's Line*, *Phaniyamma* and the classic *Mädchen in Uniform*. Here the strategy is of introducing the very role of the female as counter-cultural, or contesting the culture's most sacred ideals. The aesthetics of the film revolve around narrative strategies and positionings that allow the directors to draw out the role of the women in breaking taboos hostile to women. The directors validate this resistance of the female hero to basic cultural norms, locating feminist authority in the rejection of patriarchal values in the name of women.

Notes

Introduction

1   See the section 'Iconoclasm' in Laura Mulvey (1989) *Visual and Other Pleasures*, Bloomington: Indiana University Press – this volume includes a reprint of the essay 'Visual Pleasure and Narrative Cinema' published in *Screen* in 1975; Annette Kuhn (1982) *Women's Pictures: Feminism and Cinema*, Routledge and Kegan Paul; Mary Ann Doane (1987) *The Desire to Desire: The Woman's Film of the 40s*, Bloomington: Indiana University Press; Jane Gaines (1990) 'White Privilege and Looking Relations: Race and Gender in Feminist Film Theory', in Patricia Erens (ed.) *Issues in Feminist Film Criticism*, Bloomington: Indiana University Press.

2   See Theresa Hak Kyung Cha (ed.) (1980) *Apparatus*, New York: Tanam Press; Stephen Heath (1980) 'The Cinematic Apparatus: Technology as Historical and Cultural Form', in Teresa de Lauretis and Stephen Heath (eds) *The Cinematic Apparatus*, New York: St. Martin's Press.

3   Sergei Eisenstein (1970) *Film Essays with a Lecture*, ed. Jay Leyda, New York: Praeger, 49.

4   Teresa de Lauretis (1987) *Technologies of Gender: Essays on Theory Film and Fiction*, Bloomington: Indiana University Press, 133.

5   See Jacqueline Suter (1979) 'Feminine Discourse in Christopher Strong', *Camera Obscura: Feminism, Culture and Media Studies*, 3/4, 135–50; Claire Johnston (ed.) (1975) *The Work of Dorothy Arzner: Towards a Feminist Cinema*, London: British Film Institute.

6   See Doane (1987) and Christine Gledhill (ed.) (1987) *Home is Where the Heart is: Studies on Melodrama and the Women's Film*, London: British Film Institute.

7   See Catherine Belsey (1980) *Critical Practice*, London: Methuen.

8   Jane Gaines (1990) 'Women and Representation: Can We Enjoy Alternative Pleasure?', in Patricia Erens (ed.) *Issues in Feminist Film Criticism*, Bloomington: Indiana University Press.

9   Chris Straayer (1994) 'The Hypothetical Lesbian Heroine in Narrative Feature Film', in Diane Carson, Linda Dittmar and Janice R. Welsch (eds) *Multiple Voices in Feminist Film Criticism*, Minneapolis: University of Minnesota Press.

10 Michele Wallace (1993) 'Race, Gender and Psychoanalysis in Forties Film: *Lost Boundaries, Home of the Brave*', in Manthia Diawara (ed.) *Black American Cinema*, New York: Routledge, American Film Institute.

11 See Kaja Silverman (1988) 'The Female Authorial Voice', in *The Acoustic Mirror: The Female Voice in Psychoanalysis and Cinema*, Bloomington: Indiana University Press, 187–235 on the intrusion of the male author.

12 A spate of books devoted to women filmmakers from different areas of the world attests to this scholarly impulse: Gwendolyn Audrey Foster (1997) *Women Filmmakers of the African and Asian*

Diaspora: Decolonising the Gaze, Locating Subjectivity, Carbondale: Southern Illinois University Press; Alexandra Juhasz (2001) *Women of Vision: Histories in Feminist Film and Video*, Minneapolis: University of Minnesota Press; Diana Robin and Ira Jaffe (1999) *Redirecting the Gaze: Gender, Theory, and Cinema in the Third World*, Albany: State University of New York Press; Jacqueline Bobo (ed.) (1998) *Black Women Film and Video Artists*, New York: Routledge; Isabel Arredondo (2003) *Historia oral de las directoras de ciné Mexicanas*, Princeton: Markus Wiener, among others.

13 Claire Johnston (1975) 'Dorothy Arzner: Critical Strategies' and Pam Cook (1975) 'Approaching the Work of Dorothy Arzner', both in Claire Johnston (ed.) *The Work of Dorothy Arzner: Towards a Feminist Film Criticism*, London: British Film Institute.

14 Patrice Petro (2002) *Aftershocks of the New: Feminism and Film History*, New Brunswick: Rutgers University Press, 36.

15 Ibid., 38.

16 Judith Mayne (1995) 'A Parallax View of Lesbian Authorship', in Laura Pietropaolo and Ada Testaferri (eds) *Feminisms in the Cinema*, Bloomington: Indiana University Press, 199.

17 Alison Butler (2000) 'Feminist Theory and Women's Films at the turn of the Century', *Screen*, 41, 1, 76.

18 Catherine Grant (2000) 'www.auteur.com', *Screen*, 41, 1, 101.

19 Robert Carringer (2001) offers the most incisive critique of this practice which he calls 'the figure of the auxiliary author'. His position is that authorial context is important. See 'Collaboration and Concepts of Authorship', *PMLA*, 116, 2, 371.

20 Judith Mayne (1995) 'Mistress of Discrepancy' in *Woman at the Keyhole: Feminism and Women's Cinema*, Bloomington: Indiana University Press, 124–57.

21 See Claire Johnston (1973) 'Women's Cinema as Counter-Cinema', in Claire Johnston (ed.) *Notes on Women's Cinema*, London: Society for Education in Film and Television. Johnston called for a cinema that would intervene formally. At that time, the emphasis was on the deconstructive. The filmmakers studied here are able to make formal interventions without necessarily questioning their own processes of production, or being self-reflexive, although they may often be both.

22 Foster (1997); Anne Kaplan (1997) *Looking for the Other: Feminism, Film and the Imperial Gaze*, Routledge: New York.

23 Diana Robin and Ira Jaffe (1999) *Redirecting the Gaze: Gender, Theory, and Cinema in the Third World*, Albany: State University of New York Press.

24 See Gayatri Spivak on 'strategic essentialism', in 'Criticism, Feminism, and the Institution: Interview with Elizabeth Grosz', first published in *Thesis Eleven*, 10/11, 1984/85, reprinted in Sarah Harasym (ed.) (1990) *The Post-Colonial Critic: Interviews, Strategies, Dialogues*, New York: Routledge; see also Geetha Ramanathan (1995) on 'studied essentialism' in 'Third World Women's Texts and the Politics of Feminist Criticisms', in *College Literature*, Geetha Ramanathan and Stacey Schlau (eds), special issue: 'Third World Women's Inscriptions', 22, 1.

25 See Julia Knight (1988) *Women and the New German Cinema*, London: Verso, 1–21.

26 Elizabeth Cowie (1997) *Representing the Woman: Cinema and Psychoanalysis*, Minneapolis: University of Minnesota Press, 9.

27 See Silverman (1988).

28 Ibid., 215.

29 I am thinking primarily of Luce Irigaray's definitions here; I must add that although she speaks of registers outside the linguistic I regard Irigaray as non-essentialist; see Luce Irigaray (1985) *This Sex Which is Not One*, trans. Catherine Porter, Ithaca: Cornell University Press.

30 See Anke Gleber (1997) 'Women on the Screens and Streets of Modernity in Search of the Female Flaneur', Dudley Andrew (ed.) *The Image in Dispute: Art and Cinema in the Age of Photography*, Austin: University of Texas Press.

31 See, among others, Doane (1987).

Chapter 1

1 See, for a study of the cinematic definitions, Kristin Thompson (1990) 'The Concept of Cinematic Excess', in Leo Braudy and Marshall Cohen (eds) *Film Theory and Criticism*, fifth edition, New York: Oxford University Press, 487–98. I myself am using 'visual' in the most general sense of an element that exceeds the narrative, the feminine which assumes and subsumes visuality.

2 'It is well known that Sternberg once said he would welcome his films being projected upside down so that story and character involvement would not interfere with the spectator's undiluted appreciation of the screen image'; Mulvey (1989), 22.

3 Elisabeth Lenk (1985) 'The Self-Reflecting Woman', in Gisela Ecker (ed.) *Feminist Aesthetics*, trans. Harriet Anderson, London: The Women's Press, 55.

4 David Summers (1994) 'Form and Gender', in Norman Bryson, Michael Ann Holly and Keith Moxey (eds) *Visual Culture: Images and Interpretations*, Hanover: University Press of New England and Wesleyan University Press, 397.

5 Ibid., 393.

6 Mulvey (1989), 22.

7 De Lauretis (1987), 146.

8 Laura Mulvey (1992) 'Pandora: Topographies of the Mask and Curiosity', in Beatriz Colomina (ed.) *Sexuality and Space*, Princeton: Princeton Architectural Press, 58.

9 Anne Friedberg, '*Les Flâneurs du Mal(l)*: Cinema and the Postmodern Condition', *PMLA*, 106, 3, 428.

10 Karen Jaehne (1987) 'Hooker', *Film Comment*, 23, 3, 30.

11 Early reviewers were particular about this point; later reviewers concur: Dale Dobson (2002) www.digitallyobsessed.com/showreview.php3?ID=1223; Tracy Quan (1997) 'Hooker's Ball', www.salon.com/May 97/the life 2970530.html; Peter Brunette (1986–87) 'Review of *Working Girls*', *Film Quarterly*, 40, 2; Karen Jaehne (1987) *Film Comment*, 23, 3 25–33.

12 Two feminist films that go against the grain are Marleen Gorris's *Broken Mirrors* (1984) and Chantal Akerman's *Jeanne Dielman, 23 Quai du Commerce, 1080 Bruxelles* (1975).

13 See Gail Pheterson (ed.) (1989) *A Vindication of the Rights of Whores*, Seattle: Seal Press.

14 Knight also runs a similar discussion. She cites Margretha von Trotta as saying the process is important and that in the narrative 'how the characters and their feelings are portrayed – the stress lies not in the story but rather in the emotional flow which runs through the story'; Knight (1988), 146.

15 Leslie Fishbein (2002) 'Working Girls on Film: Images and Issues', http://clioseye.sfasu.edu/chronicles/workinggirlschron.htm.

16 Ibid..

17 Quan (1997) points out that prostitute women do get particular kinds of pleasure.

18 Luce Irigaray (1985) *Speculum of the Other Woman*, Ithaca: Cornell University Press.

19 Anon. (2002) '3 x Working Girls', www.fdk-berlin.de/arsenal/text2002/1002working.html.

20 Brunette (1986–87), 54.

21 Quan (1997); interestingly she notes that *Pretty Woman* is more about a prostitute's fantasy.

22 Brunette (1986–87), 55.

23 Marilyn Frye (1983) *The Politics of Reality: Essays in Feminist Theory*, Trumansburg: Crossing Press.

24 Jacquie Jones argues that the film justifies the abuse of the black prostitute by her 'moral inadequacy'; see 'The Construction of Black Sexuality: Towards Normalising the Black Cinematic Experience,' in Manthia Diawara (ed.) (1989) *Black American Cinema*, New York, Routledge, 254.

25 See Michelle Citron (1988) 'Women's Film Production: Going Mainstream', in E. Dierdre Pribham (ed.) *Female Spectators: Looking at Film and Television*, London: Verso, 45–64.

26 Lisa Tickner (1987) 'The Body Politic: Female Sexuality and Women Artists Since 1970', in Rozsika Parker and Griselda Pollock (eds) *Framing Feminism: Art and the Women's Movement 1970–1985*, London: Pandora Press, 263. The comparison with popular Hindi cinema and parallel cinema is uncanny and tempting but I will staunchly resist it.

27 Kobena Mercer (1994) *Welcome to the Jungle: New Positions in Black Cultural Studies*, New York: Routledge, 176. Mercer, discussing Robert Mapplethorpe's photographs of black male nudes, argues that for Mapplethorpe 'Black + Male = Erotic/Aesthetic Object', 174. However, his revision of the argument is more subtle when he comes to the conclusion that because classical aesthetics did not permit the use of classical codes to represent the black male, Mapplethorpe's inclusion of them in the Western aesthetic code and specifically through gay desiring eyes shows a certain subversiveness about dominant values, including the colonial construction of the black male.

28 Jane Gaines discusses the different spaces open to black women in this artistic economy. A discussion on Diana Ross's role as photographic model in *Mahogany* (1975) clarifies the black woman's commodification (as opposed to her aestheticisation). The essay also works through her 'blackness' as a trope and comes to conclusions that are different from Tickner's on the white female or Mercer's on the black male. See Gaines (1990), 197–216.

29 Mieke Bal (1993) 'His Master's Eye' in David Michael Levin (ed.) *Modernity and the Hegemony of Vision*, Berkeley: University of California Press, 381.

30 A vast body of scholarship has documented the destructive effect of ideals of beauty as presented by male high and popular traditions of art.

31 Mukul Kesavan (1995) *India: Review of Books*, March/April.

32 Georg Lukacs (1977) 'Realism in the Balance', trans. and ed. Ron Taylor, *Aesthetics and Politics*, London: Verso, 39.

33 See, among others, Luce Irigaray (1985) *This Sex Which Is Not One*, trans. Catherine Porter Ithaca: Cornell University Press, and Hélène Cixous and Catherine Clément (1986) *The Newly Born Woman*, trans. Betsy Wing, MN: University of Minnesota Press.

34 Lukacs (1977), 48.

35 See Colin MacCabe (1985) 'Realism and the Cinema: Notes on Some Brechtian Theses', and 'Theory and Film: Principles of Realism and Pleasure', both in *Tracking the Signifier: Theoretical Essays, Film, Linguistics, Literature*, Minneapolis: University of Minnesota Press. His now widely accepted thesis was that realism, constructed though it was, effaced the signs of its own production. The text reproduced the ideological status quo.

36 The upper part of the sari that is draped on chest and shoulders.

37 Poonam Arora and Katrina Irving (1991) 'Culturally Specific Texts, Culturally Bound Audiences: Ethnography in the Place of its Reception', *Journal of Film and Video*, 43, 1/2.

38 Mercer (1994), 177.

39 Teresa de Lauretis (1987) 'Rethinking Women's Cinema: Aesthetics and Feminist Theory', *Tech-*

nologies of Gender, Bloomington: Indiana University Press, 144.

40 Women's 'desire to be seen' is explored in a different register in the section on Julie Dash's *Illusions* in Chapter 2.

41 See Mallek Alloula (1986) *The Colonial Harem*, Minneapolis: University of Minnesota Press. Alloula discusses the nineteenth-century French fascination with Egyptian harem women who were pictured in postcards. See also Tickner (1987) and Linda Nochlin (1989) 'The Imaginary Orient', in *The Politics of Vision: Essays on Nineteenth Century Art and Society*, New York: Harper and Row, 33–60. Nochlin discusses the interesting problematic of 'realistic' orientalism, and more specifically orientalist fantasy of women.

42 Griselda Pollock talks about the nineteenth-century expansion of the image to include working-class women. In studying nineteenth-century journalists' photography of the women miners of Wigan, she notes that the effect was 'to sexualise all women who worked, to make all working women suspect as sexual and immoral'; Griselda Pollock (1994) 'Feminism/Foucault–Surveillance/Sexuality', in Norman Bryson, Michael Ann Holly and Keith Moxey (eds) *Visual Culture: Images and Interpretations*, Hanover: Wesleyan University Press, 25. In this context, it is interesting to note that modernism's bordello threatened to challenge the class codes by painting prostitutes and working-class women but succeeded similarly in sexualising them. Whether there is a new space opened up for working-class women through their aestheticisation in modernism's portrayal is the subject of another study.

43 Ibid., 33.

44 Irigaray (1985).

45 Pollock (1994), 34. She also has interesting charts regarding public/private; male bourgeois/female bourgeois that, however, do not have any bearing on this film primarily because the Indian male bourgeois is conceived of differently than the Western.

46 I am thinking of Anita Desai's and Shashi Deshpande's fiction. My point here is that the individualism of the woman is at least debated, not taken for granted, in these literary and cinematic fictions.

47 Arora & Irving (1991), 120.

48 In a fascinating close reading of Parama playing the veena, the name of the plant as Krishnapallavi and the rag that Parama plays on the veena, Arora and Irving definitely infer that Parama glosses over the 'real' in her mythologisation.

49 The notion of traditional Indian vs. Westernised readings with few qualifications is particularly troublesome.

50 Arora & Irving (1991), 113.

51 Wimal Dissanayake (1989) 'Questions of Female Subjectivity and Patriarchy: A Reading of Three Indian Women Film Directors', *East West Film Journal*, 3, 2, 80. General comments include his opinions on Aparna Sen's *36 Chowringee Lane* (1981), Prema Karanth's *Phaniyamma* (1983) and Vijaya Mehta's *Rao Saheb* (1986).

52 Ibid., 87.

53 Ibid.

54 The Indian version finds her reunited with the family, the foreign cut shows her leaving the family to work with her friend. Either way, the separation from an exclusively familial identity is significant.

55 'As far as a feminist intervention is concerned, therefore, it is not really a question of producing a "feminist" text'; Annette Kuhn (1982) *Women's Pictures: Feminism and Cinema*, London: Routledge and Kegan Paul, 13.

56 De Lauretis (1987), 135.

57 See Chris Holmlund (1996) 'The Eyes of Nelly Kaplan', *Screen*, 37, 4, 351–67.

58 Elisabeth Lenk (1985) 'The Self-Reflecting Woman', in Gisela Ecker (ed.) *Feminist Aesthetics*, trans. Harriet Anderson, London: The Women's Press, 55.

59 Gertrude Koch, 'Why Women go to Men's Films', in Gisela Ecker (ed.) *Feminist Aesthetics*, trans. Harriet Anderson, London: The Women's Press, 110.

60 Newer Bollywood films on the topic such as *Astitwa* (2000) and *Rekha* (1987), on a middle-class woman's prostitution, are aimed at educating patriarchal society on the topic.

61 See Stella Behar (1999) 'L'écriture surréaliste de Nelly Kaplan' in Georgiana M. M. Colville and Katherine Conley (ed.) *La femme s'entête*, Paris: Lachenal et Ritter, 288.

62 Holmlund (1996), 352.

63 See Meaghan Morris (1988) *The Pirate's Fiancée: Feminism, Reading, Postmodernism*, London: Verso, 1–16, 51–69.

64 Rosalind E. Krauss (1999) *Bachelors*, Cambridge: MIT Press, 17.

65 Christian Metz (1977) *The Imaginary Signifier: Psychoanalysis and the Cinema*, trans. Celia Britton, Annwyl Williams, Ben Brewster and Alfred Guzzetti, Bloomington: Indiana University Press. Regarding the spectator's identification processes he says, 'I take no part in the perceived, on the contrary, I am *all perceiving*. All perceiving as one says all powerful…', 48.

66 Lacan explains this moment of identification as 'the transformation in the subject when he assumes an image'; Jacques Lacan (1977) 'The Mirror Stage' in *Écrits: A Selection*, trans. Alan Sheridan, London: W. W. Norton, 2. In Lacan's postulation, this stage would be that of the 'ideal I' because it precedes language, and the functioning of the subject. Although Metz does not view the cinema as mirror, and it would be inaccurate to do so, it does perhaps facilitate certain identification processes as laid out by Lacan.

67 See Kaja Silverman (1999) 'On Suture', in Leo Braudy and Marshall Cohen (eds) *Film Theory and Criticism: Introductory Readings*, New York: Oxford University Press; see also Daniel Dayan (1999) 'The Tutor Code of Classical Cinema', in Leo Braudy and Marshall Cohen (eds) *Film Theory and Criticism: Introductory Readings*, New York: Oxford University Press; and Stephen Heath (1981) *Questions of Cinema*, Bloomington: Indiana University Press.

68 Jonathan Crary (1998) *Techniques of the Observer: On Vision and Modernity in the Nineteenth Century*, Cambridge: MIT Press. Crary's brilliant work on the subjectivity of vision disputes the smooth mastery afforded the Cartesian subject, for example: 'Vision and its effects are always inseparable from the possibilities of an observing subject who is both the historical product and the site of certain practices, techniques, institutions and procedures of subjectification', 5.

69 In this Dorothy Arzner film, the dancer addresses her spectators directly, thus including the viewers, and drawing attention to the systems of representation.

70 Silverman (1988).

71 Morris (1988), 2.

72 Catherine Breillat's work has also been seen in these terms.

73 Morris (1988), 2.

74 Linda Greene (1975) '*A Very Curious Girl*: Politics of a Feminist Fantasy', *Jump Cut*, 6, 13.

75 Marjorie Rosen (1976) 'Women, Sex and Power', *Millimeter*, 4, 36.

76 Naomi Gilbert (1973) 'To Be Our Own Muse: The Dialectics of a Culture Heroine', *Women and Film*, 1, 23–32.

77 Claire Johnston (1973) 'Women's Cinema as Counter-Cinema', in *Notes on Women's Cinema*, London: Society for Education in Film and Television, reprinted in Bill Nichols (ed.) (1976)

Movies and Methods: An Anthology, Berkeley: University of California Press, 211.

78 Kaplan quoted in Derek Elley (1974) 'Hiding it Under a Bushel', *Films and Filming*, 20, 4, 232, 24.

79 Ibid, 24.

80 Ibid, 23.

81 Greene (1975), 13.

82 Ibid.

83 Stella Béhar (1996) 'Belen: Gourme et Gourmandises Memoires d'une liseuse de draps ou le néo-surréalisme des années soixante-dix chez Nelly Kaplan', *Symposium: A Quarterly Journal in Modern Literature*, 50, 1, 38; translation mine.

84 This is certainly not to imply that women's treatment in say, German Expressionist film, has not been problematic. It only points to the power the woman derives from the expressionistic *mise-en-scène* in this particular sequence.

85 Brenda Roman (1973), 'Dirty Mary', *Women and Film*, 1, 69.

86 Nelly Kaplan (1997) 'Jongler avec la lumière et avec le Verbe', *Magazine littéraire*, 354, 38–9.

87 Diane Waldman (1973) 'The Eternal Return of Circe', *Velvet Light Trap*, 9, 49.

88 Karyn Kay (1973) 'The Revenge of Pirate Jenny', *Velvet Light Trap*, 9, 46–9.

89 See Kay Harris (1971) 'An Interview with Nelly Kaplan', *Women and Film*, 2, 35.

90 The French title was *Sans toit ni loi* or 'Without roof or law.'

91 Quoted in Barbara Quart (1986–87) 'Agnès Varda: A Conversation', *Film Quarterly*, 50, 2, 5.

92 Royal S. Brown (1998) 'Disc and Tape Reviews', 23, 4. Accessed through Academic Search Premier, page 3, date of access 4 October 2003.

93 Sandy Flitterman-Lewis (1990) *To Desire Differently: Feminism and French Cinema*, Urbana: University of Illinois Press, 292.

94 Brown (1998), 3.

95 Joanne Klein (1990) 'Refracting the Gaze in *The French Lieutnant's Woman, She's Gotta Have It* and *Vagabond*', paper presented at the National Women's Studies Association Mid-Atlantic conference in Rockville, Maryland.

96 Timothy Corrigan (1991) *A Cinema Without Walls: Movies and Culture After Vietnam*, New Brunswick: Rutgers University Press, 160; see also Ewa Mazierska and Laura Rascaroli (2006) 'When Women Hit the Road: Images of Female Mobility in Postmodern Europe' in *Crossing New Europe: Postmodern Travel and the European Road Movie*, London: Wallflower Press, 161–99.

97 Roger Ebert (1986) '*Vagabond*', www.suntimes.com/index/index.html; accessed 5 October 2003.

98 Flitterman-Lewis (1990), 309.

99 Jill Forbes (1986) 'Cold Venus: *Vagabond*', *Sight and Sound*, 55, 3, 209.

100 See Varda in Quart (1986–87), 8.

101 Amy Taubin (2001) 'All the girls of their age', *Village Voice*, 12 March.

102 Quoted in Flitterman-Lewis (1990), 309.

Chapter 2

1 Robert Stam and Louise Spence (1983) 'Colonialism, Racism and Representation: An Introduction', *Screen*, 24, 2, 4.

2 Paul Willemen (1994) *Looks and Frictions*, Bloomington: Indiana University Press, 180.

3 These are obviously overlapping categories.

4 Gloria T. Hull, Patricia Bell Scott and Barbara Smith (eds) (1983) *All the Women are White, All*

the Men are Black: But Some of Us are Brave, Westbury: The Feminist Press.

5   To this intent, I use 'feminist' universally, and Euro-American feminist/third world feminist/ black feminist in order to delineate specific contributions. I am aware of the difficulties of such nomenclatures but am trying to find a way between brutalising generalisations and demeaning differentiations.

6   Sumita Chakravarty (1993) *National Identity in Indian Popular Cinema 1947–1987*, Austin: University of Texas Press, 247.

7   Mercer (1994), 53–69.

8   Ibid., 243.

9   Griselda Pollock (1988) *Vision and Difference: Femininity, Feminism and the Histories of Art*, London: Routledge, 24.

10 Mercer (1994), 53–69.

11 See bell hooks (1995) 'Talking Art as the Spirit Moves Us', in *Art on my Mind: Visual Politics*, New York: The New Press, 102.

12 See, among others, Haile Gerima (1989) 'Triangular Cinema, Breaking Toys, and Dinknesh vs Lucy', in Jim Pines and Paul Willemen (eds) *Questions of Third Cinema*, London: British Film Institute; Manthia Diawara (1993) 'Black American Cinema: The New Realism' and Toni Cade Bambara (1993) 'Reading the Signs, Empowering the Eye: *Daughters of the Dust* and the Black Independent Cinema Movement', both in Manthia Diawara (ed.) *Black American Cinema*, New York: Routledge.

13 Michele Wallace (1993) 'Modernism, Postmodernism, and the Problem of the Visual in Euro– American Culture', in Hilde Hein and Carolyn Korsmeyer (eds) *Aesthetics in Feminist Perspective*, Bloomington: Indiana University Press, 205–18.

14 Ibid., 212.

15 Hal Foster (1985) *Recodings: Art, Spectacle, Cultural Politics*, Port Townsend: Bay Press, 183.

16 Clyde Taylor (1989) 'Black Cinema in the Post-Aesthetic Era', in Jim Pines and Paul Willemen (eds) *Questions of Third Cinema*, London: British Film Institute, 101.

17 Ibid. See also Taylor (1989) for a fascinating political/historical reading of Western aesthetics.

18 See Patrick Brantlinger (1990) *Crusoe's Footprints: Cultural Studies in Britain and America*, New York: Routledge.

19 Linda Williams (1994) 'Introduction', in *Viewing Positions: Ways of Seeing Film*, New Brunswick: Rutgers University Press, 2. It is important to note that some films, such as Chadha's, played a role in challenging the supremacy of that viewer, even as theorists of vision and film also began to question the solidity of the viewer.

20 Lola Young (1994) 'Mapping Male Bodies: Thoughts on Gendered and Racialised Looking', in Naomi Salaman (ed.) *What She Wants: Women Artists Look at Men*, London: Verso, 43.

21 Crary (1992).

22 See, for instance, Lisa Bloom (ed.) (1999) *With Other Eyes: Looking at Race and Gender in Visual Culture*, Minneapolis: University of Minnesota Press.

23 See Nella Larsen's *Passing* (1929) and James Weldon Johnson's *The Autobiography of an ex-Coloured Man* (1912). In mainstream film the early *Imitation of Life* (1934) has been an important influence in the genre.

24 S. V. Hartman and Farah Jasmine Griffin (1991) 'Are you as Colored as that Negro?: The Politics of Being Seen in Julie Dash's *Illusions*', *Black American Literature Forum*, 25, 2, 366.

25 Clyde Taylor (1991) discusses this especially with respect to aesthetics in 'The Re-Birth of the Aesthetic in Cinema', *Wide Angle*, 13, 3/4, 13–30.

26 Walter White (1925) 'Color Lines', in Alain Locke (ed.) *Harlem: Mecca of the New Negro*, The Survey Graphic, March 1925, 6, 6, 680–82.

27 See Donald Bogle (1988) *Blacks in American Film and TV*, New York: Garland.

28 Deborah White (1985) *Aren't I a Woman: Female Slaves in the Plantation South*, New York: Norton.

29 Gaines (1990).

30 Phyllis Rauch Klotman (ed.) (1991) *Screenplays of the African American Experience*, Bloomington: Indiana University Press, 212; all references to the screenplay of the film are from this volume.

31 Valerie Smith (1994) 'Reading the Intersection of Race and Gender in Narratives of Passing', in *Diacritics*, Judith Butler and Biddy Martin (eds) special issue: 'Critical Crossings', 24, 2/3, 53.

32 Rauch Klotman (1991), 205.

33 Hartman & Griffin (1991), 369.

34 Rauch Klotman (1991), 211.

35 Ibid., 209.

36 Mary Ann Doane (1991) 'Dark Continents: Epistemologies of Racial and Sexual Difference in Psychoanalysis and Cinema', in *Femmes Fatales: Feminism Film Theory Psychoanalysis*, New York: Routledge, 234.

37 Ironically, one of the few roles black women had in film was that of the singing entertainer; thus, Dash's point about star presence is extremely well taken.

38 *Dry Kisses Only* (1990), a video documentary does a wry job of taking us through this search, but mainly with European-American actors and directors.

39 Alexandra Juhasz (2001) 'Cheryl Dunye', in Alexandra Juhasz (ed.) *Women of Vision: Histories in Feminist Film and Video'*, Minneapolis: University of Minneapolis Press, 291; see also Juhasz's introduction for Dunye's complex relationship with feminism.

40 Ibid., 298.

41 Ibid., 291

42 David Van Leer (1997) 'Visible Silence: Spectatorship in Black Gay and Lesbian Film', in Valerie Smith (ed.) *Representing Blackness: Issues in Film and Video*, New Brunswick: Rutgers University Press, 176.

43 Anna Everett (2001) *Returning the Gaze: A Geneaology of Black Film Criticism 1909–1949*, Durham: Duke University Press.

44 See Ed Guerrero (1993) *The African American Image in Film: Framing Blackness*, Philadelphia: Temple University Press.

45 W. B. Worthen (1995) *Modern Drama: Plays, Criticism, Theory*, Fort Worth: Harcourt Brace, 627.

46 I have recapitulated only sections that are germane to my arguments in this chapter. For a detailed shot-by-shot breakdown of Lyon's analysis of the film's discussion of fantasy, see her 1980 essay, 'The Cinema of Lol. V. Stein', *Camera Obscura: Feminism, Culture and Media Studies*, 6, 6–41.

47 See Marguerite Duras (1980) 'Notes on *India Song*', *Camera Obscura: Feminism, Culture and Media Studies*, 6, 4.

48 See *City of Joy* (1992) which is a particularly unpleasant example of the imperial mission extending into the late twentieth century.

49 Martine Loutfi (1986) 'Duras' India', *Literature Film Quarterly*, 14, 3, 152.

50 Ibid., 153.

51 See, for example, Susan H. Léger (1988) 'Marguerite Duras' Cinematic Spaces', Janet Todd (ed.)

Women and Film, New York: Holmes and Meier, 241.

52 See Christine Ann Holmlund (1991) 'Displacing Limits of Difference: Gender, Race, and Colonialism in Edward Said and Homi Bhabha's Theoretical Models and Marguerite Duras' Experimental Films', *Quarterly Review of Film and Video*, 13, 1–3, 1–22; Holmlund notes the
'problems' in Duras' films.

53 See Dina Sherzer (ed.) (1996) *Cinema, Colonialism, Postcolonialism: Perspectives from the French
and Francophone Worlds*, Austin: University of Texas Press.

54 See, for instance, the even more personal *A Passage to India*; David Lean's 1984 filming of
E. M. Forster's 1924 novel where the Indian women are linked to chattering monkeys. Also the
many neo-colonial films where Chuck Norris puts paid to innumerable oriental persons.

55 Mercer (1994), 134.

56 See Lucien Taylor (ed.) (1994) *Visualising Theory: Selected Essays from Visual Anthropology Review
1990–1994*, New York: Routledge.

57 Naomi Greene (1996) 'Empire as Myth and Memory', in Dina Sherzer (ed.) *Cinema, Colonialism, Postcolonialism: Perspectives from the French and Francophone Worlds*, Austin: University of
Texas Press, 106.

58 Term first used by Frederic Strauss (1990) in 'Féminin Colonial', *Cahiers du Cinema*, 434, 29–
33.

59 Catherine Portuges (1996) 'Women Directors Interrogate French Cinema' in Dina Sherzer (ed.)
Cinema, Colonialism, Postcolonialism: Perspectives from the French and Francophone Worlds, Austin:
University of Texas Press, 80–102.

60 Of course the truly forgotten women are the colonised women, or absent at any rate from most
films of this genre.

61 E. Ann Kaplan (1997), 167.

62 Claire Denis (1997) 'Conversation with Claire Denis', Philadelphia Festival of World Cinema, 4
May.

63 Denis, quoted in Strauss (1990), 31; translation mine.

64 Denis, quoted in Portuges (1996), 84. Denis herself was raised in Cameroon.

65 See, for instance, Nikki Stiller (1990) '*Chocolat*', *Film Quarterly*, 44, 2, 9, 52–56, who in an otherwise perceptive review claims that Protée is crying because he has been denied access to the big
house and been rejected by Aimée, or Dina Sherzer's essay 'Interracial Relationships in Colonial
and Post Colonial Films' in her edited collection, who places *Chocolat* in her group of interracial
romance films.

66 See, for instance, Joan Dagle (1991, 'Effacing Race: The Discourse on Gender in *Diva*'; and
Gina Marchetti (1991) 'White Knights in Hong Kong: Race, Gender and Exotic in *Love is a
Many-Splendored Thing* and *The World of Suzie Wong*', both in *Post Script*, special issue: 'Feminist
Criticism', 10, 2.

67 Denis, cited in Portuges (1996), 84. See also Jean Jacques Annaud's *The Lover* (1992) where the
filmed version obsesses on the oriental male.

68 This is reminiscent of *Entre Nous* (1983) but with real reservations and tremendous distance
between daughter and parents.

69 Stiller (1990), 52.

70 See Peter Bates (1989) '*Chocolat*', *Cineaste*, 17, 2, 52–3, who criticises Denis for not providing
the audience with sub-titles during Protée's conversations with the Cameroonians. Denis herself
says that she did not want to show European access to spaces that they would not have entered.
Notice the scene in the film where the European and Protée struggle because the colonial wants

to bathe in the native water pipes.

71 'Shaped by [this colonial history], black masculinity is a highly contradictory formation of identity, as it is a subordinated masculinity'; Mercer (1994), 142–3.

72 Kaplan (1997), 165.

73 Gaines (1994), 184–5.

74 Young (1994), 41.

75 See Verena Lueken (1989) 'Review of *Chocolat*', *EPD Film*, 6, 9, 27.

76 William A. Vincent (1997) 'The Unreal but Visible Line: Difference and Desire for the Other in *Chocolat*', in Kenneth W. Harrow (ed.) *With Open Eyes: Women and African Cinema*, Amsterdam: Editions Rodopi, 130.

77 Marie Craven (1990) *Cinema Papers*, 81, 21–30; 55–56.

78 Also a common stereotype immediately following and during reconstruction in the United States.

79 See Hull *et al.* (1982).

80 Knight (1988), 146.

81 See Sue Harper (2000) *Women in British Cinema: Mad, Bad, Dangerous to Know*, London: Continuum, 148.

82 See Andrea Stuart (1994) 'Blackpool Illumination,' *Sight and Sound*, 4, 2, 26.

83 See Nandi Bhatia (1998) 'Women, Homelands and the Indian Diaspora', in Ralph Bauer (ed.) *The Centennial Review*, special issue: 'Locations of Culture: Identity, Home, Theory', 42, 3, 512.

84 See Stuart (1994).

85 See Farah Anwar's (1994) review of the film in *Sight and Sound*, 4, 2, 48.

86 See Lea Jacobs (1993) 'The Women's Picture and the Poetics of Melodrama', *Camera Obscura: Feminism, Culture and Media Studies*, 31.

87 Thomas Elsaesser (1992 [1972]) 'Tales of Sound and Fury: Observations on the Family Drama', in Gerald Mast, Marshall Cohen and Leo Braudy (eds) *Film Theory and Criticism*, New York: Oxford University Press, 523.

88 Ibid., 532.

89 Christine Gledhill (1996) 'An Abundance of Understatement: Documentary, Melodrama and Romance', in Christine Gledhill and Gillian Swanson (eds) *Nationalising Femininity: Culture, Sexuality and British Cinema in the Second World War*, Manchester: Manchester University Press.

90 Claudia Tate (1992) *Domestic Allegories of Political Desire: The Black Heroine's Text at the Turn of the Century*, New York: Oxford University Press.

91 Wimal Dissanayake (1993) 'The Concept of Evil in Indian Melodrama: An Evolving Dialectic', in Wimal Dissanayake (ed.) *Melodrama and Asian Cinema*, Cambridge: Cambridge University Press, 199.

92 Dolores Tierney (1997) 'Silver Slingbacks and Mexican Melodrama: *Salon Mexico* and *Danzón*', *Screen*, 38, 4, 360–71.

93 Anne Ciecko (1999) 'Representing the Spaces of Diaspora in Contemporary British Films by Women Directors', *Cinema Journal*, 38, 3, 70.

94 Ibid., 75; see also Dimitris Eleftheriotis (2000) 'Cultural Difference and Exchange: A Future for European Film', *Screen*, 41, 1, 97.

95 Ciecko (1999), 75.

96 Julian Samuel, *Indiastar: A Literary Art Magazine*, www.indiastar.com/bhaji.html.

97   Damian Cannon, *Movie Reviews U.K.*, www.film.u–net.com/Movies/Reviews/Bhaji_Beach.html.
98   Eleftheriotis (2000), 97.

Chapter 3

1   Rick Altman (1998) 'Reusable Packaging: Generic Products and the Recycling Process', in Nick Browne (ed.) *Refiguring American Film Genres: History and Theory*, Berkeley: University of California Press.

2   See Christine Gledhill (2000) 'Rethinking Genre', in Christine Gledhill and Linda Williams (eds) *Reinventing Film Studies*, London: Arnold/New York: Oxford University Press.

3   In this context it is important to note that these constraints of home are tested in all kinds of melodrama, which accounts for the huge interest in it. For newer considerations see, among others Linda Williams (1998) 'Melodrama Revised', in Nick Browne (ed.) *Refiguring American Film Genres: History and Theory*, Berkeley: University of California Press.

4   Robert Phillip Kolker (1988) 'Woman as Genre', in Janet Todd (ed.) *Women and Film*, New York: Holmes and Meier, 130.

5   Carol J. Clover (1993) 'High and Low: The Transformation of the Rape-revenge Movie', in Pam Cook and Philip Dodd (ed.) *Women and Film: A Sight and Sound Reader*, Philadelphia: Temple University Press, 76. In popular Indian film too this has been a theme.

6   Linda Williams (1989) *Hard Core: Power, Pleasure, and 'The Frenzy of the Visible'*, Berkeley: University of California Press, 229–64.

7   George Lipsitz (1998) 'Genre Anxiety and Racial Representation in 1970s Cinema', in Nick Browne (ed.) *Refiguring American Film Genres: History and Theory*, Berkeley: University of California Press, 209. Even the very progressive Euzhan Palcy's *A Dry White Season* (1989) falls into this category.

8   Nicholas Mirzoeff (1995) *Bodyscape: Art, Modernity and the Ideal Figure*, London and New York: Routledge.

9   Foster (1997).

10   Ibid., 1.

11   B. Ruby Rich (1990) 'In the Name of Feminist Film Criticism', in Patricia Erens (ed.) *Issues in Feminist Film Criticism*, Indiana University Press, Bloomington, 269.

12   See Bobo (1998); see also Foster (1997).

13   See Gaines (1990).

14   Michael Awkward (1989) *Inspiriting Influences: Tradition, Revision and Afro-American Women's Novels*, New York: Columbia University Press. Awkward defines the literal 'denigrare', 'to blacken', as 'those appropriative acts by Afro-Americans which have successfully transformed, by the addition of black expressive features, Western cultural and expressive systems to the extent that they reflect in black "mouths" and "contexts", what we might call (in Bakhtinian terms) Afro-American "intention" and "accent"', 9.

15   Toni Cade Bambara (1992) 'Preface' in Julie Dash, *Daughters of the Dust: The Making of an African American Film*, New York: The New Press, xii.

16   Julia Erhart (1996) 'Picturing What If: Julie Dash's Speculative Fiction', *Camera Obscura: Feminism, Culture and Media Studies*, 1, 38, 118.

17   Julie Dash (1992) 'Making *Daughters of the Dust*', in *Daughters of the Dust: The Making of an African American Film*, New York: The New Press, 8.

18   The two patterns in African American film are discerned by Valerie Smith who regards both these

definitions as searching for authenticity; Valerie Smith (1997) 'Introduction' in Valerie Smith (ed.) *Representing Blackness: Issues in Film and Video*, New Brunswick: Rutgers University Press, 1–2.

19 Toni Morrison (1992) *Playing in the Dark: Whiteness and the Literary Imagination*, Cambridge: Harvard University Press.

20 Despite some passing similarity of visual iconography.

21 Bambara (1993), 122.

22 Ibid., 136.

23 Karen Alexander (1993) 'Daughters of the Dust', *Sight and Sound*, 3, 9, 22.

24 See D. T. Niane (1965) *Sundiata: An Epic of Old Mali*, trans. G. D. Pickett, New York: Heinemann; see also Henry Louis Gates Jr (1985) 'Editor's Introduction: Writing "Race" and the Difference it Makes', in Henry Louis Gates Jr (ed.) *Race Writing and 'Difference'*, special issue of *Critical Inquiry*, 12, 1, 1–21.

25 Oliver Barlet (1996) *African Cinemas: Decolonising the Gaze*, trans. Chris Turner, London: Zed Books, 60.

26 Mikhail Bakhtin (1981) *The Dialogic Imagination: Four Essays*, ed. Michael Holquist, trans. Caryl Emerson and Michael Holquist, Austin: University of Texas Press, 30.

27 Title of Maya Deren's film from 1946. Dash's film evokes the aura of Deren's technique, and more generally her style.

28 See Joel R. Brouwer (1995) 'Repositioning Center and Margin in Julie Dash's *Daughters of the Dust*', *African American Review*, 29, 1, 5–17.

29 Ibid.; see also Niane (1965).

30 Note Deren's repeated injunction that the films do not comprise a symbology; see VeVe A. Clark, Millicent Hodson and Catrina Neiman (1988) 'Cinema as an Art Form', in *The Legend of Maya Deren: A Documentary Biography and Collected Works*, vol. 2, New York: Anthology Film Archives, 313–21.

31 Jacquie Jones (1993) 'The Black South in Contemporary Film', *African American Review*, 27, 1, 19.

32 Robert Farris Thompson (2000) Interview on *Daughters of the Dust* DVD, produced by Kino.

33 Erhart (1996), 121.

34 B. Ruby Rich, cited in ibid.

35 Diawara (1993), 14–19.

36 E. M. Forster's novel of 1924, *A Passage to India* (1984), filmed by David Lean. In another movie, *Apocalypse Now* (1979), Francis Ford Coppola works with this imagery.

37 See Fatimah Tobing Rony (1996) *The Third Eye: Race, Cinema and Ethnographic Spectacle*, Durham: Duke University Press, 199–208.

38 See Francette Pacteau (1999) 'Dark Continent', in Lisa Bloom (ed.) *With Other Eyes: Looking at Race and Gender in Visual Culture*, Minneapolis: University of Minnesota Press, 90.

39 See Shawn Michelle Smith (1999) 'Photographing the "American Negro": Nation, Race and Photography at the Paris Exposition of 1900', in Lisa Bloom (ed.) *With Other Eyes: Looking at Race and Gender in Visual Culture*, Minneapolis: University of Minnesota Press; Smith summarises the scholarship succinctly: 'Bound to a mythology of scientific objectivity and a system of increasing social surveillance, an invisible white gaze functioned as the arbiter of biological and cultural difference in Jim Crow America', 66.

40 Donald Bogle (1990) *Brown Sugar: America's Black Female Superstars*, New York: Da Capo Press.

41 Rony (1996), 62.

42 See bell hooks (1992) 'Dialogue: Between bell hooks and Julie Dash 26 April, 1992' in Julie
    Dash, *Daughters of the Dust: The Making of an African American Film*, New York: The New Press,
    50.

43 Peter Wollen draws a distinction between the abstract American avant-garde and the political
    European avant-garde. See Peter Wollen (1969) *Signs and Meaning in the Cinema*, Bloomington:
    Indiana University Press.

44 See, for instance, Foster (1995), 68.

45 See Greg Tate (1992) 'A Word', in Julie Dash, *Daughters of the Dust: The Making of an African
    American Film*, New York: The New Press, 71.

46 Jacqueline Bobo (1995) *Black Women as Cultural Readers*, New York: Columbia University Press,
    30.

47 Ibid., 188.

48 Ibid., 182.

49 Mona Fayad (2000) discusses this concept in relationship to Djebar's work extensively in her
    unpublished manuscript *Nationalism and Arab Women Writers*.

50 Among the most contested of terms since the post-structuralist challenge to disciplinary forma-
    tions, what constitutes history has been substantially altered by the subaltern historiographers
    in many diverse fields of inquiry. Michel Foucault (1973) *Madness and Civilisation: A History of
    Insanity in the Age of Reason*, trans. Richard Howard, New York: Random House, comes to mind
    as does Ranajit Guha's project, among others. Edward Said's description of Guha's project is as
    follows: 'The point was that if a new, or at least more authentic, history of India was to be written,
    its authors had better bring forth new material and carefully justify the importance of this mate-
    rial as sufficiently as it was necessary to displace previous historical material on India'; Edward
    Said (1988) 'Foreword', in Ranajit Guha and Gayatri Chakravorty Spivak (eds) *Selected Subaltern
    Studies*, New York: Oxford University Press, v. Like revisionist historians, feminist historians aim
    to get more history, as it were, by looking at different kinds of artifacts and moving away from
    monumental history to recording events that have not been registered by official history. Femi-
    nist artists too are claiming history as a terrain to enhance the pursuit of 'truth' however qualified
    of the past, and more simply to acknowledge the existence of women in certain spaces, certain
    periods.

51 Kumkum Sangari and Sudesh Vaid (eds) (1990) *Recasting Women: Essays in Indian Colonial His-
    tory*, New Brunswick: Rutgers University Press, 3.

52 See among others the special issue on Djebar brought out by *World Literature Today*, 70, 4,
    (1996).

53 See, among others, Mair Verthuy (1996) 'Assia Djebar: le regard dé-voilé' and Anne Donadey
    (1996) 'Rekindling the Vividness of the Past: Assia Djebar's Films and Fiction', both in *World
    Literature Today*, 70, 4.

54 See Laurence Huughe (1996) 'Écrire comme un voile': The Problematics of the Gaze in the Work
    of Assia Djebar', in *World Literature Today*, 70, 4.

55 Clarisse Zimra is an exception to the general validity of this observation. See Clarisse Zimra
    (1999) 'Sounding Off the Absent Body: Intertextual Resonances in "La femme qui pleure" and
    "La femme en morceaux"', *Research in African Literatures*, 30, 3.

56 See Donadey (1996).

57 See Mildred Mortimer (1996) 'Reappropriating the Gaze in Assia Djebar's Fiction and Film',
    World Literature Today, 70, 4: 'By granting importance to the muted conversation, to women's

silence, Djebar assumes the task completely beyond Delacroix's realm of competency, that of restoring sound to this silent study of orientalist imagery'.

58 Rony (1996).

59 Zimra (1999), 111.

60 See Clark *et al.* (1988), 607.

61 Réda Bensmaïa notes that this film's compositional style is exceptional for Algerian film; see Réda Bensmaïa (1996) '*La nouba des femmes du Mont-Chenoua*: Introduction to the Cinematic Fragment', in *World Literature Today*, 70, 4, 880.

62 See Jonathan Crary (1999) *Suspensions of Perception: Attention, Spectacle, and Modern Culture*, Cambridge, MA: MIT Press, 198–9.

63 All her commentators address this part of Djebar's project: the image of the woman with the severed hand in which Djebar places the pen is also often quoted.

64 Crary (1999), 294.

65 Ibid.

66 Ibid., 200. On the zero signifier, please see Crary's complex discussion.

67 Zimra (1999), 111.

68 Bensmaïa (1996), 883.

69 Ibid., 882

70 Mortimer (1996), 859.

71 Laurence Huughe quotes Djebar as stating that the veiled woman can be 'a potential thief within the masculine space'; (1996), 869.

72 Silverman (1988).

73 Mortimer (1996), 859.

74 See Assia Djebar (1992) 'Forbidden Gaze, Severed Sound', in *Women of Algiers in their Apartment*, trans. Marjolijn de Jäger, Charlottesville: University Press of Virginia, 138.

75 Marnia Lazreg (1994) *The Eloquence of Silence: Algerian Women in Question*, New York: Routledge, 136.

76 Mortimer (1996), 862.

77 Bensmaïa (1996), 879.

78 See Lazreg (1994), 118–142 for a nuanced discussion of women's participation in the decolonisation effort, and for a breakdown of the demographics; 77.9 percent of the total female population that participated were rural women.

79 Bensmaïa (1996), 882.

80 Mounir quoted in Jean-Marie Clerc (2001) 'La guerre d'algérie dans l'oeuvre cinématographique et littéraire d'Assia Djebar', *L'Esprit–Createur*, 41, 7, 95.

81 See Zahia Smail Salhi (2001) on how Algerian women were kept out of the benefits of liberation by the Family Law, and how both political parties, whether FIS or FLN, defined the same roles for women, in 'The Wounded Smile: Women, Politics and the Culture of Betrayal', *Critique: Journal for Critical Studies of the Middle East*, 18, 101–18.

82 Donadey (1996), 888.

83 See Danielle Marx-Scouras (1993) 'Muffled Screams/Stifled Voices', *Yale French Studies*, 82, 1, 172–83; and Evelyne Accad (1980) *Sexuality and War: Literary Masks of the Middle East*, New York: New York University Press, on women, men and war.

84 See, for instance, Maria Novaro's *Danzón*.

85 Sarah Maldoror (1977) 'On Sambizanga', in Karyn Kay and Gerald Peary (eds) *Women and the Cinema: A Critical Anthology*, New York: Dutton, 308.

86 Ibid.
87 Frantz Fanon quoted in Jane Gaines (1993) 'Fire and Desire: Race, Melodrama and Oscar Micheaux', in Manthia Diawara (ed.) *Black American Cinema*, London: Routledge, 62.
88 'Les héros ne m'intéressent pas'; Maldoror quoted in Alain Ferrari (1973) 'Le second souffle du cinéma africain', *Télécine*, 176, 7.
89 Ibid., 9.
90 Benedict Anderson (1983) *Imagined Communities: Reflections on the Origin and Spread of Nationalism*, London: Verso.
91 See Gyanendra Pandey (1980) *The Construction of Communalism in Colonial North India*, New Delhi: Oxford University Press.
92 Kumkum Sangari and Sudesh Vaid (eds) (1990) *Recasting Women in India*, New Brunswick: Rutgers University Press.
93 Homi Bhabha (1990) *Nation and Narration*, New York: Routledge.
94 Andrew Parker, Mary Russo, Doris Sommer and Patricia Yaeger (eds) (1992) *Nationalisms and Sexualities*, New York: Routledge, Chapman and Hall.
95 Evelyne Accad's insightful critique of masculine codes in the Lebanese civil struggle is worthy of comparison here as the Zimbabwean situation is not viewed as a masculinity gone awry; see Evelyne Accad (1990) *Sexuality and War: Literary Masks of the Middle East*, New York: New York University Press.
96 *California Newsreel*'s press release, www.newsreel.org/films/flame.html (accessed September 2002).
97 Ibid.
98 *Sunday Mail*, 2 June 1996, http://web.mit.edu/course/21f.853/africa-film/0171.html.
99 *California Newsreel*'s press release, www.newsreel.org/films/flame.html (accessed September 2002).
100 *Sunday Mail*, 10 June 1996, http://web.mit.edu/course/21/21f.853/africa-film/0171.html.
101 *Sunday Mail*, 4 February 1996, http://web.mit.edu/course/21/21f.853/africa-film/0171.html.
102 *Screen Africa*, www.gep.de/ezef/index–232.htm; translation from the German mine (accessed September 2002).
103 Mari Sasano (2000) 'Review of *Flame*', http://198.161.96.43/*SeeMagazine*/Issues2000/021 screen/html.
104 Martin Mhando (2000) 'Approaches to African Cinema Study', www.senseofcinema.com/contents/00/8/african.html.
105 On the practice of sati, despite her reservations about the colonial contexts, Lata Mani states, 'In other words, even the most anti-imperialist among us felt forced to acknowledge the "positive" consequences of colonial rule for certain aspects of women's lives, if not in terms of actual practice, at least at level of ideas about "women's rights"'; see Lata Mani (1990) 'Contentious Traditions: The Debate on *Sati* in Colonial India', in Abdul R. JanMohamed and David Lloyd (eds) *The Nature and Context of Minority Discourse*, New York: Oxford University Press, 320. Here, the comment is in reference not to colonial Rhodesia, but the current West.
106 Mhando (2000).
107 Ibid.
108 Mhando (2000) quotes Katrina Thompson whom I paraphrase.
109 Leonard Klady (1996) 'Flame,' *Variety*, 3 June.
110 See Sinclair's statement in *Screen Africa*, www.gep.de/ezef/index–232.htm.
111 Kenneth Harrow (1997) 'Women with Open Eyes, Women of Stone and Hammers: Western Feminism and African Feminist Filmmaking Practice', in Kenneth W. Harrow (ed.) *With Open Eyes: Women and African Cinema*, Amsterdam: Rodopi, 144.

112 Interestingly, James Berardinelli takes issue with the fact that the film is not sufficiently emotional, expecting perhaps melodrama from a woman's film; James Berardinelli (1997) http://moviereviews.colossus.net/movies/f/flame.html.

113 The women soldiers of the war say that had they been fighting a war against rape, they would not have won: 'If the war had been about rape, we would not have fought or won it', *California Newsreel*'s press release, www.newsreel.org/films/flame.html (accessed September 2002).

114 *California Newsreel*'s press release, www.newsreel.org/films/flame.html (accessed September 2002). See, in another context, Linda Brent's explanation for why she chose Mr Sands in *Incidents in the Life of a Slave Girl* by Harriet Jacobs.

115 We know that rape survivors did marry the rapists in war situations for economic reasons, and for safety reasons. Usually, however, the rapist is assumed to be from the enemy.

116 Barlet (1996), 53.

Chapter 4

1 Silverman (1988).

2 Mary Ann Doane (1980) 'The Voice in the Cinema: The Articulation of Body and Space', *Yale French Studies*, 60, 34.

3 Jacques Derrida (1976) *Of Grammatology*, trans. Gayatri Chakravorty Spivak, Baltimore: Johns Hopkins University Press.

4 Doane (1980), 33–50.

5 See Kathryn Kalinak cited in Pamela Robertson Wojcik (2001) 'The Girl and the Phonograph: Or the Vamp and the Machine Revisited', in Pamela Robertson Wojcik and Arthur Knight (eds) *Soundtrack Available: Essays on Film and Popular Music*, Durham: Duke University Press.

6 See Tania Modleski (1992, 'Time and Desire in the Woman's Film', in Gerald Mast, Marshall Cohen and Leo Braudy (eds) *Film Theory and Criticism: Introductory Readings*, fourth edition, New York: Oxford University Press.

7 Ibid.; the last description is Modleski's.

8 See Linda Williams (1994) 'A Jury of Their Peers: Questions of Silence, Speech, and Judgement in Marleen Gorris's *A Question of Silence*', in Diane Carson, Linda Dittmar and Janice R. Welsch (eds) *Multiple Voices in Feminist Film Criticism*, Minneapolis: University of Minnesota Press.

9 See Geetha Ramanathan (1992) 'Murder as Speech: Narrative Subjectivity in Marleen Gorris's *A Question of Silence*', *Genders*, 15, 58–71.

10 Irigaray (1985).

11 See Monique Wittig's (1973) *Les Guerilleres*, trans. David Le Vay, New York: Avon Books, for an insistence on the body as speech act.

12 Julia Kristeva (1986) 'Revolution in Poetic Language', in *The Kristeva Reader*, ed. Toril Moi, New York: Columbia University Press, 89–137.

13 Carol Flynn (1986) 'The "Problem" of Femininity in Theories of Film Music', *Screen*, 27, 6, 58.

14 Linda Dittmar (1994) 'The Articulating Self: Difference as Resistance in *Black Girl, Ramparts of Clay*, and *Salt of Earth*', in Diane Carson, Linda Dittmar and Janice R. Welsch (eds) *Multiple Voices in Feminist Film Criticism*, Minneapolis: University of Minnesota Press, 392.

15 Also a tendency in women's writing; see for example the work of Monique Wittig, Luce Irigaray and Toni Morrison.

16 See, for example, Golden Age cinema in Mexico of the 1940s, and the 'women's film' of the 1940s and 1950s in the US.

17 See Ana López (1994) 'Tears and Desire: Women and Melodrama in the "Old" Mexican Cinema' and Julianne Burton-Carvajal (1994) 'Portrait(s) of Teresa: Gender Politics and the Reluctant Revival of Melodrama in Cuban Film' both in Diane Carson, Linda Dittmar and Janice R. Welsch (eds) *Multiple Voices in Feminist Film Criticism*, Minneapolis: University of Minnesota Press.

18 Peter Aspden (1992) 'Review of *Danzón*', *Sight and Sound*, 2, 41, 7.

19 Dolores Tierney (1997) 'Silver Sling-backs and Mexican Melodrama: *Salon Mexico* and *Danzón*', *Screen*, 38, 4, 360–72.

20 For a fascinating essay on Novaro's *Lola* (1990) see Diane Sippl (1999) 'Al Cine de las Mexicanas: *Lola* in the Limelight', in Diane Robin and Ira Jaffe (eds) *Redirecting the Gaze: Gender, Theory, and Cinema in the Third World*, Albany: SUNY University Press.

21 Jacqueline Rose (1988) 'Sexuality and Vision', in Hal Foster (ed.) *Vision and Visuality*, Bay Press: Seattle, 116.

22 Doris Sommer (1991) *Foundational Fictions: The National Romances of Latin America*, Berkeley: University of California Press; see, in particular, 'Irresistible Romance', 1–30.

23 Djelal Kadir (1986) *Questing Fictions: Latin America's Family Romance*, Minneapolis: University of Minnesota Press: 'This metaphor [of the journey] is a way of saying that *quest* in Latin America figures as family history; that the errantry which resulted in the discovery of the New World has become internalised by that world's imagination; that the first voyagers' error which led to the necessity of *inventing* a reality for an unexpected world, the happenstance discovery, serves as precedent for the ever-errant inventiveness of Latin American fictions. Indeed these fictions trace the imaginative outlines of an errant family history in endless errancy', 11.

24 Ana López notes that the master narratives are religion, nationalism and modernisation; (1994), 256.

25 See Daniel Kotheschulte (1995) *Filmdienst*, 58, 16, 18, who notes that this is not a dance film.

26 See Agnès Varda's *Vagabond*. The Varda film is different in that the road movie itself is seen as alternate, while Julia of *Danzón* embarks on the journey for different reasons.

27 For comprehensive definitions of the 'imperfect cinema' see Michael Chanan (1983) *Twenty Five Years of the New Latin American Cinema*, London: British Film Institute, 9–12, 18–27, 28–33.

28 'Raped, defiled and abused, Malintzin/Malinche is the violated mother of modern Mexico, la chingada – the fucked one – or la vendida – the sellout'; López (1994), 257. See also Carl J. Mora (1985) 'Feminine Images in Mexican Cinema: The Family Melodrama; Sara Garcia, *The Mother of Mexico* and the Prostitute', *Studies in Latin American Popular Culture*, 4, 233. He discusses the space of the 'bitch goddess as the space of cabaret contrasted with the domestic space of the "saintly mother"'.

29 See *Mona Lisa* (1986) or *Eyes Wide Shut* (1999).

30 Recall that Odysseus is told, 'trust a woman never'.

31 Claudia Schaeffer, among others, notes that the filming is different in Vera Cruz; see Claudia Schaeffer (1999) 'Framing the Feminine: From Frida to *Danzón*', in *Revista canadiense de estudios hispanicos*, 23, 2, 289–310.

32 See Serge Daney (1992) 'Falling Out of Love', *Sight and Sound*, 2, 3, 14–18.

33 Schaeffer (1999), 306.

34 Fredric Jameson (1986) 'On Magic Realism in Film', *Critical Inquiry*, 12, 2, 311: 'The possibility of magic realism as a formal mode is constitutively dependent on a type of historical raw material in which disjunction is structurally present.'

35 See Mayne's work on the relationship between the woman and the image: Judith Mayne (1990) *The Woman at the Keyhole: Feminism and Women's Cinema*, Bloomington: Indiana University

Press, 124–54.

36 Ravi Vasudevan (1989) 'The Melodramatic Mode and the Commercial Hindi Cinema', *Screen*, 10, 3, 50.

37 Laura Mulvey (1975) 'Visual Pleasure and Narrative Cinema', *Screen*, 16, 6–18.

38 Tierney (1997), 361; note also that certain Golden Age cabareteras also linked 'music to the subjectivity of the female protagonist', 365.

39 '…an extra layer of narrational authority, this "other" voice telling/singing the story, standing both inside and outside the filmic text'; Vasudevan (1989), 45.

40 Ginette Vincendeau (1989) 'Melodramatic Realism: On Some French Women's Films in the 1930s', *Screen*, 30, 3, 52.

41 Lent (1991) 'Review of *Danzón*', *Variety*, 29 April.

42 'Heterosexual critics of queers' "role-playing" ought to look at themselves in the mirror on their way out for a night on the town to see who's in drag. The answer is, everybody is. Perhaps the main difference between heterosexuals and queers is that when queers go forth in drag, they know they are playing'; Marilyn Frye (1983) *The Politics of Reality: Essays in Feminist Theory*, Trumansburg, New York: The Crossing Press, 29.

43 Tierney (1997), 370.

44 'Traveller, moving through sea and sky/you leave hearts behind/that beat with passion/and vibrate with song/Then a thousand deceptions/I too/I loved you/I kissed you, then I lost you/I pray to God that at last/you'll get tired of travelling/and finally want to stay/What will I do without you?/What will the future bring?/I kissed you then I lost you/How can I forget you?/I might die without you/My moon and my sun will/go with you.'

45 See Silverman (1988); also, in discussing 'third world women', and their relationship to voice and subjectivity, Amy Lawrence argues that the positions available to them are different from first world subjectivities and requires a kind of cultural travelling. Novaro does undertake a kind of cultural travelling, but in a mode different from that employed by independent filmmaker Trinh T. Minh-ha; see Amy Lawrence (1992) 'Women's Voices in Third World Cinema', in Rick Altman (ed.) *Sound Theory/Sound Practice*, New York: Routledge.

46 Jean Franco (1986) 'The Incorporation of Women: A Comparison of North American and Mexican Popular Narrative', in Tania Modleski (ed.) *Studies in Entertainment: Critical Approaches to Mass Culture*, Bloomington: Indiana University Press.

47 Vasudevan (1989), 38.

48 See Randolph D. Pope (1996) 'The Spanish American Novel', in Robert Gonzalez Echevarria and Enrique Pupo Walker (eds) *The Cambridge History of Latin American Literature: Volume 2, The Twentieth Century*, Cambridge: Cambridge University Press, 248.

49 Jameson (1986), 303.

50 While seeming to have some resemblance to Judith Butler's idea of 'performing' femininity, this is different in that 'essential' femininity is not questioned by the character, and ontological femininity, not to be confused with essential femininity, is not questioned by the auteur; see Judith Butler (1990) *Gender Trouble: Feminism and the Subversion of Identity*, New York: Routledge.

51 See Guy Gauthier (1991) '*Danzón*', *La Revue du Cinema*, 477, 38. Gauthier notes the sensuality of the tropical port and claims that Novaro maintains a fine balance between exoticisation and the conventions of the old Mexican film.

52 Schaeffer (1999), 303.

53 For comparison, see Sun Axelsson (1992) 'Raffinerat enkelt om kvinnlig Orfeu', *Chaplin*, 3, 96.

54 Schaeffer (1999), 303; Tierney (1997), 370.

55 Schaeffer (1999), 306.

56 A feminist film that explores this theme in the US-Chicana context is Allison Anders' *Mi Vida Loca* (1993).

57 Schaeffer (1999), 306.

58 Novaro quoted in Tim Golden (1992) '*Danzón* Glides to a Soft Mexican Rhythm', *New York Times*, 11 October.

59 Other critics have also had difficulty with the film's 'feminism', including Janet Maslin of the *New York Times*. Novaro suggests that there might be difficulties with cultural translation here, a view with which I concur.

60 See Jean-Francois Pigoullie (1992) 'Danser, dit-elle', *Cahiers du Cinéma*, 41, 55–6.

61 Julia Kristeva (1980) *Desire in Language: A Semiotic Approach to Literature and Art*, ed. Leon S. Roudiez, trans. Thomas Gora, Alice Jardine and Leon S. Roudiez, New York: Columbia University Press, 6.

62 Elissa J. Rashkin (2001) *Women Filmmakers in Mexico: The Country of Which We Dream*, Austin: University of Texas Press, 168.

63 Ibid., 184; for a more detailed breakdown than one summarised here on different groups' reception of the film.

64 Franco (1986), 132.

65 Mario Valdes (1995) 'Hermeneutica de la representacion filmica de la mujer: *La Regenta, Que he hecho yo para merecer esto y Danzón*', *Revista Canadiense de Estudios Hispanicos*, 20, 1, 80.

66 For a very specific and accurate reading of the looks in the dance, including the lesson with Suzy where Julia plays the role of the man, and Suzy objects to looking away, see Francoise Aude (1992) 'Une femme a principes: *Danzón*', *Positif*, 372, 20.

67 Dittmar (1994).

68 See Rashkin (2001) for a fascinating discussion on the effects of globalisation on Mexico, particularly urban Mexico and the cinema that emerges called 'garbage cinema' which refuses to 'prettify' urban decay and its impact on the people.

69 Rashkin attributes it to Foucault via Jean Franco.

70 A popular trope in feminist film: Lizzie Borden's *Born in Flames* (1983), Deepa Mehta's *Fire* (1996) and Ingrid Sinclair's *Flame* (1996). Rage against the powers that be links all four films.

71 Nelly Richard (1995) 'Women's Art Practice and the Critique of Signs', in Gerard Mosquera (ed.) *Beyond the Fantastic: Contemporary Art Criticism from Latin America*, London: The Institute of International Visual Arts, 149.

72 Rotberg quoted in Isabel Arredondo (2001) *Palabra de Mujer: Historia oral de las directoras de cine mexicanas (1988–1994)*, Iberoamericana: Vervuert, Universidad Autónoma de Aguascalientes, 185.

73 Nelly Richard (1995), 'Chile, Women and Dissidence', in Mosquera (ed.), 139.

74 David R. Maciel and Joanne Hershfield (1999) 'Women and Gender Representation in the Contemporary Cinema of Mexico', in David R. Maciel and Joanne Hershfield (eds) *Mexico's Cinema: A Century of Film and Filmmakers*, Wilmington: Scholarly Resources Imprint, 262.

75 Rotberg quoted in Arredondo (2001), 180.

76 Ibid., 185.

77 Mae Gwendolyn Henderson (1990) in 'Speaking in Tongues: Dialogics, Dialectics, and the Black Woman Writer's Literary Tradition', *Reading Black, Reading Feminist: A Critical Anthology*, ed. Henry Louis Gates, New York: Penguin.

78 Dittmar (1994), 396.

79 Viola Shafik (1998) *Arab Cinema: History and Cultural Identity*, Cairo: The American University in Cairo Press, 101–20.

80 Amy Lawrence (1992) 'Women's Voices in Third World Cinema', in Rick Altman (ed.) *Sound Theory/Sound Practice*. New York: Routledge.

81 Malek Alloula (1986) *The Colonial Harem*, Minneapolis: University of Minnesota Press.

82 S. M. (1994) 'Notes sûr d'autres films,' *Cahiers du Cinéma*, 483, 69.

83 Laura Mulvey (1995) 'Moving Bodies,' *Sight and Sound*, 19, 3, 18–20.

84 Anon. (1994) 'Review of *Les silences du palais*', *Positif*, 401/2, 199–200.

85 Kay Armatage (1995) 'Review of *Les silences du Palais*', *Cineaction*, 36, 27.

86 See Thierry Gendron (1996) '*Les silences du palais* de Moufida Tlatli', *Cinébulles*, 15, 2, 53–4.

87 See Leila Ahmed (1992) *Women and Gender in Islam: Historical Roots of a Modern Debate*, New Haven: Yale University Press.

88 See Gayatri Chakravorty Spivak (1988) 'Can the Subaltern Speak?', in Cary Nelson and Lawrence Grossberg (eds) *Marxism and the Interpretation of Culture*, Urbana: University of Illinois Press, 296. Her complex formulation pertains to how the desire to represent a particular group may end up turning that group into the 'object of investigation'. The sentence that Spivak formulates is as follows: 'White men are saving brown women from brown men.'

89 Interestingly despite Sadaam's progressive record for the education of women, little attention was paid to that. As far as Arab women's issues in the media go, almost everyone was appalled that women were not permitted at the funeral of King Hassan of Jordan.

90 See Amitava Kumar (1998) 'Indian Women in the Theatre of the West', in *Deep Focus*, Geetha Ramanathan (ed.) special issue: 'Third World Women's Film', 8, 3/4, 13–23.

91 See Poonam Arora (1994) 'The Production of Third World Subjects for First World Consumption: *Salaam Bombay and Parama*', in Diane Carson, Linda Dittmar and Janice R. Welsch (eds) *Multiple Voices in Feminist Film Criticism*, Minneapolis: University of Minnesota Press.

92 Paul Scott (1979) *The Raj Quartet*, New York: Harper Collins-Avon, including *The Jewel in the Crown*, televised on public television, had a huge audience in the US in 1987. It harked back to a time when the British were in power in India, but offered no political critique.

93 Tlatli's training as an editor enables her to use editing as a sophisticated aesthetic tool.

94 Tlatli quoted in Mulvey (1995), 20.

95 Maureen Turim (1989) *Flashbacks in Film: Memory and History*, New York: Routledge, 57.

96 See Jodi Brooks (1995) 'Between Contemplation and Distraction: Cinema, Obsession and Involuntary Memory', in Laleen Jayamanne (ed.) *Kiss Me Deadly: Feminism and Cinema for the Moment*, Sydney: Power Publications.

97 See Michel Chion (1994) *Audio Vision: Sound on Screen*, ed. and trans. Claudia Gorbman, New York: Columbia University Press, 182. I have reworked his concept of decentering which notes that the visual and audio go in different directions, and because of this dialogue is less centred. While this is true of Tlatli, the auditory becomes more important, an important distinction.

98 Note Tlatli's own mother's silence about her life.

99 In another famous mother/daughter film, *Imitation of Life* (1934), race becomes the term to be put under erasure.

100 Nancy Chodorow (1997) 'The Psychodynamics of the Family', in Linda Nicholson (ed.) *The Second Wave: A Reader in Feminist Theory*, New York: Routledge, 181–98.

101 Gayatri Chakravorty Spivak (1993) 'Women in Difference', in *Outside in the Teaching Machine*, New York: Routledge, 93.

102 Shafik (1998), 107.

103 See Mona Fayad (1998) 'Architectures of Identity: Divergent Feminisms in Two Films by Arab Women', in *Deep Focus*, Geetha Ramanathan (ed.) special issue: 'Third World Women's Film', 8, 3/4, 33.

104 Aparna Sen says that *Parama* was the film that shook the Bengali public the most.

105 Sati was abolished in 1829.

106 See Rajeswari Sunder Rajan (1990) 'The Subject of Sati: Pain and Death in the Contemporary Discourse on Sati', *The Yale Journal of Criticism*, 3, 2, 5. In a rich discussion on interpretations of sati, Sunder Rajan discusses the feminist reading: 'If one subscribes to a liberal ideology of the freedom of choice one must sometimes grant sati the dubious status of existential suicide. To refuse to do so is to find oneself, as feminists have done, in another bind, that of viewing the sati as inexorably a victim and thereby emptying her subjectivity of any function or agency.'

107 The burning of the widow on the husband's funeral pyre. For statistics and historical contextualisation, see Lata Mani (1990) 'Contentious Traditions: The Debate on Sati in Colonial India', in Abdul R. JanMohamed and David Lloyd (eds) *The Nature and Context of Minority Discourse*, New York: Oxford University Press, 319–57.

108 See Mani (1990) on how Rammohan Roy, the British and the fundamentalist Hindus are equally unconcerned with her.

109 I use this awkward formulation instead of female sati to give the woman some identity other than that of being burned.

110 This is definitely changing in Bollywood, as can be seen with the recent blockbuster *Devdas* (2002) and the earlier more progressive *Astitva* (2000).

111 In pointed contrast to what is expected of the woman. Not only can the man remarry when his wife is dead, apparently he can when his wife is alive.

112 Such as that actively deployed on behalf of Afghani women at the moment.

113 Sunder Rajan (1990), 6.

114 The shocking way in which lynchings in the US were regarded as public spectacles come to mind.

115 See Ananya (1999) 'Dancing Death by Fire: In Search of Roop Kanwar', *Women and Performance: A Journal of Feminist Theory*, 11, 81–102.

116 Michel Foucault's (1978) *I, Pierre Riviere*, trans. Frank Jellinek, New York: Pantheon, remains the foundational text for this kind of discursive construction.

117 See Vijay Mishra (2002) *Bollywood Cinema: Temples of Desire*, New York: Routledge, ix–xxiii and 203–35.

118 'The choice for the concerned feminist analysis in this predicament … as one between subject-constitution (i.e. 'she wanted to die') and object formation (i.e. 'she must be saved from dying'), is a paralysing one'; Sunder Rajan (1990), 5–6.

119 In a realistic film the problematic that I am labouring would not obtain, nor in a symbolic film that did not have aspirations to social commentary at the diegetic level.

120 Lalitha Gopalan (1997) 'Coitus Interruptus and Love Story in Indian Cinema', in Vidya Dehejia (ed.) *Representing the Body: Gender Issues in Indian Art*, New Delhi: Kali for Women.

121 See Catherine Mackinnon (1997) 'Sexuality', in Linda Nicholson (ed.) *The Second Wave: A Reader in Feminist Theory*, New York: London.

122 Juliane Burton-Carvajal (1993) 'Regarding Rape: Fictions of Origin and Film Spectatorship', in John King, Ana M. Lopez and Manuel Alvorado (eds) *Mediating Two Worlds: Cinematic Encounters in the Americas*, London: British Film Institute, 261.

123 Sunder Rajan (1990), 7.

124 Many partition rape survivors were never accepted back by their families.

125 Agni pareeksha – test by fire, Sita comes through it alive and the woman undergoing it is supposed to become a goddess.

126 See K. Sangai and S. Vaid (1981) 'Sati in Modern India: A Report', *Economic and Political Weekly*, 16, 3, 1285, on the primary motivations behind compulsory sati.

127 Montesquieu apparently envisioned the woman reuniting with the husband in the afterlife in sexual terms. See Christopher Betts (1997) 'Constructing Utilitarianism: Montesquieu on *Suttee* in the *Lettres Persanes*', *French Studies: A Quarterly Review*, 51, 1, 19–29.

128 Satyajit Ray's *Devi* (1960) illustrates this. A father-in-law sublimates his desire for his daughter-in-law by deifying her; thus effectively preventing her from having sex with his son, her husband.

129 Writings on sati erroneously emphasise the youth of the women, making the necessity for the suppression of their sexuality all too important.

130 This is not meant to imply that women who are raped do not survive, but that in many instances, women do get badly hurt.

131 Sen quoted in Brinda Bose (1997) 'Sex, Lies and the Genderscape: The Cinema of Aparna Sen', *Women: A Cultural Review*, 8, 3, 324.

132 Ibid., 323.

133 Quoted in ibid. The other two films are *36 Chowringee Lane* (1981) and *Parama* (1987).

Chapter 5

1 Doane (1987), 12.

2 Linda Williams (1992) 'When the Woman Looks', in Gerald Mast, Marshall Cohen and Leo Braudy (eds) *Film Theory and Criticism: Introductory Readings*, New York: Oxford University Press, 561.

3 Kristeva (1980), 50

4 Teresa de Lauretis (1984) *Feminism, Semiotics and Cinema*, Bloomington: Indiana University Press, 103–58.

5 Hal Foster (2001) 'Violation and Veiling in Surrealist Photography: Woman as Fetish, as Shattered Object, as Phallus', in Jennifer Mundy (ed.) *Surrealism: Desire Unbound*, Princeton: Princeton University Press, 203.

6 Ibid., 221.

7 Michel Foucault (1978) *The History of Sexuality*, vol. 1, trans. Robert Hurley, New York: Pantheon, 83.

8 Flitterman-Lewis (1990).

9 See, for example, Yvonne Rainer's film *The Man Who Envied Women* (1985).

10 Germaine Dulac (1978) 'The Avant-Garde Cinema', in P. Adams Sitney (ed.) *The Avant–Garde Film: A Reader of Theory and Criticism*, New York: New York University Press, 48.

11 Chantal Akerman's *Jeanne Dielman, 23 Quai du Commerce, 1080 Bruxelles* (1975) and Marleen Gorris's *A Question of Silence* (1982) are two examples of films that come to mind that seem to echo the desire of this early text.

12 Katherine Conley (2001) 'Anamorphic Love: The Surrealist Poetry of Desire' in Jennifer Mundy (ed.) *Surrealism: Desire Unbound*, Princeton: Princeton University Press, 101.

13 See for example, Oscar Dominguez's 'Electrosexual Sewing Machine' from 1934, in Jennifer Mundy (ed.) (2001) *Surrealism: Desire Unbound*, Princeton: Princeton University Press, 244.

14 Hal Foster (1993) *Compulsive Beauty*, Cambridge: MIT Press, 8.

15 See Xaviere Gauthier (1971) *Surrealisme et sexualite*, Paris: Gallimard.

16 Foster (2001), 203.

17 See, for analogous implications, Whitney Chadwick (1985) *Women Artists and the Surrealist Movement*, Boston: Little, Brown, 33.

18 See Jean Franco (1986) 'The Incorporation of Women: A Comparison of North American and Mexican Popular Narrative', in Tania Modleski (ed.) *Studies in Entertainment: Critical Approaches to Mass Culture*, Bloomington: Indiana University Press.

19 *Nea: Young Emmanuelle* (1976) by Nelly Kaplan is an almost textbook version of this movement.

20 For a detailed breakdown of the sequences, see Flitterman-Lewis (1990), 106–7.

21 The surrealists, of course, changed that with their painting of the da Vinci work.

22 Fiona Carson contextualises this trope for us in the history of art in the following way: 'In the seamless trajectory of Western art history, one might be forgiven for assuming that art is the province of men and that the place of woman is in the picture, as model or muse.' Music and literature would seem to fit equally seamlessly in this formulation. See Fiona Carson (2001) 'Feminist Debate and Fine Art Practices', in Fiona Carson and Claire Pajaczkowska (eds) *Feminist Visual Culture*, New York: Routledge.

23 The scene in *Citizen Kane* (1941) where Susan Alexander sings follows up on the male master squeezing the art out of the female.

24 Lis Rhodes and Felicity Sparrow, (1986) 'Her Image Fades as her Voice Rises', in Charlotte Brunsdon (ed.) *Films for Women*, London: British Film Institute, 197.

25 Sandy Flitterman–Lewis, (1990), 103.

26 Doane (1987).

27 B. Ruby Rich (1997) 'An/Other View of Latin American Cinema', in Michael Martin (ed.) *New Latin American Cinema: Theories, Practices and Transcontinental Articulations*, vol. 1, Detroit: Wayne State University Press, 284.

28 For an early discussion of *Vidas Secas* see Randal Johnson and Robert Stam (1988) 'The Cinema of Hunger: Nelson Perreira dos Santos's *Vidas Secas*', in Randal Johnson and Robert Stam (eds) *Brazilian Cinema*, Austin: University of Texas Press.

29 See Robert Stam (1997) *Tropical Multiculturalism: A Comparative History of Race in Brazilian Cinema and Culture*, Durham: Duke University Press, 293.

30 See Michael Martin (1997) 'Suzana Amaral on Filmmaking, the State, and Social Relations in Brazil: An Interview', in Michael Martin (ed.) *New Latin American Cinema: Theories, Practices and Transcontinental Articulations*, vol. 1, Detroit: Wayne State University Press.

31 Ismael Xavier suggests that tropicalismo critiqued both right and left politics, and introduced the shocking and parodic within the allegorical motifs of the historic Cinema Novo: 'The discontinuities and the enigmatic tone of its [tropicalismo], representations were analysed by intellectuals as a modern version of allegorical schemes'; Ismael Xavier (1997) *Allegories of Underdevelopment: Aesthetics and Politics in Modern Brazilian Cinema*, Minneapolis: University of Minnesota Press, 7.

32 B.Ruby Rich, (1997), 282.

33 Ibid., 284.

34 Ibid., 285.

35 José Carlos Avellar (1997) 'Backwards Blindness: Brazilian Cinema of the 1980s', in Ann Marie Stock (ed.) *Framing Latin American Cinema: Contemporary Critical Perspectives*, Minneapolis: University of Minnesota Press, 53.

36 The idea that all third world cultural production is inevitably a national allegory, a proposition advanced by Fredric Jameson about literature, still holds some currency with film critics including Ismael Xavier, but has also been challenged, notably by Aijaz Ahmed. In the terrain of film, I especially take objection to it because so much 'third cinema' has tried to speak of the marginal, rather than the national. Interestingly, in relationship to gender issues, the same thesis has been proposed about, say, Fassbinder's females and more relevantly, about Cuban cinema. In a complex formulation, Marvin D'Lugo contends that 'as the films of the last decade attest, despite such (historic and social), change, that fundamental notion of transparency – the textual motivation of the audience to read the discourse of nation through female characters – has remained an indelible constant'; see Marvin D'Lugo (1997) 'Transparent Women: Gender and Nation in Cuban Cinema', in Michael Martin (ed.) *New Latin American Cinema: Theories, Practices and Transcontinental Articulations*, vol. 2, Detroit: Wayne State University Press, 156.

37 See Xavier (1997).

38 The military coup took place in 1964 and civilian rule was restored in 1984.

39 See Robert Stam and Ismael Xavier (1990) 'Transformation of National Allegory: Brazilian Cinema from Dictatorship to Redemocratisation', in Robert Sklar and Charles Musser (eds) *Resisting Images: Essays on Cinema and History*, Philadelphia: Temple University Press.

40 Ibid.; Glauber Rocha's film *Terra em Transe* (1967) marks the difference between the national allegory and the parodic, yet its basic visual aesthetic is comparable.

41 Quoted in Dennis West (1987) '*The Hour of the Star*: An Interview with Suzana Amaral', *Cineaste*, 15, 4, 45.

42 The narrator of the novel's self-absorption and self-reflexivity, as well as his class position, make it a meditation on himself in some senses; indeed the novel is comparable to the script of Tomás Gutiérrez Alea's *Memories of Underdevelopment* (1968).

43 Cileine I. De Lourenco (1998) 'Of Knowledge, Gender, Ethnicity and Class: *The Hour of the Star*', in *Deep Focus*, Geetha Ramanathan (ed.) special issue: 'Third World Women's Film', 8, 3/4, 87.

44 The mirror image has a fetishised place in women's film history for signalling a certain kind of self-consciousness, and for producing the mirror image instead of being the mirror image.

45 For the woman of colour, or the mixed race woman, invisibility is to be feared. 'To be looked at' is not necessarily viewed as objectification nor does it imply the loss of control it does for the female hero of Hollywood films; see my discussion of Julie Dash's *Illusions* in chapter two.

46 Giuliana Bruno (1995) 'Streetwalking Around Plato's Cave,' in Laura Pietropaolo and Ada Testaferi (eds) *Feminisms in the Cinema*, Bloomington: Indiana University Press, 156.

47 Ibid., 163.

48 See Elice Munerato and Maria Helena Darcy de Oliveira (1988) 'When Women Film', in Randal Johnson and Robert Stam (eds) *Brazilian Cinema*, Austin: University of Texas Press, 340–50.

49 Fabio Barreto's film *Lucia* (1988) is a case in point of the 'glamourisation' of the peasant woman; thankfully, she does ride off instead of marrying the rich ranchero, newly returned from the US.

50 Quoted in West (1987), 45.

51 See Jacqueline Bobo (1998), 'Black Women's Films: Genesis of a Tradition', in Jacqueline Bobo (ed.) *Black Women Film and Video Artists*, New York: Routledge, 12.

52 See Geetha Ramanathan (2000) 'Aesthetics as Woman: Aparna Sen's *Parama*', *Quarterly Review of Film and Video*, 17, 1, 63–74 for a discussion of how the theme works in film, and its bases in Western art history.

53 Kathleen Collins (1991) *Losing Ground* in Phyllis Rauch Klotman (ed.) *Screenplays of the African American Experience*, Bloomington: Indiana University Press, 151.

54 See Arora (1994), 301.

55 See Burton-Carvajal (1994), 314.

56 Crary (1998), 20.

57 Collins (1991), 178.

58 Kaja Silverman (1996) 'Political Ecstasy', in *The Threshold of the Visible World*, New York: Routledge.

59 Ibid., 87.

Chapter 6

1 Silverman (1988).

2 Constance Penley (1989) *The Future of an Illusion: Film, Feminism, and Psychoanalysis*, Minneapolis: University of Minnesota Press, 28.

3 Feminist film scholarship has devoted a lot of energy to Hollywood's casting of the mother/daughter relationship, especially the film *Stella Dallas* (1937); see Janet McCabe (2005) *Feminist Film Studies: Writing the Woman into Cinema*, London: Wallflower Press.

4 Meerapfel's filmography shows her lasting interest in migration, and the condition of the migrant subject.

5 Márta Mészáros's *Girl* (1964) also employs this device which is deployed metaphorically in *Malou*. Camille Billops's *Finding Christa* (1991), a 'documentary', makes a more radical intervention in that the narrative is organised around the mother's looking for a daughter she had given up for adoption. Diane Kurys' *Entre Nous* (1983) invites comparison to these films. Here, the daughter's voice does not enter until the end, quite as in the later film *A Man in Love* (1987) where the female narrator's voice does not divulge itself until the last sequences. Kurys then includes the daughter's desire to know the mother but does not allow it to dominate. There is a generous acknowledgement that the story may not be complete because it is the daughter's perspective.

6 Elizabeth Grosz (1994) *Volatile Bodies: Towards a Corporeal Feminism*, Bloomington: Indiana University Press; see 3–62, 86–115.

7 Luce Irigaray's work has helped establish the multiplicity of femininity,

8 Grosz (1994), 14.

9 Deepa Mehta's *Fire* (1996) follows this option through to the discomfiture of many lesbian viewers.

10 See Silverman (1988).

11 See Derrida (1976).

12 See Mladen Dolar (1996) 'The Object Voice', in Renate Salecl and Slavoj Zizek (eds) *Gaze and Voice as Love Objects*, Durham: Duke University Press.

13 See Lawrence (1994); also the films of Minh-ha, Djebar, Sen etc.

14 Andreas Huyssen (1986) 'Mass Culture as Woman: Modernism's Other', in *After the Great Divide: Modernism, Mass Culture, Postmodernism*, Bloomington: Indiana University Press.

15 Judith Mayne (1990) *The Woman at the Keyhole: Feminism and Women's Cinema*, Bloomington: Indiana University Press.

16 Penley (1989).

17 Homi Bhabha speaks of this in the colonial context.

18 The type of mimicry Malou practices is to be distinguished from Judith Butler's notion of perfor-

mativity. Butler (1990) suggests that performance is integral to the constitution of gender identities, while here the corporeal is important to the constitution of gender identity. I understand Butler's work as a way of finding a way out of the patriarchal imposition of body and the essential through performativity. The film makes a plea to reclaim the corporeal.

19   See Mladen Dolar (1996) 'At First Sight', in Renate Salecl and Slavoj Zizek (eds) *Gaze and Voice as Love Objects*, Durham: Duke University Press, 135.

20   Grosz, (1994) xii.

21   See Laura Mulvey (1989) 'Boundaries', in *Visual and Other Pleasures*, Bloomington: Indiana University Press on Propp and narrative.

22   Lizzie Borden's *Born in Flames*.

23   Julie Dash's *Illusions*; Cheryl Dunye's *The Watermelon Woman*.

24   The Griffith canon.

25   See Geetha Ramanathan (1996) *Sexual Politics and the Male Playwright: The Portrayal of Women in Ten Contemporary Plays*, Jefferson: McFarland.

26   Rosalind Krauss (1988) 'The Im/Pulse to See', in Hal Foster (ed.) *Vision and Visuality*, Seattle: Bay Press, drives towards the conclusion that many of the optical effects captured by modern art imbricate women in problematic ways, but does not make a statement to that effect. Krauss (1999) *Bachelors*, Cambridge: MIT Press, develops the idea more elaborately.

27   Joan Mellen (1973) *Women and their Sexuality in the New Film*, New York: Horizon.

28   B. Ruby Rich (1998) 'She Says, He Says: The Power of the Narrator in Modernist Film Politics', *Chick Flicks: Theories and Memories of the Feminist Film Movement*, Durham: Duke University Press, 252.

29   See Susan Sniader Lanser (1996) 'Towards a Feminist Poetics of Narrative Voice', in David H. Richter (ed.) *Narrative/Theory*, New York: Longman, 186.

30   *Antonia's Line* review in *Variety*, 26 June–9 July 1996, 81.

31   The video cover of the Orion release quotes Daphne Davis of *Movies and Videos* as saying the film is 'as compelling as the irresistible comic magic of *Like Water for Cholcolate*'; see also Alan Stone's (1996) review of the film, 'A Second Nature', in the *Boston Review*; http://bostonreview. mit.edu/br21.3/stone.html.

32   Paula Rabinowitz (2001) 'Great Lady Painters, Inc.: Icons of Feminism, Modernism and the Nation', in Jani Scandura and Michael Thurston (eds) *Modernism, Inc.: Body, Memory, Capital*, New York: New York University Press, 195.

33   Consider *Iphigeneia at Aulis*.

34   Quoted in Robert Sklar (1996) 'The Lighter Side of Feminism: An Interview with Marleen Gorris,' *Cineaste*, 22, 1, 26–8.

35   See J'Nan Morse Sellery (2001/02) 'Women's Communities and the Magical Realist Gaze of *Antonia's Line*', *Philological Papers*, 48, 115–24.

36   See Karen Jaehne (1996) '*Antonia's Line*', *Film Quarterly*, 50, 1, 27–31 on Gorris's indebtedness to both Flemish and Dutch traditions.

37   Teresa Brennan (1996) 'The Contexts of Vision From a Specific Standpoint', in Martin Jay and Teresa Brennan (eds) *Vision in Context: Historical and Contemporary Perspectives on Sight*, New York: Routledge, 223.

38   Literally 'magischer Blick'; see Marli Feldvoss (1996) '*Antonias Welt*', *EPD Film*, 13, 9, 37.

39   Brennan (1996), 223.

40   Jaehne (1996), 28.

41   Rabinowitz (2001), 195.

42 Gotthold Ephraim Lessing (1967) 'Laocoon', in *Laocoon, Nathan the Wise and Minna Von Barn-helm*, ed. William A. Steel, New York: Dutton, 55.

43 Janet Soskice (1996), 'Sight and Vision in Medieval Christian Thought', in Martin Jay and Teresa Brennan (eds) *Vision in Context: Historical and Contemporary Perspectives on Sight*, New York: Routledge, 35.

44 See Nicholas Mirzoeff (1995) *Bodyscape: Art, Modernity and the Ideal Figure*, London: Routledge, 118–26.

45 Stone (1996).

46 See Sellery (2001/02), 115

47 Feldvoss (1996).

48 See Madan Gopal Singh (1995) 'The Space of Encounter: A Re-reading of *Sant Tukaram*', in Aruna Vasudev (ed.) *Frames of Mind: Reflections on Indian Cinema*, New Delhi: Indian Council for Cultural Relations, UBSPD.

49 The discussion is of John Akomfrah.

50 Madan Gopal Singh's terms.

51 Indeed, one of the filmmakers that Madan Gopal Singh studies in his essay, Rithwik Ghatak, mythologises women in *Megha Dhaka Tara* (1960) in an almost allegorical movement from the realistic to the mythological, albeit not of the D. G. Phalke register. An equally disturbing ele-ment of the film is the girl's symbolic mingling with the elements; i.e., her death, and her exist-ence in a timeless space.

52 See Maithili Rao (1995) 'To Be a Woman', *Frames of Mind: Reflections on Indian Cinema*, in Aruna Vasudev (ed.) *Frames of Mind: Reflections on Indian Cinema*, New Delhi: Indian Council for Cultural Relations, UBSPD; Rao discusses especially the genre of the vengeful Kali.

53 Aruna Vasudev discusses the West's role in promoting the realistic mode, borrowed as it initially was from the West, and the second-class status it holds in Western aesthetic criteria as politi-cal rather than artistic. See Aruna Vasudev (1995) 'Ideologies of Underdevelopment', in Aruna Vasudev (ed.) *Frames of Mind: Reflections on Indian Cinema*, New Delhi: Indian Council for Cultural Relations, UBSPD. This is as true of mainstream feminist aesthetic standards where black women's films are concerned. Third world filmmaker Glauber Rocha and third cinema filmmaker Haile Gerima have also spoken of an 'aesthetics of hunger' or an 'aesthetics of under-development.'

54 Although this is a project in many third world feminist narratives, the semiotics of silence and secrecy being deployed in say, *I, Rigoberta Menchu* (1983), also glamourises a dangerous notion that cannot be retrieved with any integrity except through history.

55 See MacCabe (1985); this now widely accepted thesis was, in brief, that realism constructed though it was, effaced the signs of its own production which had the effect of reproducing the ideological status quo.

56 See Geeta Kapur (1993) 'Cultural Creativity in the First Decade: The Example of Satyajit Ray', *Journal of Arts and Ideas*, 23–4, 17–50. She notes that Ray, in using a realist aesthetic, paradoxi-cally through his great influence impedes the development of modalities that would be able to record the interiority of the subaltern.

57 I understand Singh's term to mean a self-consciousness of the medium outside of the constraints of the reflection of reality model.

58 While dominant Hollywood cinema is said to place the woman as object of the male gaze, dominant Hindi and Tamil cinema in many cases presents the woman as alluring of the male gaze as opposed to parallel cinema where the woman seems to desire to evade the male gaze at

least within the diegesis. The roles that Shabana Azmi plays in Shyam Benegal's films as in *Ankur* (1974) illustrate the latter. Any hit on-screen would provide evidence of the former, for example *Khamoshi* (1996) in Hindi or *Gnanapazam* (1996) in Tamil. For a more detailed and very different discussion of the way Laura Mulvey's thesis is played out in mainstream Hindi cinema, see Ravi Vasudevan (1989) 'The Melodramatic Mode and the Commercial Hindi Cinema', *Screen*, 10, 3, and more generally his work on the topic.

59 Ashish Rajadhyaksha and Paul Willeman (1999) *Encyclopedia of Indian Film*, revised edition, Chicago: Fitzroy Dearborn, 456.

60 Ibid.

61 See T. G. Vaidyanathan (1999) *Hours in the Dark*, New Delhi: Oxford University Press. The constructed nature of sexuality has been documented both in the Western world and in India itself; see Foucault (1978) and Sudhir Kakar (1990) *Intimate Relations: Exploring Indian Sexuality*, Chicago: University of Chicago Press.

62 Laura Mulvey (1989a) 'The Oedipus Myth: Beyond the Riddles of the Sphinx', in *Visual and Other Pleasures*, Bloomington: Indiana University Press.

63 More extreme male plots are depicted by Peter Brooks and Leo Bersani.

64 Laura Mulvey (1989b) 'Changes: Thoughts on Myth, Narrative and Historical Experience', in *Visual and Other Pleasures*, Bloomington: Indiana University Press.

65 Carving out a different place is substantively different than 'finding' one.

66 The explosive secret of *Chinatown* (1974) that provides the enigma is thus substantially different from knowledge that is regarded as needing to be published.

67 Laura Mulvey (1989a), 179.

68 See Roland Barthes (1994) *S/Z, Oeuvres Complétes: Tome II 1966–73*, Paris: Editions du Seuil, 567.

69 See Fredric Jameson (1996) 'On the Sexual Production of Subjectivity; or, Saint Augustine as a Social Democrat', in Renate Salecl and Slavoj Zizek (eds) *Gaze and Voice as Love Objects*, Durham: Duke University Press.

70 Patricia White calls it a femme flick because of this feature. See Patricia White (1999) *Uninvited: Classical Hollywood Cinema and Lesbian Representability*, Bloomington: Indiana University Press, 16.

71 Chris Straayer (1996) *Deviant Eyes Deviant Bodies: Sexual Re-orientations in Film and Video*, New York: Columbia University Press, 118.

72 See B. Ruby Rich (1998) 'From Repressive Tolerance to Erotic Liberation: *Mädchen in Uniform*', in *Chick Flicks: Theories and Memories of the Feminist Film Movement*, Durham: Duke University Press.

73 B. Ruby Rich's analysis of how all the teachers work towards the same end is indispensable to an understanding of the film. See Rich (1998), 179–207.

74 Ibid., 185.

75 Literally, 'schwärmt sich für'.

76 The film had some suturing looks censored, and the print that I am using may not be the latest restored one; however I do not believe that it would materially affect this part of the interpretation that does not rely on narrative suturing. The video I am using is distributed by Janus Collection in the International Collection series.

77 Rich (1998), 186.

78 In the many times I have shown the film, students insist on the either/or model. The refusal to accept the maternal and the erotic is shown in a theme that has emerged over the last two years

in students' conversations about the film: sexual abuse.

79   Richard Dyer (1990) *As You See It: Studies on Lesbian and Gay Film*, London: Routledge, 37.

80   Straayer (1996), 124.

81   White (1999), 94–136.

82   Dyer (1990), 40. Regarding the 'feminine' lesbian ideal that Sagan portrays, it is interesting that the woman originally cast as von Bernburg, Margarete Melzer, was rejected in favour of Dorothea Wieck who eventually played the role. The former was not sufficiently 'feminine-looking'.

83   See Julia Kristeva (1980) 'Motherhood According to Giovanni Bellini', in *Desire in Language: A Semiotic Approach to Literature and Art*, New York: Columbia University Press.

Index